PHOTOGRAPHY
THE GROUNDBREAKING MOMENTS

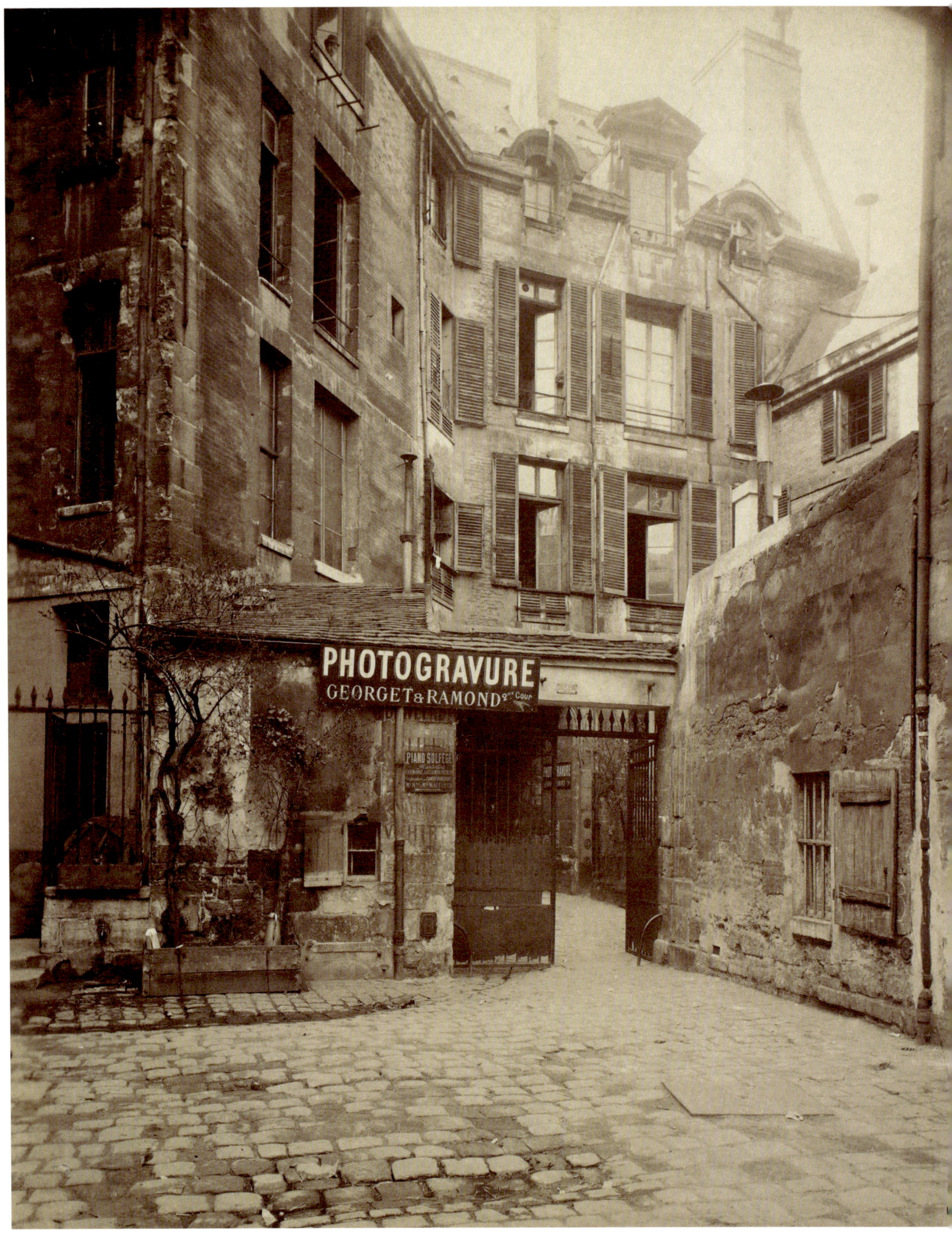

PHOTOGRAVURE
GEORGET & RAMOND 2me Cour
PIANO SOLFÈGE

PHOTOGRAPHY
THE GROUNDBREAKING MOMENTS

FLORIAN HEINE

PRESTEL
Munich · London · New York

CONTENT

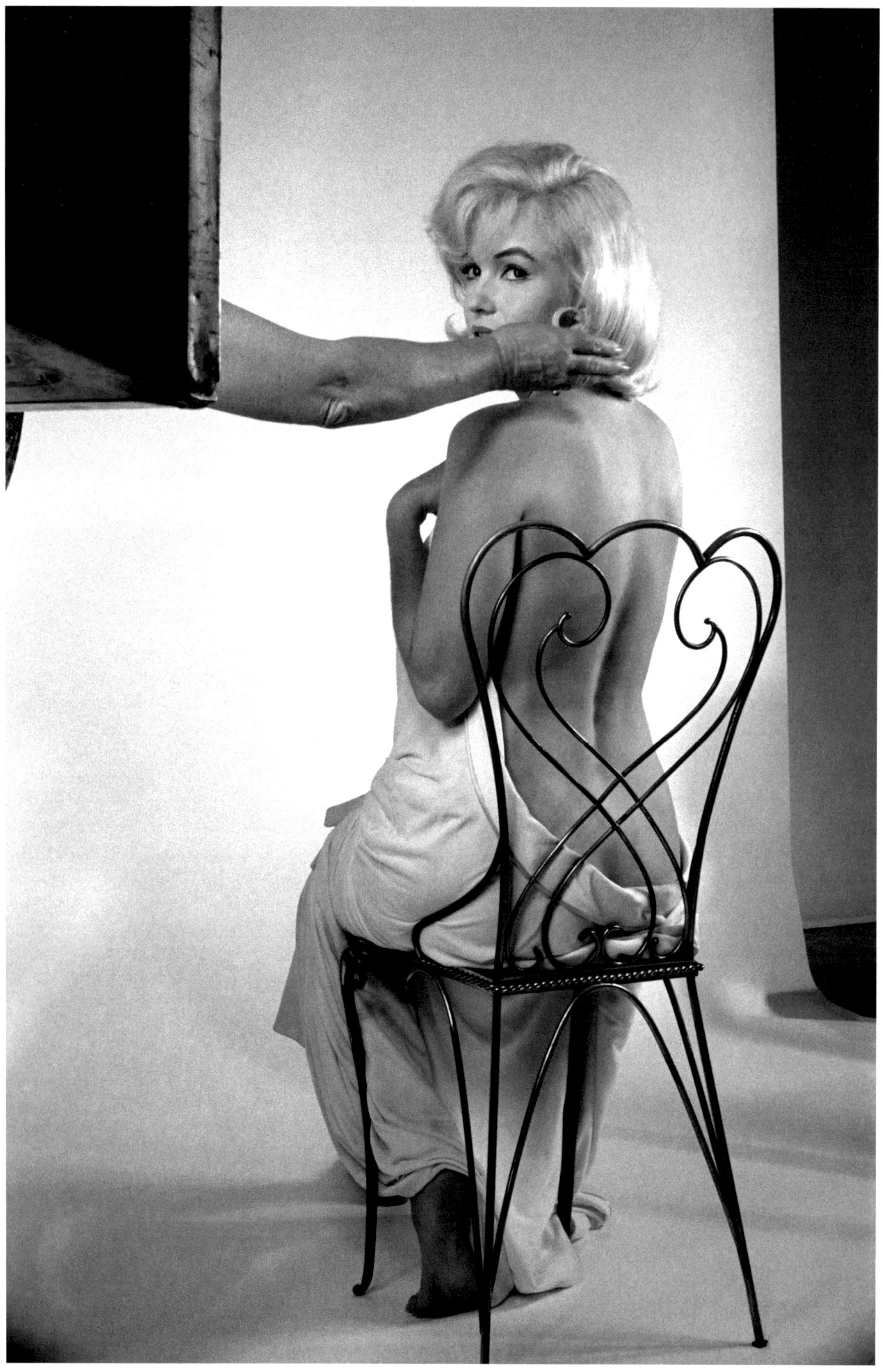

INTRODUCTION

"Those who are ignorant of photography, rather than those who cannot read, will be the true illiterates of the future." This comment, made by the photographer and Bauhaus teacher László Moholy-Nagy in 1927, seems more relevant than ever today. It has never been easier to take photos, and photography is not only all pervasive but also widely recognized as a significant artistic medium. From the very beginning, photography was a mass medium and a mass phenomenon, and never more so than now, when every cell phone is equipped with a camera and it is possible to photograph anything at any time. Joseph Beuys's observation that everyone is an artist becomes a real possibility through photography. And so it seems all the more important that we should be aware of the history of this medium, this art form, so as not to be among the "illiterates of the future."

In *Groundbreaking Moments in Photography*, the history of photography is not told in the usual chronological fashion. The book is subdivided according to genres and styles, which are described in detail. Some genres are familiar from the field of painting, while others arose because of the specific opportunities provided by photography, such as street photography and photojournalism. The borders are fluid, because very few photographers limit themselves to a single genre, but prefer to experiment with a variety of genres.

During its almost 180-year history, from its beginnings in the 19th century to the invention of digital photography in 1974 and its technical sophistication today, photography has continued to develop technologically at a rapid pace. What has remained, however, is the fact that despite all the technology it is still the photographer who determines what a photo looks like. "The tool of photography is the photographer, not the camera" (Eve Arnold). Ultimately, technique is only a means to an end. During each era photographers have always made use of the technology that was available to them and that seemed most suitable for their purpose and for the task of creating their type of pictures. For the viewer, it really makes no difference what sort of camera was used to take the photo. What is more important is whether the picture tells a story, evokes a mood, or depicts a person—in fact, arouses emotions. *Groundbreaking Moments in Photography* aims above all to encourage a love of photography—whether in taking photographs or viewing them. In the words of the British photographer Martin Parr: "Photography is the most accessible, democratic medium available in the world. This has to be celebrated, and we must continually remind photographers of this."

left——EVE ARNOLD: MARILYN MONROE, STUDIO SESSIONS, LOS ANGELES | 1960

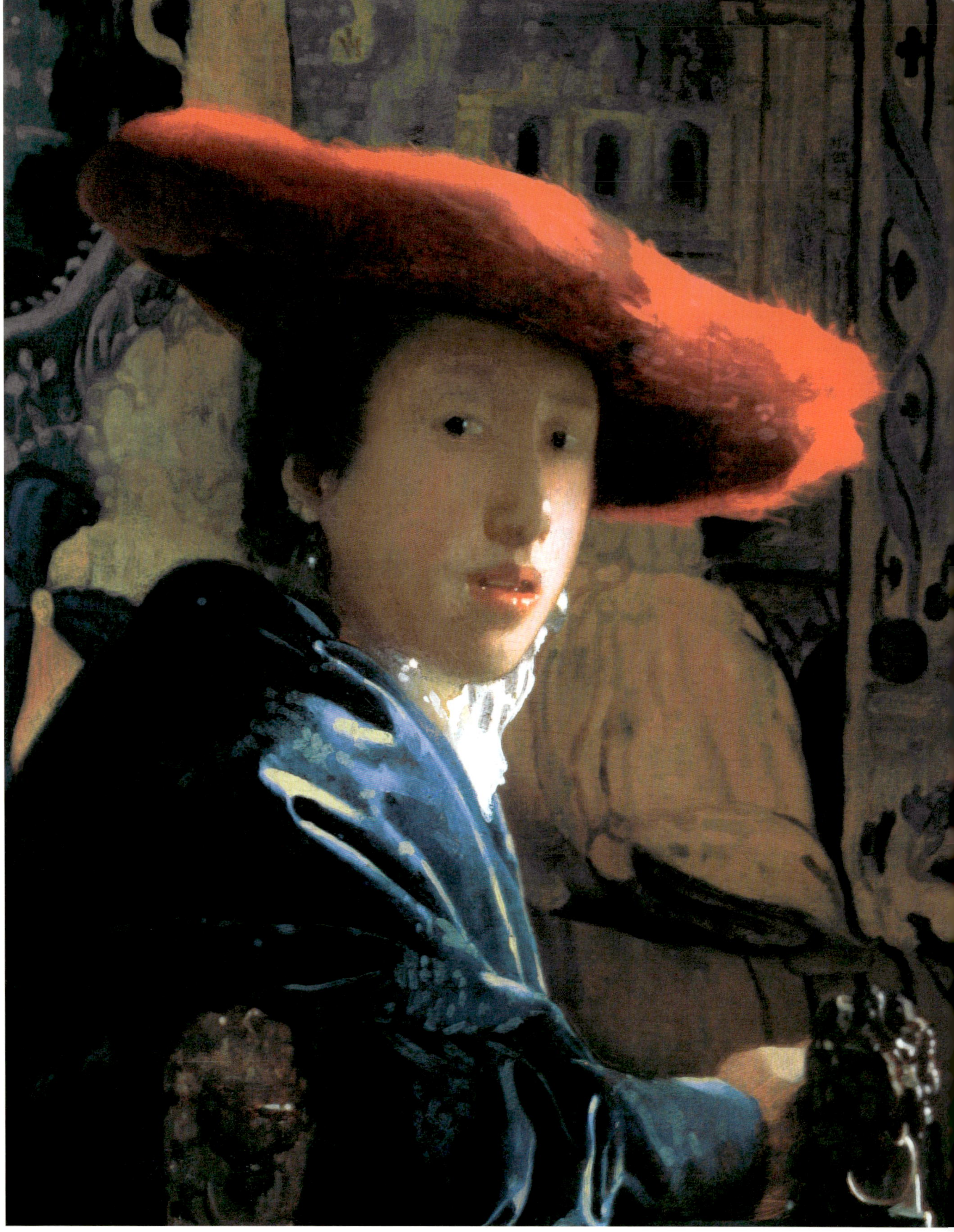

c. 1420–c. 1480 Jean Fouquet   1471–1528 Albrecht Dürer

BEFORE PHOTOGRAPHY

"The spirits have sought to fix these fleeting images; they have made a subtle substance by means of which a picture is formed in the twinkling of an eye. They coat a piece of canvas with this substance, and place it in front of the object to be taken. The first effect of this cloth is similar to that of a mirror, but by means of its viscous nature the prepared canvas [...] retains a facsimile of the image. The mirror represents images faithfully, but retains none; our canvas reflects them no less faithfully, but retains them all. This impression of the image is instantaneous. The canvas is then removed and deposited in a dark place. An hour later the impression is dry, and you have a picture the more precious in that no art can imitate its truthfulness."

This quotation reads like a somewhat romanticized account of the creation of a photograph. Surprisingly, it is an excerpt of the novel *Giphantie* by the French writer Tiphaigne de la Roche (1722–1774), which was published in 1760, almost 80 years before the first photograph was produced. This fictional description shows that the desire to create pictures without the involvement of a skilled artist existed long before the invention of photography.

From the Renaissance onwards, painters sought devices that would both make their work easier and also solve problems such as the correct representation of perspective and proportions. The grid used by the German artist Albrecht Dürer (1471–1528) is one example (fig. p. 10, above). Concave mirrors were already in use before that, allowing the projection of a scene onto a surface, on which it could then be traced. The *Grandes Chroniques de France* by the French painter Jean Fouquet (*c.* 1420–*c.* 1480) includes remarkable illuminations such as *The Arrival of Emperor Charles IV in St. Denis* (fig. p. 11). This shows a paved street that is so warped that the picture looks like an image created by a wide-angle lens. While there are no records regarding the use of optical devices in Fouquet's work, this depiction strongly suggests that Fouquet used a mirror projection for the illustration. Why else would he paint with such systematic distortion, unless he were using an optical projection?

The most important and best-known optical device used by artists was the camera obscura, which was already in use in classical times. Originally, it consisted of a darkened room (a "camera obscura") in which rays of light were projected through a hole in one wall onto the opposite wall. In order to turn

left—**Jan Vermeer: Girl with the Red Hat** | c. 1666/67 | oil on canvas | 23.2 x 18.1 cm | Washington | National Gallery of Art

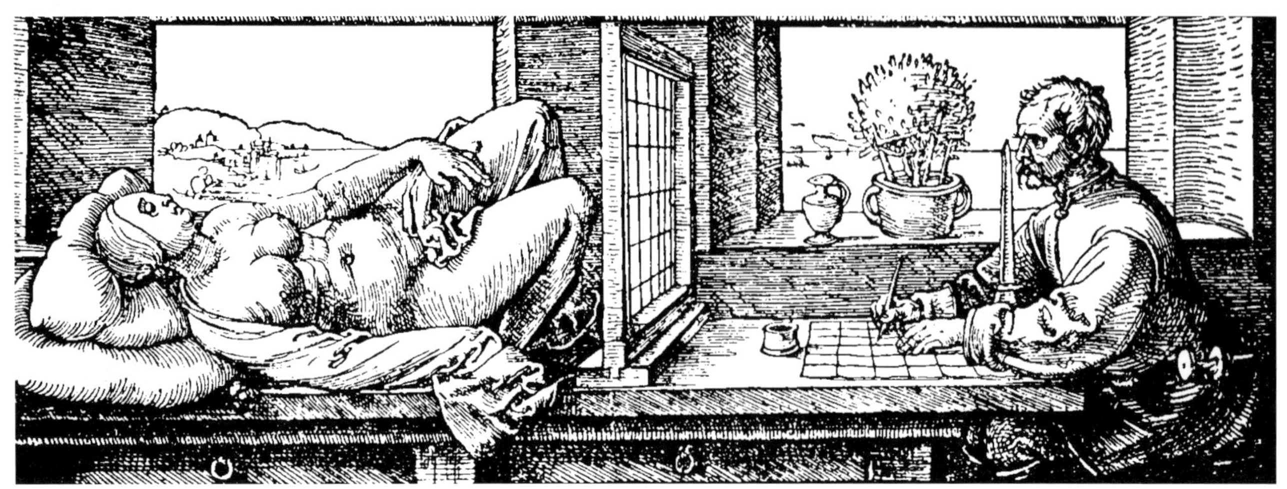

the camera obscura into a practical tool for artists, it was reduced to a portable box—and so the precursor to the modern camera was created. Light enters the box through a lens and, by means of a mirror, is projected onto a glass pane, from which the image it creates can be copied (right). This method was used by a large number of painters, the Dutch artist Jan Vermeer (1632–1675) and the Venetian Canaletto (1697–1768) being among the most famous.

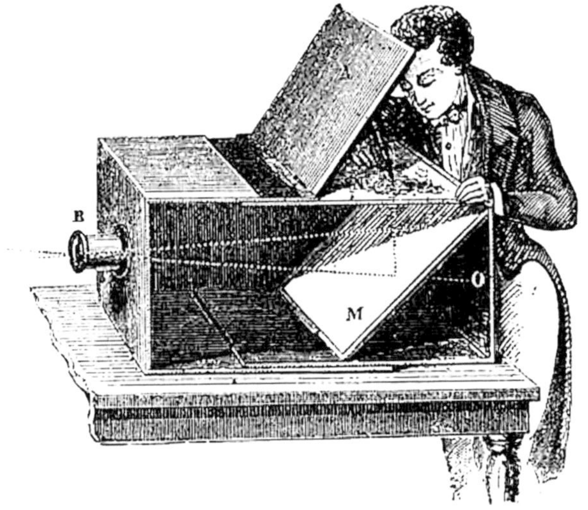

In his painting *Girl with the Red Hat* (fig. p. 8), which is remarkably small (23 x 18 cm, 9 x 7 in) and would therefore have been well suited to the size of a camera obscura, Vermeer appears to have copied the image projected onto a pane of glass very faithfully, so that the pointillist painting visible, for example, in the lions' heads on the armrests on the left and right, is the result of the variations in focus created by the camera obscura he used. Unlike many of his colleagues who used a camera obscura, Vermeer did not "correct" the blurs and inaccuracies caused by the lenses of the time, but instead replicated precisely these subtle visual effects in his paintings.

Canaletto used a camera obscura to help him to paint his views of Venice (fig. p. 12) and London. He transferred the comparatively small images produced by the camera obscura onto canvas, and used these as a basis for his paintings. To this day, we can see with just how accurately he captured scenes by comparing his paintings with photos of the same views (fig. p. 13).

The increasingly accurate paintings that resulted from the use of the camera obscura awakened a

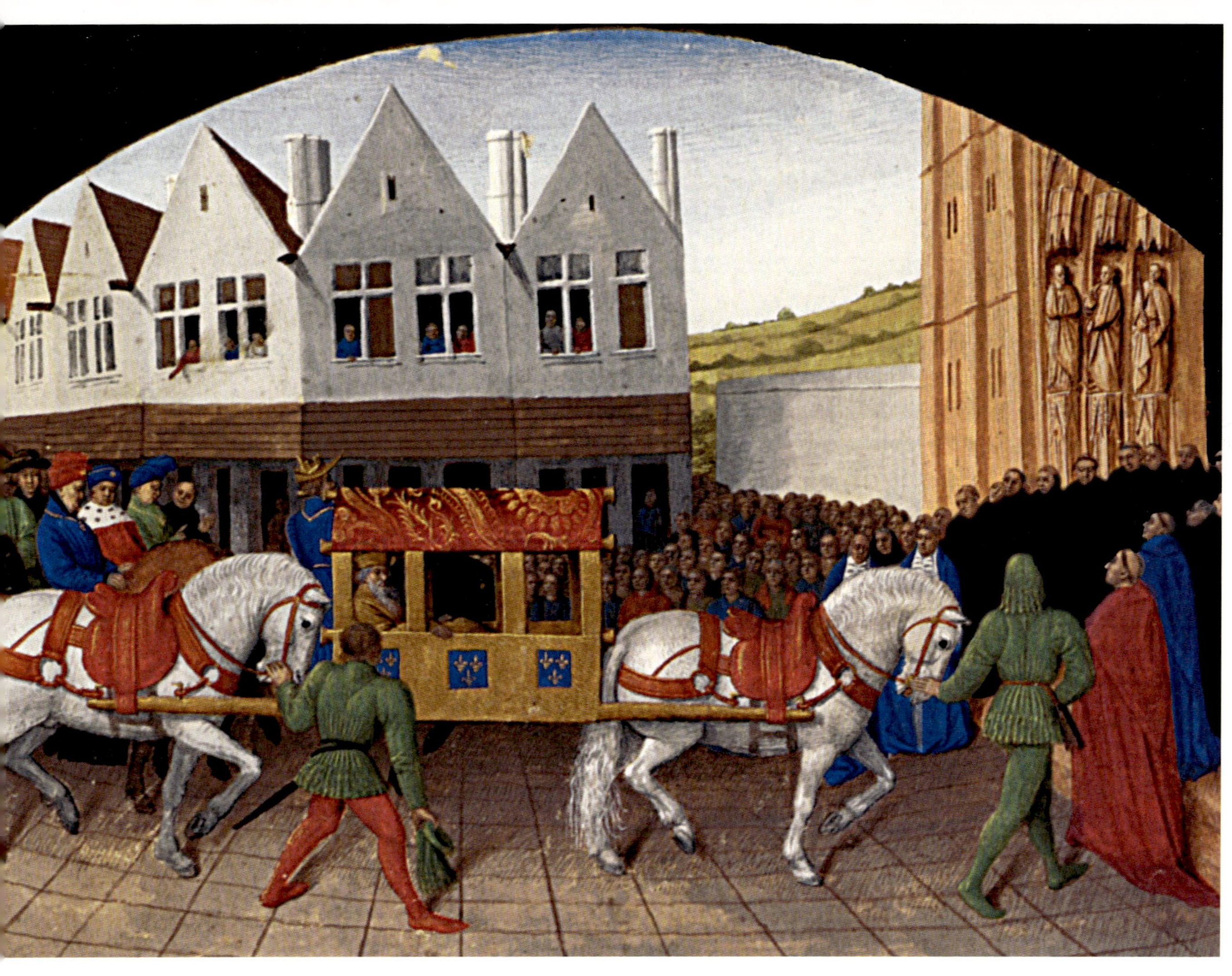

left, above——ALBRECHT DÜRER: THE GRID | from *The Art of Measurement* | 1525
left, below——A CAMERA OBSCURA | 19th-century illustration
above——JEAN FOUQUET: THE ARRIVAL OF EMPEROR CHARLES IV IN ST. DENIS
from *Grandes Chroniques de France* | c. 1455–60 | Paris | Bibliothèque Nationale
de France | Département des Manuscrits Français 6465 | fol. 442 (Livre
de Charles V)

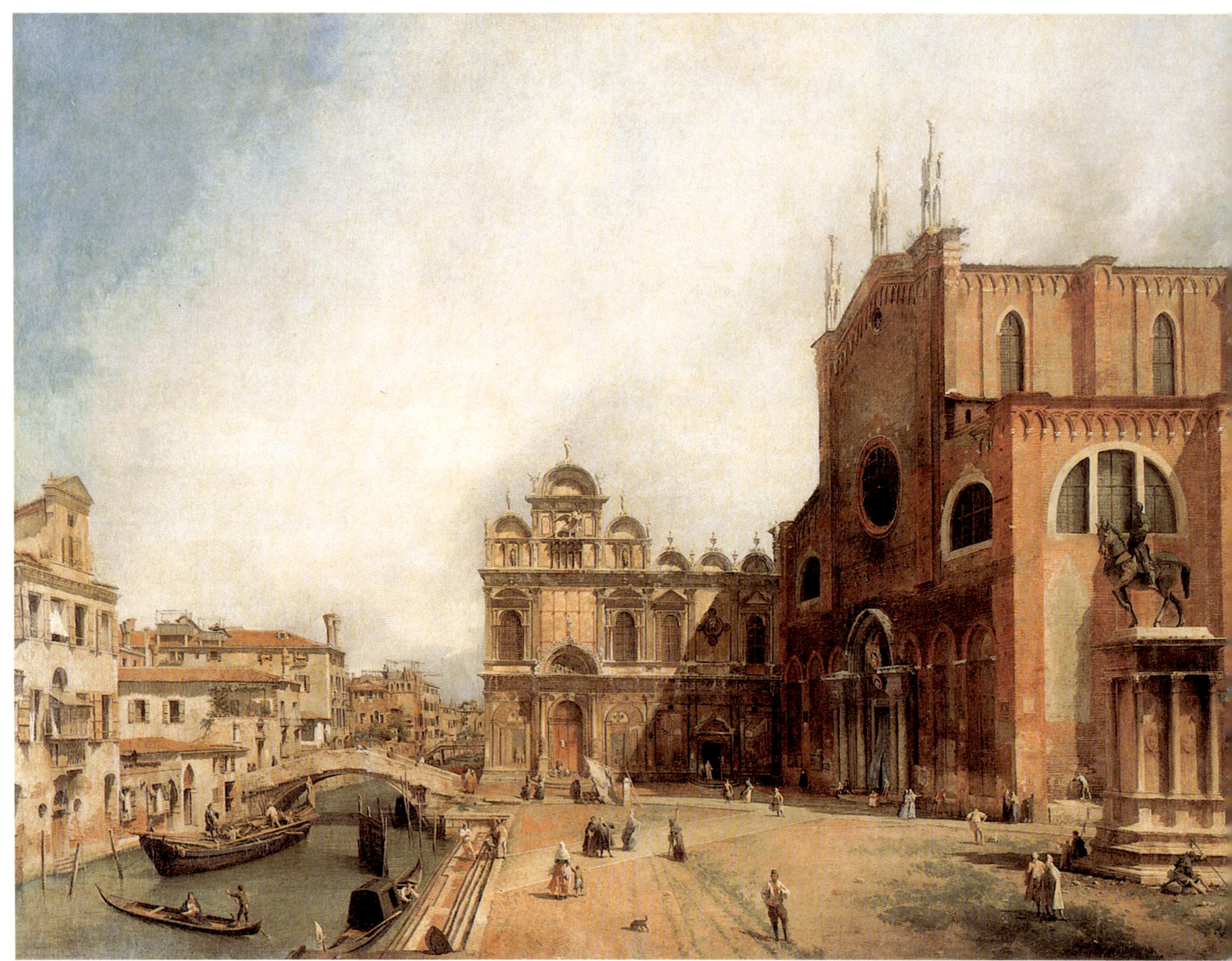

desire to create an image without the laborious intermediate step of drawing. And once the optical pre-conditions were in place thanks to the camera obscura, all that was needed was a chemical process that would, so to speak, automate the drawing process. The German chemist Johann Heinrich Schulze (1687–1744) made a major contribution when he discovered the light sensitivity of silver salts. The English chemist Thomas Wedgwood (1771–1805), son of the famous potter, was the first person to realize the importance of this discovery in connection with the camera obscura. He began to

experiment with the camera obscura and silver salts in 1799, with the aim of facilitating the process of making preliminary drawings for the decoration of tableware. He coated white leather and paper with silver nitrate and placed objects, such as leaves, on them—their traces remained in the form of the first photograms in history. They were visible for only a few minutes, however, before turning black. Wedgwood could not find a way to fix the images, to make them permanent. The foundations, however, had been laid, and it would only be a matter of time until photography proper was invented.

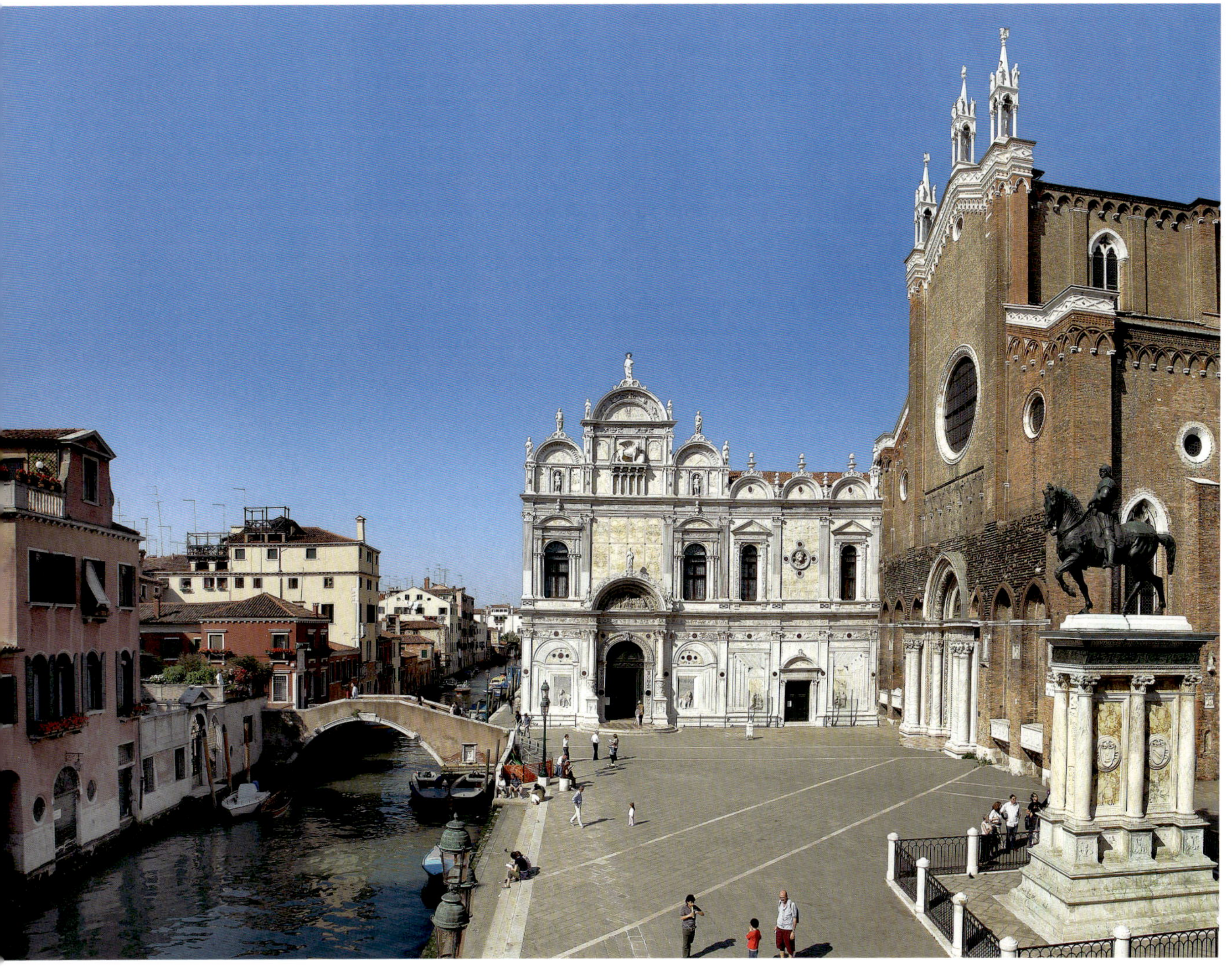

left——**CANALETTO: CAMPO SANTI GIOVANNI E PAOLO** | c. 1726 | oil on
canvas | 125 x 165 cm | Dresden | Galerie Alter Meister

above——**FLORIAN HEINE: CAMPO SANTI GIOVANNI E PAOLO** | Venice 2009

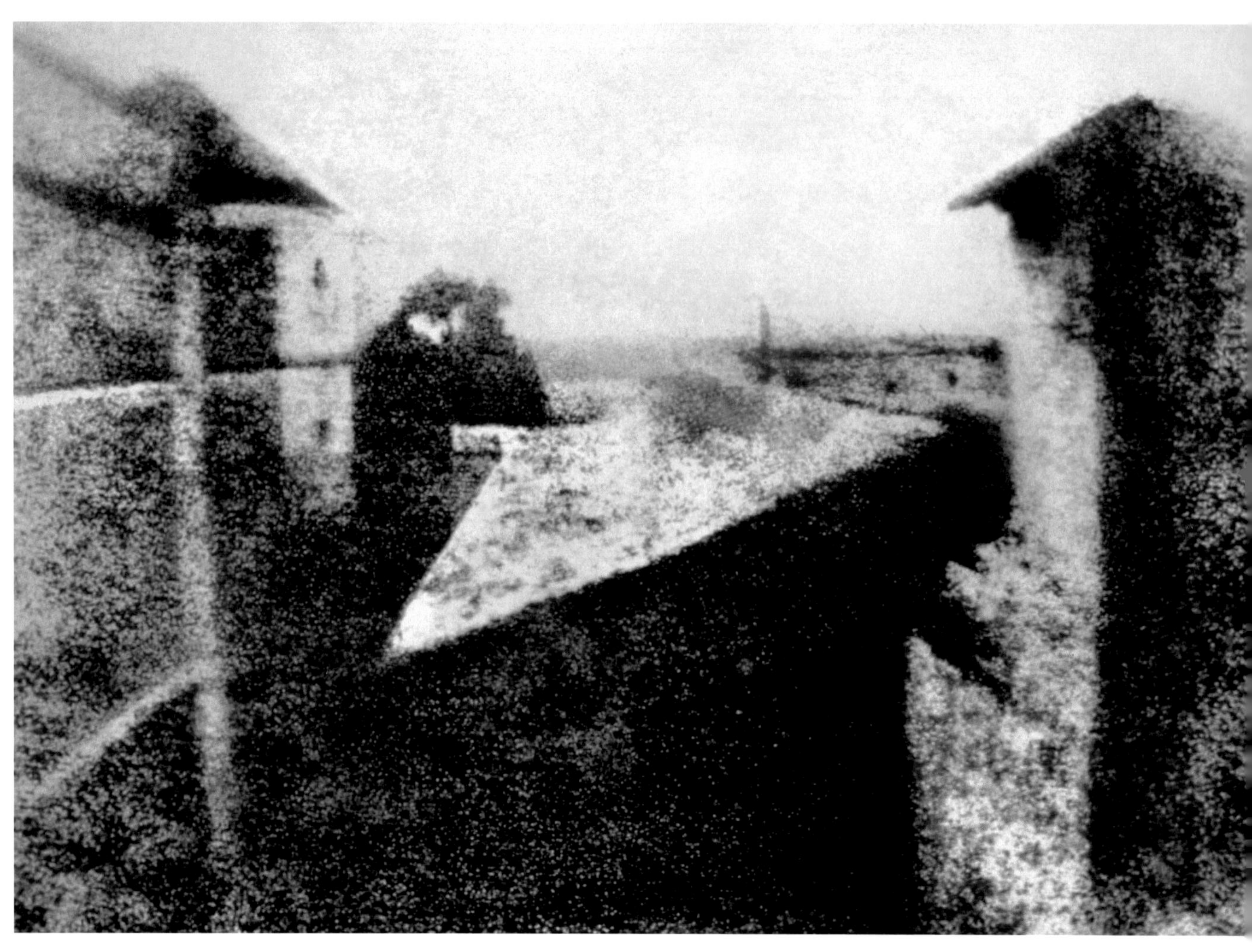

1765–1833 Nicéphore Niépce **1771–1805 Thomas Wedgewood**

THE INVENTION OF PHOTOGRAPHY

"How charming it would be if it were possible to cause these natural images to imprint themselves durably, and remain fixed on paper." Frustrated by his insufficient skill as an artist, William Henry Fox Talbot (1800–1877) wanted to improve the quality of the drawings he made during his honeymoon at Lake Como in 1883. For Talbot, as for many other would-be artists, photography was the solution to this problem. The difference between Talbot and the others was that he actually went on to invent photography. He was not the only person to come up with this idea, however. Unbeknownst to Talbot, several others were working towards the solution of the same problem; the invention of photography must have been in the air at the beginning of the 19th century. When the method was officially presented to the world by Louis Jacques Mandé Daguerre (1787–1851) on August 19, 1839, he was only one of several who claimed to be the inventors of photography. Not only Talbot and Daguerre, but also Nicéphore Niépce (1765–1833), Hippolyte Bayard (1801–1887) (see *Self-Portraits*), Hercule Florence (1804–1879), who

was a Frenchman living in Brazil, and the Norwegian Hans Thøger Winter (1787–1851), all invented photography independently of one another, or at least claimed to have done so after the publication of Daguerre's method.

Talbot had made several attempts before he succeeded in creating the first photograms on paper in 1834, dipping paper in a salt solution before sensitizing it with a solution of silver nitrate. In 1835 he succeeded in taking a picture of his house using his little camera obscura, making it "the first known instance of a house painting its own portrait" (fig. p. 16). Satisfied with his achievement, he then turned his mind to other things.

Nicéphore Niépce faced the same problem as Talbot: he could not draw. At first, he tried to make lithography stones light sensitive in order to expose them in the camera obscura. These attempts were not successful, but he continued his research and, as early as 1816, described a picture of a birdhouse that he had clearly succeeded in photographing: "The possibility of drawing in this way seems to me to have been all but proved." Unfortunately, this picture has been lost. Extant, however, is the "heliograph" (as Niépce called it) entitled *View from the Window in Le Gras* (left), created by Niépce in 1826 or 1827, and therefore today considered the first (surviving) photograph. He produced it us-

left——Nicéphore Niépce: View from the Window in Le Gras
1826/27 | Gernsheim Collection | The University of Texas at Austin

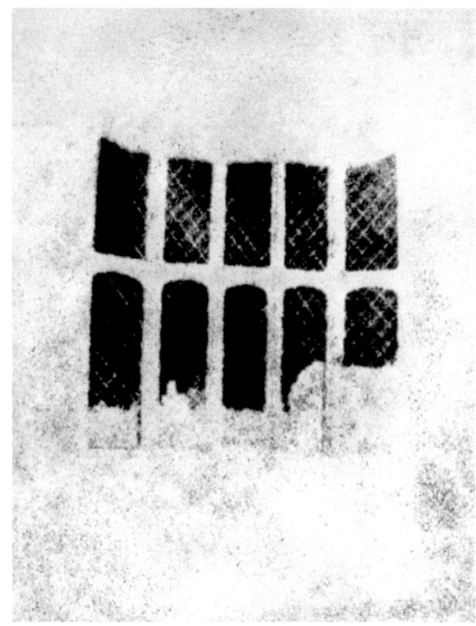

ing a tin plate made sensitive to light with a layer of asphalt, which he exposed for eight hours.

In 1829, Niépce was introduced to Louis Daguerre by the lens dealer they had in common. Daguerre was a successful Paris businessman who made his money from presenting dioramas; he hoped that the possibility of creating permanent images from the camera obscura would facilitate his work creating expansive views for his dioramas. The two men decided to work together.

When Niépce died in 1833, Daguerre continued to do research on his own. Niépce's method proved to be groundbreaking but, simultaneously, impracticable. Daguerre, on the other hand, experimented with silver-coated copper plates, which he steamed with iodine crystals. His breakthrough occurred in the fall of 1834: as a result of a coincidence, he decided to develop the exposed plates using mercury vapor. This resulted in extremely detailed images with fine tonal nuances. It would take another three years, however, before he managed to fix the images permanently using a strong saline solution. One of his first pictures shows the Boulevard du Temple, which appears to be deserted (right); only a bootblack and his customer are to be seen on what was generally a lively street—this is because these two were the only people to stay still for long enough to be captured

on the plate, which required a long exposure time. It was then that Daguerre was ready to present the process to the public. In January 1839, he introduced his "daguerreotypes" to a commission of the Académie des Sciences in Paris, which included the statesman and director of the observatory François Arago, and the German scientist Alexander von Humboldt. Full of enthusiasm, they suggested that Daguerre transfer the rights of his invention to the state (and thus to the public) in return for a life annuity for him and for Niépce's son. That very same month, a Parisian daily newspaper praised the advantages of photography in almost prophetic terms: "This discovery verges on the miraculous. [...] You will come to see how far removed pencil and paintbrush are from the truth of the daguerreotype. But drawers and painters need not despair: M. Daguerre's results differ from their work and can, in many respects, not replace it."

On August 19, 1839, Daguerre's method was published, thus firing the official starting shot for the development of photography. At the same time, a book by Daguerre was published in more than 30 editions and distributed from New York to Tokyo. It not only described his method in detail, but also

left——**WILLIAM HENRY FOX TALBOT: WINDOW (LACOCK ABBEY)** | 1835 Fox Talbot Museum | Lacock Abbey

right——**LOUIS JACQUES MANDÉ DAGUERRE: BOULEVARD DU TEMPLE** 1838 | Bayerisches Nationalmuseum | Munich

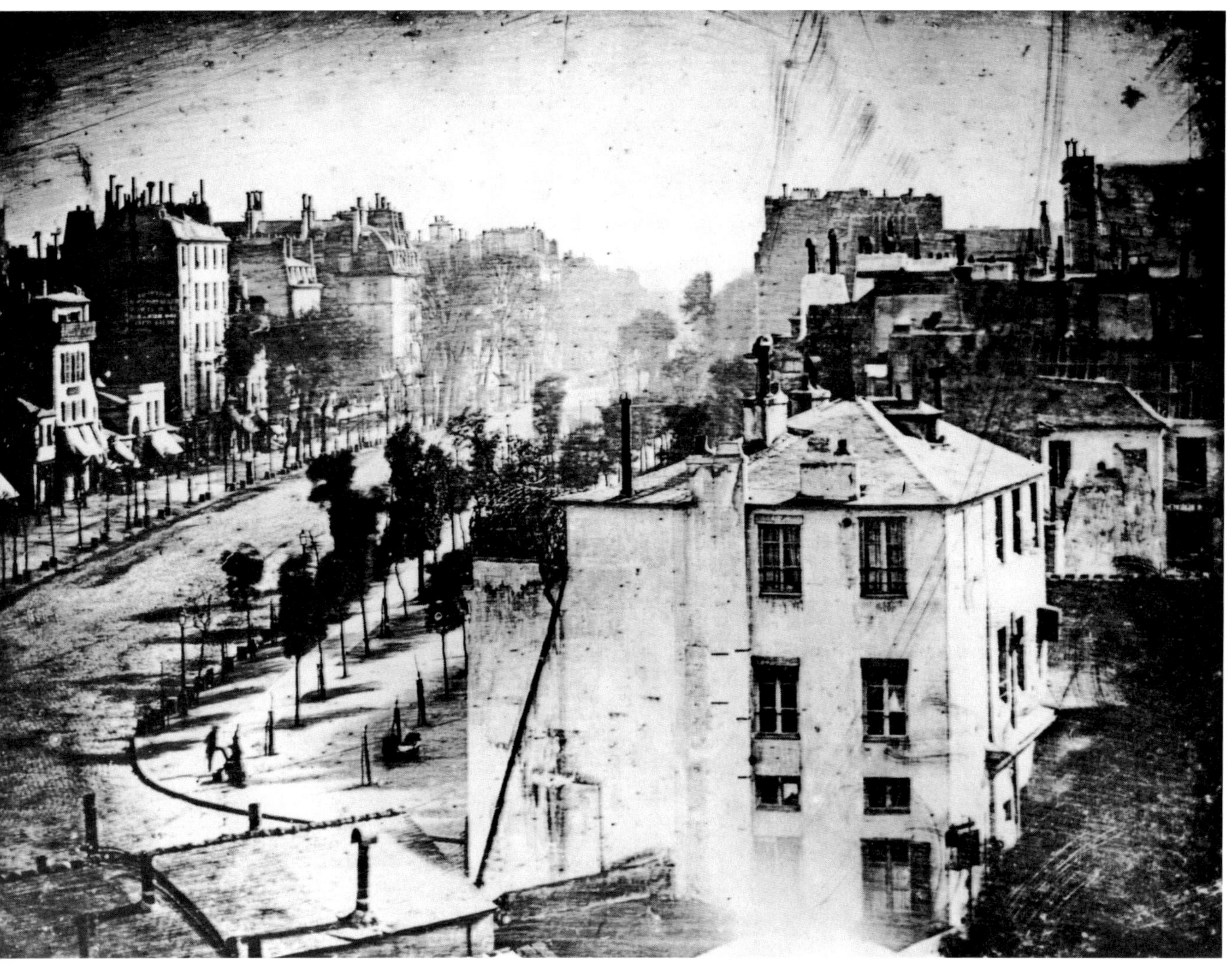

included construction drawings of the necessary equipment. The rapid spread of his ideas shows that people already longed for something like photography. "A few days later, opticians' shops were besieged by amateurs desperate to own daguerreotype devices, and everywhere cameras were being pointed at buildings," wrote one eyewitness. Daguerre's book claimed that this "procedure is no more difficult than saddling and bridling a horse," which is remarkable considering the complexity of the method. A veritable daguerreotype-mania took hold of the public (fig. p. 19),

and continued to flourish for several years thanks to a steady drop in prices. In Paris alone, more than 2,000 appliances and 500,000 plates were sold in 1846. Critical voices were to be heard among the euphoric choruses, however, complaining about the long exposure time, which made pictures of movement impossible and portraits difficult. It was also said that "Daguerre's invention has tremendous scientific value, but only limited artistic value." This was the beginning of a long debate about whether photography is an art or not, "because in everything that

"Photography should not be confused with painting. The former, like the latter, is a representational art form that has its own aesthetic."

relates to true art, it is the power of imagination and observation, rather than the anxious copying of the external, that has an effect on us." And many early daguerreotypes do indeed have little connection to art; they are fascinating primarily for the technical conditions under which they were made at that time, rather than for their artistic expression. It took some time for photography to develop its own language, one that would allow it to grow into an entirely new artistic medium. The inventor of the *carte de visite*, Alphonse Eugène Disdéri (1819–1889) (see *Portraits*), wrote in 1864 that "photography should not be confused with painting. The former, like the latter, is a representational art form that has its own aesthetic."

The problem of long exposure times was steadily improved thanks to the refinements made by many amateurs. The exposure time required in 1839 was 15 minutes, but this was soon reduced to less than a minute as a result of the development of better lenses and of emulsions more sensitive to light.

There was another problem with the daguerreotype, however, and this was impossible to solve. The finished photographs were extremely fragile and unique—they could not be reproduced.

The photographic method of William Henry Fox Talbot did not suffer from this drawback. When Talbot heard about Daguerre's developments in Paris, he thought again about his own method.

He rapidly set about writing the paper "Some account of the art of photogenic drawing [...] by which natural objects may be made to delineate themselves without the aid of the artist's pencil," which he presented to the Royal Society in London in January 1939. But, as is well known, he crossed the finishing line too late, and so Daguerre was, at least initially, given all the credit.

Yet Talbot achieved something that would become more important in photography than the daguerreotype: the positive-negative method. He called his pictures calotypes (from the Greek *kalos*, beautiful), and received a patent for them in 1841. Talbot covered paper sensitized by a silver-nitrate solution with a solution of gallic acid and silver nitrate, making it even more light sensitive, and then exposed it. This resulted in a so-called latent image that had been exposed but was not yet visible. The paper was developed again in the same solution, leading to noticeably shorter exposure times. The exposed areas turned dark, and unexposed sections remained light; it was, in other words, a negative. Talbot then washed the picture in a bath of solution not dissimilar to modern-day fixing agent. Next, he

right——**Théodor Maurisset: La Daguerreotypomanie** | December 1839

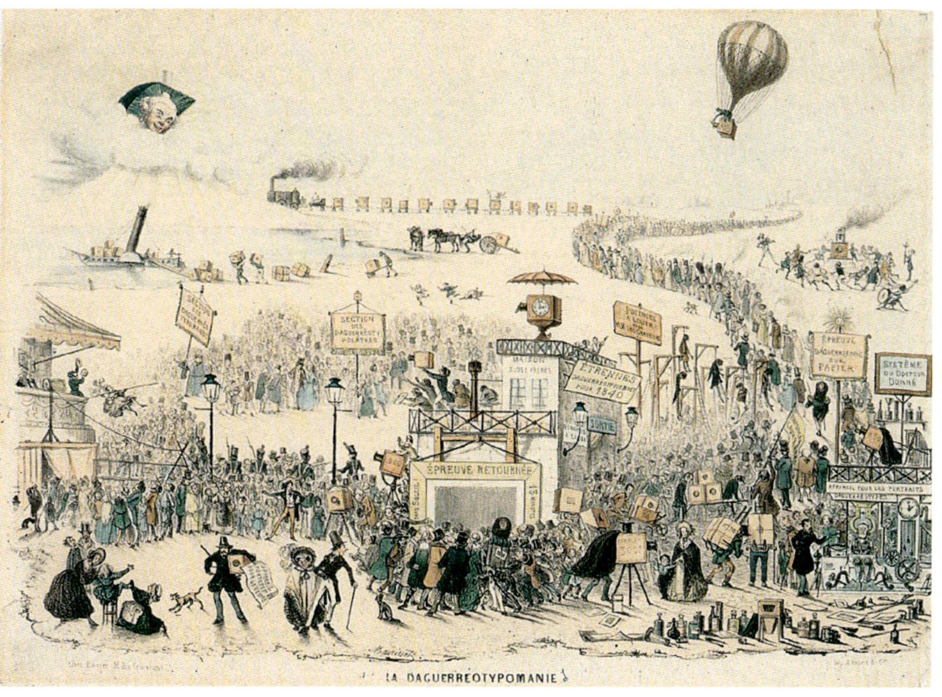

made the negative transparent using beeswax. In order to create a picture true to the original, a print of the negative had to be made; renewed exposure caused the tonal values to be reversed. This process, though involved, had the advantage that an unlimited number of copies of the negative could be made. As a result of the fibrous structure of paper, calotypes were not as brilliant and rich in nuances as were daguerreotypes. The simplicity of the method and the reproducibility of the image, however, would be highly influential. And yet this form of photography, which also became known as talbotype, spread only very slowly because Talbot charged a high license fee for the use of his patent, and mercilessly prosecuted infringements. His method became popular among amateurs (because of the lower costs), and soon among artists too, who valued its painterly effects.

Although Daguerre's method was at first the more successful, Talbot's would finally emerge victorious: the daguerreotype disappeared from the face of the earth. At the 1856 annual exhibition of London's Photographic Society, only three of the 606 images exhibited were daguerreotypes. To this day, analogue photography is based on the negative-positive method invented by Talbot.

It must also be said that even the term "photography" also had two inventors. One was Talbot's friend and natural scientist Sir John Hershel (fig. p. 29), and the other was Hercule Florence in Brazil, who used the term in his notebooks two years before Hershel.

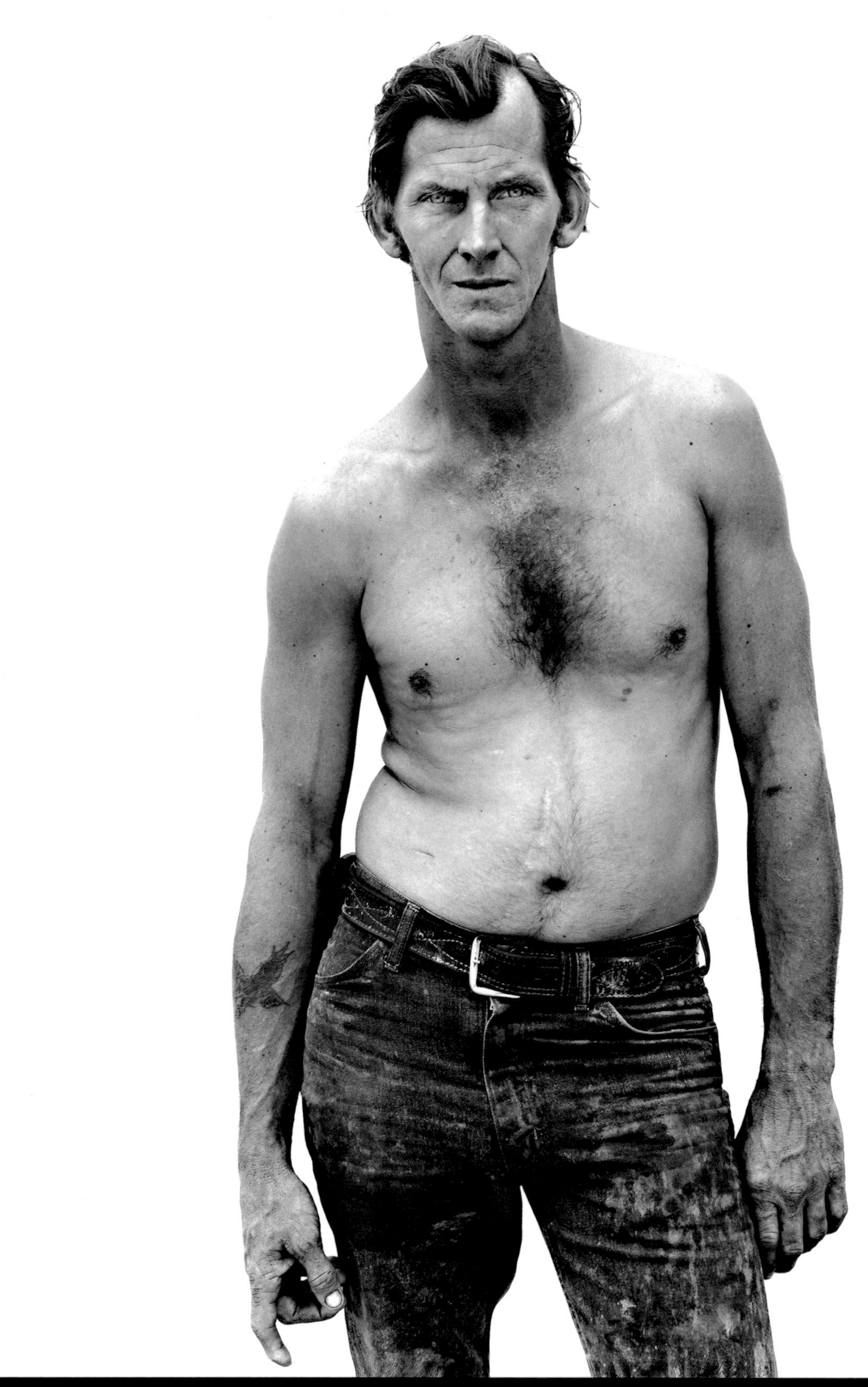

1787–1851 Louis Jacques Mandé Daguerre   1798–1863 Eugène Delacroix   1802–1870 David Octavius Hill

PORTRAITS

Photography was a mass phenomenon from the moment it was officially announced to the public in August 1839. People could be seen everywhere with the cumbersome equipment they used to capture images of their surroundings. Cameras were sold, built, and modified by individuals all over the world. There was an enormous enthusiasm for a device with which the user could create images more accurately than any artist. The only thing that dampened this enthusiasm was the long exposure times needed, which made it difficult—if not impossible—to take portraits. But as soon as it became technically possible to shorten the exposure times appreciably, the process aroused even greater interest and enthusiasm. The portrait, previously the prerogative of the prosperous classes, was now democratized and the middle classes, who were then in the process of asserting themselves politically and socially, acquired their own (inexpensive) form of representation.

Initially, however, things did not look at all promising. In April 1840 the optical scientist Jean-Baptiste-François Soleil (1798–1878) noted in a book on the subject of daguerreotypes: "Our hopes regarding the creation of portraits have so far not been fulfilled [...] I know that to date no portrait has been produced in which the eyes are open and the posture and facial expression are natural." This was not surprising, because even Daguerre himself doubted that his process was suitable for portraits, since the exposure times of up to a quarter of an hour were far too long. Nonetheless, Daguerre apparently did attempt to produce portraits. In 1998 the French photo-historian Marc Pagneux found what he considered to be rather a strange-looking daguerreotype at a flea market. His research proved that it was the oldest known photographic portrait. It was produced in 1837, in other words two years before the official announcement of the invention of photography. This tiny daguerreotype (it measures 5.8 x 4.5 cm, 2¼ x 1¾ in) shows a friend of Daguerre's, the artist Nicolas Huet (fig. p. 23, right). There were probably two reasons why Daguerre decided not to display this portrait with the other pictures in the Académie des Sciences. Firstly, he could see that it would not be possible to produce a proper portrait photo with long exposure times. Secondly, he may have decided to present it to the public at a later date, when the technology had improved, in order to establish yet another milestone. Daguerre clearly failed to take into account the enormous speed with which the daguerreotype process was to develop as a result of the ideas and

left—RICHARD AVEDON: BILLY MUDD, TRUCKER, ALTO, TEXAS, MAY 7, 1981

1819—Carlsbad Decrees
1826—First photography
1827—Death of Ludwig van Beethoven
1831—Nat Turner's Rebellion in Virginia
1815–1879 Julia Margaret Cameron
1820–1910 Nadar
1832–1856 John Beasley Greene

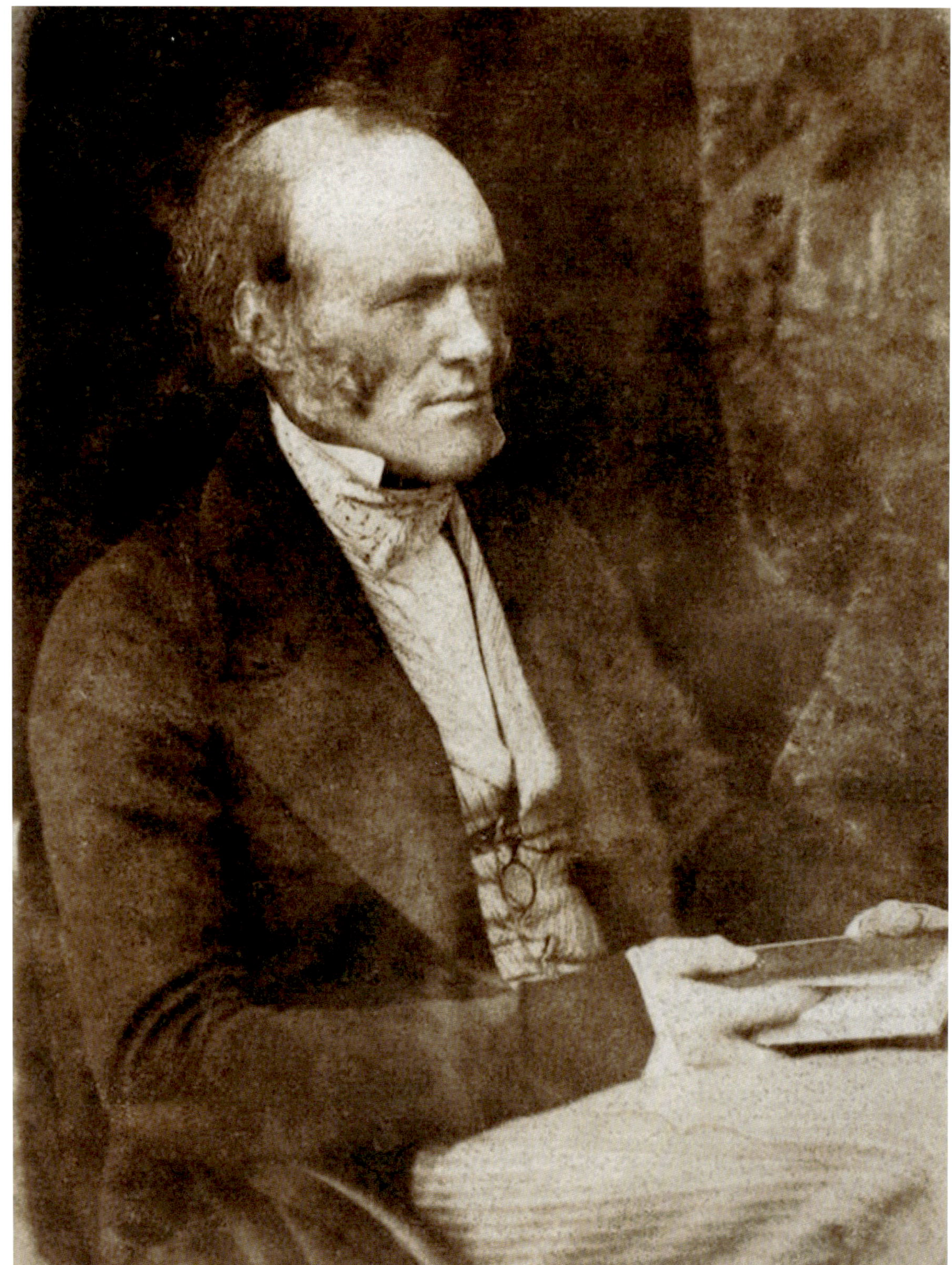

"Photography fascinates the greatest minds and yet it can be carried out by any fool."

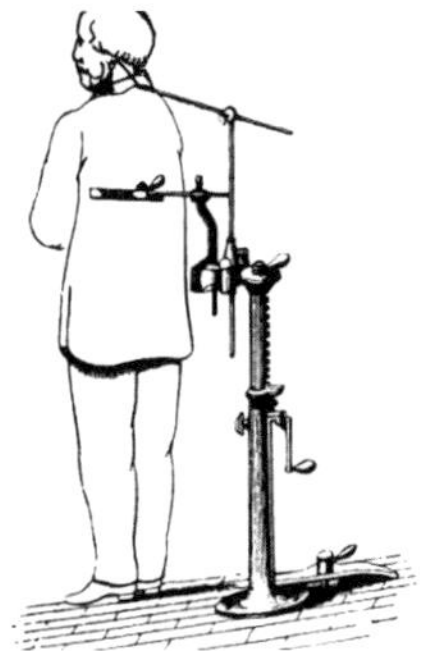 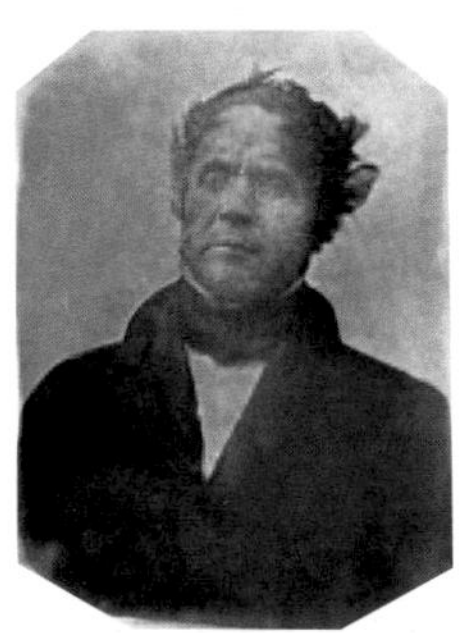

experiments of countless keen amateur inventors. Even after exposure times had been considerably shortened, sitting for a portrait remained quite an arduous process. For the sitting, the "victims" were forced into uncomfortable harnesses so that they did not move and spoil the picture (above right). During the long exposure time, they were subjected to bright sunlight and blinding mirrors, which were meant to shine as much light as possible onto the face. And last but not least, faces were coated with white powder in order to increase the contrasts.

In spite of these tortuous procedures, however, portrait studios mushroomed everywhere and it became very fashionable to have one's daguerreotype portrait taken. In the United States in particular, photography was greeted with great excitement. By early 1840, for example, the first "daguerreotype portrait studio" opened in New York. At last, less prosperous citizens also had the chance of having their portrait taken, and they took advantage of opportunity with enormous enthusiasm. It has been estimated that in the United States alone, of the 30 million photographs taken between 1840 and 1860, 95 percent were portraits. The new technique, a symbol of the self-representation of the young democracy, also offered career opportunities within the country's less rigid social system. All that was required was a small amount of starting capital, as well as a basic knowledge of the technology and chemistry involved in using the equipment—but otherwise no particular craftsmanship or artistic skills. The French photographer and journalist Nadar unflatteringly described the new medium as follows: "Photography fascinates the greatest minds and yet it can be carried out by any fool."

Early portrait photography cannot yet be described as an art; it was often more a case of overcoming technical difficulties than of responding creatively to artistic challenges. The portrait studios had a stock of backgrounds and props that they used repeatedly, so that portraits quickly became stereotyped. There were exceptions, however, including the photos taken by the Scottish artist David Octavius

above left——**Head and body support** | 19th-century illustration

above right——**Louis Jacques Mandé Daguerre: Nicolas Huet** | 1837 5.8 x 4.5 cm | daguerreotype

left——**David Octavius Hill: Charles Lyell** | 1843–1847 | Royal Photographic Society | London

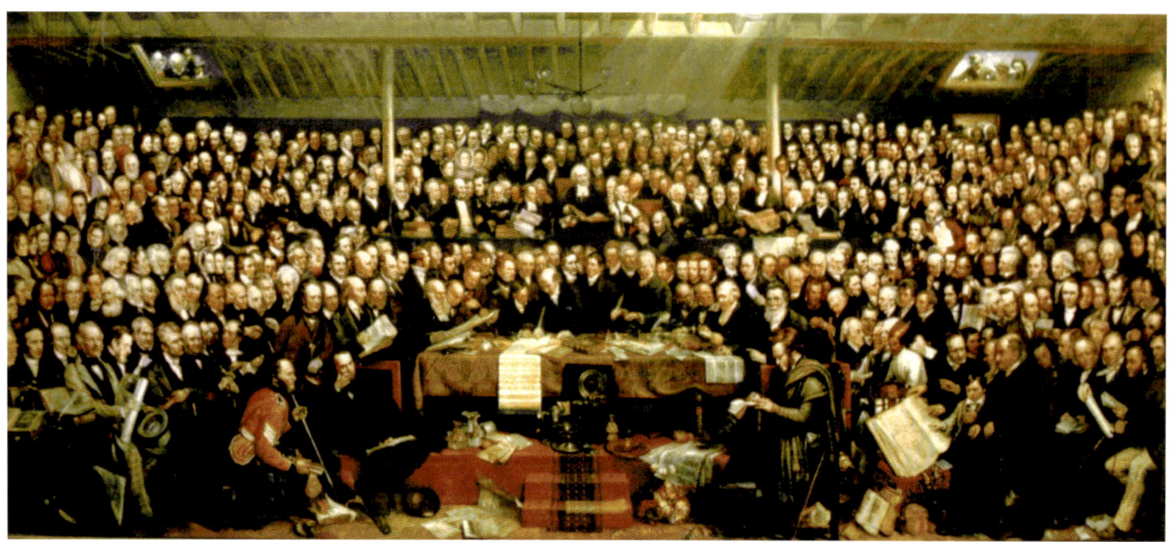

Hill (1802–1870) and his colleague Robert Adamson (1821–1848), who worked with the calotype process developed by Henry Fox Talbot. In 1843 Hill was commissioned to paint a group portrait of the 457 men and women attending the First General Assembly of the Free Church of Scotland in Edinburgh (above). For this, the two pioneers produced more than 1,500 group and individual portraits that served as a reference for the vast painting. Hill was responsible for the artistic part, while the younger Adamson was in charge of the photo technology. Here too the exposure times varied from three and six minutes. In spite of this (or perhaps because of it), the portraits the two artists produced are characterized by a particular intensity. During the short period of their partnership until Adamson's early death in 1848, they produced over 3,000 calotypes showing not only the members of the Church but also farmers, sailors, and scientists (fig. p. 22), and scenes of everyday life. Hill did not complete the painting until 1866.

The quality of portrait photos changed not only because of technological improvements, but above all because of the person who stood behind the camera. In 1854 the caricaturist and writer Gaspard-Félix Tournachon (1820–1910), known as Nadar, opened his first photo studio in Paris. It became the meet-ing place of the Parisian bohemian scene, whose members liked to be photographed by him. In his portraits, Nadar mostly dispensed with decorative frills and placed his models in front of a neutral background. The people in his pictures accordingly look all the more intense (fig. p. 27). This prompted the German-born French photographer Gisèle Freund (1908/1912–2000), to observe in her ground-breaking dissertation of 1936: "Photography, on the cusp of its development, and using technology that was still primitive, experienced an artistic perfection that has never been achieved again in this manner." This applies, however, only to exceptional characters like Nadar or his colleague Étienne Carjat (1828–1906), interestingly enough also a caricaturist. Nadar was always interested in the latest developments, not only in photography (see *Night Photography*), but also in painting. It is therefore not surprising that in 1874 the first exhibition was held in his studio of

above——**DAVID OCTAVIUS HILL: FIRST GENERAL ASSEMBLY OF THE FREE CHURCH OF SCOTLAND** | 1843–1866 | oil on canvas | 153 x 345 cm | Free Church of Scotland | Edinburgh

"Photography, on the cusp of its development, and using technology that was still primitive, experienced an artistic perfection that has never been achieved again in this manner."

works by the young artists who would soon form the avant-garde of French art: the Impressionists surrounding Claude Monet and Camille Pissarro. Portrait photography became a real mass phenomenon with the introduction of the *carte de visite,* a photographic calling card in the convenient size of 6 x 9 cm (just under 2½ x 3½) that usually showed a full-length portrait (fig. p. 28). It was invented by Adolphe Eugène Disdéri (1819–1889), who developed a camera with which several photos could be taken on the same plate. With this process, which was patented in 1854, it became even cheaper to have one's photo taken and virtually everyone in the middle and upper classes had a *carte de visite* made to be exchanged during social encounters. This proved the ruin of the miniature portrait painters in particular, who were already suffering under the competition of photography. Many of these artists exchanged their paintbrush for a camera and worked as portrait photographers instead. Those who did not keep up with developments lost their customers and their livelihood.

One of the few women who became involved in photography at a relatively early stage in its development was Julia Margaret Cameron (1815–1879). She was introduced to photography when, at the age of 48,

she was given a camera by her daughter; in time she became one of the most celebrated woman photographers of the 19th century. Apart from religious allegories typical of the era, she created above all portraits that where artistically far superior to the broad mass of studio photographs. But her pictures were also dependent on long exposure times, as can clearly be seen in her portrait of Sir John Herschel (fig. p. 29). It is obvious that Herschel looked back and forth while the photo was being taken, his blurred eyes giving him the appearance of a seer. That, however, seems only appropriate, for he was the person who introduced Henry Fox Talbot to the pioneering method of fixing pictures, and he also introduced the terms "negative," "positive," and "photography."

In the second half of the 20th century, portrait photography was characterized by two contrasting approaches. One was the so-called "environmental portrait," whose most famous exponent was the American photographer Arnold Newman (1918–2006). Newman felt it was important to present subjects in their own environment or with their personal belongings. He considered that the surroundings in his elaborately designed compositions told the viewer more about a person than a mere portrait shot could. But even Newman realized that it was possible

"In front of the camera lens I am simultaneously the person I consider myself to be, the person I would like to be, and the person the photographer thinks I am and whom he makes use of in order to demonstrate his skill."

to photograph only the external shell of an individual: "Any photographic attempt to show the complete person is nonsense. We can only show [...] what the surface reveals. The inner life is seldom revealed, sometimes not even to oneself." In one of his most famous portraits (fig. p. 30), he nonetheless attempts to look "beneath the surface." In 1963, Newman was commissioned by the magazine *Newsweek* to make a portrait of the German industrial tycoon Alfried Krupp, who had been sentenced to twelve years' imprisonment during the Nuremberg Trials at the end of the Third Reich because of his company's use of forced labor. Newman, who was of Jewish descent, originally wanted to refuse the contract, but he finally agreed. In Krupp he encountered a distinguished elderly gentleman who bore no resemblance to his idea of a war criminal. Krupp had a high opinion of Newman's portraits and gave him a free hand. Newman placed him on a platform above one of the production halls and set the lighting to the right and left. When he asked Krupp to lean forward he had him in the right light. "It was as if I had photographed the devil," commented Newman later in an interview. The greenish coloring that emanated from the neon lighting in the hall contributed in no small measure to the menacing, ghostly atmosphere. Krupp was not enthusiastic. "After this portrait I was persona non grata in Germany," observed Newman.

Richard Avedon (1923–2004) employed a contrasting style. Avedon was initially famous for his fashion photography (see *Fashion Photography*), but went on to become one of the most important portraitists of the 20th century. In contrast to Newman's environmental portraits, Avedon's portraits are highly puristic: "I work from a series of Nos: No to distracting details, No to a carefully chosen light, No to props. All these Nos force me to a Yes." That was how Avedon described his minimalist approach. "I have [...] no accessories, just a white background, the person I am interested in, and what happens between us." Avedon adopted this purism, which recalls the work of Nadar, not only in his portraits of famous people but also for his famous series *In the American West*, for which he photographed hundreds of unknown people between 1979 and 1985. The example of the trucker Billy Mudd (fig. p. 20), whom Avedon portrayed in 1981 during the course of this project, shows how portraits can penetrate beneath the surface and have a profound effect on people. When Mudd saw himself on a three-meter-high print at the first exhibition in the

right——**Nadar: Nadar's Mother** | 1853 | Menil Foundation | Houston

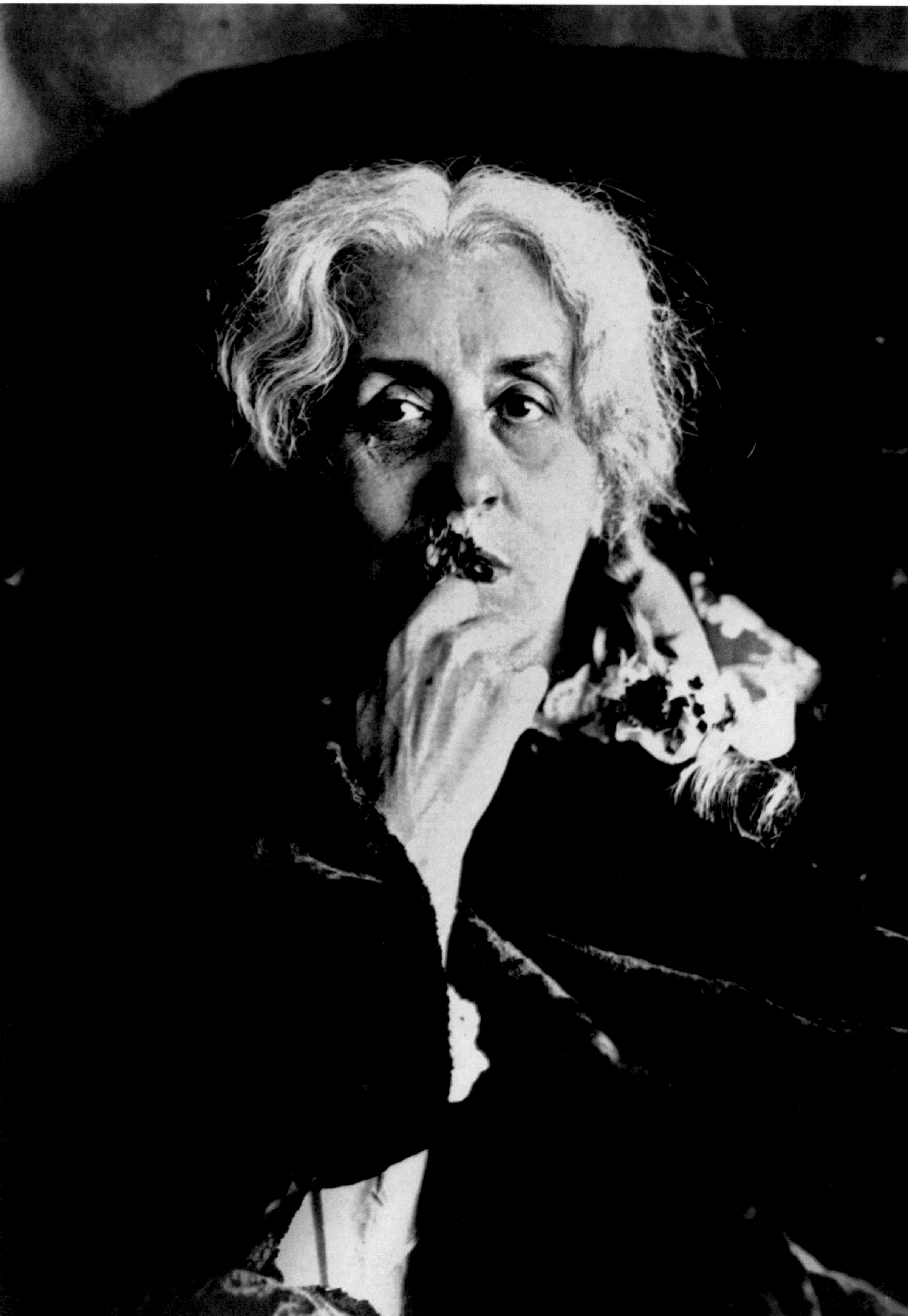

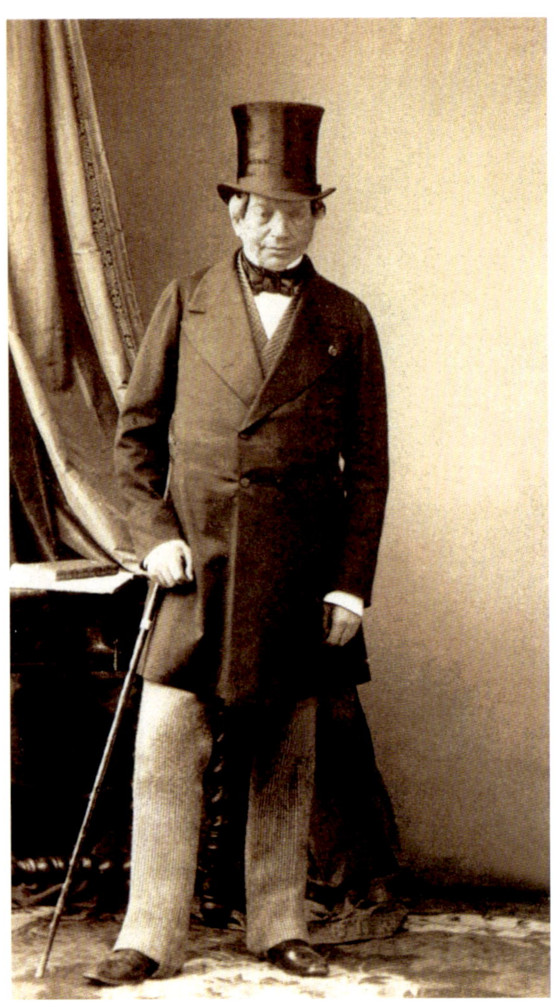

Amon Carter Museum in Fort Worth in 1985, he experienced a feeling not of delight or surprise but of fear: "It was like an out-of-the-body experience. It frightened me. I suddenly saw myself as a mirror could never reflect me [...] It was so enormous that I looked at myself and thought I was dead." Billy Mudd, who transported dynamite, was suffering from severe depression at the time and had already tried to commit suicide. Avedon had clearly found his sensitive spot: "I felt how I took hold of myself and said to myself: Well, son, you've got to change your life."

The example of Roger Ballen (b. 1950) shows the way in which "straightforward" portraits can also amount to a political provocation. Between 1986 and 1993, the American geologist and photographer, who lives and works in South Africa, took photos for his book *Platteland* in the rural Transvaal in South Africa. During his trips as a geologist, he came across a white underclass that had hitherto been ignored and ostracized by official Apartheid policy. Until these photos were taken, the white citizens were always regarded as prosperous, educated, and unquestionably superior to the black population. Ballen's pictures show the other side of the coin (fig. p. 31). In that time of political upheaval, these portraits were political dynamite. The consequences for Ballen, who was white, were correspondingly violent. He was ejected from the South African Artists' Association and was repeatedly subject to threats of murder.

The portrait represents one of the most fascinating challenges facing a photographer; and, as we have seen, it can also be a challenge for the person being photographed. It is always a question of a blend of likeness and honesty, or, as the French critic Roland Barthes put it: "In front of the camera lens I am simultaneously the person I consider myself to be, the person I would like to be, and the person the photographer thinks I am and whom he makes use of in order to demonstrate his skill."

left——**Adolphe Eugène Disderi: F. C. Canrobert** | c. 1860

right——**Julia Margaret Cameron: The Astronomer Sir John Herschel** | 1867 | 30.2 x 23.2 cm | Royal Photographic Society

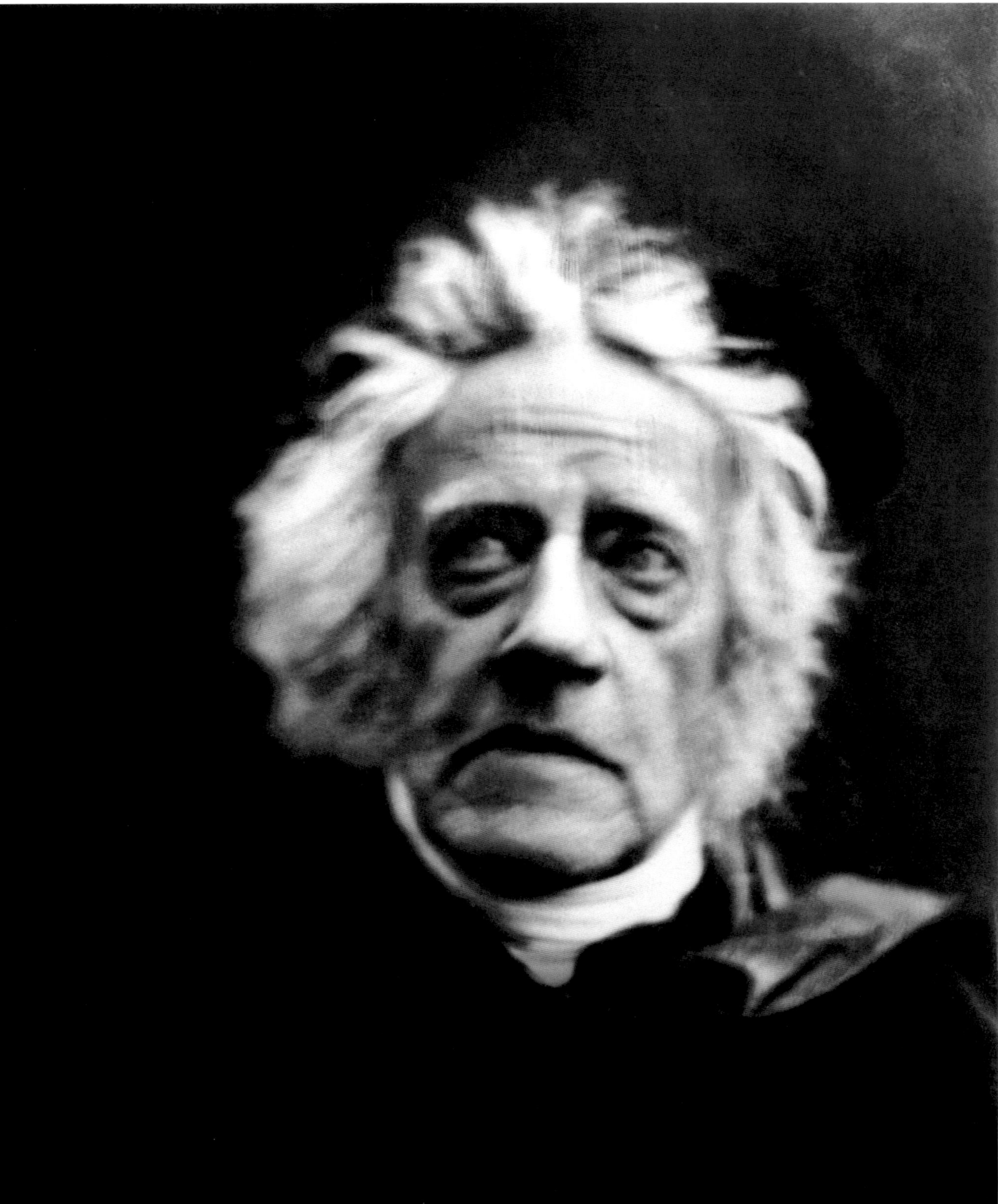

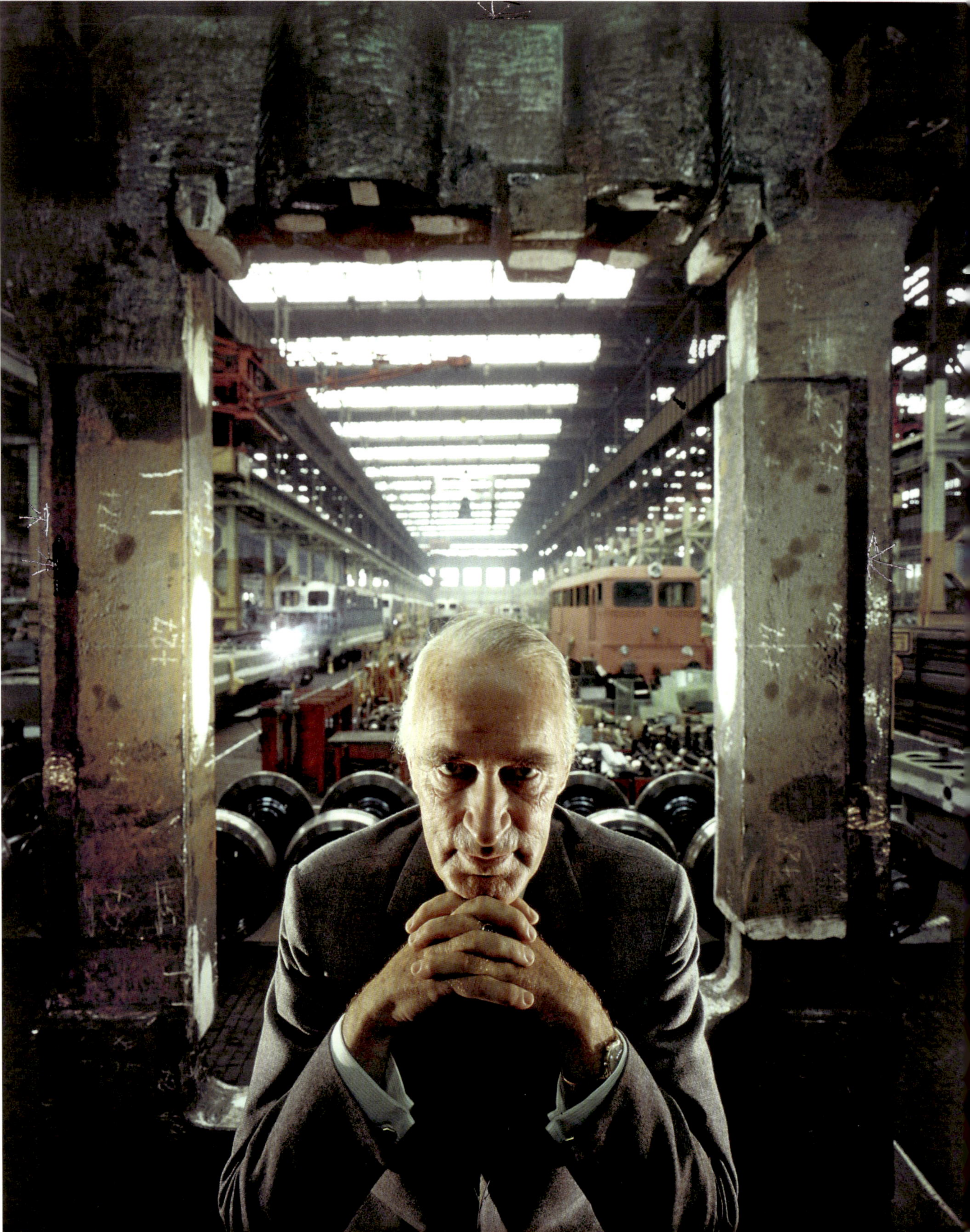

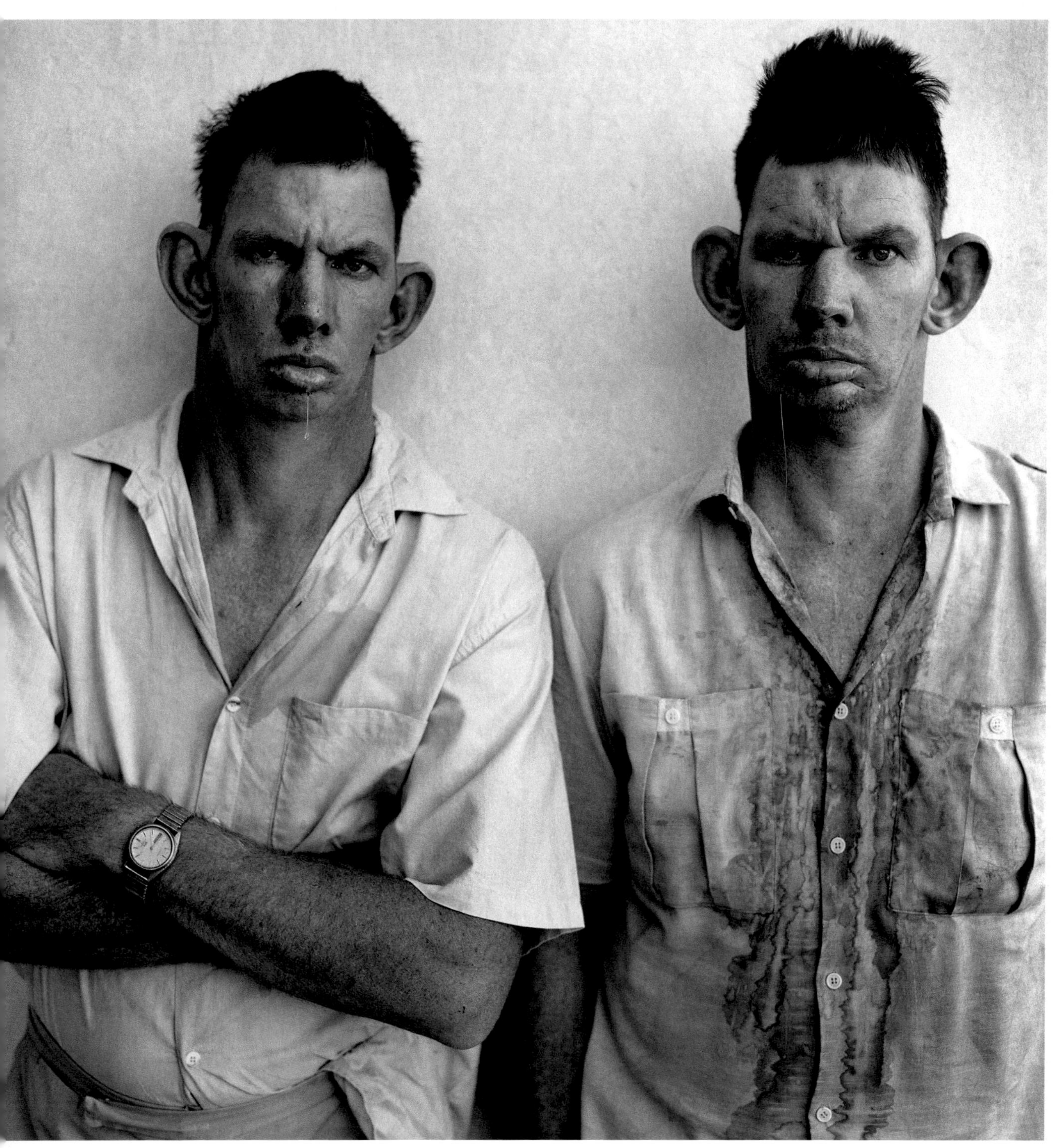

above——**Roger Ballen: Dresie and Casie** | Western Transvaal | 1993

left——**Arnold Newman: Alfried Krupp** | 1963

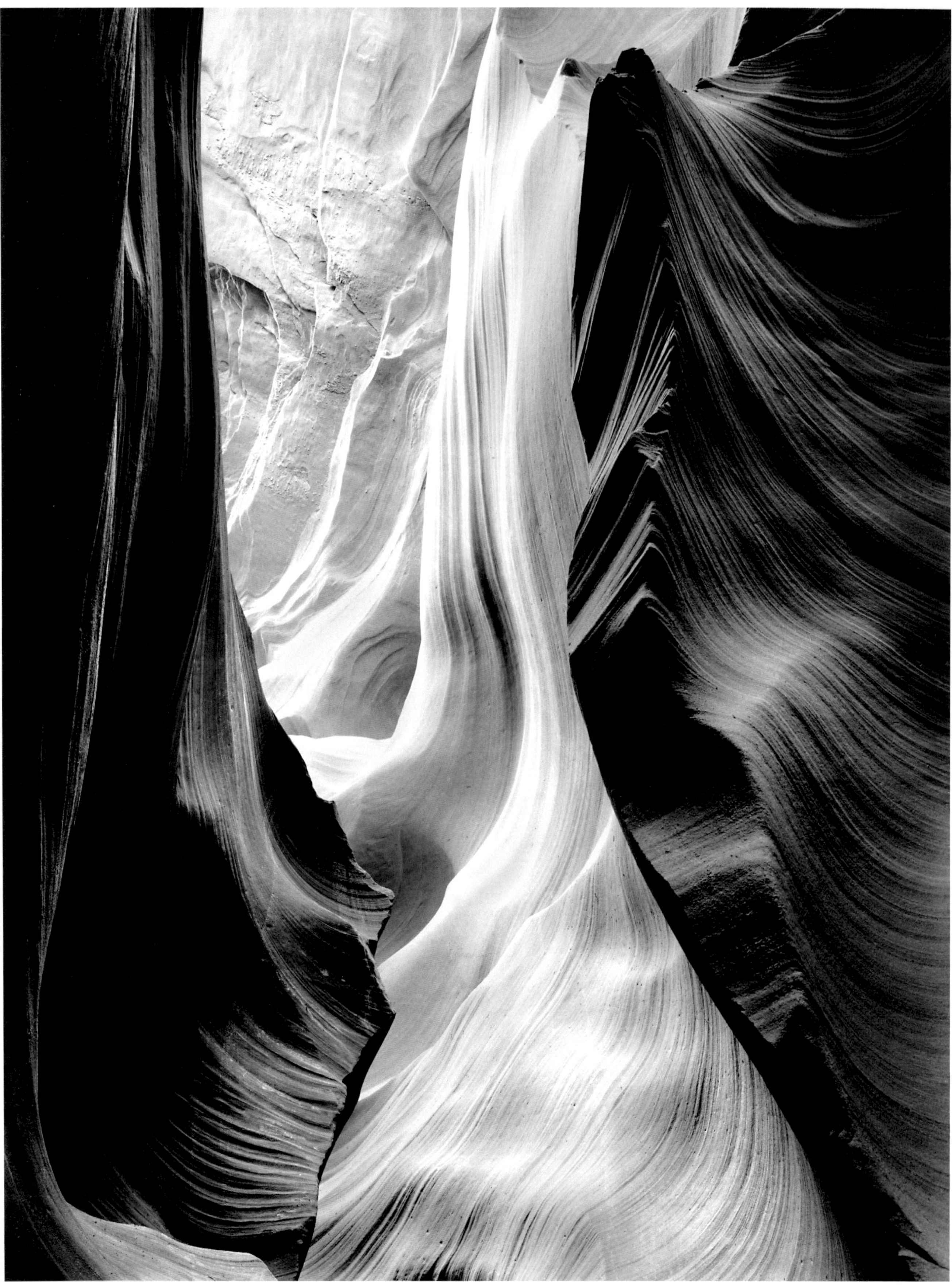

1771–1805 Thomas Wedgewood   1787–1851 Louis Jacques Mandé Daguerre   1800–1877 William Fox Talbot

LANDSCAPES

When Daguerre presented his daguerreotype to the Académie des Sciences in January 1839, his invention provoked great excitement. A Parisian daily newspaper immediately recognized its potential for what remains to this day one of the most important uses of photography: "Travelers, soon you will have the opportunity to purchase the machine invented by M. Daguerre for something like a couple of hundred francs. That will allow you to bring home to France the world's most beautiful memorials and landscape views." Landscapes and cityscapes soon became popular subjects; here, the long exposure times (which initially made portraits difficult and images of movement impossible) did not pose a problem. The voluminous camera equipment did require a high degree of enthusiasm on the photographer's part, however: together with all the necessary accessories, the basic daguerreotype equipment weighed about 50 kg (110 lb) (fig. p. 35, below). Shortly after the daguerreotype had been

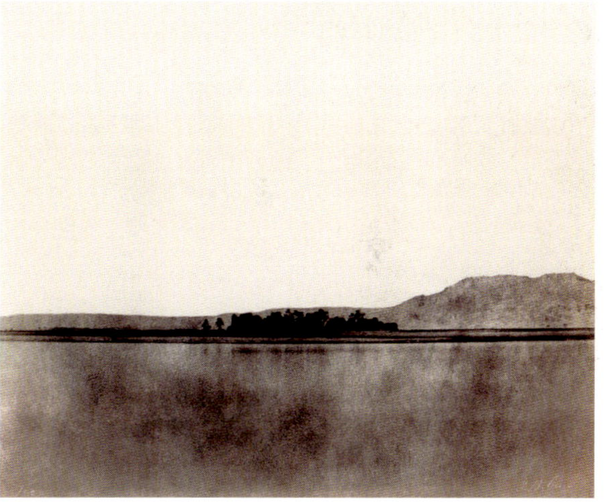

formally introduced to the public in August 1839, photographers set out to all parts of the world in order to bring back pictures of exotic locations to be viewed in the safety and comfort of European homes and exhibition spaces. The first photographs of the Sphinx in Egypt were taken as early as November 1839.

Egypt and the Middle East were of particular interest to many French photographers because of the enthusiasm generated by Napoleon's Egyptian campaign. John Beasley Greene (1832–1856), an American archeologist and photographer born in

left——**Bruce Barnbaum: Wall with Two Ridges** | Lower Antelope Canyon 1983
right——**John Beasley Greene: The Nile in Front of the Theban Hills** | 1853/54 | 23.1 x 30.3 cm | Gilman Collection | Metropolitan Museum of Art | New York

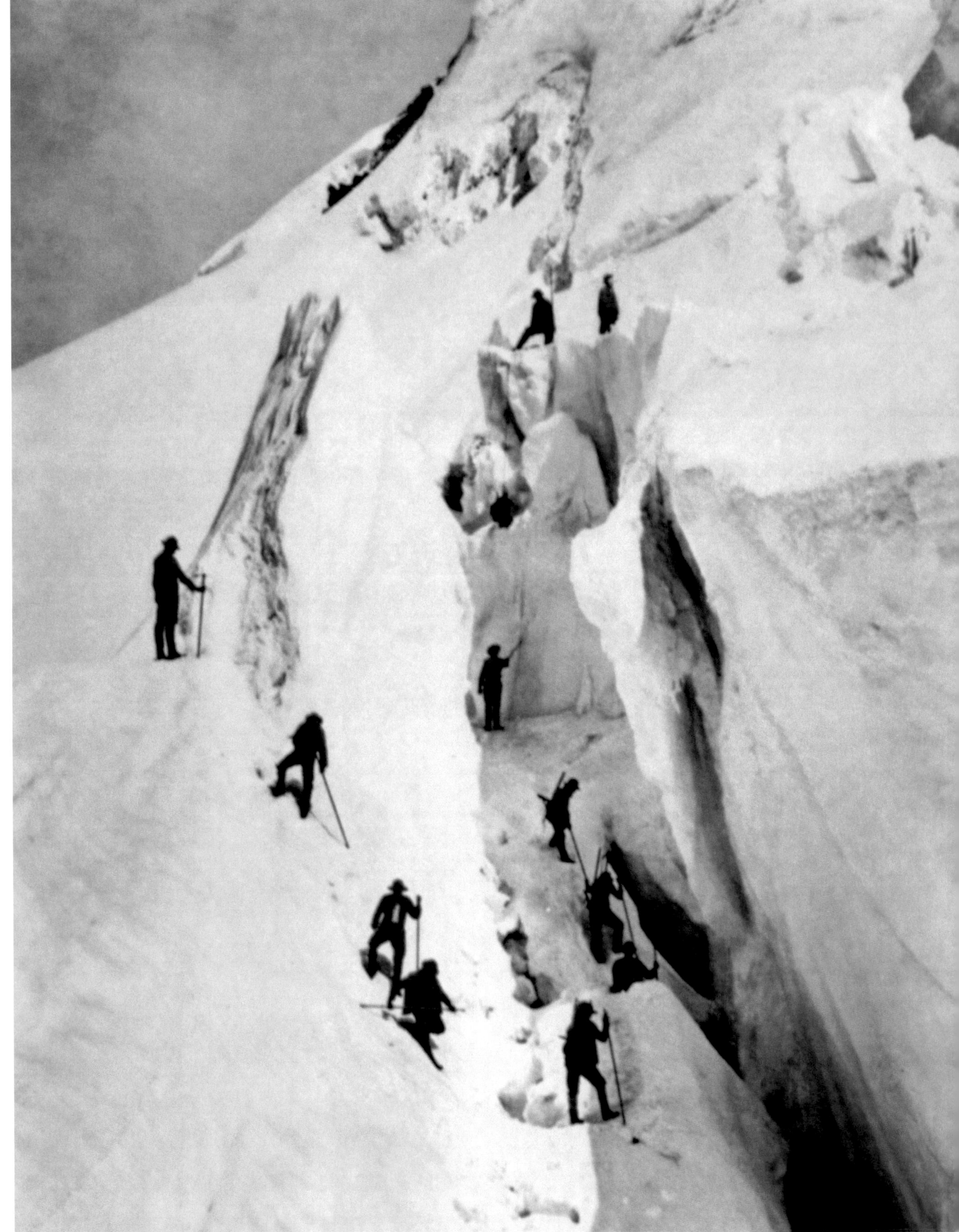

1814–1876 Louis-Auguste Bisson   **1832–1856 John Beasley Greene**   **1843–1942 William Henry Jackson**

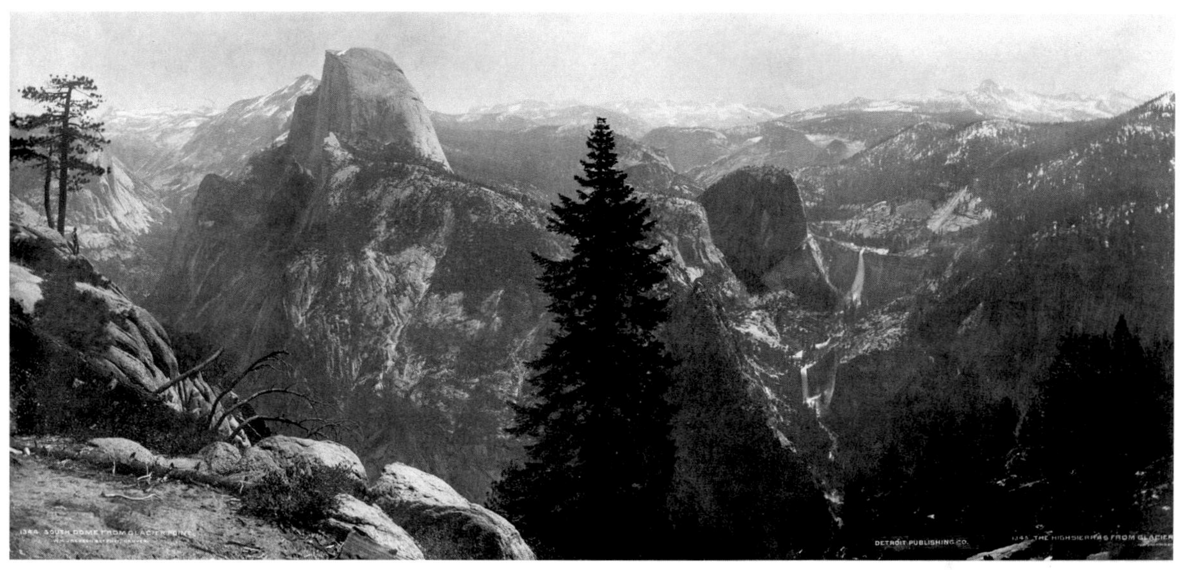

France, traveled to Egypt at the tender age of 21. His views of the Nile are remarkable for their graphic restraint, which sets them apart from those of his contemporaries. Whereas most photographers took their cue from landscape painting, Greene appears to have developed a distinctively *photographic* eye early on. He achieved an intensity that makes the photo reproduced here (fig. p. 33) an early masterpiece of landscape photography, thanks to its reduced composition. In Paris, 90 of his photographs were published in the book *Le Nil: Monuments, paysages, explorations photographiques* (1854). His publisher, Louis Désiré Blanquart-Evrard (1802–1872), was one of the first to recognize the economic potential of the reproduction of photographs. The former cloth merchant developed a technique with which he could produce up to 300 copies of a negative per day, which were pasted into books. His publishing company, Imprimerie Photographique Blanquart-Evrard, is considered to have been the first fine-art publisher for photography. In addition, Blanquart-Evrard developed the most important

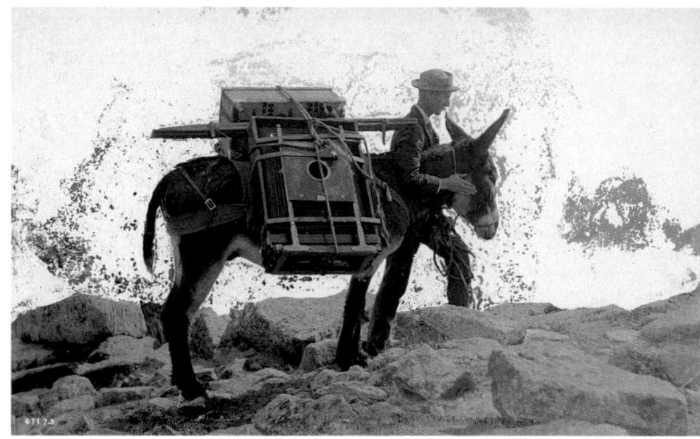

left——**Bisson Brothers: The Ascent of Mont-Blanc** | 1861
International Museum of Photography | Rochester

top——**William Jackson: Yellowstone** | c. 1870 | International
Museum of Photography | Rochester

above——**William Jackson: Photographic Equipment** | 1873
International Museum of Photography | Rochester

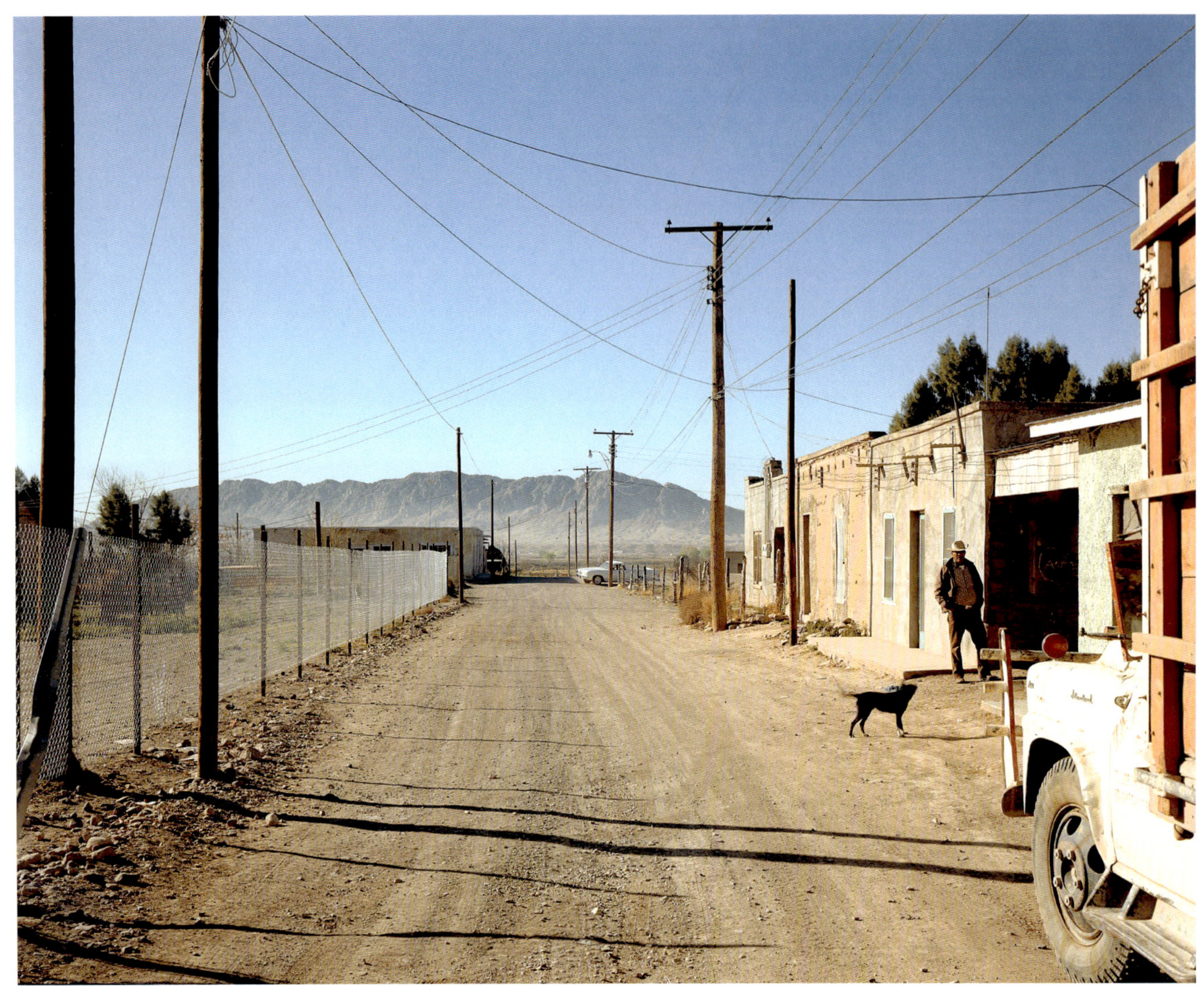

photographic paper of the 19th century, known as albumen paper.

Until the advent of mass tourism, it was photographers who introduced people to faraway countries. Their photographs told of exotic lands and untouched nature, and photographers went to tremendous trouble to get them. In 1850/51 Frederick Scott Archer (1813–1857) and Greene's teacher, Gustave Le Gray (1820–1884), developed the so-called wet-plate collodion method, which retained its primacy until the 1880s. This combined the advantages of both of the earlier methods, the daguerreotype and the calotype, so that photographic prints made using this process exhibit a wide tonal range and sharpness of detail, and can also be reproduced endlessly. The disadvantage lay in the amount of effort required: a damp layer of collodion was applied to a glass plate and next sensitized using silver nitrate; once it had been prepared in this way, the still-damp

above——STEPHEN SHORE: PRESIDIO, TEXAS, FEBRUARY 21, 1975
1975–2004 | chromogenic print | 43.2 x 55.2 cm

plate was inserted into the camera and then had to be developed immediately after exposure. This was a very laborious process even under studio conditions; when working outdoors, photographers had to take a darkroom-tent or a suitably adapted vehicle with them (fig. p. 49). Photographers accepted these inconveniences because of the prospect of producing spectacular, high-quality pictures.

The brothers Louis-Auguste (1814–1876) and Auguste-Rosalie (1826–1900) Bisson set themselves an extraordinary challenge in 1861, using this laborious process to produce photographs of their ascent of Mont Blanc (fig. p. 34). Just 75 years after the first ascent of the mountain, 25 men dragged equipment weighing more than 250 kg (550 lb) to the summit of the highest mountain in Europe in order to take the first high-altitude mountain photographs in history. In addition to the bulky equipment, there was the problem of the preparation of the glass plates and the immediate development of the photographs on site. Before taking a photograph, they had to heat the plates so that the silver would not crystallize due to the cold, and then had to melt snow for the wash. The result was an array of impressive photographs of the summit, as well as of the ascent and descent.

In the 1880s, the laborious collodion wet-plate process was also used for the photographic exploration of the western regions of America. As photographs were reproduced only as contact prints at the time, photographers had to carry around different sizes of cameras with which they exposed glass plates up to 50 x 60 cm (just under 20 x 24 in) in size to create different print sizes. William Henry Jackson (1843–1942) used this method to capture the untouched natural environment of the Rocky Mountains (fig. p. 35 above) and the famous geysers of Yellowstone. When his photographs were presented to Congress in Washington, politicians, enchanted by the great natural beauty of the region, recognized the value of untouched landscapes and in 1872 passed legislation to protect this extraordinary landscape. Yellowstone became the first national park in the United States. For a long time, landscape photography hardly changed: it focused on showing magnificent landscapes and unspoilt nature in photographs that were as spectacular as possible. Photographers like Ansel Adams and later Bruce Barnbaum (b. 1943) became famous for their impressive black-and-white pictures (fig. p. 32). Landscape photography was, for many years, a conservative genre. Radical changes did not take place until the 1970s, when color photography became standard and photographers discovered new subjects. Photographers like Robert Frank and William Eggleston acted as trailblazers. This young generation of photographers did not seek out the spectacular but the normal, the commonplace.

"Art is a fragment of creation,
seen through a temperament."

Stephen Shore (b. 1947) is one of the exponents of the new landscape photography (fig. p. 36). Shore explores everyday reality in the form of landscapes made by human hand, such as streets and parking lots, gas stations and motels. He draws inspiration from Eugène Atget, a photographer in Paris at the turn of the century (see *Straight Photography*). Fascinated by Atget's apparent lack of artistic pretensions, Shore does not use unusual angles, so that his photographs and their restrained compositions feel as normal, even banal, as his subjects. Shore attempts to document the "this is what it's like"; in other words, as a documentary photographer he steps behind the pictures and allows the objects and landscapes to speak directly to the viewer. Both in form and content, Atget's consistent approach had a particularly strong impact on photographers whose work has a documentary character and who are associated with the so-called "Becher School" (see *Conceptual Photography*).

The work of the British photographer Rob Carter (b. 1968) shows how something as thoroughly representational as landscape can be interpreted in an abstract manner. In his series *Travelling Still,* he shows landscapes in passing (right). As suggested by the title, Carter wants to communicate the impression of movement and the experience of travel. "The flowers along the edges of the fields are no longer flowers [...] but red and white stripes; there are no dots anymore, everything becomes stripes; grain fields become long streaks; clover fields appear as long green braids." This was not written by Carter, but by the novelist Victor Hugo (1802–1885), describing the impressions he gathered on a rail journey. Carter's photographs make us feel as though we were looking at the landscape through the window of a passing train, as described by Hugo. In fact, his photographs are not taken in motion, but by using a fixed camera with a revolving lens. This creates a visual spectacle of colors whose abstract forms still hint at the landscapes they depict.

How landscapes are seen, which landscapes inspire photographers to depict them, and how varied the approach to this photographic genre has become, all depend on the individual photographer. In this respect, Émile Zola's (1840–1902) observation is not just a good definition of art in general, but of landscape photography in particular: "Art is a fragment of creation, seen through a temperament."

right——ROB CARTER: TRAVELLING STILL, TULIP FIELD HOLLAND XIV
2006 | cibachrome

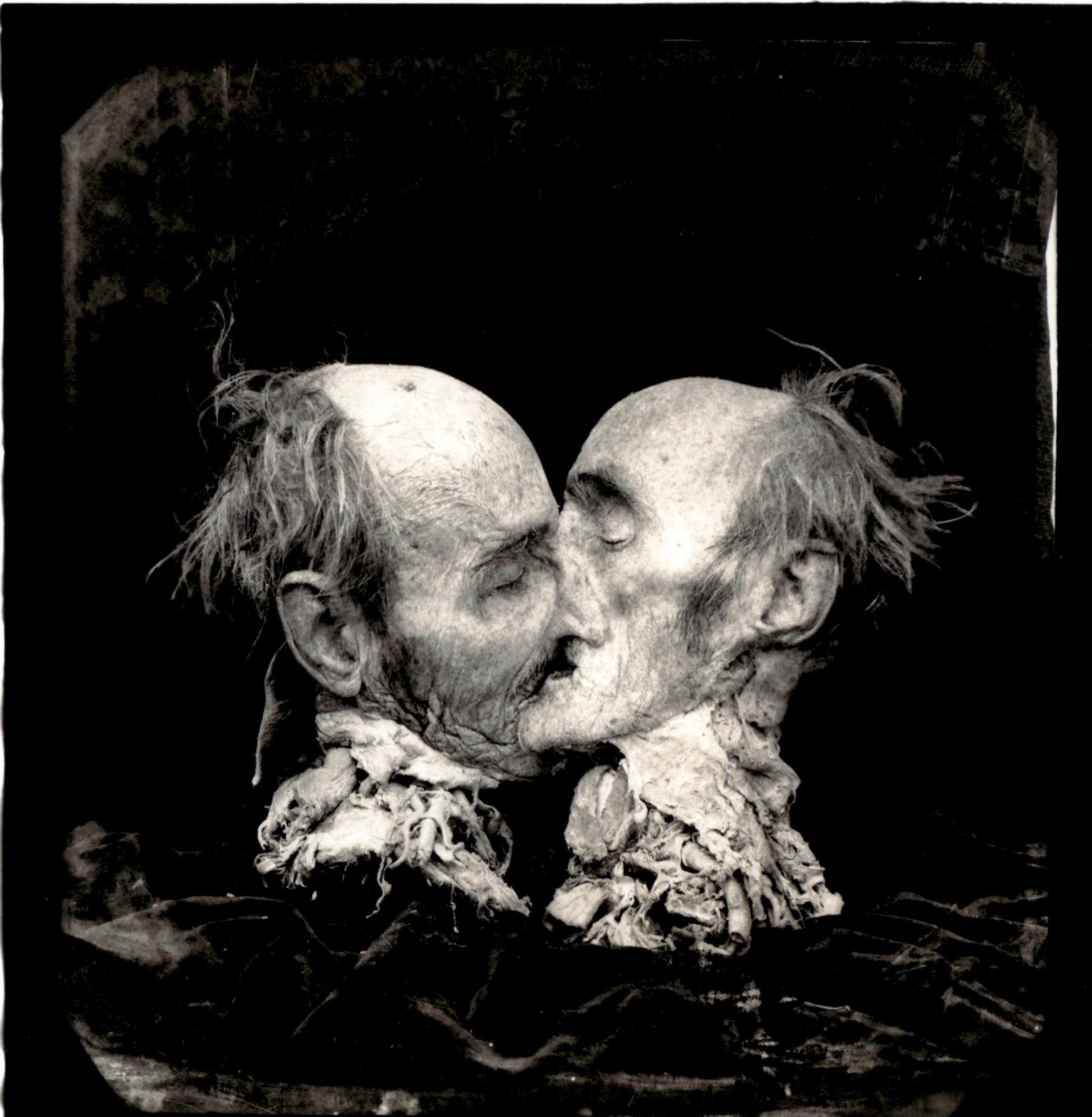

1931–2007 Bernd Becher   1939–today Joel-Peter Witkin   1946–1989 Robert Mapplethorpe

STILL LIFES

The term "still life," which derives from the Dutch *stilleven*, refers to pictures in which still, or lifeless, objects are depicted. Arranged artistically, they allow the painter to celebrate materiality, form, color, and the interplay of light and shadow. This definition of the still life also applies to photography. Photographic still lifes range from those of the early years of the medium, still heavily influenced by the traditions of painting, to contemporary advertising (product) photography. The variety is boundless; strictly speaking, almost every photo of an inanimate object is a still life. The following examples show that, despite its traditional associations, this genre remains modern to this day.

One of the most important creators of classic still lifes in 20th-century photography was Robert Mapplethorpe (1946–1989). He became famous for his nude photographs and those of sadomasochistic practices in New York's gay scene (see *The Nude*). Conservative groups often took advantage of the opening days of his exhibitions to stage demonstra-

tions against what they considered to be pornographic pictures. Mapplethorpe also became celebrated, however, because of the other main aspect of his creativity: perfectly staged flower still lifes (fig. p. 42–43). A perfectionist, he was "obsessed with beauty." In restrained compositions that draw their power from graphic precision and perfect lighting, Mapplethorpe usually concentrated on individual flowers, or groups of just a few carefully arranged flowers. His still lifes are typical of a strand of photography in the 1980s in which design and a cool, detached form of representation played an important role.

It was largely through the accessibility of his flower still lifes, and the great popularity he enjoyed as a result, that Mapplethorpe achieved increasing recognition for photography as an art form, and thus as museum worthy: "His work walks a tightrope: it is hard and romantic; it dares to balance on the border of art and kitsch. Only artists are willing to take that risk" (Els Barents).

The still lifes of the London-based German photographer Wolfgang Tillmans (b. 1968) stand in stark contrast to Mapplethorpe's carefully staged images. If Mapplethorpe's still lifes can be regarded as aesthetic expressions of the mood of New York in the 1980s, Tillmans' photographs represent the mood of London in the 1990s: "I wanted to give my

left——JOEL-PETER WITKIN: THE KISS, NEW MEXICO | 1982
following pages——ROBERT MAPPLETHORPE: TULIPS | 1987

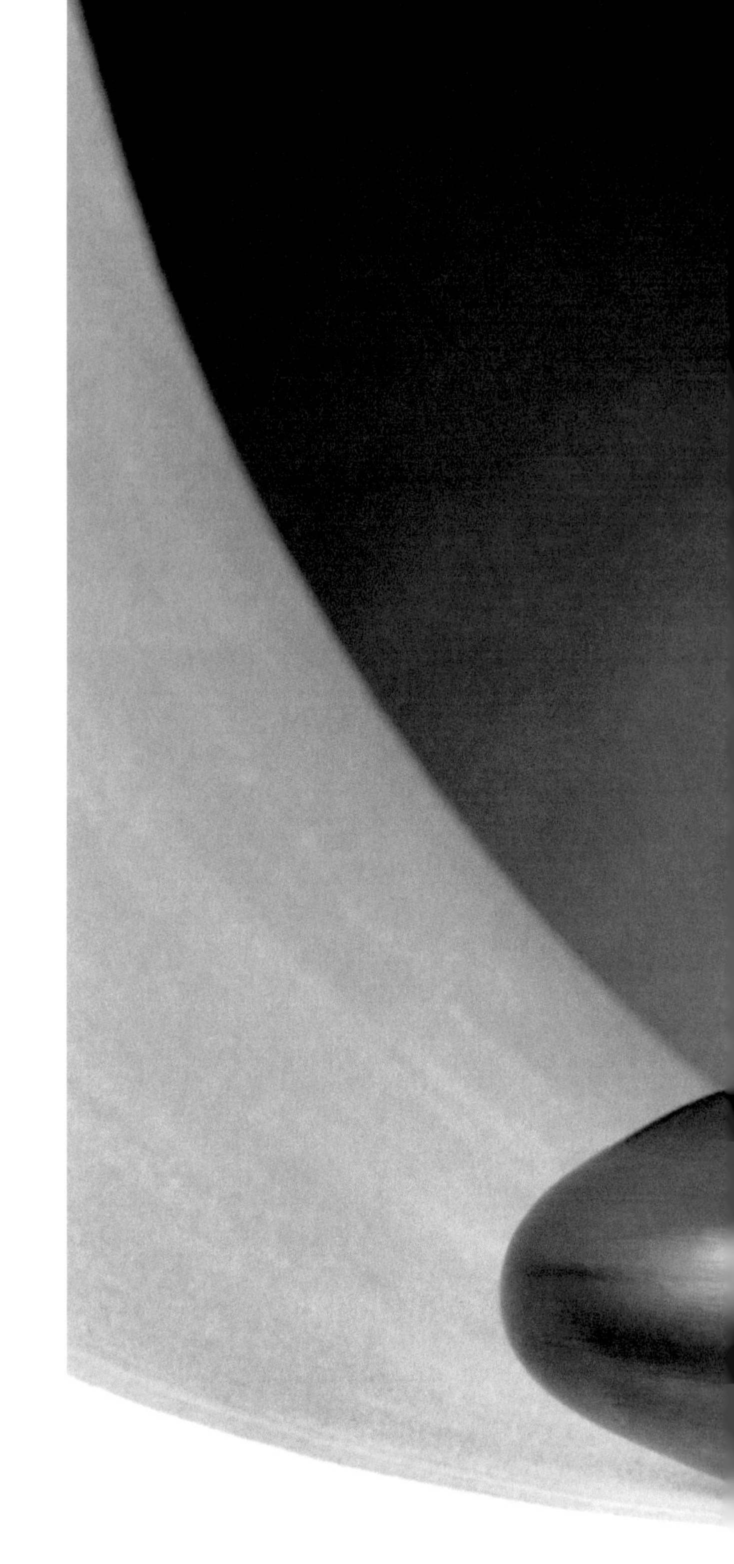

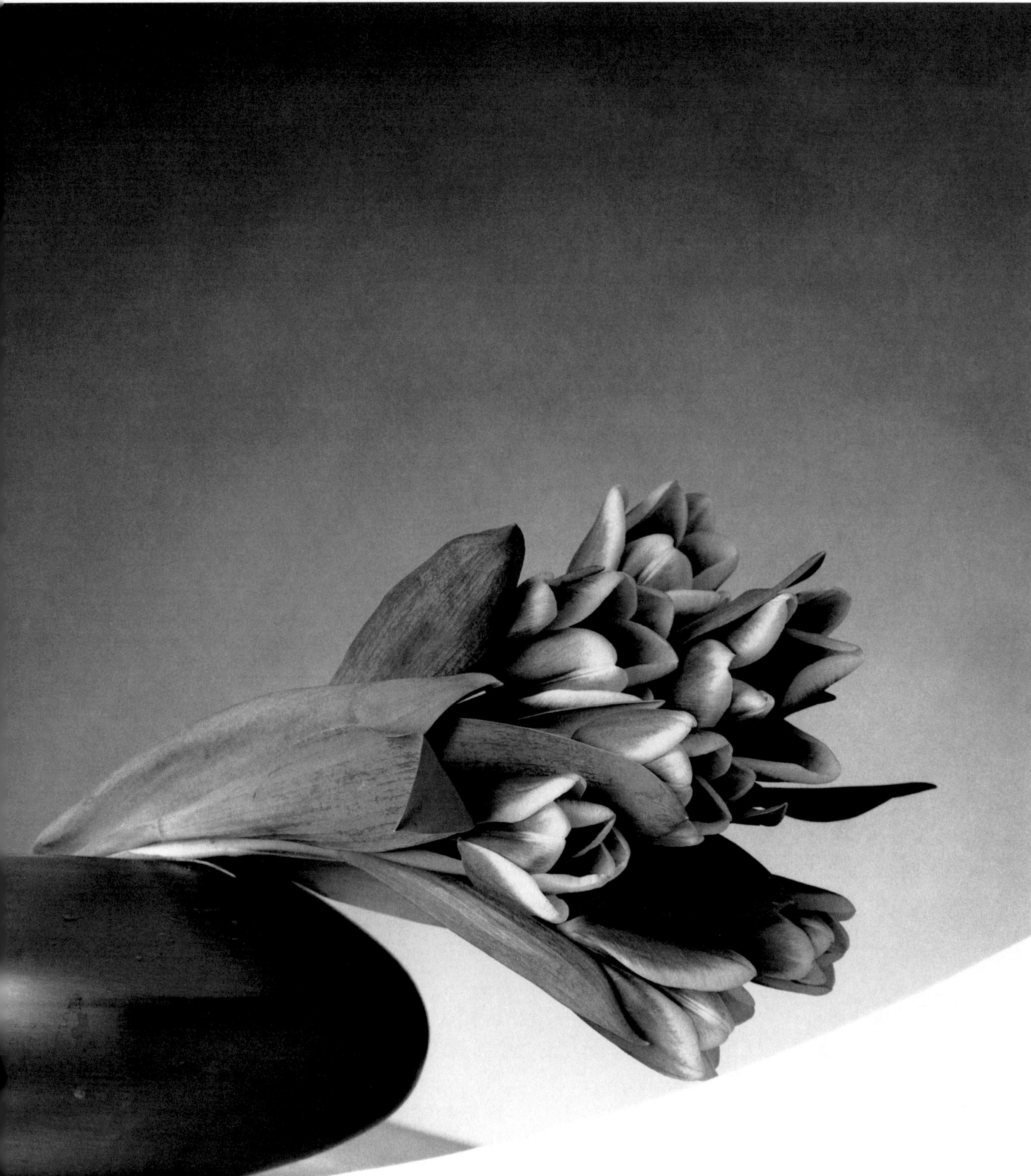

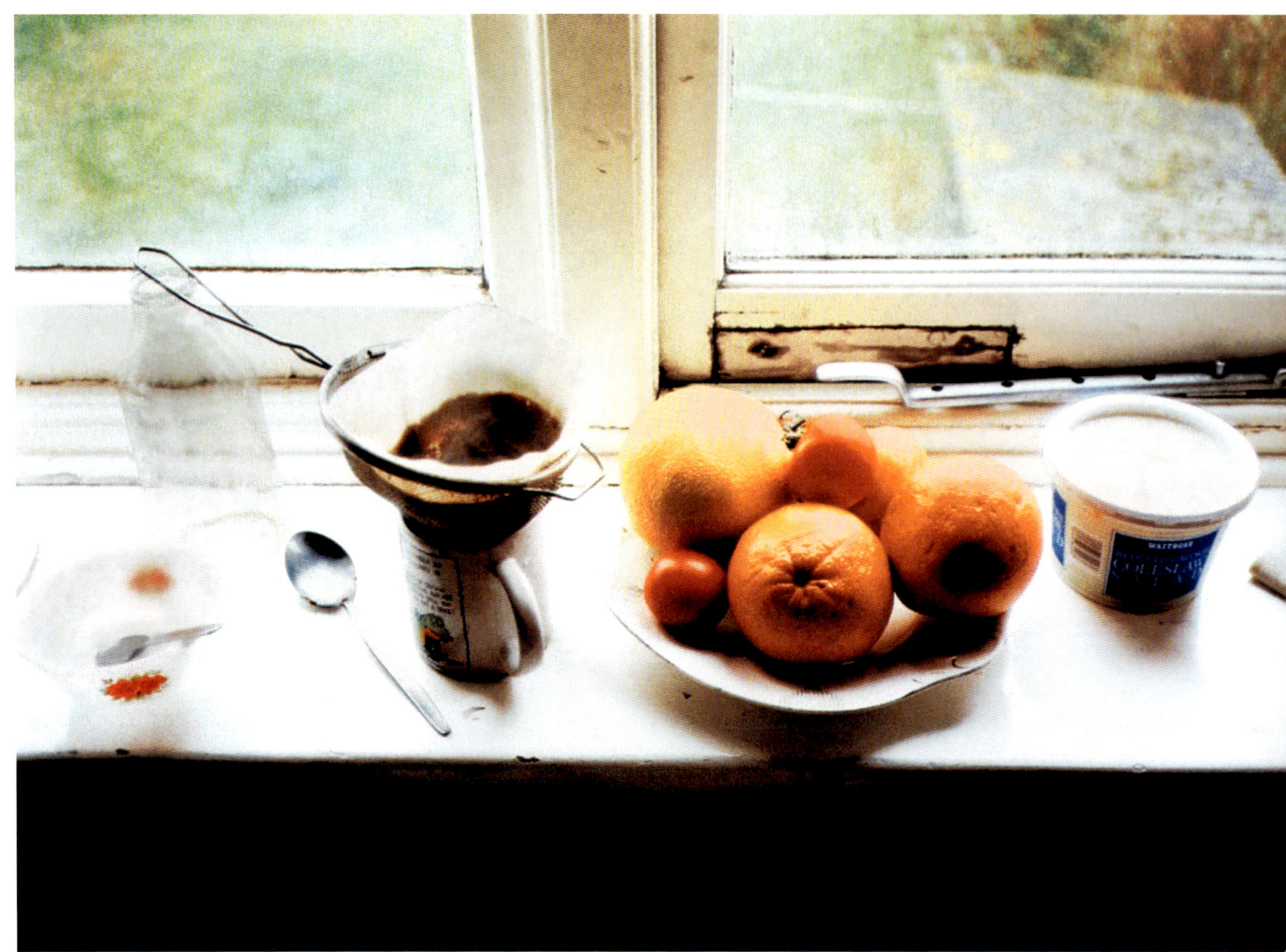

photographs a position that I could not find in this way anywhere else. I did not feel represented by the pictorial world that existed at the time."

Tillmans' approach is comparable to that described by William Eggleston's "democratic gaze" (see *Color Photography*), for the "unprivileged gaze" is the key term in the work of Tillmans. He starts from the assumption that "it's all pretty much the same with regard to materiality. Even uninteresting stuff, such as snow, consists of matter in the very same way that a diamond or a human does." From this point of view, Tillmans' still lifes of mundane objects from his everyday surroundings are just one aspect of his art, alongside portraits and other kinds of photographs. "Taking photographs of a still life of recently bought fruit arranged on a window sill felt just as existential as photographing sweaty bodies in nightclubs." Looking at his still lifes (above), one does not immediately see evidence to support the claim that his photographs are "carefully composed." Viewers are often quick to think "I could do

above——WOLFGANG TILLMANS: STILL LIFE TALBOT RD. | 1991

"Viewers are often quick to think 'I could do that with my camera.' That may well be the case, but to think this way would be to miss the point."

that with my camera." That may well be the case, but to think this way would be to miss the point. In contemporary art photography, the photo itself is not the only important consideration. The context and the concept behind the photo are also significant. Tillmans' art cannot be fully understood by looking at the individual photograph, but by looking at groups of photographs. These are presented in his installations, which aim to reproduce his world in its plurality. This results in a kind of personal iconography that is not necessarily fully accessible to the viewer.

In French, the term for "still life" is *nature morte*: dead nature. Few photographers have interpreted the concept of "dead nature" quite as literally as the American photographer Joel-Peter Witkin (b. 1939) has done in his almost alchemistic-looking photographs. Bizarre, dark, creepy, and macabre are the adjectives often used to describe Witkin's pictures. He developed an interest in the unusual and the abnormal at an early age, watching with relish the "freak shows" of Coney Island: "The freak show became my home, my real environment filled with living phantasies." Pictorial elements in Witkin's work include "freaks of every kind, idiots, dwarves, giants [...] All the people who were born without arms, legs, eyes, breasts, genitals, ears, noses, lips"—

not to forget corpses and parts of dead bodies. In his search for subjects for his photographs, Witkin came across a head that had been sawed in half, in the collection of an anatomical institution. He used this head in his 1982 photo *The Kiss* (fig. p. 40) For Witkin, this head with the two virtually identical profiles is a symbol of the different psychological aspects of human life, such as good and bad, Eros and Thanatos. In this photograph, Witkin explores the idea of a myth in which this human, whose two halves have long been separated, celebrate a mystical reunification in a kiss.

Witkin does not aim to shock people with his photographs. Instead, religion and philosophy, mythology and mysticism are integral elements of his artistic oeuvre, which is closer to the art of Hieronymus Bosch, Giuseppe Arcimboldo, or Francisco Goya than it is to photography. And yet his photographs are more shocking than are paintings showing similar subjects. The issue of how "real" the reality depicted in photography is plays an important role in this respect. The shock experienced by some when faced with horror is sublimated when the subject is painted. But that which is recorded in a photo must actually have been present in front of the camera's lens, and was thus not just a figment of a painter's imagination.

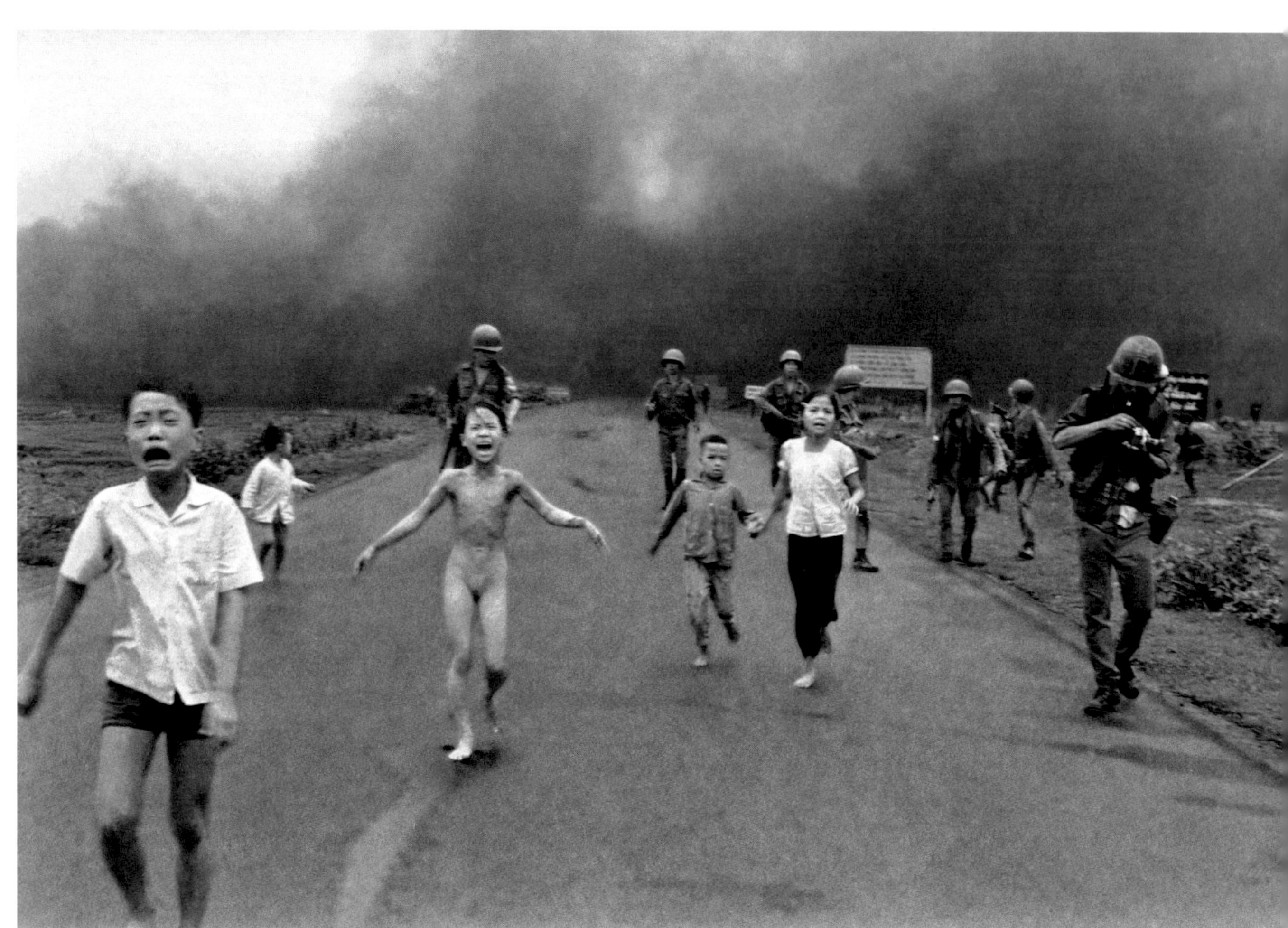

1814–1876 Louis-Auguste Bisson   **1819–1869 Roger Fenton**   **1830–1904 Étienne-Jules Marey**

WAR PHOTOGRAPHY

When Roger Fenton (1819–1869) traveled to the Crimea to take photographs of the war between Russia and the alliance formed by the United Kingdom, France, and the Ottoman Empire, he arrived with several hundred kilos of photographic equipment. Five large-format cameras, 700 glass plates, and the chemicals and equipment needed for the collodion wet-plate process (see *Landscapes*) were stowed away in his photographic wagon, which had been converted into a darkroom (fig. p. 49). Fenton was one of the first photographers who aimed to document a war. This was in fact barely possible with the photographic equipment available at the time, or at least it was not possible in the way we imagine it nowadays. "No dead bodies," Prince Albert had instructed Fenton, and Fenton complied. His photographs include portraits of officers and teams, tent camps, and harbor facilities. One of his most famous images, *Valley of the Shadow of Death* (fig. p. 48), which depicts the valley where an English cavalry brigade had suffered terrible losses, is strewn merely with cannon balls

(probably by Fenton himself), not with men and horses. Several weeks passed before his photographs were made public in London. They were shown in galleries in London and Paris and printed in newspapers as wood engravings because photographs could not be reproduced in newspapers at that time. In 2010, when the American photographer and Pulitzer prizewinner Damon Winter (b. 1974) accompanied US soldiers in Afghanistan for the *New York Times*, he took photos with his 140-gram smartphone (fig. p. 50)—and as a result he was accused of not showing the men sufficient respect. Winter's intention, however, was to create as close a connection as possible to the soldiers while he documented their everyday experiences of war. As the soldiers took photographs of themselves with their cell phones, using one himself appeared to him to be a good way to be less intrusive. In the final analysis, the technical element is irrelevant; what counts is how photographers transform what they see into images. War photography has developed between these two extremes over the course of the last 150 years. With its many facets, it has become a genre of its own within photography. The strangely contemplative effect of photographs by the likes of Roger Fenton are rooted in another era. War photography as we know it today did not become possible until cameras were small enough to be carried by hand, and films were

left——Nick Ut: 8.6.1972, Trang Bang; Phan Thi Kim Phuc (center) flees with other children after South Vietnamese planes mistakenly dropped napalm on South Vietnamese troops and civilians | 1972

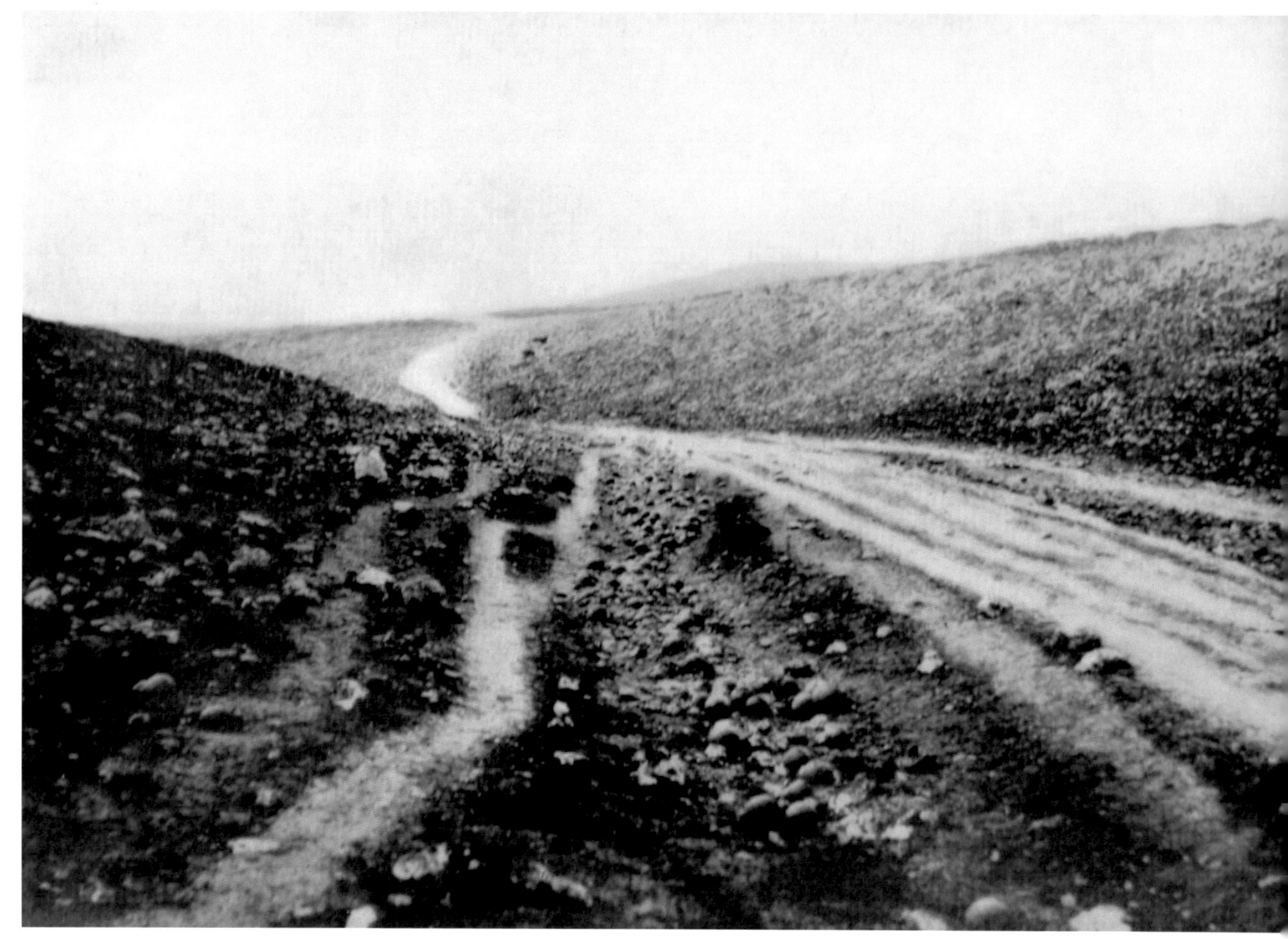

sensitive enough to capture events actually taking place. Whereas Fenton and the photographers of the American Civil War—such as Matthew Brady (*c.* 1822–1896) and Alexander Gardner (1821–1882)—could take photographs only of the aftermath, the photographers of the 20th century were able to take pictures while the events were actually unfolding. Perhaps the most famous war photographer is Robert Capa (1913–1954), whose motto "If your photograph isn't good enough, you weren't close enough" had a profound effect on war photographers. His photographs of a dying soldier during the Spanish

Civil War (fig. p. 52) and of the invasion of France by the Allies on D-Day are typical of this approach to war reporting. The dying soldier became one of the best-known war photographs, despite the fact that doubts were repeatedly voiced about its authenticity. Capa himself remarked: "In Spain, you don't need to use tricks to take photographs. [...] Reality is the best photograph." But Capa was not just somebody who took risks and launched himself head over heels into the battlefield. He had an additional aim: the true power of his oeuvre lies in the fact that he, as a humanist photographer, also

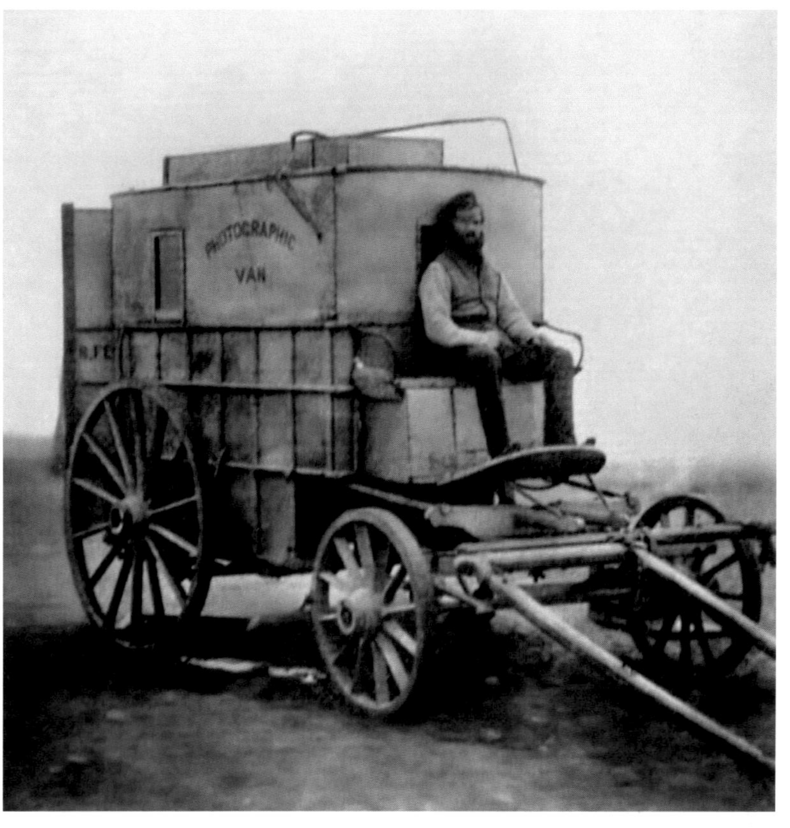

reported on the suffering of civilian populations during war, away from the battlefield.

Indeed, in addition to the documentation of warfare itself, coverage of the effects of war on civilian populations is often the focus of war photographers. Politi-cians and military leaders often attempt to control coverage of a conflict by using "embedded" journalists or photojournalists, who, to all intents and purposes, become part of the army to which they are attached. A picture by the Vietnamese photographer Nick Ut (b. 1951) gained tragic fame in this context (fig. p. 46). It shows a girl called Kim Phuc, crying and naked as she flees from a napalm attack during the Vietnam War. Time and again, photographs such as these cause readers in the safety of their homes to think about the real purpose and the actual conditions of combat missions. The publication of photographs

left——**ROGER FENTON: VALLEY OF THE SHADOW OF DEATH** | 1855
Getty Museum
right——**ROGER FENTON: PHOTOGRAPHIC VAN**

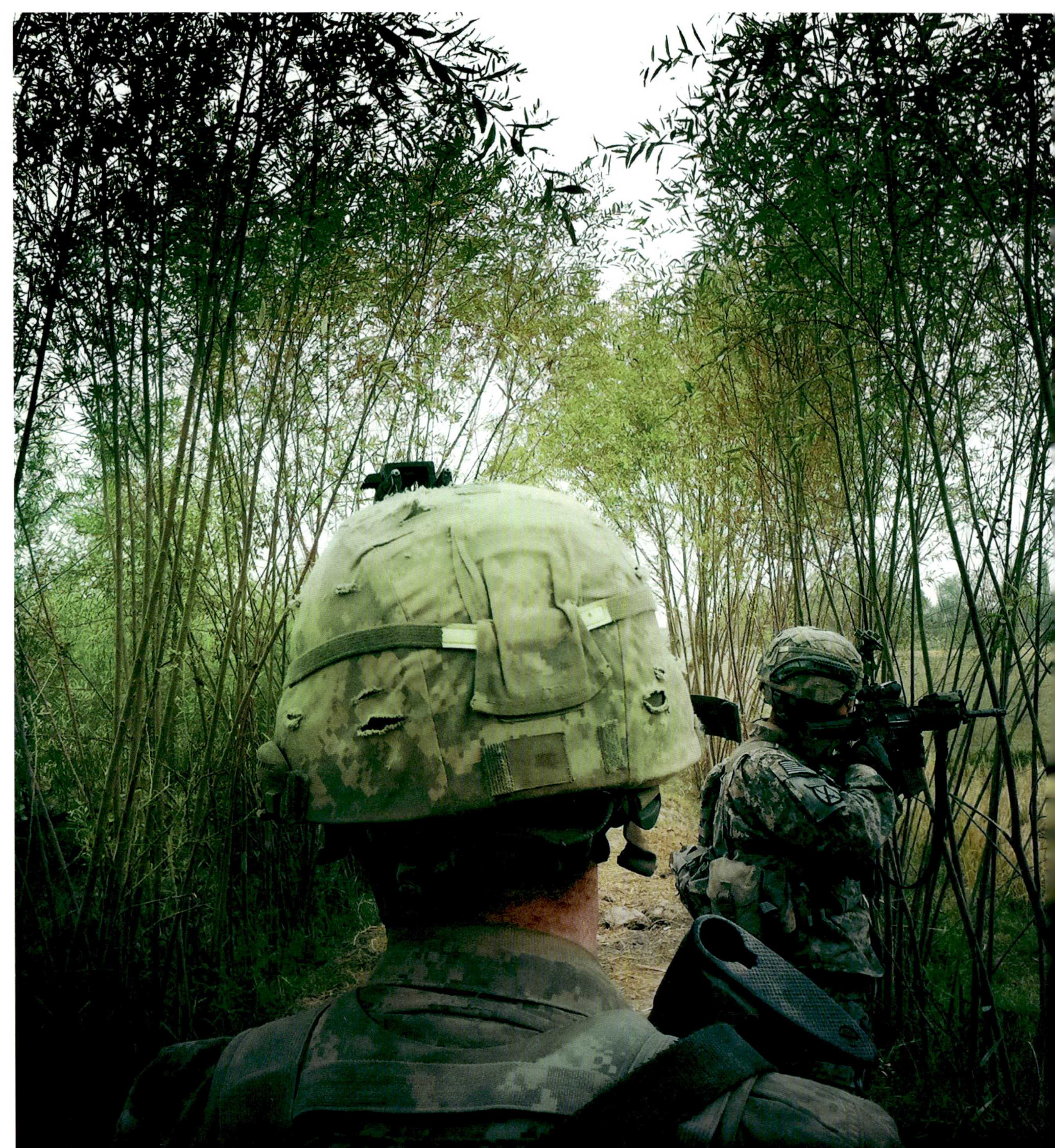

1886–1958 Edward Weston   **1896–1963 Martin Munkácsi**   **1906–1979 Philippe Halsman**

like these provides the opportunity to make clear, through their emotional power, what actually happens in a war. And yet photographers who take such emotionally charged photographs always attract heavy criticism for allegedly making money from the suffering of other people. However, the possibility of reducing people's suffering arises only if conflicts and their consequences are revealed by the media. The charge that photographers frame war atrocities in as aesthetically pleasing a way as possible in order to profit from them takes too narrow a view. Artists such as Francisco Goya (1746–1828), who depicted the horrors of the Spanish war against Napoleon, are seldom accused of depicting war for financial reasons. Photographers must pay attention to both the content and the composition of their photographs because the more powerful an image is the more deeply it makes an impression and so the more likely

it is to change hearts and minds. And only photographs that are moving find their way into the media, from where they can have an effect. Photographs that become milestones of war photography are those that reach beyond the specific circumstances in which they were created and become universal symbols. It is no coincidence that Goya's paintings and etchings are frequently cited as references by photographers the debates about the artistic quality of war photographs. This is because Goya successfully shaped the brutality, madness, and absurdity of war, the darkest aspects of humanity, into a form that is generally accessible and that transcends a specific conflict.

James Nachtwey (b. 1948), who studied the history of art and is well acquainted with Goya's art, is, together with Robert Capa and Don McCullin, one of the most celebrated war photographers of the 20th century. He repeatedly took photographs of conflicts all over the world: "I have been a witness, and these pictures are my testimony. The events I have recorded should not be forgotten and must not be repeated." Nachtwey attempted to capture the decisive moment in which the history of war and suffering coalesces into a picture. He, more than just about anybody else, was able to take photo-

left——**Damon Winter: While on Patrol to Clear its Way out of Nahr-i-Sufi, the 2nd Platoon Came under Fire** | 2010

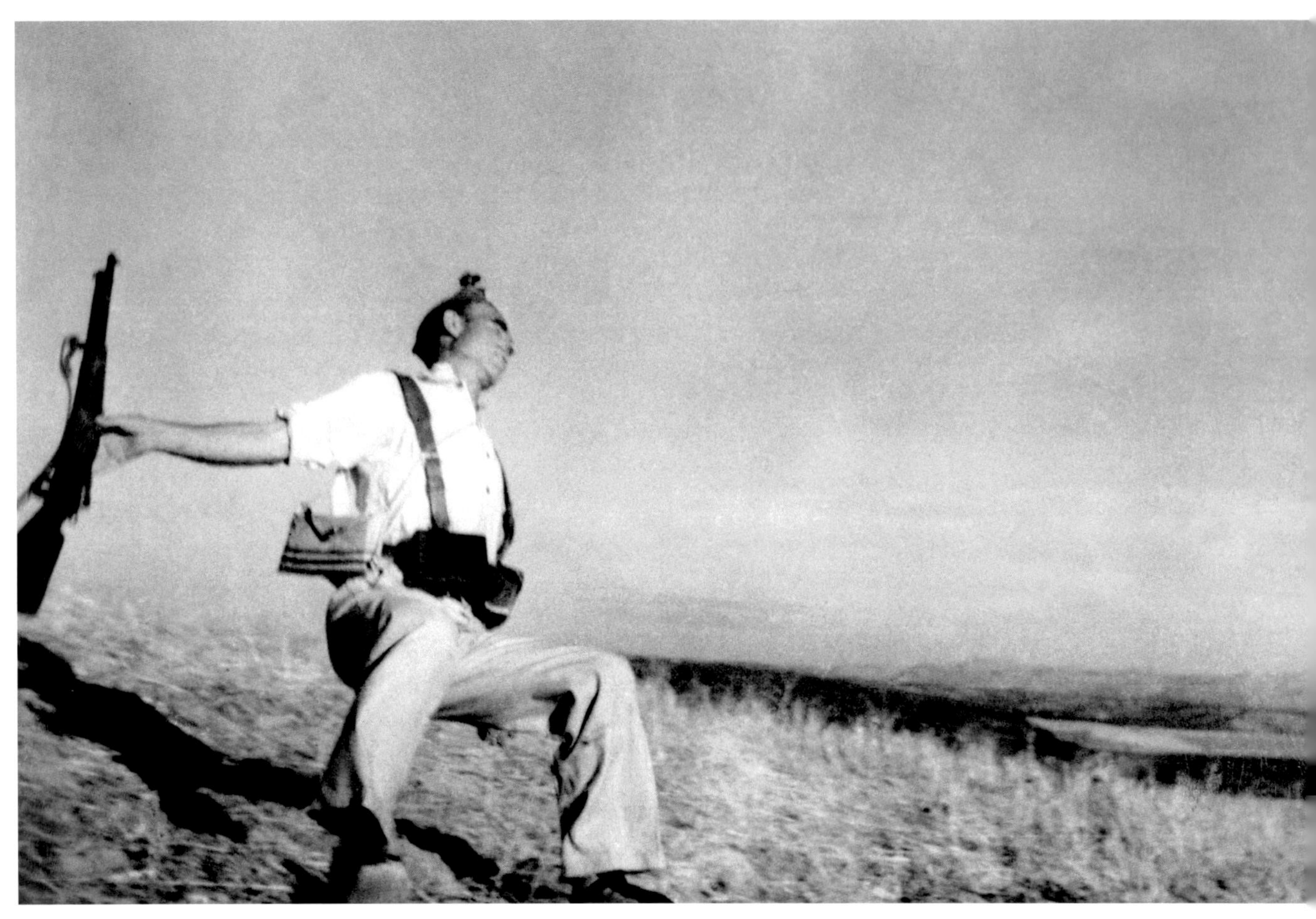

above——ROBERT CAPA: DEATH OF A REPUBLICAN SOLDIER | 1936
opposite, left——DON MCCULLIN: TURKISH CYPRIOT WOMAN MOURNING
THE DEATH OF HER HUSBAND IN GHAZIVERAM, CYPRUS | 1964
opposite, right——JAMES NACHTWEY: KOSOVO | 1999

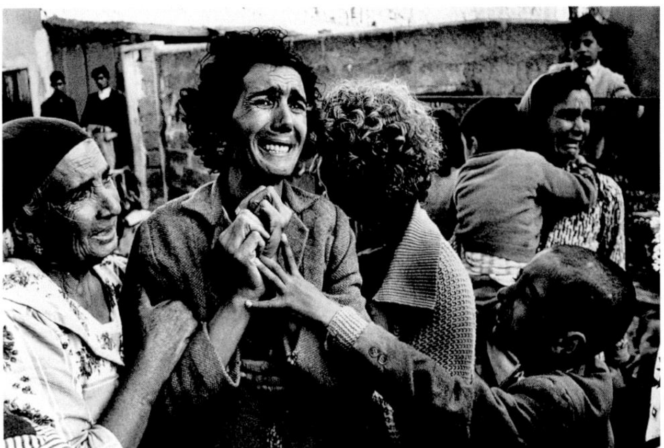

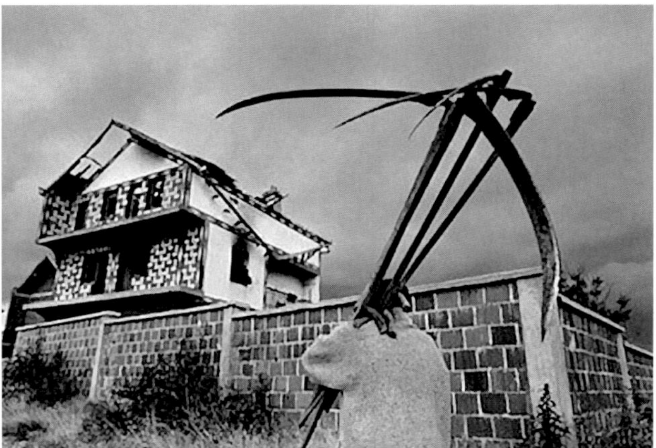

graphs whose artistic quality could be compared to that of Goya's paintings and etchings. In the photo reproduced here (above, right), Nachtwey refers to a symbol of death that has been used since the Middle Ages: the reaper. His best photographs work even if the viewer does not know their precise political context. Nachtwey's photographs of war and misery have symbolic qualities and are eloquent about people and about their ability to both suffer and inflict suffering.

"If you can't feel what you're looking at, then you're never going to get others to feel anything when they look at your pictures," claimed the British war photographer Don McCullin (b. 1935). This quotation reveals the dilemma of war photography and of war photographers. They are in the difficult position of having to become emotionally involved with what they see in order to create an appropriate impression of it (above, right). The psychological strain they experience is often comparable to that experienced by soldiers. McCullin himself retired from the "business of war" and went on to take other types of photograph, such as landscapes in his native Somerset, in order to leave behind the nightmares he suffered as a result of his experience of war. "It brings me a kind of peace until I hear the local hunters shooting. Gunfire is a prelude to war for me. I feel I'm back there on some godforsaken road passing dying soldiers lying in culverts." Photographers have no choice but to capture the events that are actually taking place. This makes it all the more challenging to take photographs of war that can, like other great artworks, stand alone and become symbols of opposition to war. They then become what most war photographers aim to create: anti-war photographs, as James Nachtwey put it.

"Art has nothing to do with established morality. On the contrary, art stands in opposition to what is normally considered ethical or moral, because it must call everything into question again."

A still life by Oliviero Toscani (b. 1942) is a very different type of anti-war photograph (right). Used in a poster campaign by the clothing label Benetton in 1994, it has become one of the most controversial contributions to the theme of war and photography. Toscani, who became famous for his provocative advertising posters for Benetton, is not a war photographer. And yet this photo is an image of war, and an anti-war picture. In 1993 Toscani received a letter from a Yugoslavian student, demanding that he do something about the war in her country. Via the Benetton representative in Yugoslavia and the Red Cross, Toscani obtained clothing that had belonged to Marinko Gagro, a soldier who had been killed, from the latter's father. In a letter, the soldier's father gave Toscani permission to take photographs of the items of clothing: "I, Gojko Gagro, father of Marinko Gagro [...] would like the name of my dead son Marinko, and all that is left of him, to be used for peace and against war." Toscani photographed the blood-stained trousers and T-shirt (in which the entry hole of a bullet is visible) as though they were holy relics, a "symbol of a person who died in these clothes," said Toscani; "It was like a report, only more than that."

Reactions to it ranged from severe condemnation to somber admiration. Toscani did not regard the poster as an advertising campaign for a clothing manufacturer, but as an artistic opportunity to draw international attention to the real problem: the bloody war in Yugoslavia. Toscani was successful in creating an artistic interpretation, and in this way triggered strong emotional responses. This allowed him to achieve his aim of reinvigorating debates about the war. "Art has nothing to do with established morality. On the contrary, art stands in opposition to what is normally considered ethical or moral, because it must call everything into question again" (Oliviero Toscani).

above——**Oliviero Toscani: Clothes of the Killed Croatian Soldier Marinko Gagro** | 1993

IZJAVA: JA OTAC, GOJKO GAGRO, POGINULOG MARINKA GAGRE ROD. 1963. GOD. U BLATNICI OPĆINA ČITLUK, SUGLASAN SAM DA SE UZMU PODACI MOGA POK. MARINKA U SVRHU PLAKATA ZA MIR U BORBI PROTIV RATA.

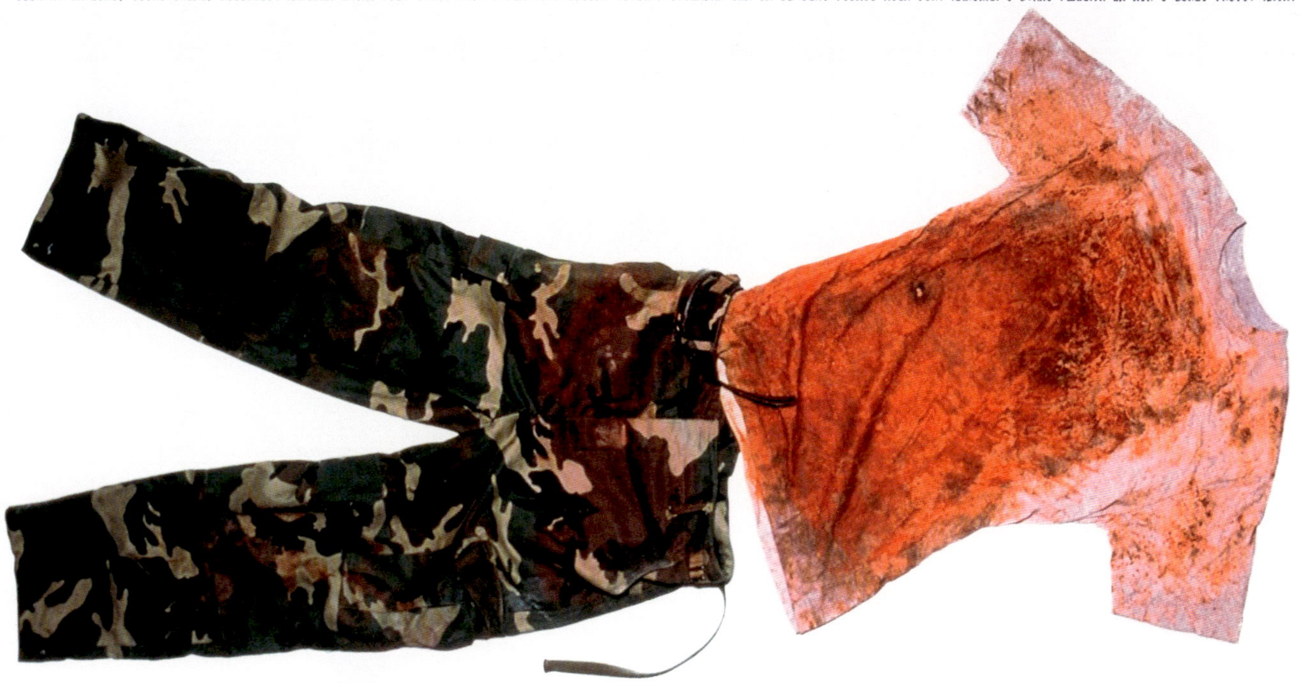

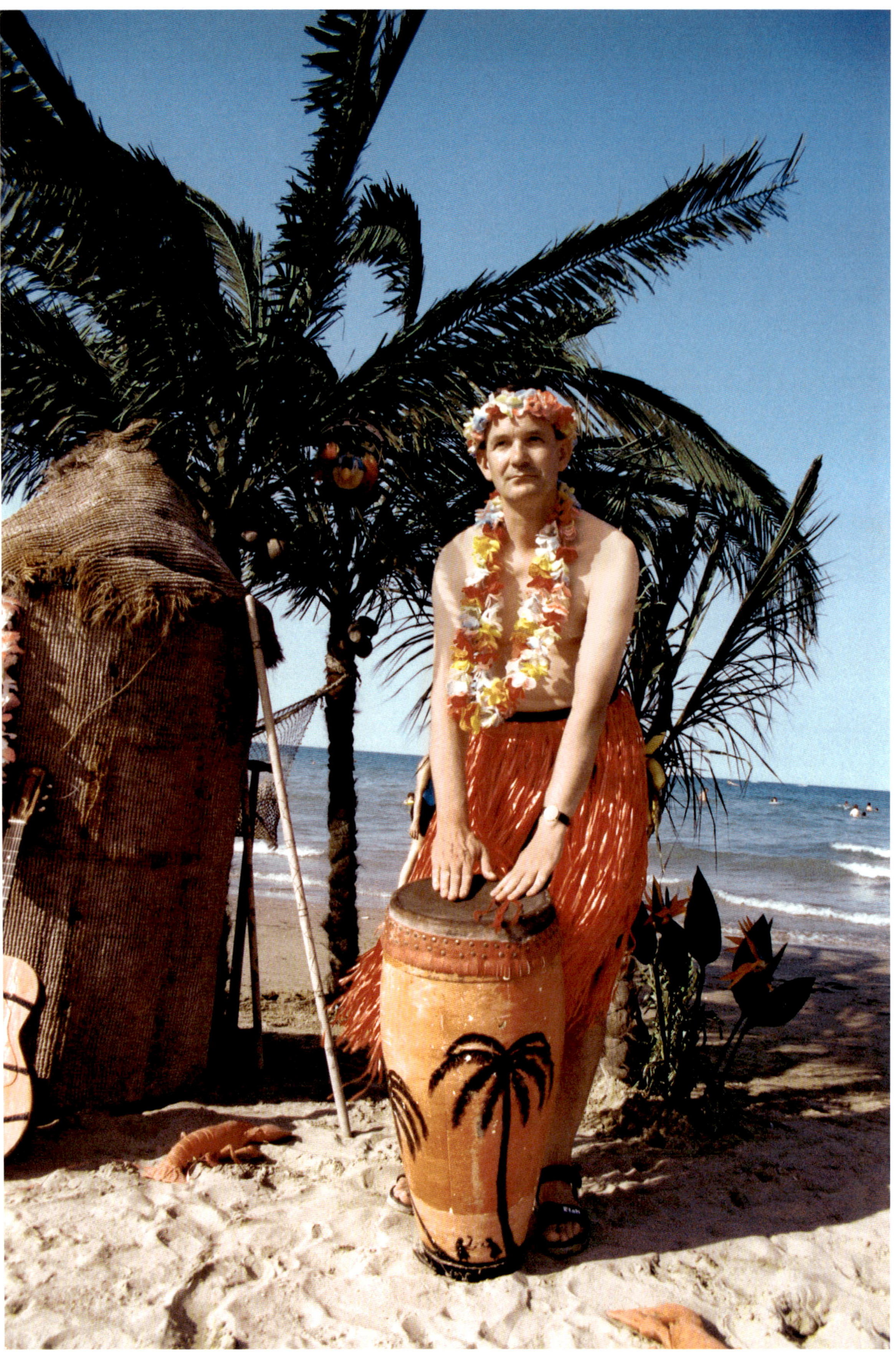

SELF-PORTRAITS

The classic self-portrait shows an artist with the tools of his trade. For a painter these are his paintbrush and palette, for a photographer his camera. The self-portraits shown here go beyond this normal self-representation and tell us a great deal about the photographers and their working methods. They are the work of photographers who in their own unique way all occupy a special place in the history of photography. "The body of the man you see portrayed overleaf is that of Monsieur Bayard. [...] The government, which had given M. Daguerre much too much, declared that it could do nothing for M. Bayard. And so the unfortunate man drowned himself." This obituary is printed on the back of the photo *Self-Portrait as a Drowned Man* (right), which was created in 1840 by the French finance official Hippolyte Bayard (1801–1887). One of the pioneers of the invention of photography, Bayard developed a direct positive process by making ordinary paper light sensitive through treating it with silver chloride, which turns black when exposed to light. Then he made it light sensitive once more and

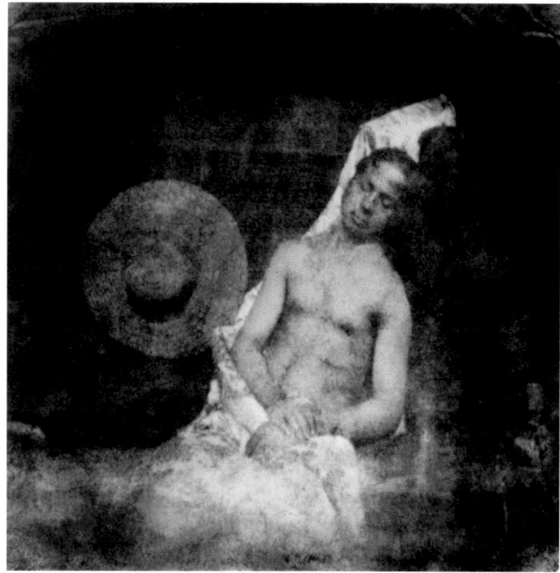

the exposure in the camera bleached the black areas again according to the intensity of the light. Thus he created a positive photograph that, however, could not be reproduced. It was a very promising method and was considerably cheaper than the daguerreotype process. Before the latter was presented to the general public in August 1839, Bayard exhibited 30 of his photographs in June of the same year in Paris. It was the first photographic exhibition in history, and took

left——**Martin Parr: Self-Portrait, Foto Alfredo, Rimini** | 1999

right——**Hippolyte Bayard: Self-Portrait as a Drowned Man** | 1840

21 x 24.7 cm | Société Française de Photographie | Paris

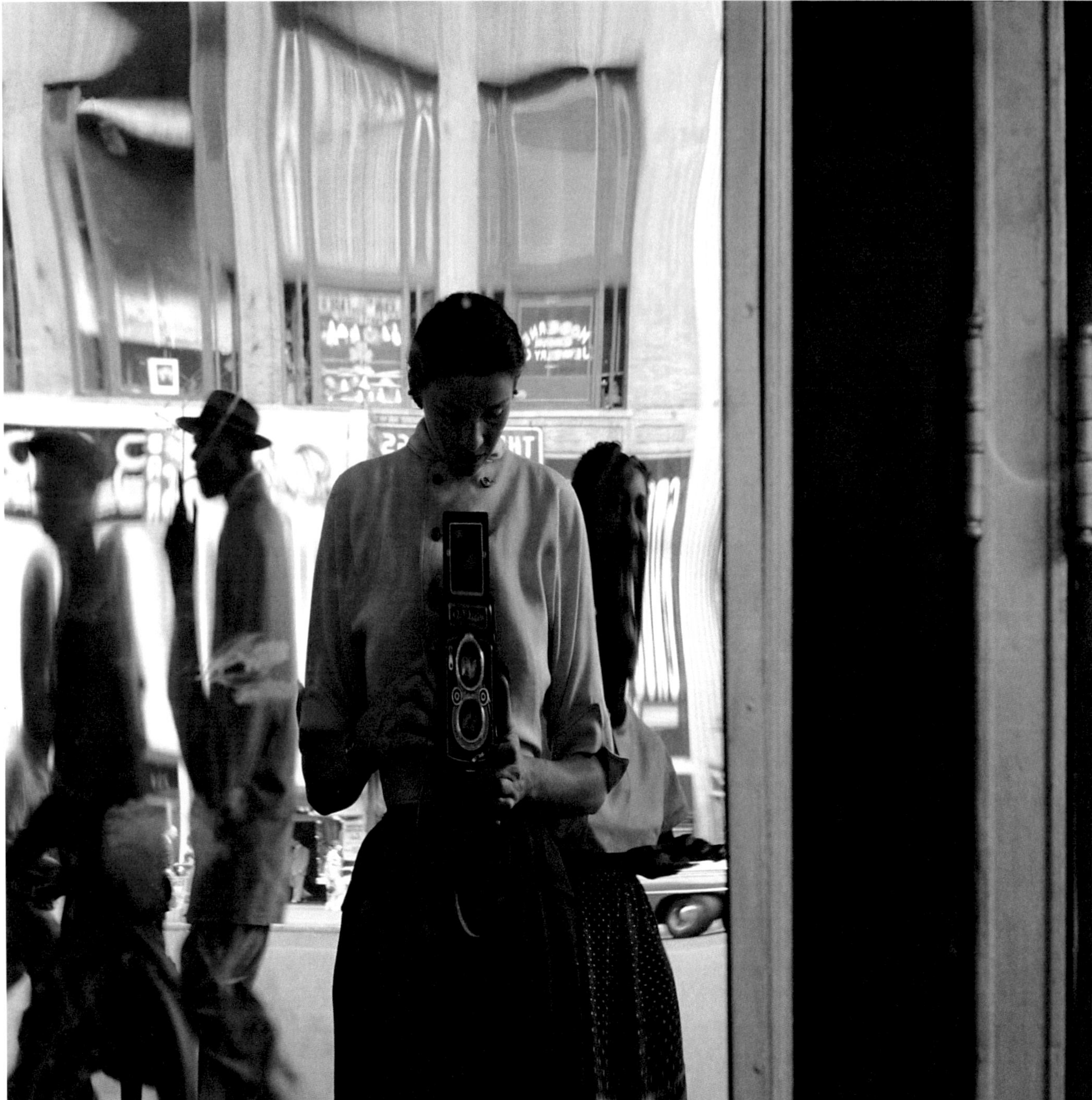

place even before photography had been officially announced. It is no longer possible to establish why Bayard nonetheless failed to receive support from official bodies. After all, he too invented photography, alongside Daguerre and Henry Fox Talbot. He appears, however, to have had a keen sense of humor. Once he had come to terms with the mortifying lack of official recognition, he made an ironic comment on his situation through photography itself. His self-portrait, one of the first in history, is pure irony despite the criticism it contains, if only for its title: *Self-Portrait as a Drowned Man*. Yet in spite of his initial difficulties, Bayard became a successful photographer who later mostly used the technique developed by Talbot. In 1851 he was one of the founding members of the Société Héliographique, which still exists today under the name of the Société Française de Photographie; among other duties, it administers Bayard's estate. The self-portrait always embodies an artist's individual point of view at a precise point in time. The *Self-Portrait* (fig. p. 60) of 1901/02 by Edward Steichen

(1879–1972) is one such statement of an attitude. Born in Luxembourg in 1879, Edward (Éduard Jean) Steichen emigrated to America in 1881 with his parents. At the beginning of the 20th century he was one of the most important figures in American photography, alongside Alfred Stieglitz (see *Pictorialism*). He edited the journal *Camera Work* with Stieglitz and created his own photographs in the Pictorialist style. His self-portrait dates from this period and reveals the divided nature of Pictorialism with remarkable clarity. This self-portrait is a declaration of his desire to establish photography as an art in its own right; yet he does this by showing photography's close links to traditional art: he shows himself holding a paintbrush and palette, as a photographer and a painter.

Steichen abandoned Pictorialism after World War I and underwent a change from being a purely artistic photographer to being a commercial one. In 1911 he produced the first modern fashion photos, and in 1922 became chief photographer for the magazines *Vanity Fair* and *Vogue*. Many of his colleagues from the art scene deplored his move to commercial photography; they felt he had betrayed the artistic cause. For Steichen himself, his work as a fashion and advertising photographer and as a portraitist of high society represented new challenges. His portraits of artists and actors became world famous, and his fashion shots were trend setting, as was the way he moved effort-

left——EVE ARNOLD: SELF-PORTRAIT IN A DISTORTING MIRROR, NEW YORK | 1950

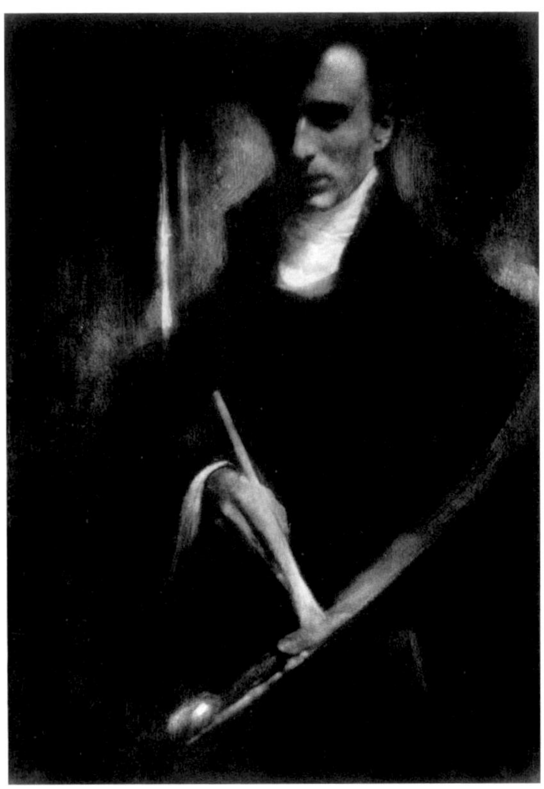

lessly between artistic and commercial photography, a very common practice today.

In 1938, Steichen retired from active photography. In 1947, at the age of 67, he began his second career as head of the department of photography at the Museum of Modern Art in New York. Until he left in 1962, he was one of the central figures in US photography and organized over 60 frequently pioneering exhibitions. The year 1955 saw the opening of *The Family of Man*, the most successful photographic exhibition of all time, which, curated by Steichen, attracted over nine million visitors. After the experiences of World War II, he wanted to use photography as a medium to show that men and women throughout the world, despite their many differences, all shared the same needs and dreams. He saw the 503 photos from 68 countries "as a mirror of the universal elements and emotions in the everydayness of life—as a mirror of the essential oneness of mankind throughout the world" (Edward Steichen). Among the numerous unknown photographers, there were also many famous ones, including Richard Avedon, Robert Frank, Garry Winogrand, August Sander, and Elliott Erwitt. In 2003 *The Family of Man* was added to UNESCO's Memory of the World Register, and is now on permanent display in the Château de Clervaux in Steichen's home country of Luxembourg.

Also represented in the exhibition is the American photographer Eve Arnold (1912–2012) (fig. p. 58). She is an example of the many photographers whose names are mostly only known in specialist circles, but whose works have become icons. In a shop window we see the reflection of a photographer who becomes part of the scenery between all the other people. This is typical of Arnold's working method; she always operated as inconspicuously and discreetly as possible. Eve Arnold is one of the most important photographers of the twentieth century, and a pioneer of photojournalism. She was the first woman to join the famous Magnum photo agency (see p. 114), and she had a decisive influence on its style. She photographed "the usual and the unusual." Her particular interest was women, although she refused to be taken over by the supporters of feminism. "I didn't want to be a

"His self-portrait is a declaration of his desire to establish photography as an art in its own right: he shows himself holding a paintbrush and palette, as a photographer and a painter."

woman photographer as such; that would only have restricted me. I wanted to make use of my approach as a woman and my personality in the interpretation of what I was photographing." She photographed Queen Elizabeth II and Marlene Dietrich, as well as Malcolm X and – repeatedly – Marilyn Monroe (fig. p. 6). The two of them had met during their early years and a profound familiarity developed, permitting her to photograph such private moments. Arnold did not take star photos as such, but sensitively accompanied the person standing before her camera in her "Portraits in Action."

Arnold's interest was not only focused on famous personalities; it also applied to ordinary people. She took photos in Afghanistan and in the Soviet Union, and she was one of the first Western photographers to travel through China. Robert Capa described Arnold's photographic range as follows: "Arnold's work falls metaphorically between Marlene Dietrich's legs and the bitter lives of migratory potato pickers."

Martin Parr (b. 1952) (see *Comic Photography*) is not simply a photographer; actually, it might be more accurate to describe him as a hunter-gatherer in the field of photography. His photos brought a new dynamism to documentary photography, and he himself collects everything possible and "impossible" related to photography and mass culture. That starts with clocks with the face of Saddam Hussein via "boring postcards" to photobooks; to date he has produced two volumes dedicated to the history of the photobook. His passion for collecting even extends to himself, and has accordingly led to his series *Self-Portraits* (fig. pp. 56, 62 and 63). These are not self-portraits in the strict sense of the word, though Parr, who is always searching for quirky subjects in everyday life, describes them as such. During his travels around the world, he got local photographers to photograph him in their own style and according to their own methods. His sole requirement was that he should follow the instructions of the photographer concerned in each case and put on as neutral an expression as possible, so that the photos would be comparable. The result is a series of portraits of Parr that are sometimes bizarre, sometimes elegant, and sometimes comical. For Parr, the pictures are also an act of homage to the little photo studios that use every possible technique from retouching to digital manipulation in their attempt to make the customer appear—as they see it—as advantageously as possible.

left——**Edward Steichen: Self-Portrait** | 1901/02 | Chicago Institute of Art | Chicago
next pages: left——**Martin Parr: Self-Portrait, New York** | 1999
next pages: right——**Martin Parr: Self-Portrait, Honey Rose Studio, Mexico City** | 1999

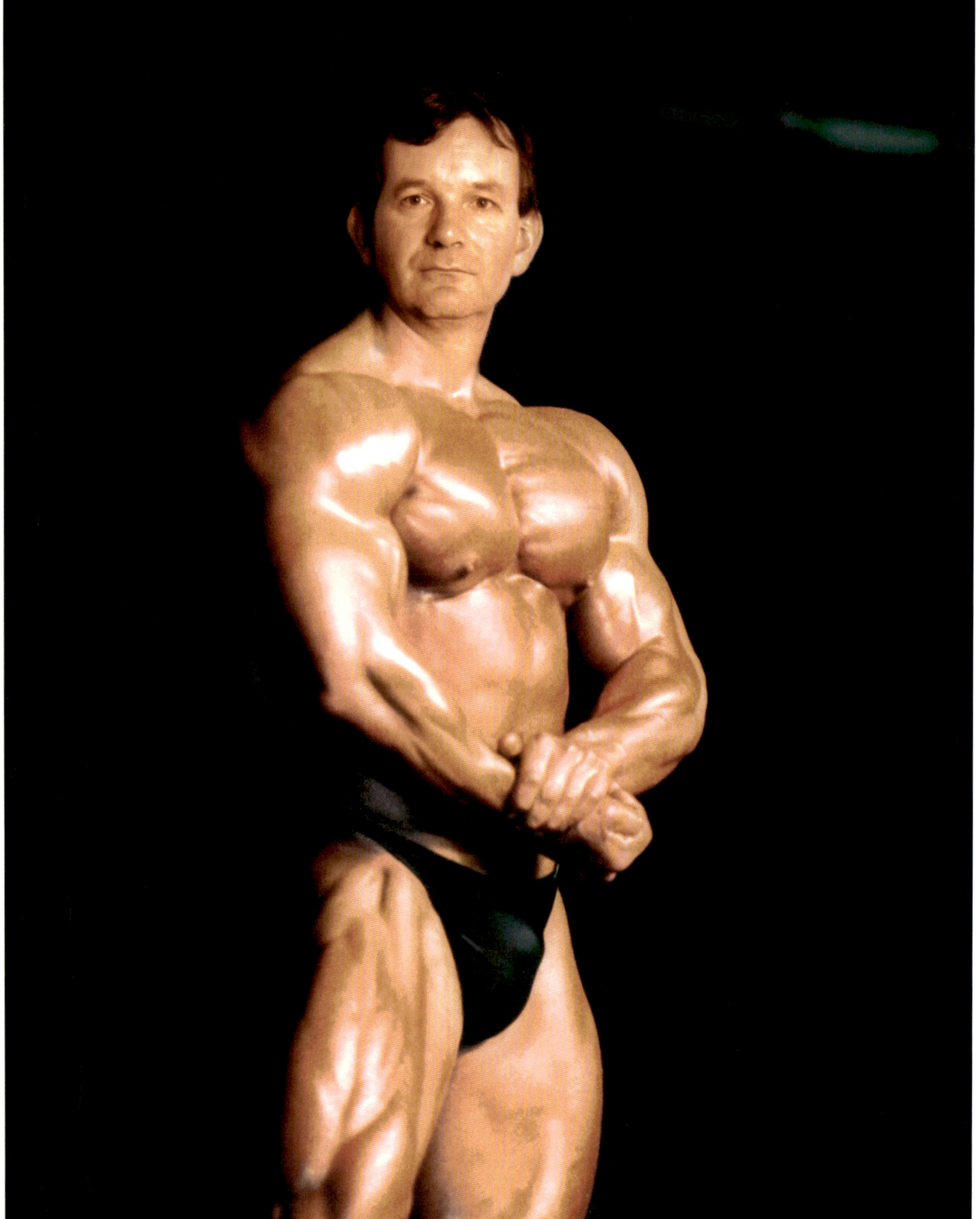

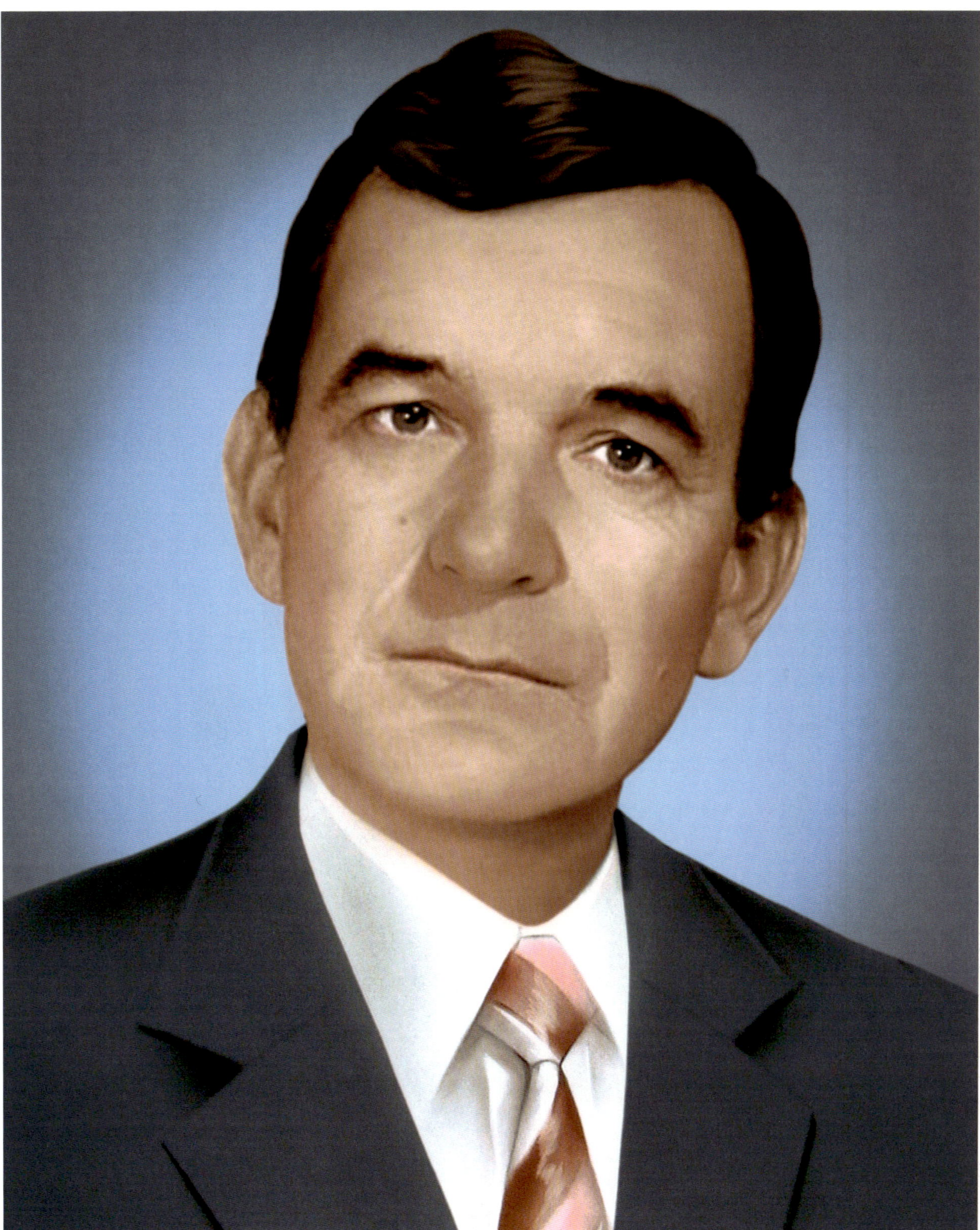

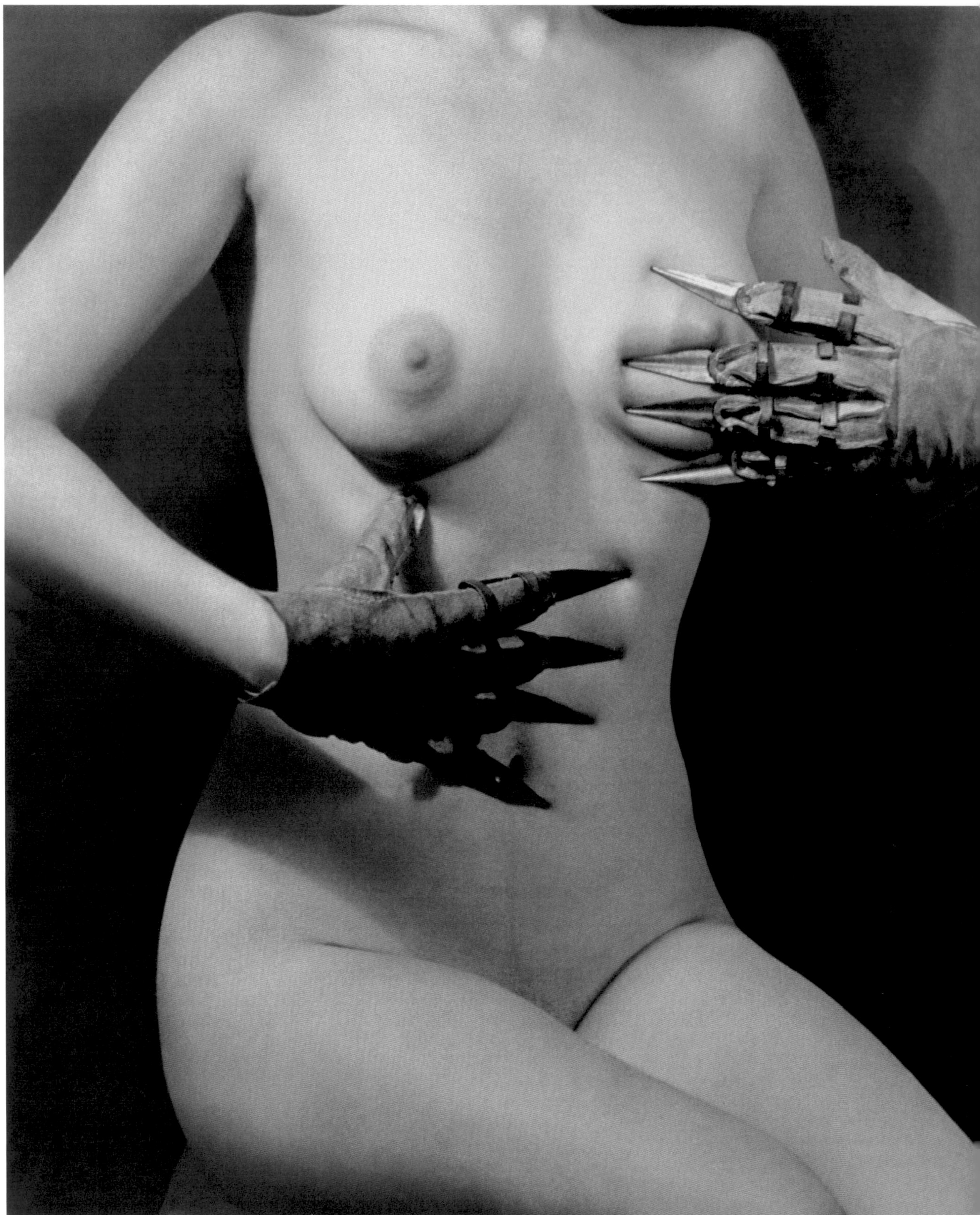

THE NUDE

"I look passionately and without tiring at these photographs of nude people, this admirable poem, the human body." Eugène Delacroix (1798–1863) was not the only 19th-century painter to be enthusiastic about the "new type of pictures" created by photographers, which he saw as an alternative to lengthy and expensive sessions with live models. These painters recognized the advantages afforded by the modern "sketchbook" created by photography, in particular nude photography. A veritable photographic industry soon developed, with photographers offering catalogues of nude models in the classic poses of the academy.

And not only artists observed nude photographs "passionately and without tiring": everyday people, too, liked to look at them. Under the cloak of artistic pretensions, some photographers therefore added an erotic charge to the fairly matter-of-fact photographs created for artists by adding a suitable setting and by draping the figures in a way that revealed more than it concealed. The claim that they were creating "artistic" images helped these photographers to bypass the stringent laws that aimed to ensure moral probity at the time. Nude photography developed between these two poles: the artistically refined and the voyeuristically pornographic. Nude photography can be aesthetically pleasing, erotic, provocative, artistic, educational, and much more besides.

The American photographer Paul Outerbridge (1896–1958) established a boundary between nude and pornographic photography that applies as much to viewers as it does to photographers: "Nudity is a state of fact; lewdity, to coin a phrase, is a state of mind," said Outerbridge, who created the most controversial nude photographs of his day. At a time when all overt sexuality was censored in American films, this highly successful advertising photographer created nude photographs that became precursors and icons of the fetish scene. *Woman with Claws* (left) from 1937 became one of his best-known photographs. Gloves (in this case custom made), top hats, and masks were some of the accessories he used to give his cool and distant-looking images an erotic charge. These photos were taken in color, which was still very unusual at the time. An eccentric perfectionist, who lived with a snake, he used the extremely laborious and expensive Cabro process; he claimed that each picture cost 150 dollars to make—it was his

left——**Paul Outerbridge: Woman with Claws** | 1937 | 87 x 66.2 cm
The J. Paul Getty Museum | Los Angeles

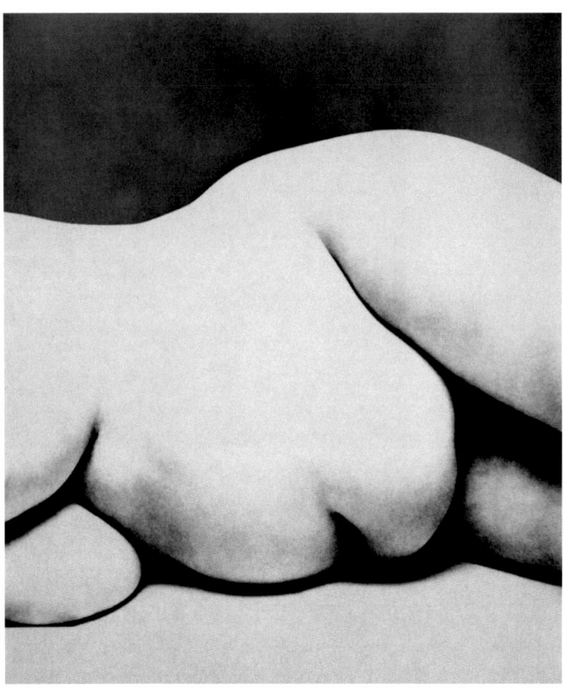

aim to create "the best color photographs that had ever been made by anybody anywhere." He was, in fact, successful in this respect, though this special feature of his work faded into the background with the introduction of better and less expensive color film, such as Kodachrome. Outerbridge continued to be a successful advertising photographer, but his nude pictures were rarely shown because they were considered too offensive. With their high prices, they were in any case primarily the province of well-endowed collectors.

In 1949/50, Irving Penn (1917–2009) created the series of nude photographs entitled *Nudes* (above). Consisting of photographs of more or less voluptuous women, taken at a time when slim models were usual, it represents his "search for the sculptural." For Penn, this series was an attempt to break out of the constraints of commercial photography and to develop as an artist. His photographs of nude models are remarkable for their emphasis on the sculptural quality of the figures, and also for the total absence of a demeaning or salacious gaze. This is the result of the rigorous composition, the models having to be posed in the square format of his Rolleiflex camera. For Penn, these images were

a self-prescribed course with several different aims. They allowed him to experiment with the possibilities offered by the square format he preferred above all others, and also to reduce his reluctance to "get too close" to his models. "As 'objects', I had selected professional models who worked for painters and sculptors; most of them were soft and fleshy, some of them positively voluptuous. What was most important, however, was that they felt comfortable in their bodies. [...] The relationship between us was purely professional, without the slightest hint of sexuality. Anything else would have made these pictures impossible." Despite their artistic integrity, Penn did not exhibit these photographs. Just one was reproduced in the July 1950 issue of *Vogue*, and two others in his first book, entitled *Moments Preserved*, published in 1960. After that, he locked them away, "for fear that the audience might be shocked by them." This worry was not unfounded at the time, considering that he had had to remove pictures from this series from a package sent to the editor of the British edition of *Vogue* because they fell foul of American laws regulating the postal service at the time. It was not until 1980 that Penn exhibited the entire series in New York.

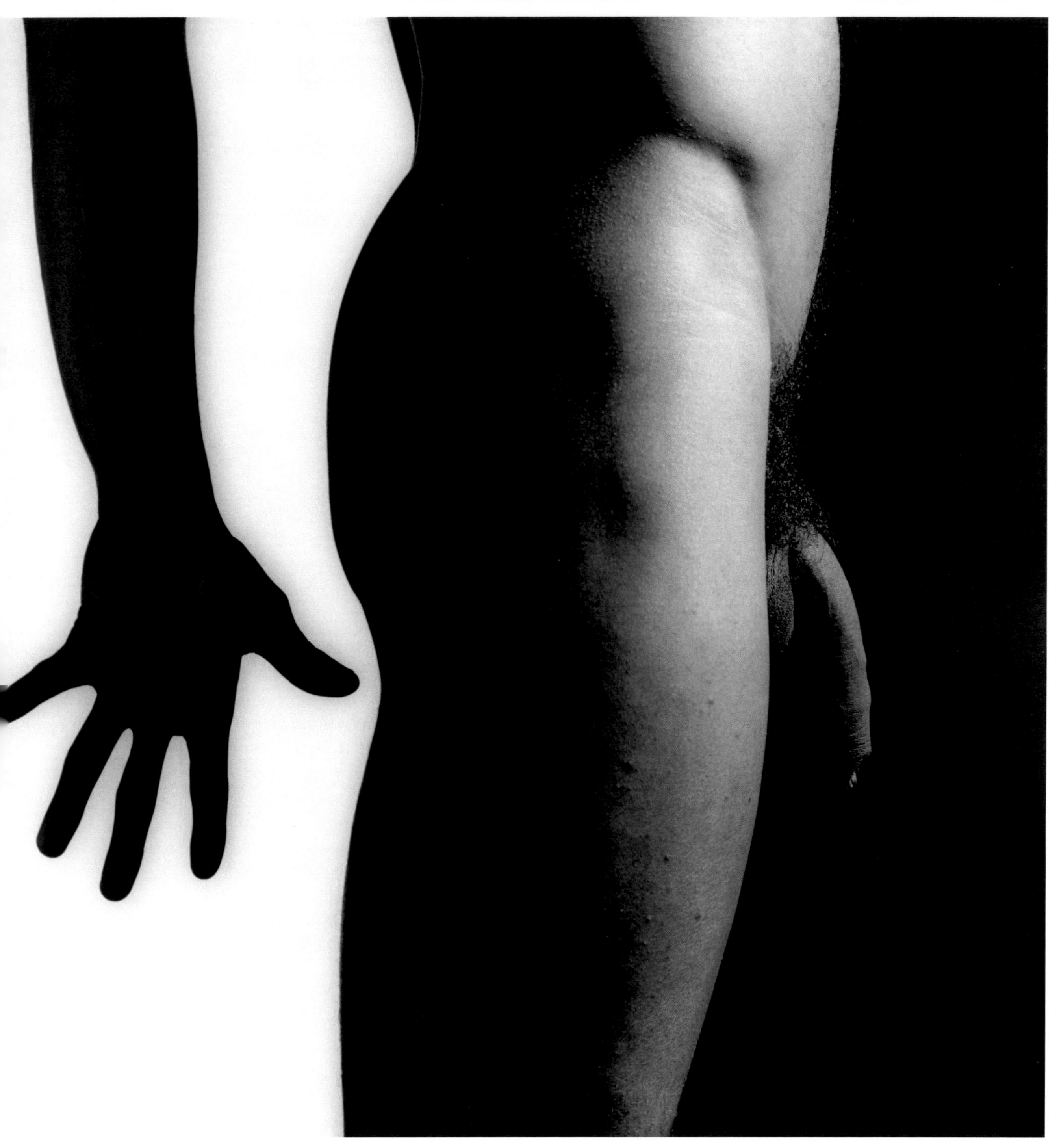

left——**IRVING PENN: NUDE NO. 151** | 1949/50 | 47.3 x 45.7 cm | The Metropolitan Museum of Art | New York
above——**ROBERT MAPPLETHORPE: UNTITLED** | 1981

"In a number of countries nude representations are still subject to considerably stricter regulation than are depictions of violence. That raises the question: Which is more offensive: a weapon or a bared breast?"

Robert Mapplethorpe (1946–1989) would almost certainly never have considered using models such as those depicted in Penn's photographs. He was interested in flawless bodies, which he captured in perfect poses in simple but aesthetically pleasing photographs (fig. p. 67). The first female world champion body builder, Lisa Lyon, was one of his favorite models. Mapplethorpe, who also became famous for his controversial pictures of the gay hardcore scene, succeeded in making erotic male nudes (which had hitherto been quite rare in photography) popular through his visually pleasing images of men. Here too he had a preference for elegant, flawless models, most of whom were part of his circle of friends. Nude photography was long the prerogative of male photographers; for many years, among the legions of male nude photographers, there were only a handful of women. In photography, as in painting, the "male gaze" was predominant. When women did photograph nude subjects, they initially did not used male models, which would have been a reversal of this gaze. Female photographers also often worked with female subjects, though they did so differently from their male colleagues. They attempted to redefine the female body, to challenge the male gaze. One of the most famous female photographers to engage in nude photography is Bettina Rheims (b. 1952), who became well known after the publication of her book *Chambre close* (right). She observed: "I am a woman,

and I am a feminist. I take photographs of women and for women. My view of women is not voyeuristic and not male." Rheims has examined various sexual orientations, too, in her photographic series, such as her *Gender Studies*, created in 2011. She took pictures of men and women whose sexual identity is not fixed, such as Andrej Pejić who works as a model for both men's and women's fashion. He observed: "I sometimes feel more male and sometimes more female. Lots of people probably find me more female at the moment, but I'm both."

Through the works of Bettina Rheims and of photographers with a social agenda, nude photography can gain a socio-political aspect: they can cause certain subjects that have until now been cloaked in silence to be discussed by the wider public, so that they will no longer be considered taboo. Nowadays, nude representations are virtually omnipresent. And yet in a number of countries they are still (particularly regarding those who are underage) subject to considerably stricter regulation than are, for example, depictions of violence. That raises the question: Which is more offensive: a weapon or a bared breast?

right——**Bettina Rheims: 25 Avril I, Paris** | 1991

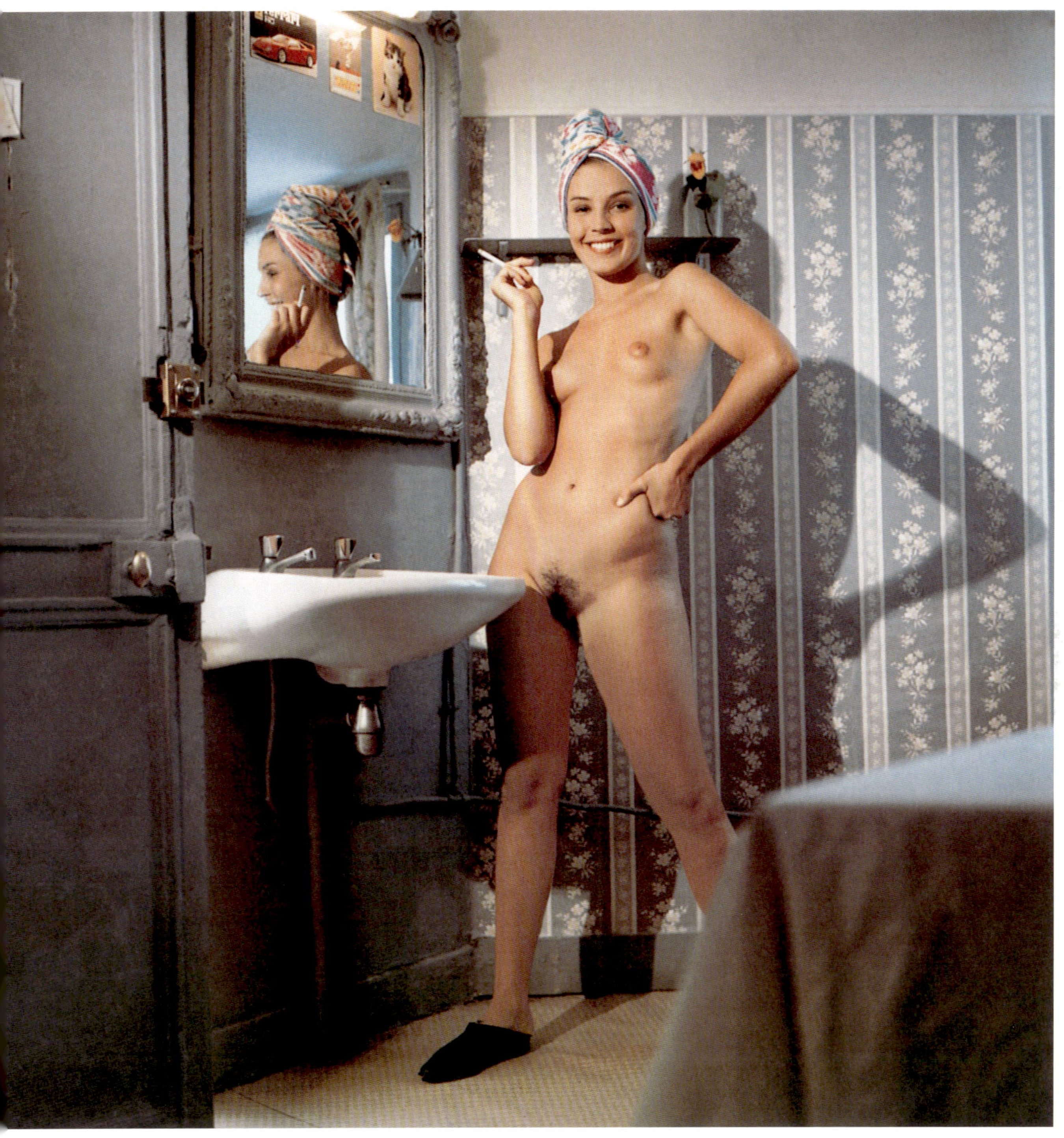

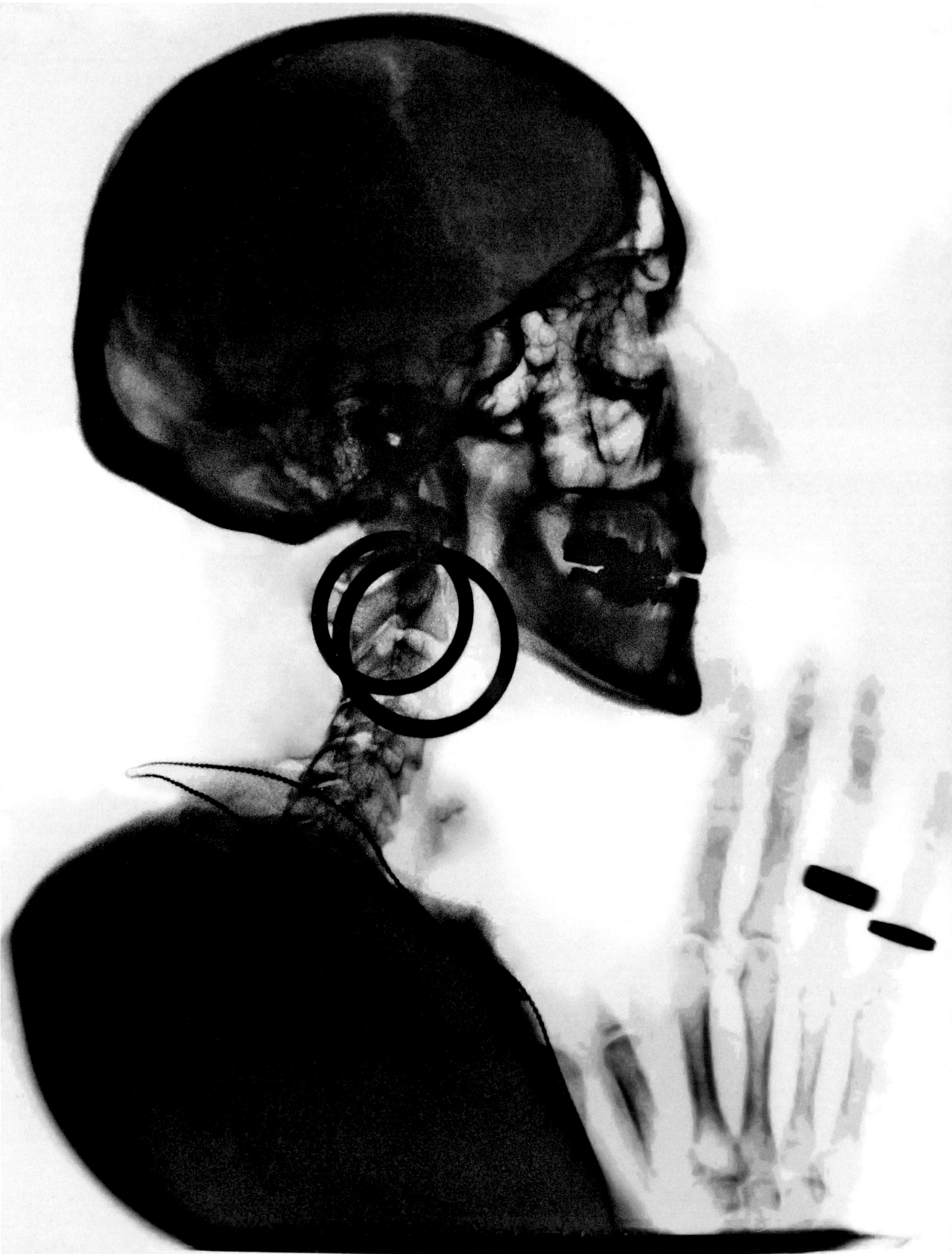

X-RAY PHOTOGRAPHY

When the French scientist and statesman François Arago (1786–1853) provided considerable support for the invention of the daguerreotype in 1839, he was already keen to emphasize the scientific value that he predicted this invention would have. He could never have imagined, however, just how strong the bond between photography and science would become in 1895. While he was experimenting with cathode rays, Wilhelm Conrad Röntgen (1845–1923) chanced upon the effect of a previously unknown type of ray that was able to penetrate certain kinds of solids. When he presented his discovery of X-rays ("X" stood for "unknown") at the physics institute in Würzburg in Germany, he used an image of his colleague Albert von Kölliker's hand (fig. p. 72). This illustrates the defining quality of X-ray photography: flesh is reduced to a mere shadow, whereas bone is visible. Other objects, such as rings, are also left clearly visible by the rays.

A scientific and photographic sensation, Röntgen's discovery was a milestone in modern medicine, of which X-ray photography is now an integral part. More than a thousand articles on this phenomenon were published worldwide within the first year of the invention's publication. As Röntgen decided not to patent his invention, further developments followed in quick succession. Soon, X-ray machines were used in their thousands of hospitals, clinics, and surgeries, and in 1901 Röntgen was awarded the first Nobel Prize in physics for his discovery.

X-ray photography is not limited to scientific uses, however. It also finds application in art, as the idiosyncratic self-portrait of the German-born Swiss artist Meret Oppenheim (1913–1985) shows (left). She had an X-ray photograph showing her head and hand made in 1964. We can see the black shapes of her earrings, and the rings on the fingers she holds up. Oppenheim, who became known as "the muse of the Surrealists" following a series of nude pictures, *Erotique voilée*, by Man Ray in 1933, was also committed to Surrealism in her own work.

In this extraordinary self-portrait, she takes very seriously the challenge voiced by many portrait photographers that one must "look beyond the surface"—it would be hard to interpret this demand more literally. Oppenheim's X-ray photograph can be read in a variety of ways. On the one hand, it represents a macabre look into her own future: as with mummified corpses and other bodies buried with

left——**MERET OPPENHEIM: X-RAY OF MY SKULL** | 1964 | Levy Galerie Hamburg

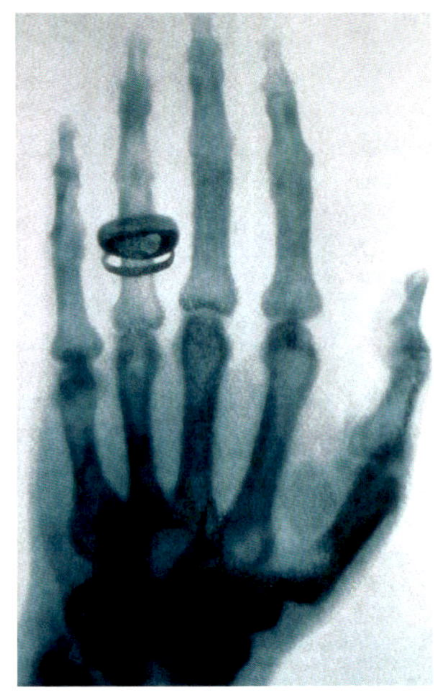

"I'm interested in how things work, and X-rays show what's happening under the surface. Plus, they look cool."

grave goods, all that will remain long after death are the bones and, if present, jewelry. Her self-portrait can also be seen as a variation on the classic *vanitas* image, a genre that reached its apogee in the still-life painting of the Netherlands in the 17th century. In this, as in Oppenheim's picture, the human skull acts as a warning against the presumption of humankind in the face of the transience of its own existence. Oppenheim's X-ray image, in other words, can be interpreted as a modern *memento mori*.

The use of the X-ray machine by fashion photographer Helmut Newton (1920–2004) is more ironic. Born in Berlin and famous for his fashion and nude photography, Newton created a series of X-ray pictures for the jewelry company Van Cleef & Arpels in 1979. The almost surreally bent foot is inside a high-heeled shoe, which is clearly visible, including its internal construction. Here too the subject of eternity appears to have influenced the choice of technique, as with Meret Oppenheim's self-portrait. What remains of humans (including models) after death are bones—and jewelry. In this particular case, this is supplemented by high-heeled shoes, which were typical of Newton's models.

The British photographer Nick Veasey (b. 1962) has also adapted the technique of X-ray photography to his own purposes and now, unusually among photographers, he uses it exclusively. In his pictures, the interior structures of objects otherwise hidden from view reveal themselves. He has visually penetrated all sorts of things, from spiders, flowers, and hats to motor scooters, cars, an airplane, and a bus. "I'm interested in how things work, and X-rays show what's happening under the surface. Plus, they look cool."

For his picture of the fully occupied bus (fig. pp. 74–75), he utilized the kind of X-ray machine used at ports and border crossings to check the contents of trucks. To take these X-ray photographs of humans, Veasey uses either skeletons in special rubber suits or dead bodies that have been donated to science. The bus and the skeletons were captured separately for this photograph, and then merged digitally. It was used as an advertisement for a clinic, and appeared on the side of a real-life bus.

Veasey is interested in more than simply creating "cool" pictures, however. In his X-ray photographs of human bodies in particular, he wants to draw attention to the fact that all humans are the same "on the inside," thus creating a highly unusual critique of society's obsession with external appearances. The dream shared by many artists that art can penetrate people to the very core of their being was never closer to being realized than through X-ray photography—though this was almost certainly not the use for which it was envisaged.

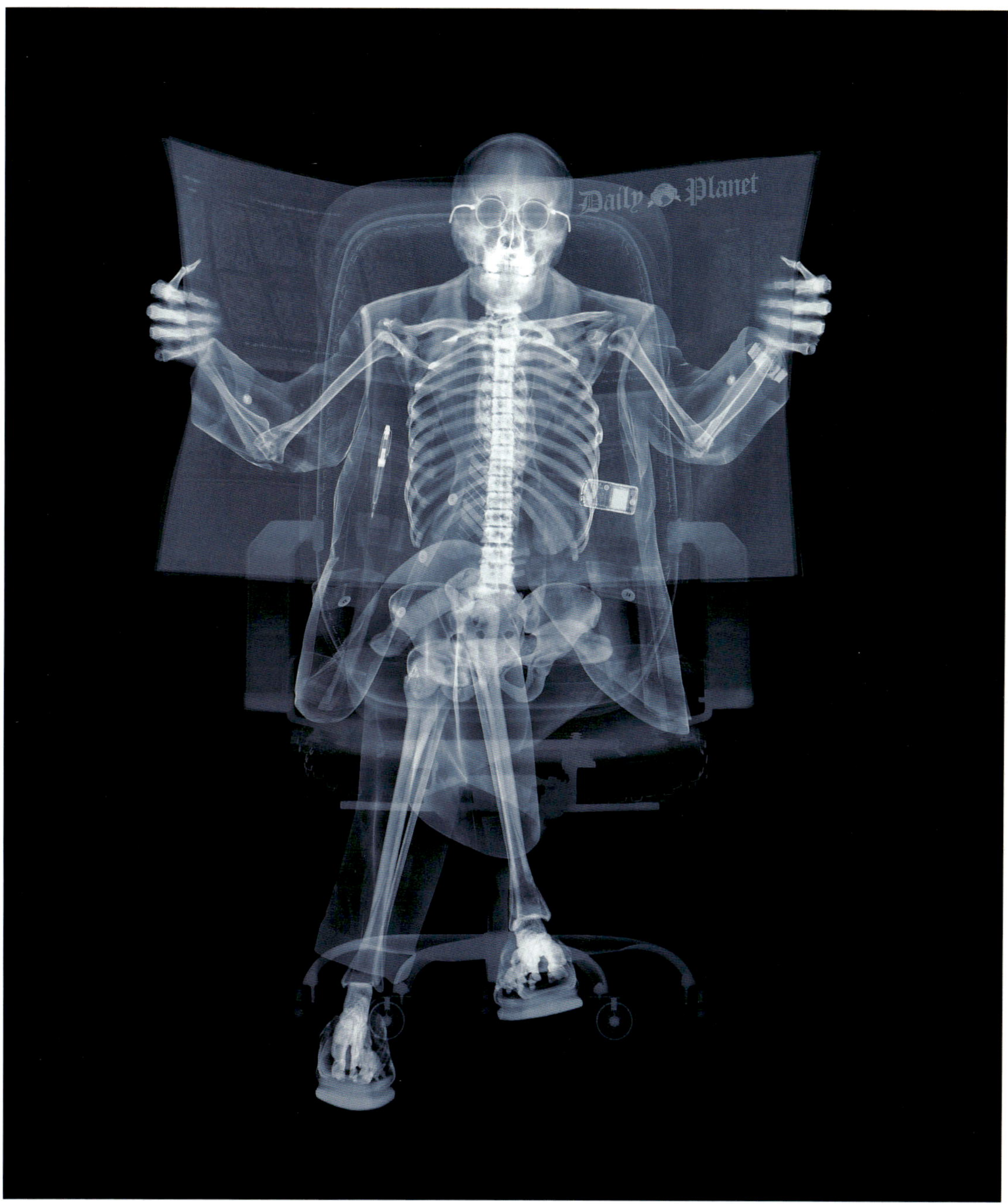

left——WILHELM CONRAD RÖNTGEN: HAND OF ALBERT VON KÖLLIKER 1895

above——NICK VEASEY: SKELETON READING PAPER | 2008

following pages——NICK VEASEY: BUS | September 1998 | 150 x 60 cm

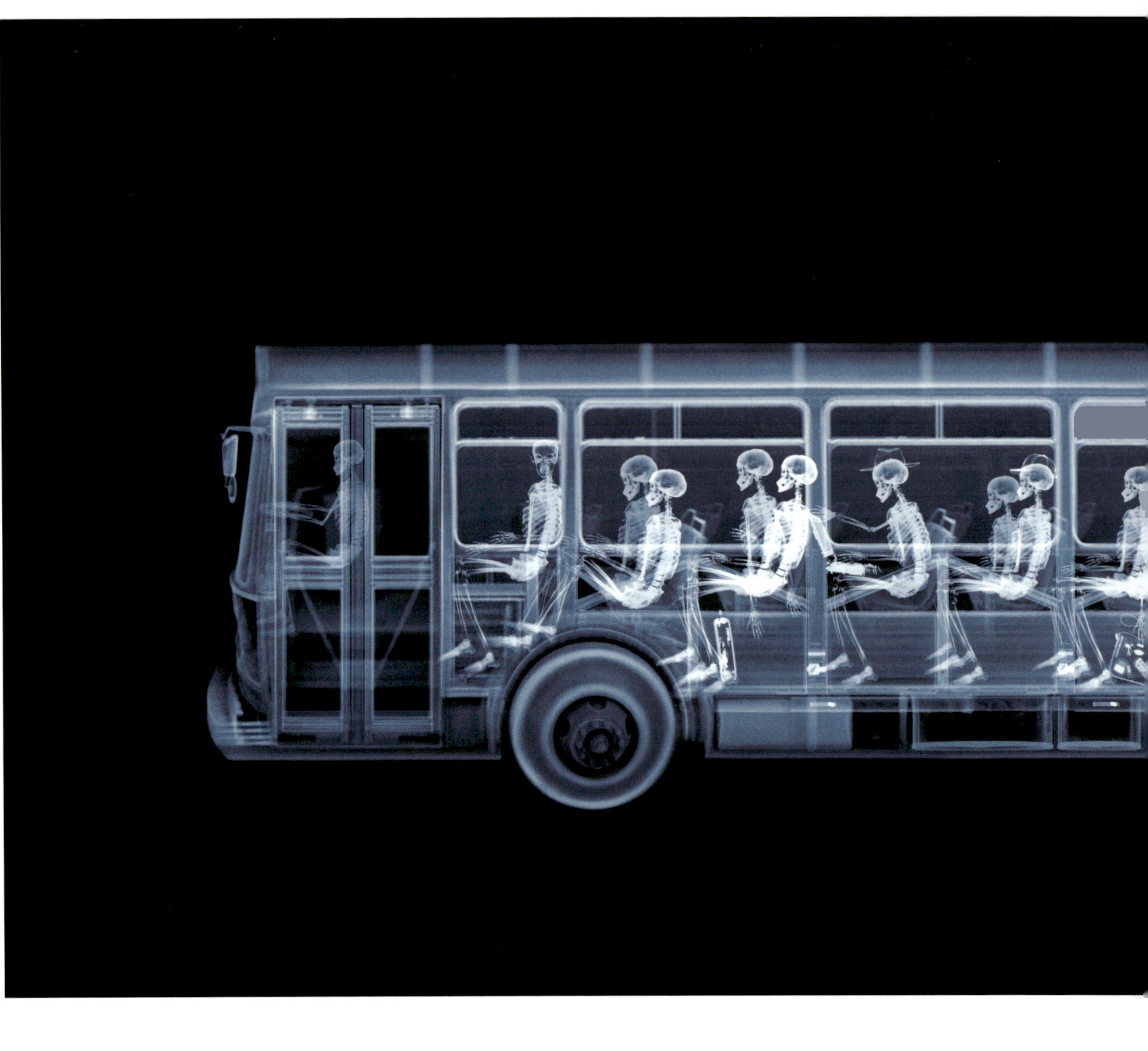

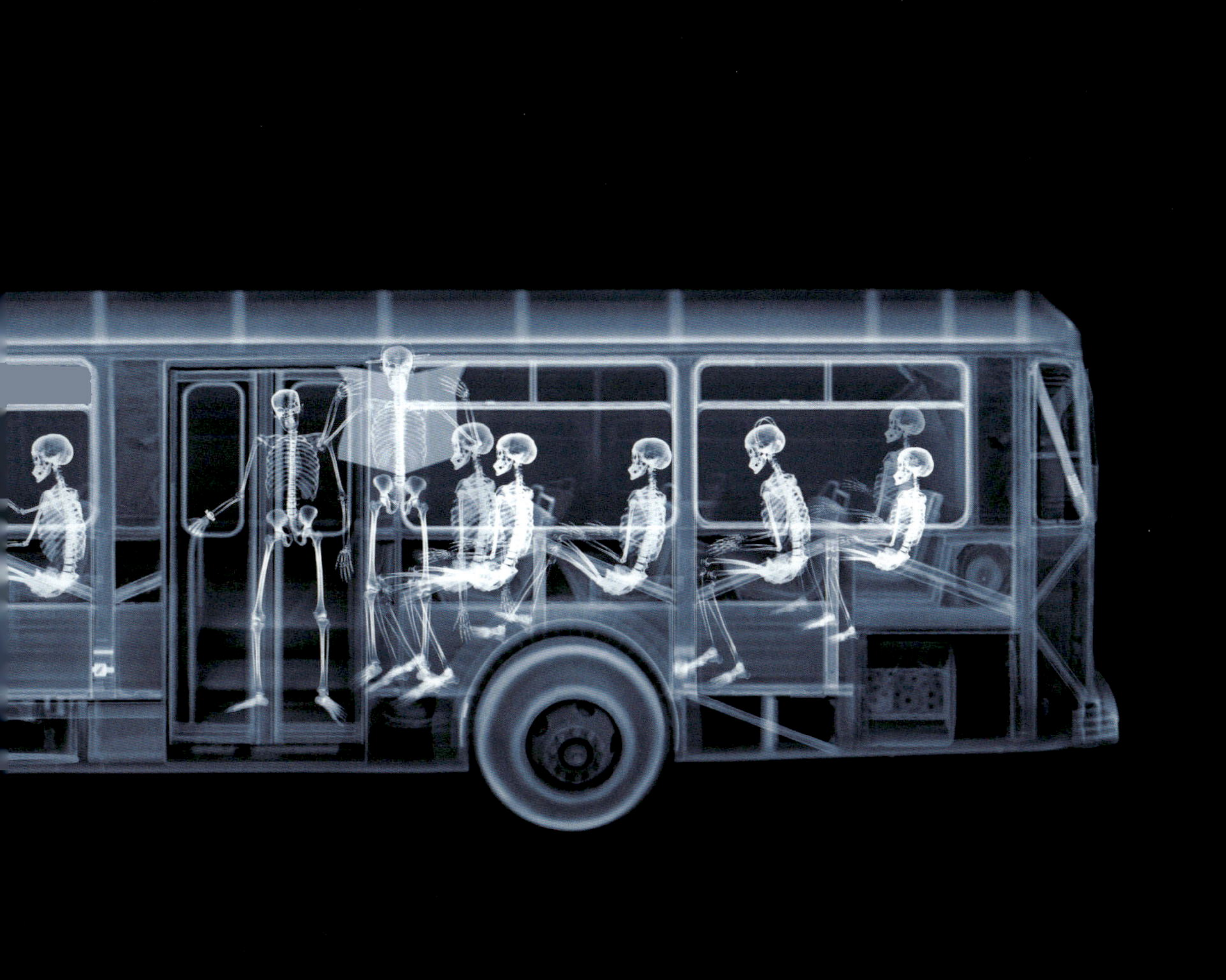

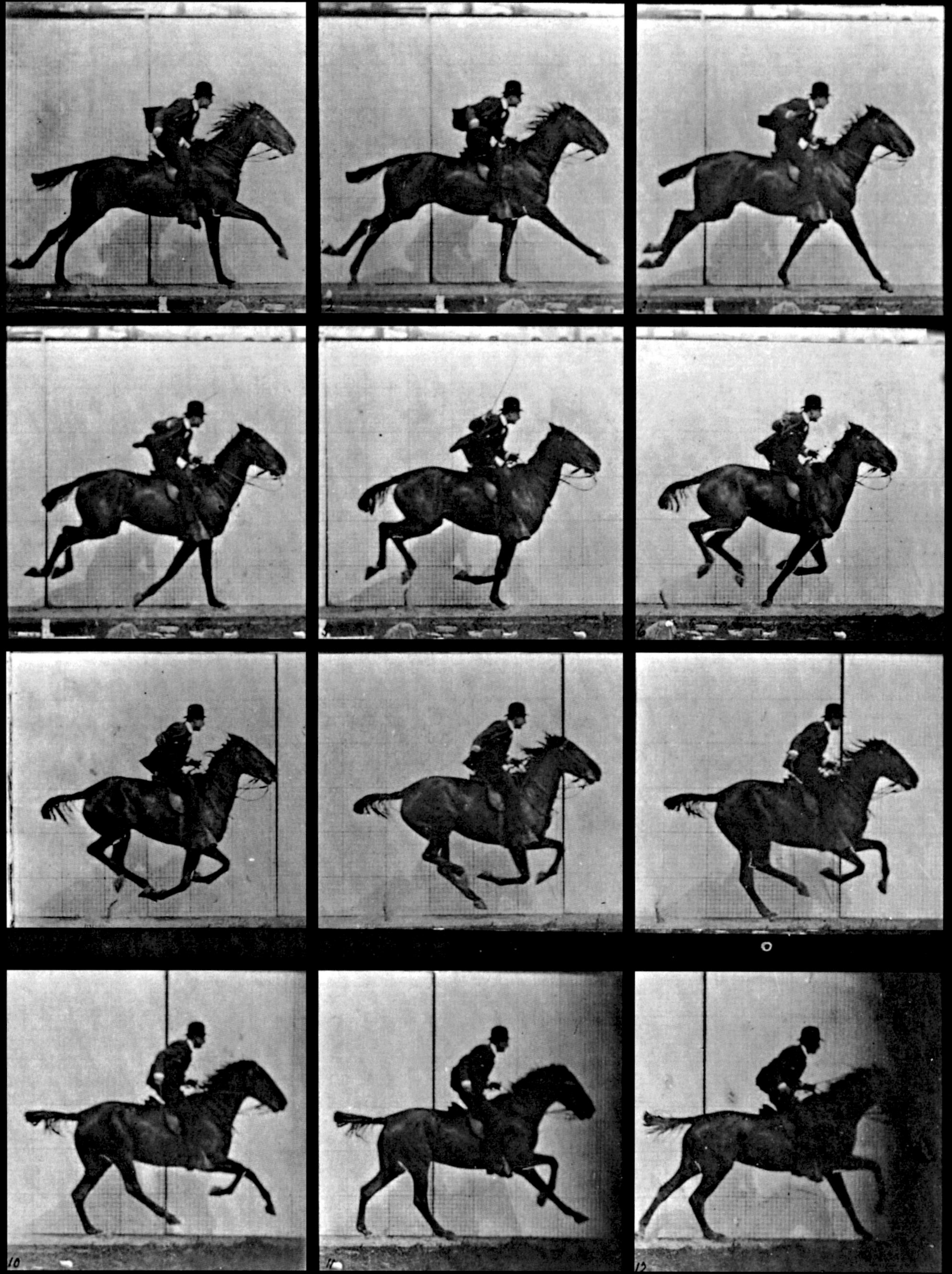

CHRONOPHOTOGRAPHY

The camera sees more than the human eye. During the early stages in the development of photography, this statement applied above all to the countless details that could be made out on daguerreotypes with the help of a magnifying glass. What the long exposure times ruled out, however, was the representation of any form of movement. An observer noted in 1839: "The free movement of an object [...] remains beyond the scope of that chemical process that can control space but not time." This situation changed as exposure times became shorter, and as more powerful lenses and more sensitive emulsions were developed. The camera could now also control time: it could "freeze" rapid movements and thus see even more than with the naked human eye. In the early days of photography, it had been sufficient to remove the lens cover and put it back on again after an exposure of several minutes, so that a few seconds more or less made no appreciable difference. In the case of the new technologies, it was a matter of seconds or fractions of a second,

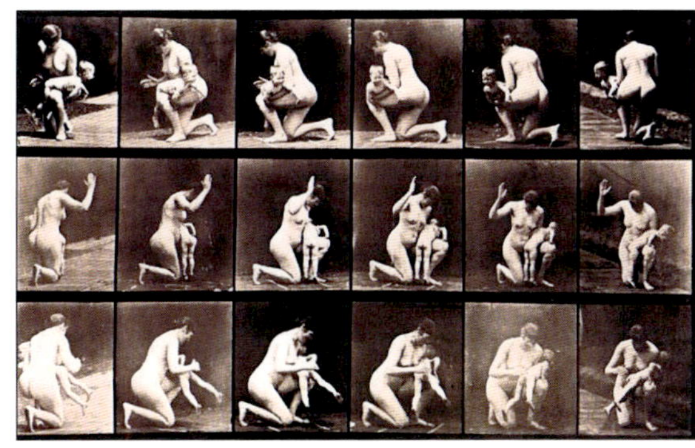

and these could no longer simply be measured by hand. Here, in fact, another photographic innovation had to be introduced: the camera shutter. One of the first photographers to develop a camera shutter was the Englishman Eadweard Muybridge (1830–1904). In 1869 he was commissioned by the former governor of California, Leland Stanford, to photograph his favorite horse, *Occident*, trotting quickly. Muybridge began to tackle this completely new task the same year. The horse had to be persuaded to trot in front of a long line of white sheets intended to reflect as much light as possible. Muybridge created an ingenious system consisting of trip-wires (activated by the horse) linked to shutters he himself had devised for the purpose that were capable of a shutter speed of 1/500 second,

left——**Eadweard Muybridge: Galloping Horse** | 1878

right——**Eadweard Muybridge: Mother Spanking her Child** | 1887

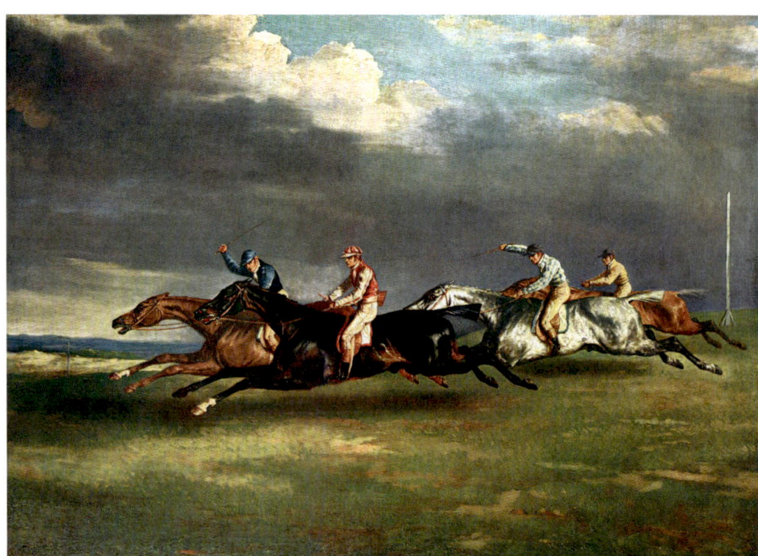

which enabled him to capture the horse's movements as it was trotting.

However, it was the photos of horses that Muybridge took for Stanford in 1878 that made him world famous (fig. p. 76). Stanford wanted to clarify once and for all how a horse's legs move when it is galloping. So Muybridge developed an experiment with which he made the first photo series of a galloping horse. He linked up 12 cameras in series, again using trip-wires but now connected to electrical shutters that were now capable of a speed of less than 1/2000 second. For the first time it was possible to see in which phase of the gallop the horse had all four legs in the air at the same time. For the viewers of the time, the pictures appeared confusing, because galloping horses had hitherto been depicted with their legs extended to the front and the back (above). Muybridge subsequently took photos of all sorts of human and animal movements using shutters that were controlled by clockwork, including a woman who was spanking a child (fig. p. 77). He published them in 1878 in a volume entitled *Animal Locomotion*, which was intended to serve as an atlas for artists of the movements of people and animals. Muybridge also presented his photos in a rotating drum, where they could be observed through a slit. When the drum was rotated,

the viewer could see the horse apparently running—the idea and basis of film had been created. In 1883 the inventor and photographer Étienne-Jules Marey (1830–1904) developed a camera that enabled him to produce several exposures on a single plate (right, above). In order to be able to analyze human movement, he dressed his models in black suits on which white lines corresponding to parts of the body had been drawn (right, below). This echoes the modern technique of capturing motion used in order to digitalize movements for film. Marey's photos influenced avant-garde artists such as the Italian Futurists, notably Umberto Boccioni (1882–1916) and Giacomo Balla (1871–1958), one result being the latter's *Dynamism of a Dog on a Lead* (fig. p. 81), which shows several phases of movement simultaneously.

The research of Muybridge and Marey finally led to the possibility of taking snapshots. Jacques Henri Lartigue (1894–1986) did not produce any ultra-quick shots, but he was one of the first to explore the technical and design opportunities offered by snapshot photography—and while he was still a teenager. In 1912 he photographed a racing car during a race (fig. pp. 82–83). Every detail in the picture confirms the impression of speed: the blurred spectators, the car that rockets out of the

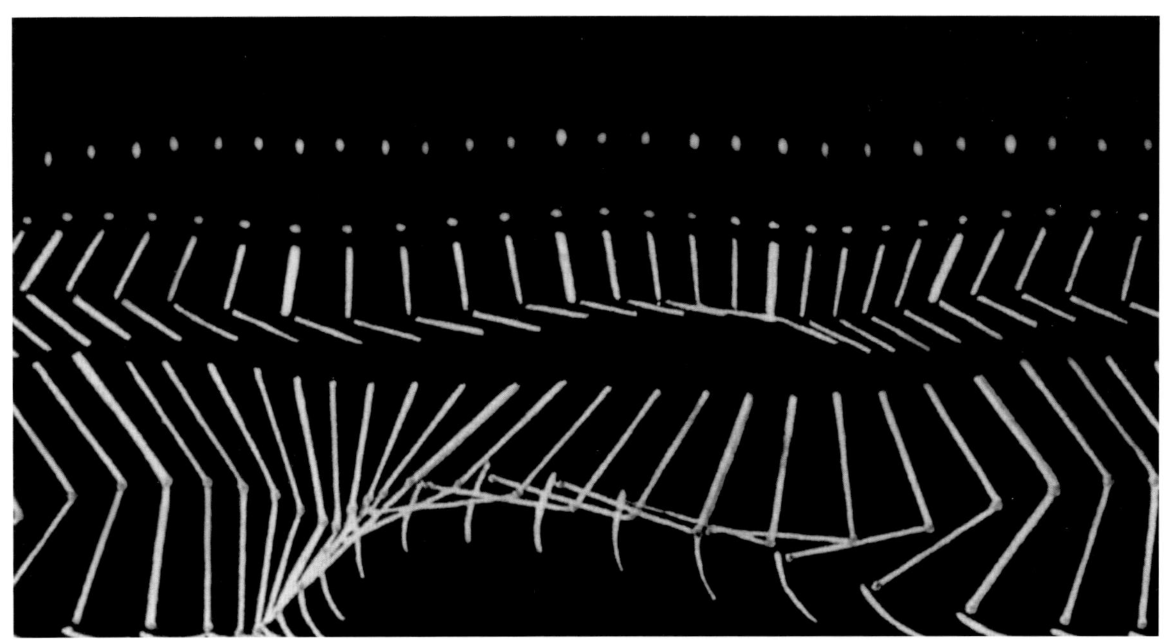

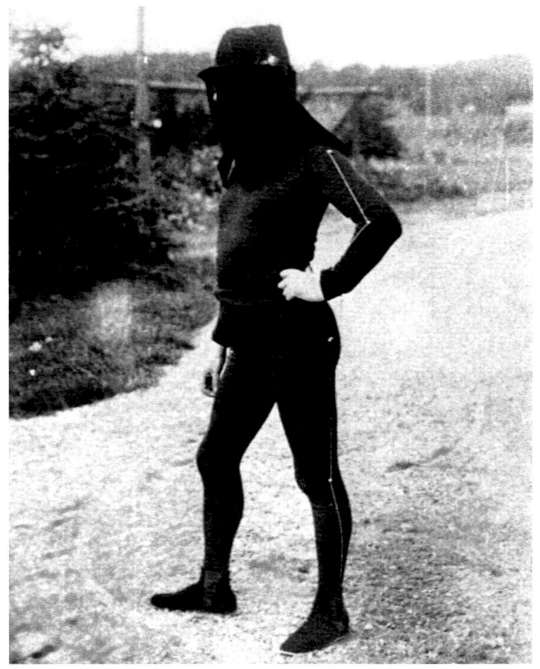

left——**Théodore Gericault: Horse Race at Epsom** | 1820 | oil on
canvas | 29 x 41 cm | Musée des Beaux Arts | Caen
above——**Étienne-Jules Marey: Movement Study** | 1884
right——**Étienne-Jules Marey: Model in a Black Suit with White
Stripes for Movement Studies** | 1884

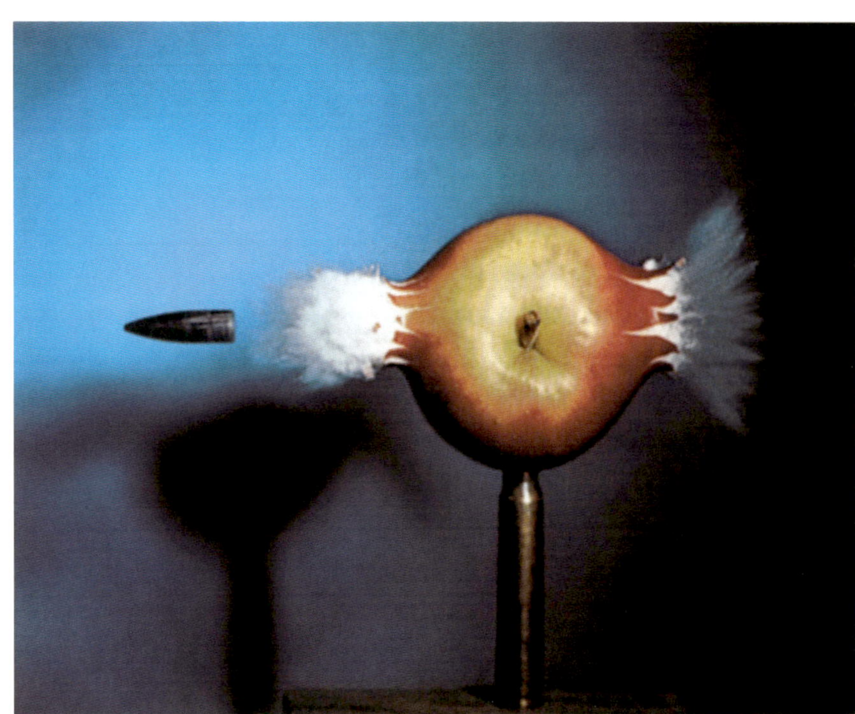

picture, and above all the distorted tires. The elliptical form of the tires is the result of the camera technology. Lartigue used a camera with a horizontal focal-plane shutter, which does not expose the entire picture surface at the same time, but moves line by line, so to speak, across the negative—fast enough, of course, for the time lapse not to be visible under normal circumstances. In the case of fast movement, however, the picture is distorted. Here the camera shutter closed while the car continued to move, and as a result of the movement, the tires were exposed at different times and therefore on different places of the negative. The so-called "rolling-shutter effect" results in the tires appearing in this pronounced elliptical form. With this photograph, Lartigue created an early icon in the representation of speed.

Harold E. Edgerton (1903–1990), a professor at the Massachusetts Institute of Technology, chose another way of making time stand still (above). His photos of movement sequences and shots, taking with extremely short exposure times, were the result not of a rapid shutter movement but of the use of electronic flashes with extremely short flash times, a technique he began developing in 1938. Shutters widely available today can achieve times of up to 1/8000 second, but Edgerton's flashes enable the photographer to achieve exposures of a millionth of a second. Here the camera shutter is opened in a darkened room and the exposure takes place via the production of these ultra-rapid flashes. This enabled him to photograph things that moved faster than the speed of sound and thereby revealed to the human eye yet another dimension that was previously unthinkable.

above——HAROLD E. EDGERTON: SHOT THROUGH AN APPLE | 1964
right——GIACOMO BALLA: DYNAMISM OF A DOG ON A LEAD | 1912
90.8 x 110 cm | Albright-Knox-Gallery | Buffalo | New York
following pages——JACQUES HENRI LARTIGUE: RACING CAR | 1912

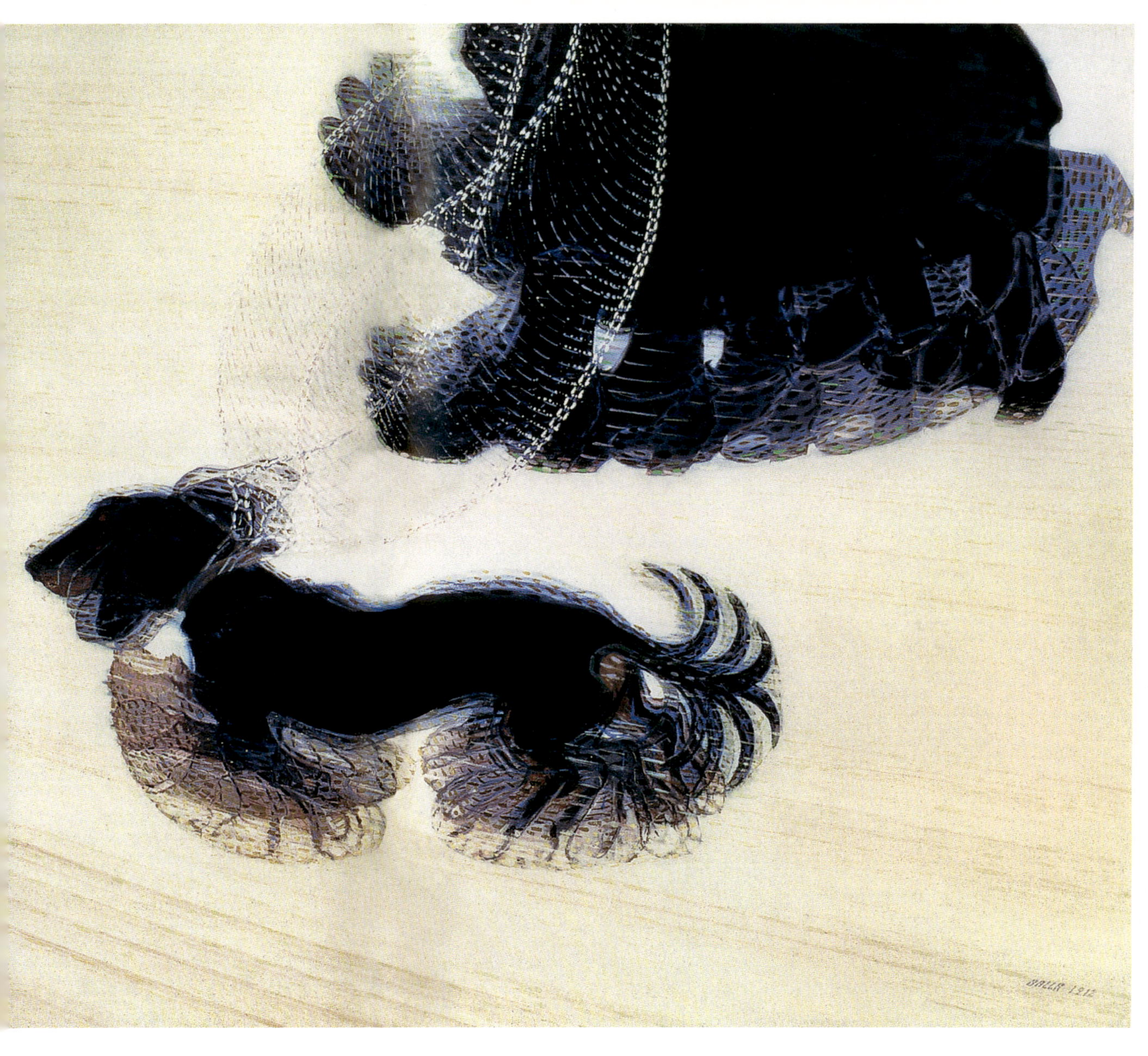

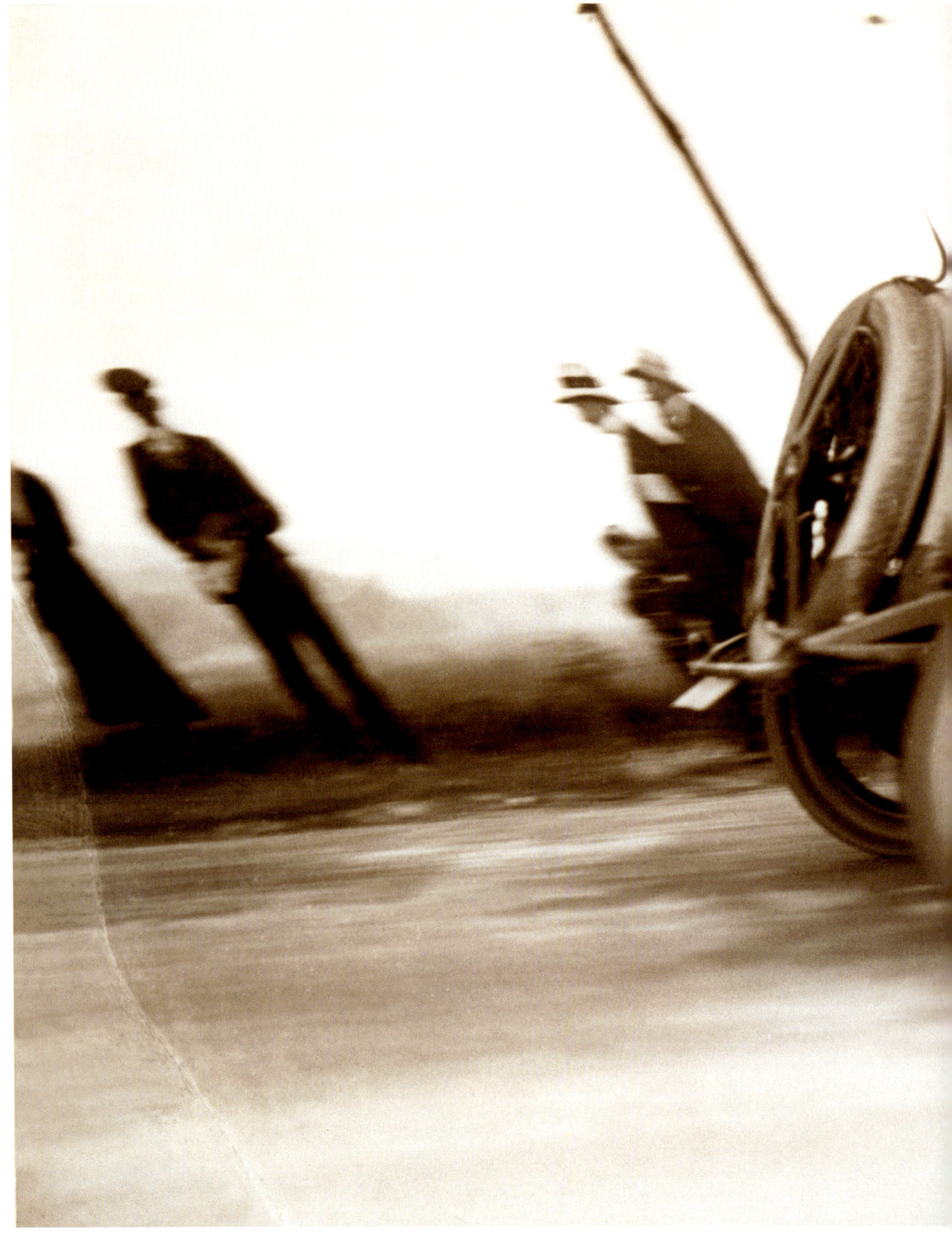

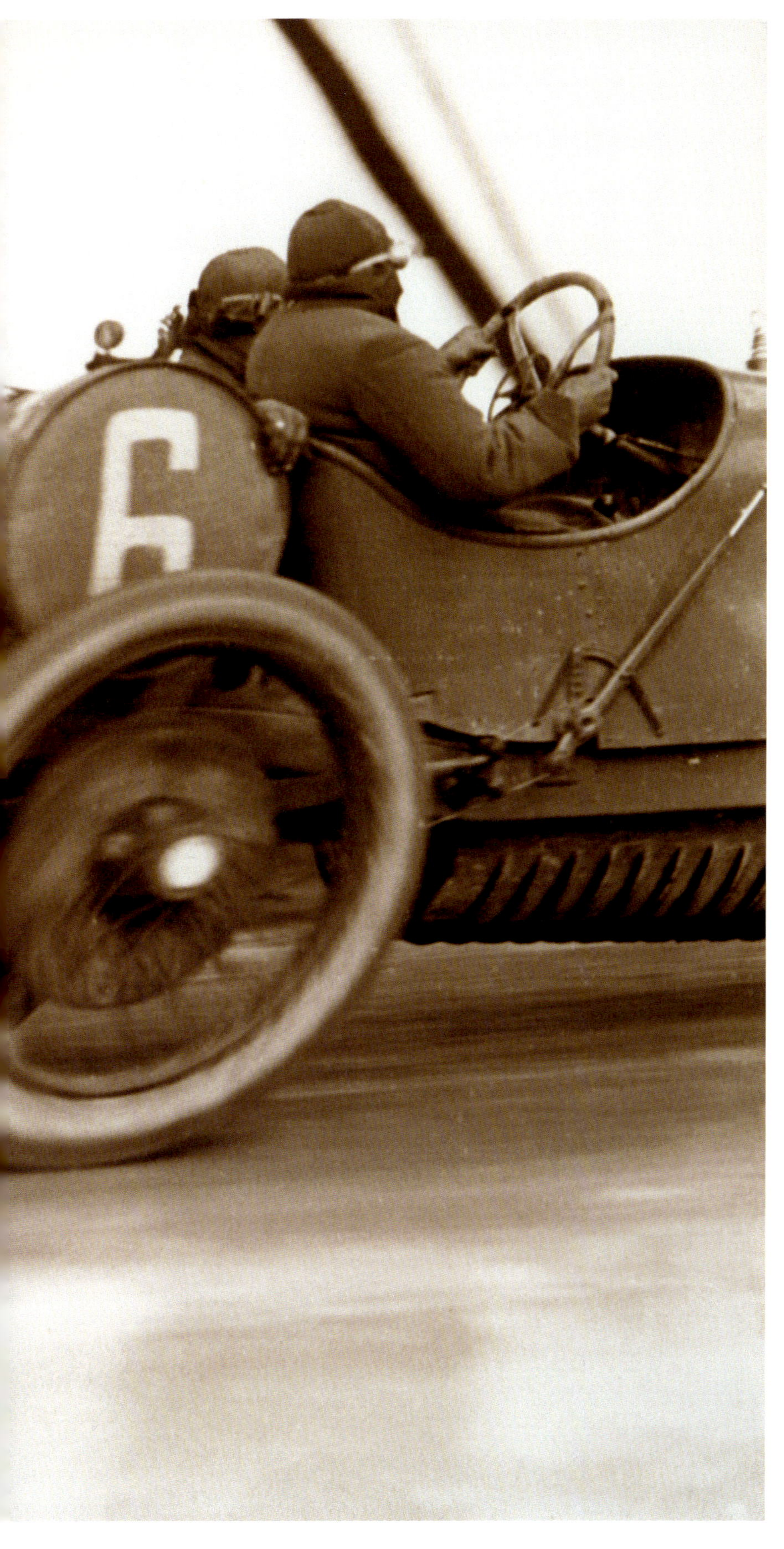

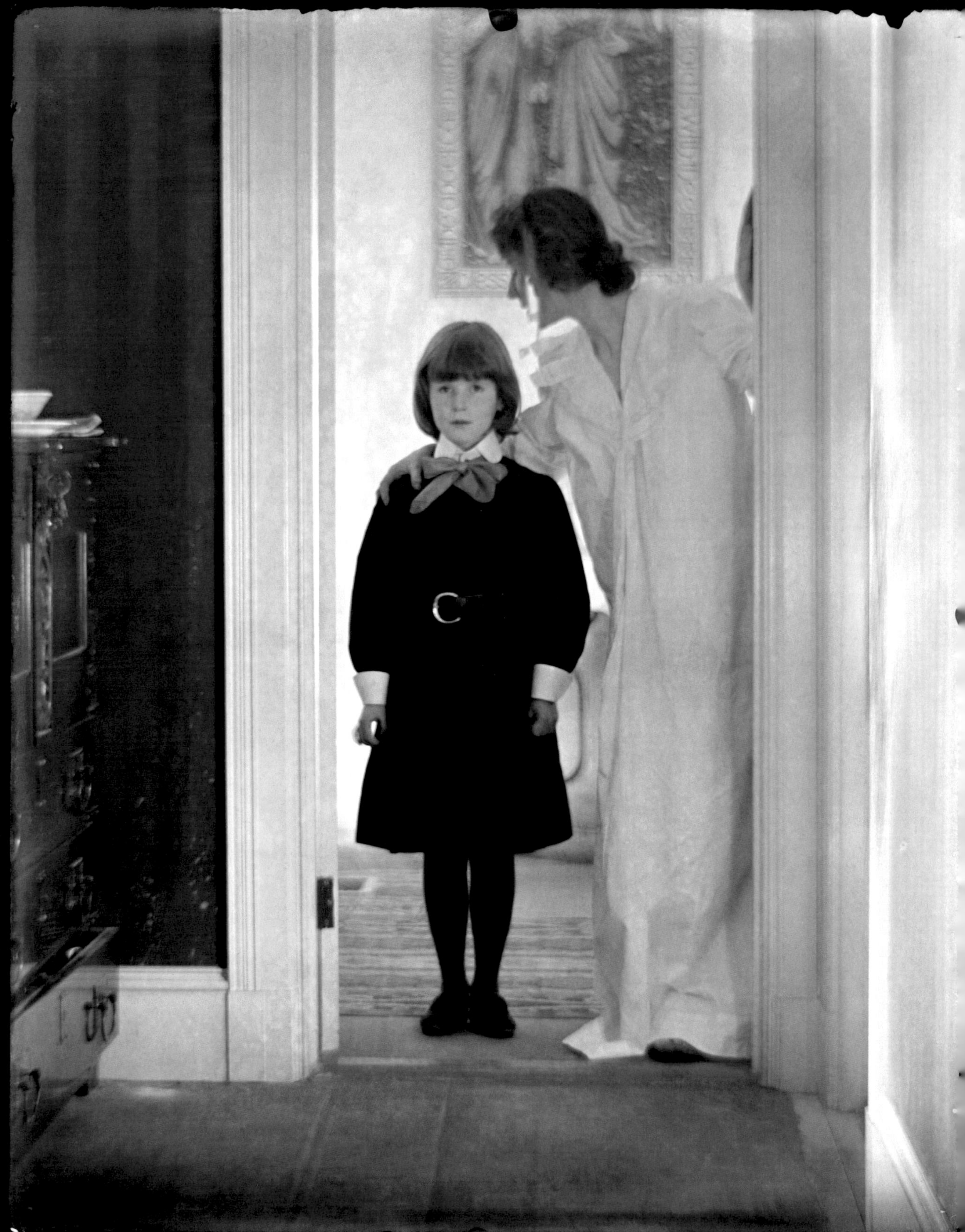

PICTORIALISM

Ever since its invention, the question as to whether or not photography is an art has been the subject of keen debate. Painting and sculpture were the acknowledged art forms. Could a technical and chemical process that demanded nothing more than a little practical skill quickly acquired be art? Many felt that the process of taking a picture with a camera was too mechanical. After all, the artist acknowledged in the case of an engraving was the person who had drawn the original design, whereas the engraver was regarded simply as a craftsman. This argument continues to have currency to this day, and the debate has indeed been given additional relevance by the development of digital photography. What is photography, what is art, and when (if ever) is photography art? It is remarkable that it was precisely because of improvements in lenses and films that controversy erupted once before, towards the end of the 19th century. For increasing accuracy and the possibilities of mass reproduction appeared to undermine the artistic nature of photography. To counteract this, some photographers attempted to take photographs that were not reproducible, that were instead akin to paintings. By the end of the 19th century, Impressionism and Symbolism had become established in the world of art. Fine-art photographers wanted to achieve similar effects, and named themselves "Pictorialists" in order to emphasize their proximity to painters.

They felt that the technically brilliant and highly detailed photographs that could now be made obscured the personal style of the photographer. For this reason, they used manual development and printing processes such as the gum bichromate process and the bromoil process, hoping to make it "as easy to differentiate the styles of leading photographers as it is to tell apart Rembrandt and Reynolds" (Alfred Stieglitz). To this end, emulsions of light-sensitive chromate salts, color pigments, and gum arabic (hence the term "gum bichromate process") were applied to the paper. After the copy had been made, painterly touches were applied to the pictures by hand so that they looked like paintings or prints. In some cases, photographers used etching needles and similar tools on the negatives. The aim was the creation of a unique image.

How far this manipulation went in some cases is illustrated by *Struggle*, created by France's leading Pictorialist, Robert Demachy (1859–1936), in 1904 (fig. p. 86). This shows a female nude caught in a

left——**Gertrude Käsebier: Blessed Art Thou Among Women**
c. 1900 | Museum of Modern Art | New York

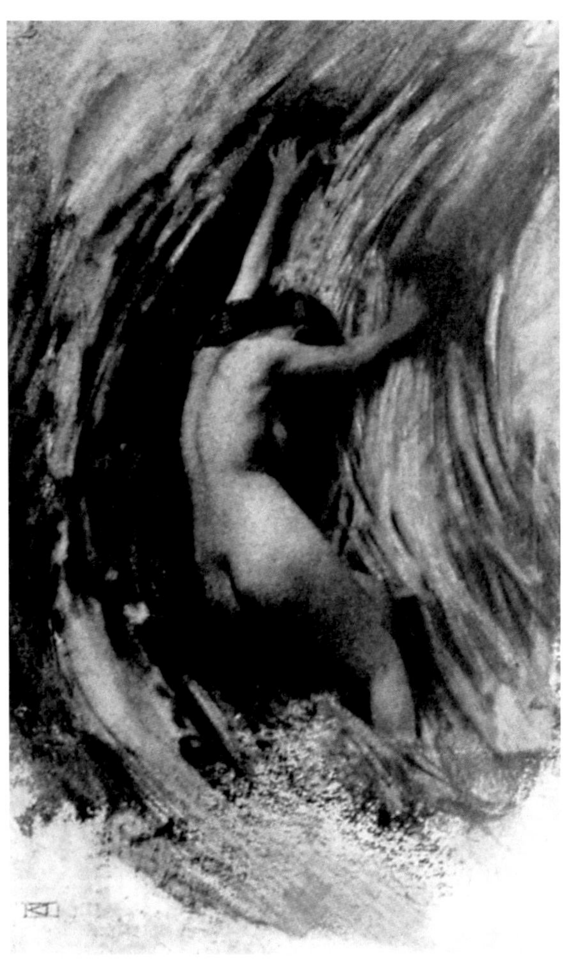

wave, the latter not photographed but worked into the emulsion using a paintbrush. For this ex-banker from Paris, photographs that had not been manipulated did not qualify as art. He too felt the need for a "creative hand" through which a simple photograph could become a unique work of art.

Pictorialism was the first photographic style to achieve international recognition. One of the most famous and most talented exponents was the Austria-based German photographer Heinrich Kühn (1866–1944) (opposite, left). He too applied the gum bichromate method masterfully and, furthermore, experimented with the use of eyeglass lenses instead of standard camera lenses in order to avoid the sharp focus considered undesirable by the Pictorialists. Kühn developed several soft-focus lenses and perforated diaphragms that gave the photographer full control of soft focus. In cooperation with an optician, he developed a soft-focus lens (the Imagon) that continued to be produced until the 1990s. Kühn was also one of a small number of fine-art photographers to make use of color in his photographs.

The most important figure in this new form of fine-art photography was the New York-born Alfred Stieglitz (1864–1946). Having spent several years in Europe, during which he studied engineering in Berlin, he returned to New York in 1889. After various activities in the New York photography scene, he founded the Photo-Secession in 1902. Members of this association, which was modeled on European art groups, included Edward Steichen and Gertrude Käsebier. Stieglitz opened his famous gallery 291 (named after the street number of its Fifth Avenue address in New York) in 1905. In 1903 he had founded the journal *Camera Work*, which continued to be published until 1917. The gallery and the periodical were the main platforms for the Pic-

left——**ROBERT DEMACHY: STRUGGLE** | 1904 | published in *Camera Work* January, 1904 | Musée d'Orsay | Paris

right——**HEINRICH KÜHN: PICNIC ON A HILL** | between 1912 and 1915 Musée d'Orsay | Paris

far right——**ALFRED STIEGLITZ: WINTER, FIFTH AVENUE, NEW YORK** 1893 | The Museum of Modern Art | New York

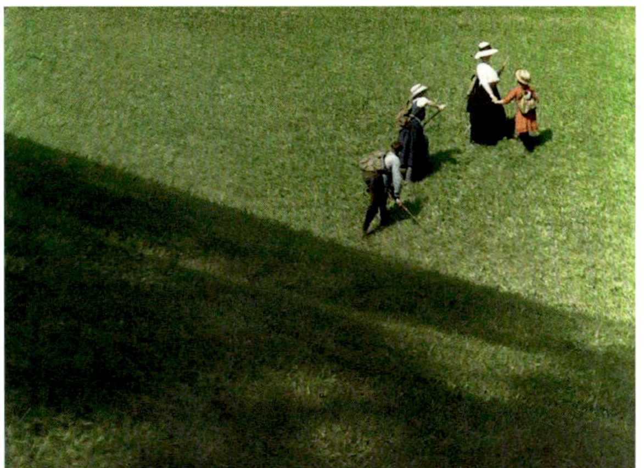

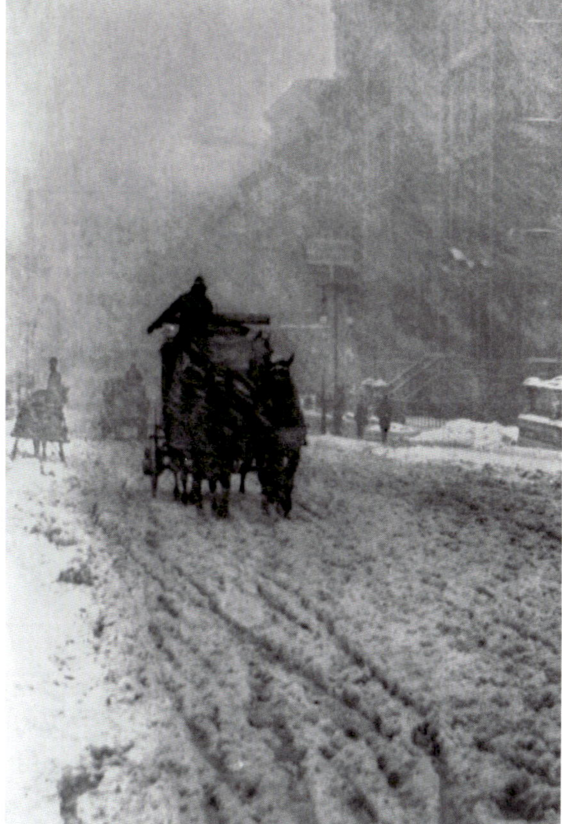

torialists and, later, for avant-garde art in the United States; Stieglitz was the first to exhibit modern European art, notably Impressionism and Cubism, in the United States. The first issue of *Camera Work* was dedicated to the photographer Gertrude Käsebier (1852–1934), who selected easily recognized scenes and positioned them within the history of art by giving them traditional titles. *Blessed Art Thou Among Women* (fig. p. 84) from *c.* 1900 represents her personal take on the representation of the Virgin Mary. Käsebier attempted to gain recognition of her photographs as artworks by making explicit the reference to familiar subjects in painting.

The flamboyant Edward Steichen (1879–1973), who was a co-founder of the Photo-Secession, would have a profound effect on the development of photography throughout his career. He had trained as a painter and photographer, and his self-portrait of 1901/02 (fig. p. 58) is unique in the clarity with which it reflects the Pictorialists' ambition to transform photography into an independent art form using the methods of painting.

But photography's attempts to assert itself as an art form in its own right using methods borrowed from painting would eventually turn out to be a dead end, precisely because this attitude confined photography to the role of painting's poor cousin. Stieglitz may have sensed this, for his approach differed from that of his colleagues. In his view, the photographer's eye, rather than the many forms of artistic manipulation possible during the printing process, was photography's most important artistic tool. *Winter, Fifth Avenue* (above, right) from 1893 is one of the most famous photographs from this period. Stieglitz stood in a flurry of snow for hours in order to capture this picture, and simply enlarged one section of the negative in order to heighten the pictorial atmosphere.

Stieglitz recognized that photography would not be able to emancipate itself from painting through Pictorialism, and that he would have to set a new course instead. It is therefore no surprise that it was in *Camera Work*, the Pictorialists' most important platform, that this photographic development took place. The last (double) issue of the magazine, published in 1917, was dedicated to the work of the young New Yorker Paul Strand, who led the way in a new direction: "straight photography."

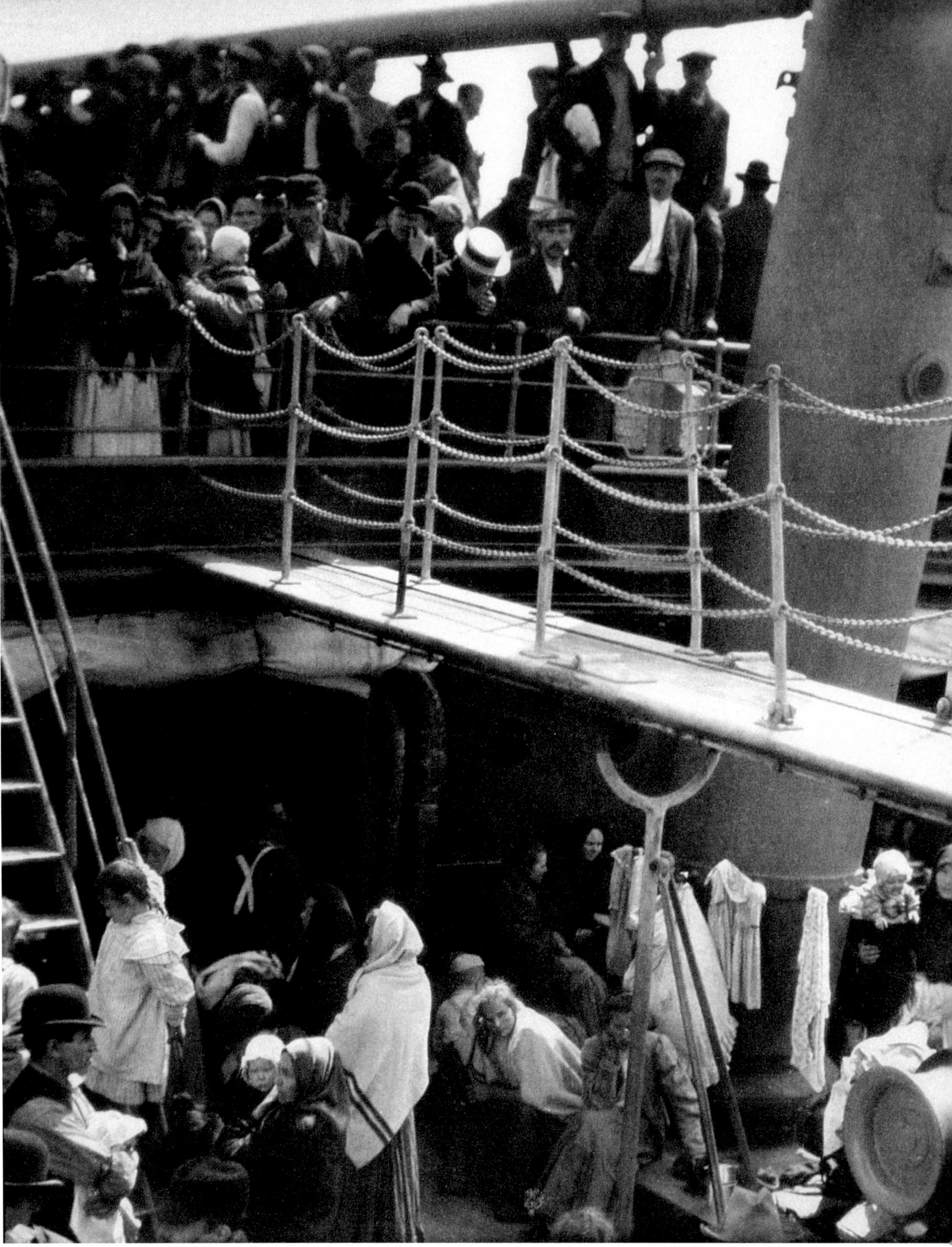

STRAIGHT PHOTOGRAPHY

Alfred Stieglitz's change of approach is directly linked to a photo that he took on board the *Kaiser Wilhelm II* in 1907. While crossing the ocean from Europe to America, he spotted a subject he felt he had to photograph immediately: "I saw the relationship between forms; I saw a picture that consisted of forms that expressed my attitude to life." For Stieglitz, *The Steerage* (left) was a crucially important work. He recognized that "the key elements of photography: camera, lens, emulsion" were all that was necessary to create a picture. No manipulation in the darkroom, no elaborate printing processes, and no standing around in a snowstorm for hours, as he had done for *Winter, Fifth Avenue* (fig. p. 87, right). And in contrast to that picture, he found *The Steerage* so perfect that he printed the entire negative. From now on he wanted to "take photos that looked like photos"—the idea of "straight photography" had been born.

Although it seems perfectly normal to the present-day viewer, it amounted to a revolution at the time. The critic Sadakichi Hartmann, a friend of Stieglitz's, explained the shift from art to reality, and thus the specific characteristics of photography, as follows: "Painting composes by allowing the imagination free rein. The photographer interprets by means of his spontaneous powers of judgment. He composes through his eyes." And it was precisely one such composition that Stieglitz recognized and recorded on the *Kaiser Wilhelm II*.

Stieglitz himself gave his enthusiastic support to this new trend in the last issue of his journal *Camera Work* in 1917, which he dedicated to the young Paul Strand (1890–1976). Strand had studied photography under Lewis Hine (1874–1940), the most famous documentary photographer of the time. Strand's photos, which attracted a great deal of attention, can be divided into two groups easily distinguished from each other in terms both of technique and form. One group focuses on the city, with its streets and people; with these photos Strand became one of the cofounders of street photography (see *Street Photography*). The other group consists of strictly formal shots of subjects that illustrate Strand's interpretation of straight photography. *The White Fence* (fig. p. 90) of 1916, for example, shows a simple fence behind which there is a garden and two houses that gradually become blurred. By focusing on the fence, Strand turned it into an aesthetic object. There is no manipulation of the print and no artistic-sounding title, just pure pho-

left—**ALFRED STIEGLITZ: THE STEERAGE** | 1907 | Museum of Modern Art | New York

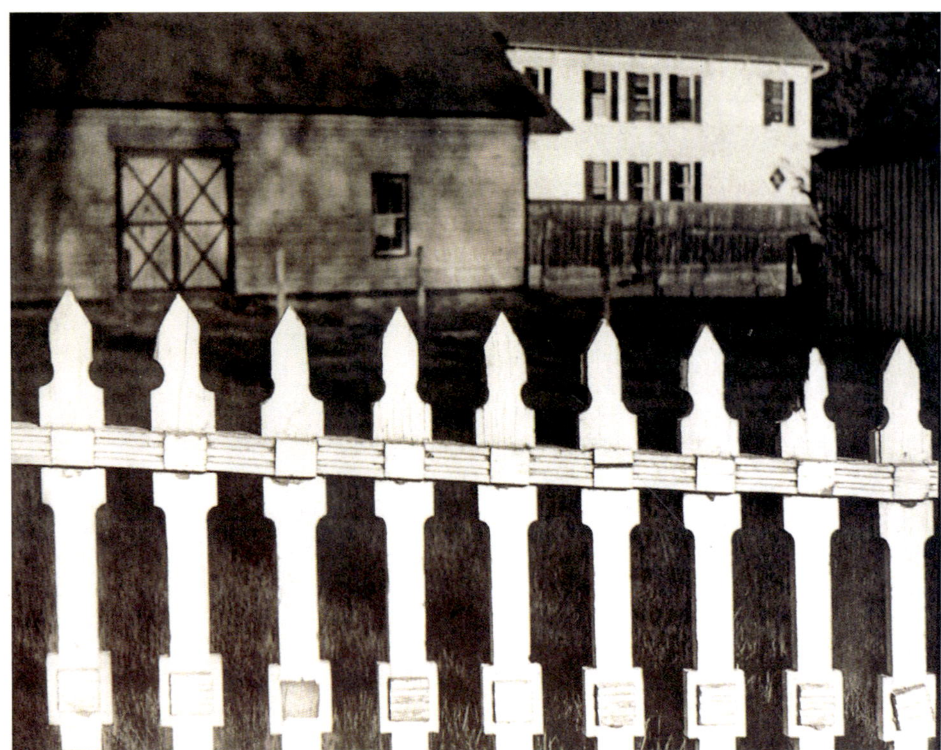

tography. Strand photographed simple objects that can be recognized as such, "or one can treat them as abstract forms in order to evoke a specific feeling without any obligation regarding the objectivity of the shot."

Strand's pictures were accompanied by an essay in which he explained his approach to photography. Its central statement was: "The legitimation of photography, like that of all media, lies in the complete uniqueness of its means." Although this sounds simple, almost trite, it was a completely new idea in art photography at the time. Strand passed a harsh verdict on the work of his predecessors in *Camera Work*: "The full effectiveness of any medium depends on how straight it is used, and all attempts to mix end in dead things like color printing, rubber printing, oil printing, etc." (It would be interesting to hear Strand's opinion of the opportunities presented by today's digital photography!)

Perhaps it was also through his teacher Lewis Hine that Strand came to this conclusion, for the latter had long been a "straight" photographer. For Hine, photography was not really art, but a form of documentation in the struggle for social reform. Strand developed between the two "cornerstones" of American photography, Stieglitz representing the artistic side and Hine the documentary.

With Strand's photographs, which Stieglitz described as "brutal, direct, clean, and without deceit," we find the beginnings of a *photographic* approach to art photography. In this respect, the change from Pictorialism to straight photography was the most important artistic development in photography since the demise of the daguerreotype. In the discussion about art and photography, Strand had a highly individual and very interesting approach, which he formulated thus in 1922: "The discussion surrounding the question as to whether

above——**Paul Strand: The White Fence, Port Kent, New York**
1916 | Museum of Modern Art | New York

"The discussion surrounding the question as to whether photography is an art or not has contributed to the fact that fortunately no one knows exactly what art is."

photography is an art or not [...] has contributed to the fact that fortunately no one knows exactly what art is."

The new approach also established itself in the western regions of the United States. Edward Weston (1886–1958), who like virtually all other photographers of the era initially made a study of Pictorialism, eagerly adopted the ideas of straight photography. He also became convinced that "real photography can only be achieved through realism." Weston was one of the first to formulate what many photographers of the last century had to be aware of because of the technical requirements, and which is common knowledge today: a photo is formed in the head. Before he releases the shutter, the photographer must check all the factors and envision what the final result will look like. Weston's landscapes, still lifes, and nudes are characterized by a perfect rendering of materiality, by sharp definition, and by precise focus. The close-up shots of objects such as lettuce leaves or green peppers, whose form and volume he puts into perfect focus, sometimes look like abstract sculptures. Weston arouses in the viewer completely new associations by means of this transformation of familiar objects, this "alienation effect" (fig. p. 92).

While the debate about art and photography, the "pictorial" and "straight," was being pursued in the United States, in Paris Eugène Atget (1857–1927) had long been taking photographs that were as "straight" as Stieglitz and Strand had wanted (fig. p. 93). Although his photographic technique was regarded as out-of-date even in his day, Atget was in is own way one of the most advanced photographers of his time. This became clear, however, only at the end of his life, since he made little fuss about his photographs. When his "discoverer," Man Ray, wanted to publish some of his photos in the magazine *La Révolution surréaliste* in 1926, Atget commented: "Don't mention my name. The pictures I take are only documents." Atget recorded his city in those times of change and sold his photographs to artists as references for their paintings.

Everything that straight photography required—clarity, directness, crispness of focus, and no darkroom manipulation—could be found in Atget's photos. He worked with a large-format camera with glass plates measuring 18 x 24 cm (7 x 9½ in) and a slightly wide-angle lens. The result was an abundance of detail and clear focus. The long exposure times required by his equipment means that there are very few people on his pictures. Furthermore, he mostly took his photos in the early morning hours, when the streets were still relatively quiet. His scenes do not look deserted, however, but as if someone had just left or was about to appear at

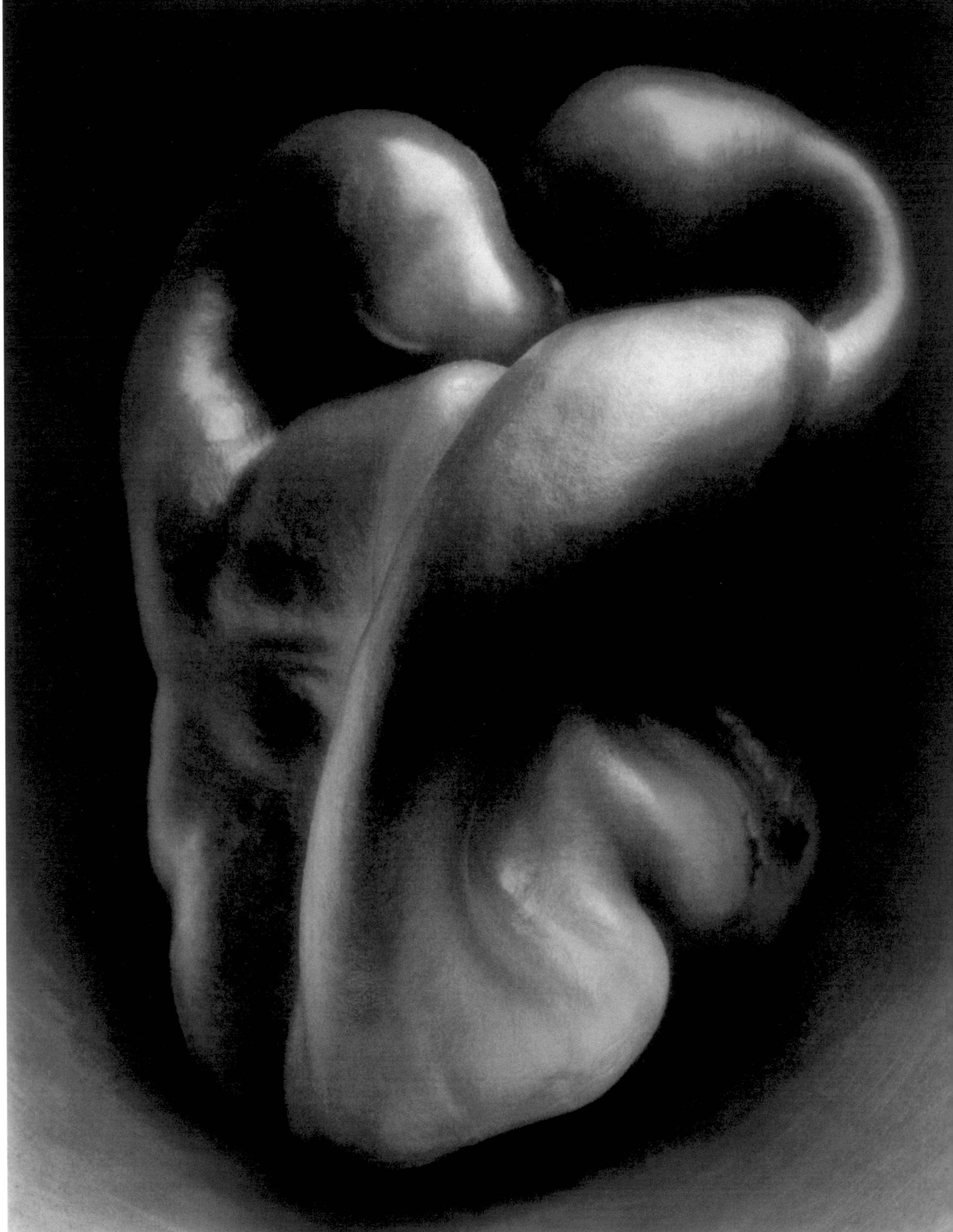

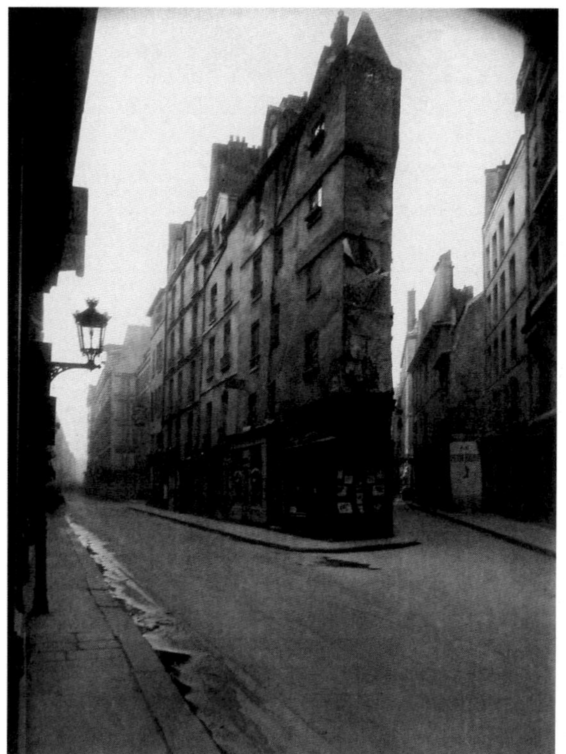

any minute. In his best pictures, Atget achieved an extraordinary liveliness by concentrating on objects and including a wealth of detail. Through Man Ray and his assistant, Berenice Abbott, who acquired part of Atget's estate, Atget's photos also became famous in the United States and had a lasting influence on the younger generation.

In straight photography, photography emancipated itself from painting and achieved a new independence, enabling it to develop with its own means and possibilities. It formed the artistic basis for the younger generation of photographers, including Walker Evans (1903–1975). During the Great Depression in America, Evans became famous for the images showing the poverty of the land workers, photographs he took on behalf of the government. He adopted the ideas and aesthetics of Strand's work and developed them further. His aim was to produce neither documentary nor journalistic photography; he saw himself instead as an artist who

aimed to show in his photographs "the ubiquitous in a socially influenced world" (fig. pp. 94–95). Evans wanted to create an impersonal art in which the subject stands on its own and is not influenced by the photographer. He believed that photographers should step back from their subjects and abandon the desire to produce art. He saw himself as the heir of Eugène Atget, whose photographs he knew through Berenice Abbott.

In Europe, the development of photography was on the whole more diverse than it was in the United States, since there were new artistic impulses from various countries such as Russia and Czechoslovakia. But straight photography did lead to important changes in Germany, where it was primarily photographers like August Sander (see *Conceptual Photography*), Karl Blossfeld, and Albert Renger-Patzsch (see *The Photobook*) who implemented the "New Vision" in their photographs and thus exerted an influence that lasted until modern times, as can still be seen in the photography of the "Becher School" (see *Conceptual Photography*).

left——**Edward Weston: Bell Pepper no. 30** | 1930
right——**Eugène Atget: A Corner, Rue de Seine** | 1924 | George Eastman House | Rochester
following pages ——**Walker Evans: Street Scene, Vicksburg, Mississippi** | 1936

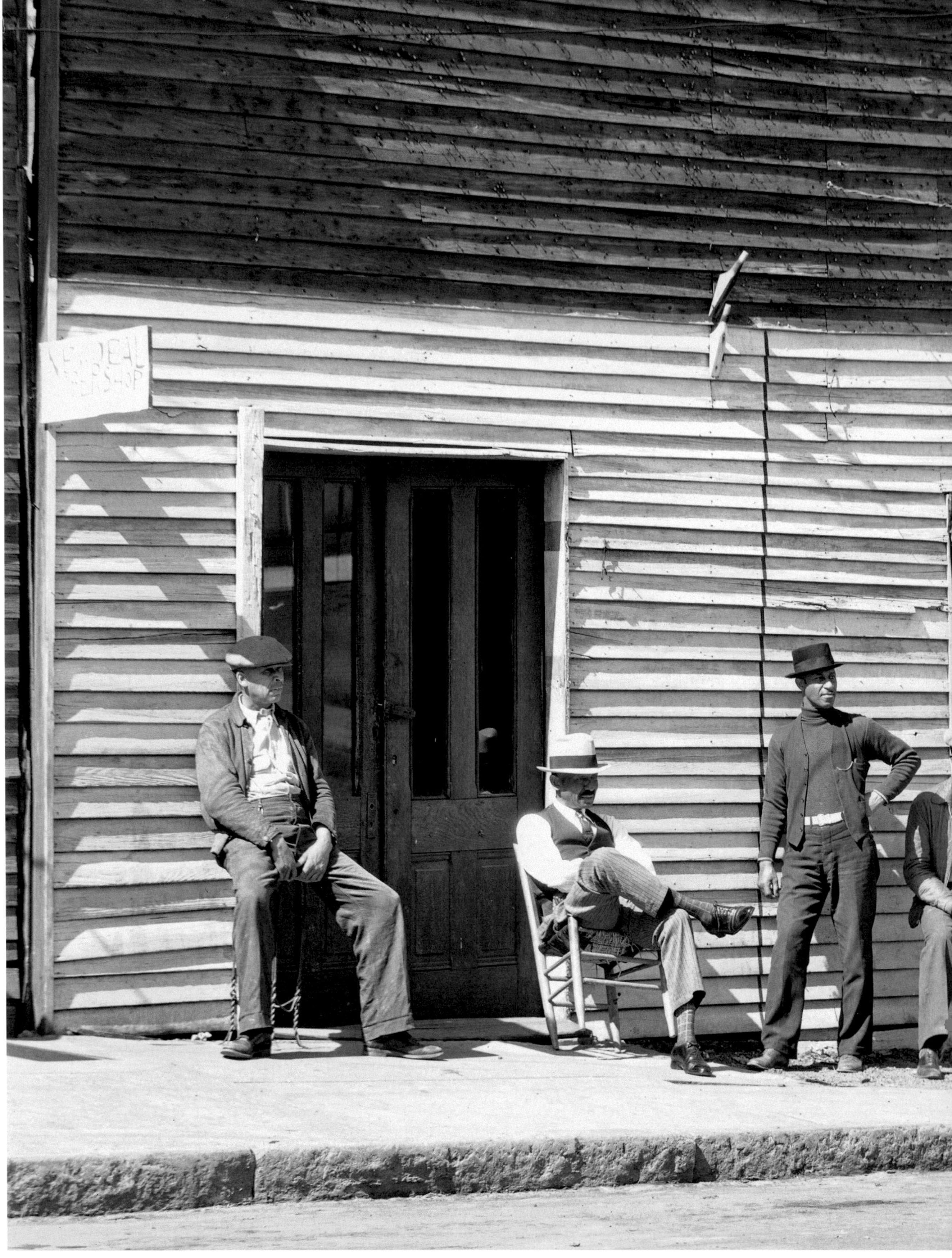

NEW DEAL
BARBER SHOP

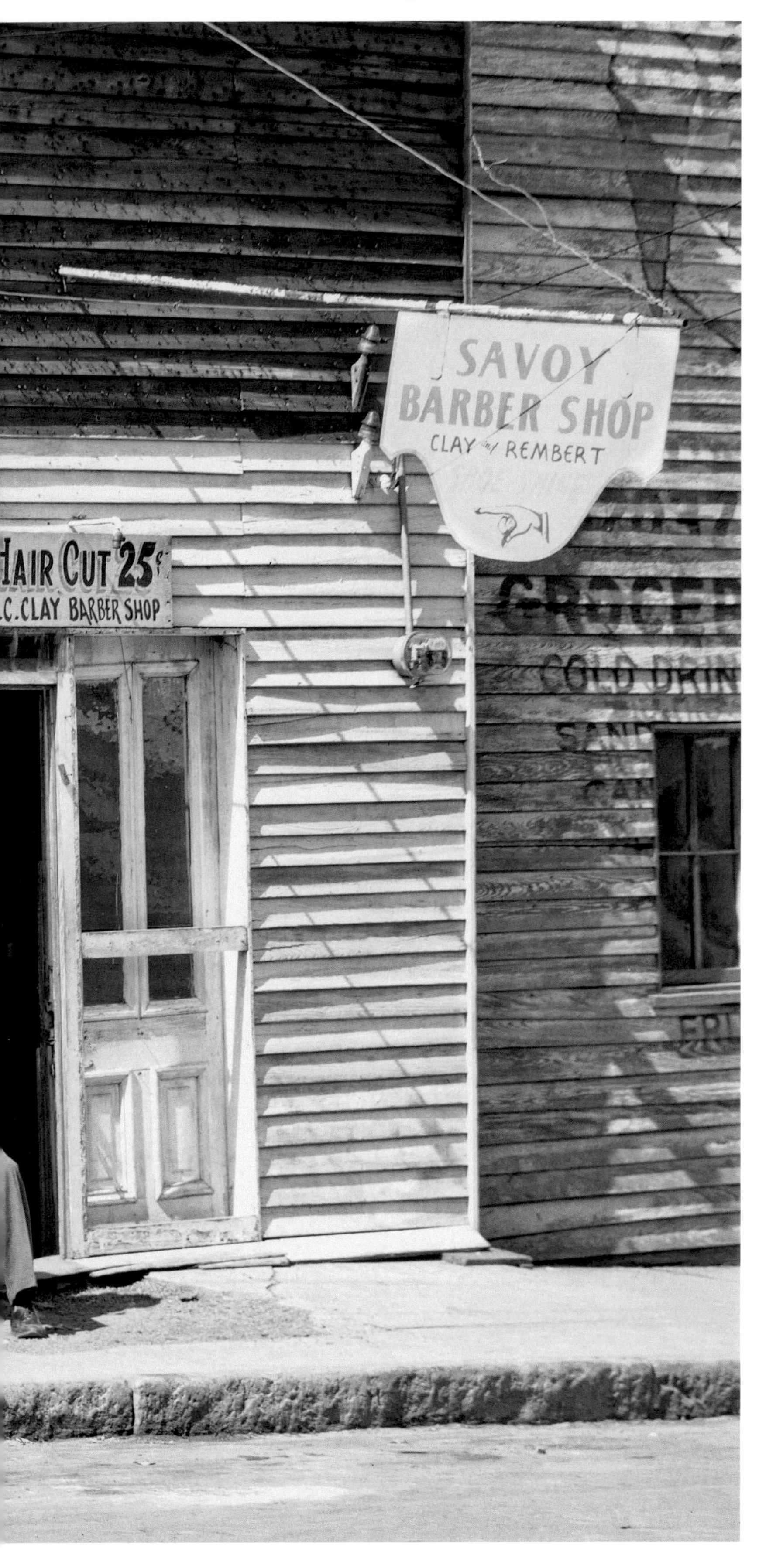

SAVOY
BARBER SHOP
CLAY and REMBERT
HAIR CUT 25¢
C. CLAY BARBER SHOP
GROCER
COLD DRIN
SAN
CAN
FRI

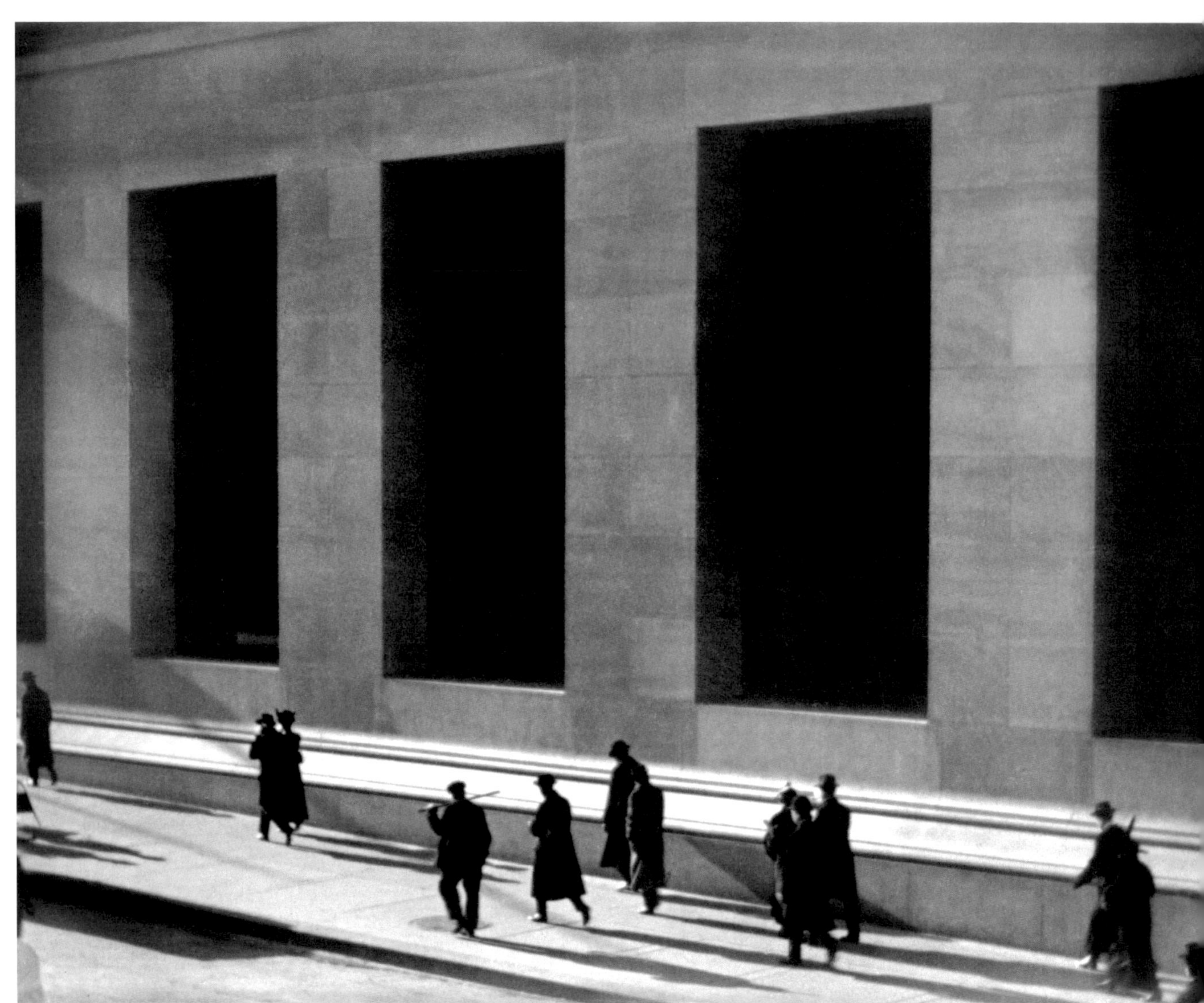

STREET PHOTOGRAPHY

Technical advances in photography have allowed new genres, like reportage and street photography, to develop alongside classical ones, such as portraits and landscapes—largely because photography, unlike art, can capture the fleeting moment. Street photography is generally defined as the photography of urban spaces. It is related to reportage, but distinguished from it by being less subject-oriented and by having artistic rather than purely utilitarian aims (though the boundaries between the two are fluid). The photographer makes use of reality and turns it into his or her own pictorial reality. Often, people and objects that are not in fact connected to one another are captured in a moment in which a special relationship exists fleetingly between them. The skill lies in the ability to separate such a moment from the continuum of time, and so create a new reality from it. The photographic historian Naomi Rosenblum defines street photography as the art of "picking out a lyrical moment from the normality of everyday existence," the term "lyrical" being interpreted in different ways at different times.

Paul Strand (1890–1976) established the founda-tions of this new genre with the photographs he published in the last issue of *Camera Work*, in 1917. An advocate of straight photography, he declared that art and photography should be based on everyday life and deal with current issues. Strand's subjects are people in the context of urban spaces, though they are not treated as individuals but as parts of an anonymous mass. Strand's street photographs can be divided into two types. The first consists of his portraits, in which individual people are picked out of whatever is going on around them, and photographed without their knowledge (fig. p. 98). The second type consists of street photography in which the inhabitants of the city are the subjects of his pictures, but are positioned within a greater context. His *Wall Street* (left) of 1915, which some consider to be Strand's most powerful photograph, is a striking example. Dominated by the high wall with its deep-black voids, it could be read primarily as a graphic interplay of surfaces. This impressive structure also determines its message, for the outlines of the people are sketchy and dominated by the monumental architecture: individuals are lost in the anonymity of the big city. Strand's pioneering contribution was to use photography to articulate the relationship between people and urban environments, while also calling this relationship into question. His photographs both

left——PAUL STRAND: WALL STREET, NEW YORK | 1915

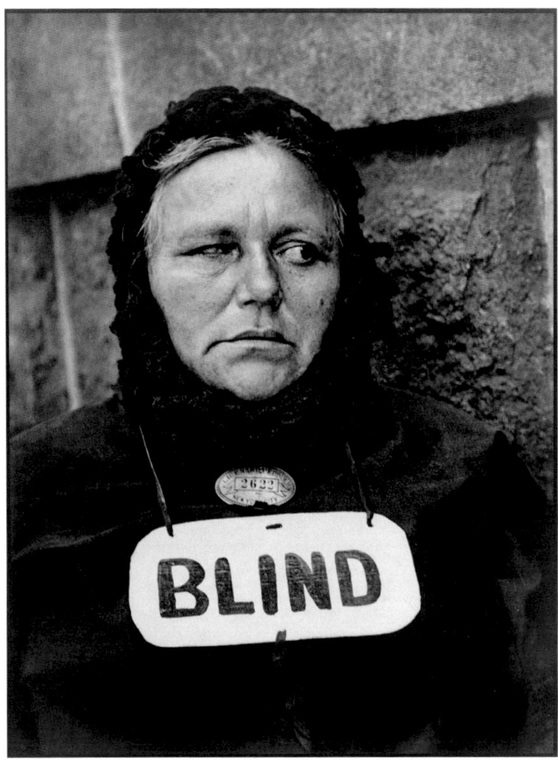

"…because at every step in the real world, a chasm of poetry can appear beneath one's feet."

represent the beginning of street photography and simultaneously, in their clarity and distinctiveness, constitute its first apogee.

In the United States, street photography quickly became, among other things, a tool for social criticism. This can be seen in the work of Paul Strand and Walker Evans (see *Straight Photography*). European photographers, on the other hand, pursued a more poetic approach that owed a lot to its early exponents.

The Hungarian former stock-exchange employee André Kertész (1894–1985), who moved to Paris in 1925, was a trailblazer of European street photography. He worked as a photographer for a variety of newspapers, and in doing so developed his own distinctive style. This relied on the use of small, hand-held cameras, which had not yet achieved recognition among his professional colleagues. Kertész was one of the first photographers in Paris to work with a Leica small-format camera, which made its debut in 1924 and which would become

the standard for street photography. It was the ideal tool for him, a *"flâneur* with a camera," to capture everyday subjects. He did so without the objectivity and social concerns advocated by American street photography, however: "I took photographs of real life—not as it was, but as I felt it. That is the most important thing: not to analyze, but to feel." Kertész looked for the special in the everyday. He wanted his pictures to tell little anecdotes, and he wanted the interactions of the people in his photographs to stimulate the viewer to imagine a "before" and an "after," thus essentially integrating the viewer into the picture as a witness, almost a participant (right). In this way, Kertész (along with Strand and Evans in the United States) created the foundation

above——**PAUL STRAND: BLIND WOMAN, NEW YORK** | 1916
right——**ANDRÉ KERTÉSZ: THE FLOWER SELLER, PARIS** | 1928 | Estate of André Kertesz

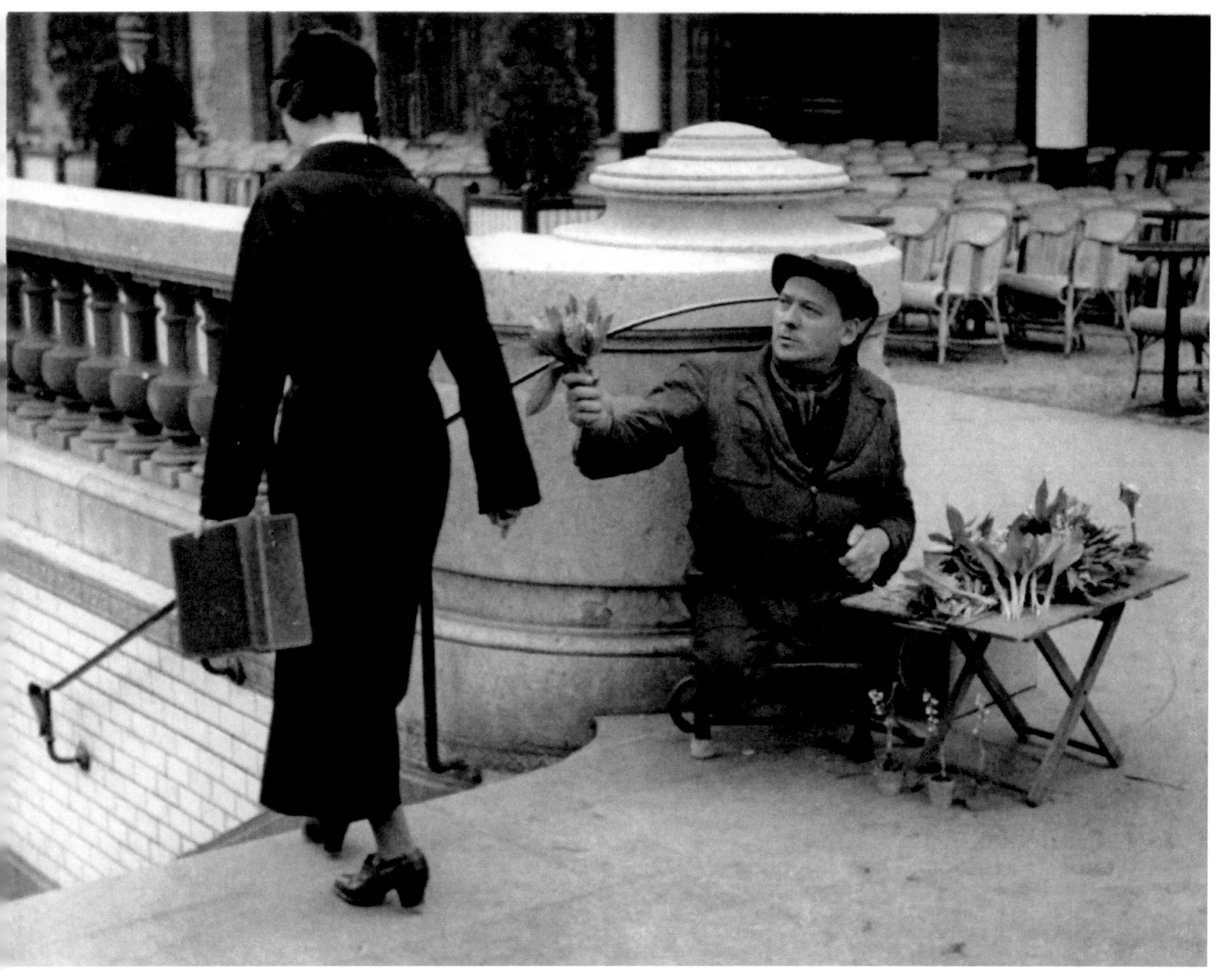

of this exclusively photographic genre in which the photographer wanders the streets with eyes wide open, always ready to react at the right moment, "because at every step in the real world, a chasm of poetry can appear beneath one's feet" (André Kertész). With Henri Cartier-Bresson (1908–2004), this new, poetic way of taking photographs achieved international renown. His style of photography established a standard against which that of others was measured, and he became one of the most famous and most influential photographers of the 20th century (see *The Photobook*). His stated aim was to capture the "decisive moment," the moment in which reality and perfect composition intersect (figs. pp. 100 and 153). He composed his pictures only through the viewfinder, never altering or cropping photographs afterwards. He even decreed that a section of the unexposed area surrounding the negative should remain. That is why the photo reproduced here has a narrow black frame.

With street photography, the street became a stage and people became actors in a brief scene about

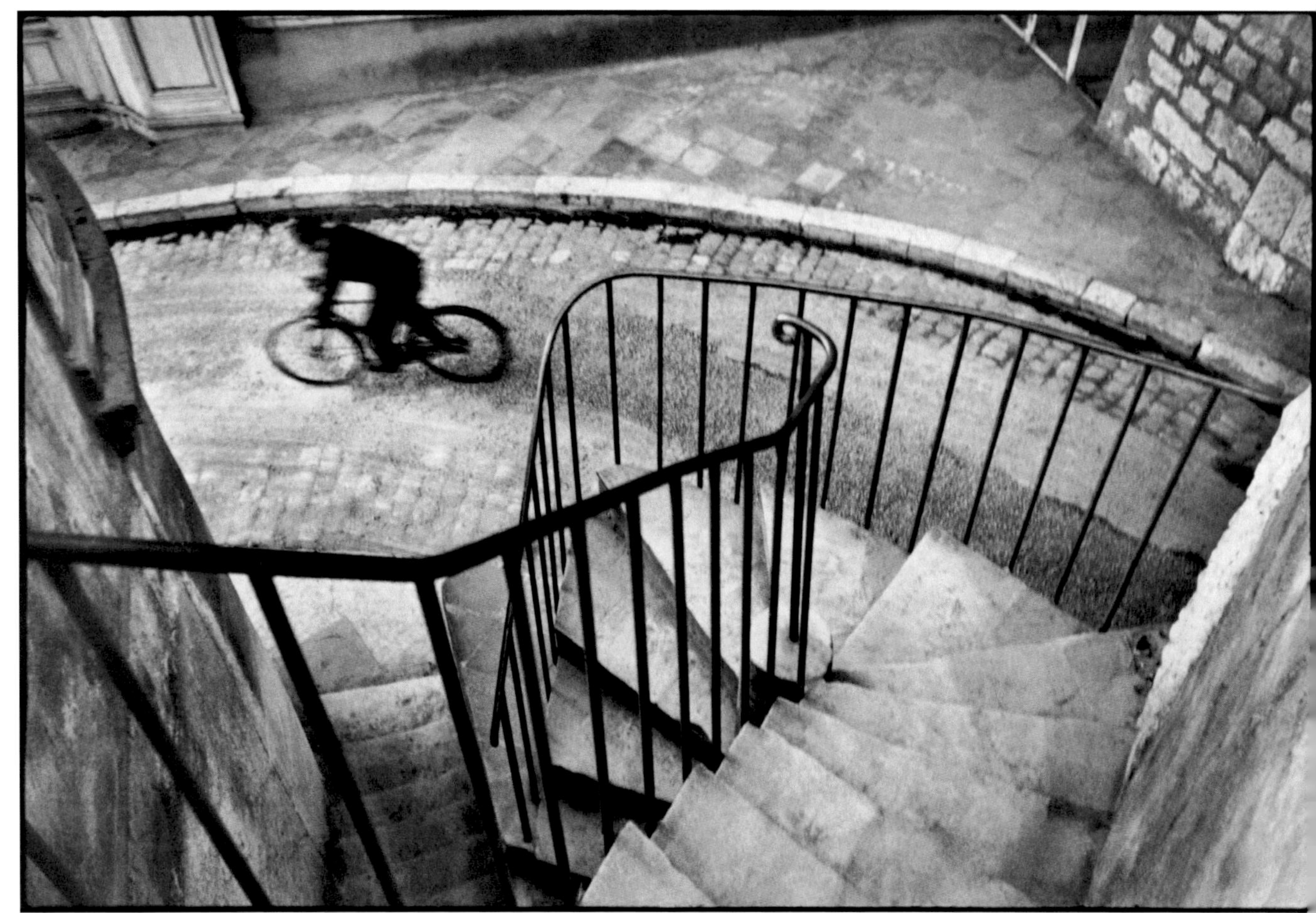

which they knew nothing. Only the photographer recognizes the performance, and records it using a camera. The American Garry Winogrand (1928–1984) was one of the most important photographers to work in the genre of street photography. His virtually obsessive way of taking photographs acted as a counterpoint to the method of Cartier-Bresson and Frank. For Winogrand, the very act of taking a photo was important, similar to the act of painting for Jackson Pollock: "I take photographs in order to find out what it looks like when it has been photographed." For Winogrand, the fascination of photography lies in its ability to see, in a fraction of a second, more than the human eye can (fig. p. 103). He does not take any particular position in his pho-

tographs, leaving viewers completely free to form their own associations: "I have nothing to say in my pictures." He wanted nothing more than to commit a fragment of reality to film, and "if the picture means something or other to somebody or other at some point in the future, all the better." Winogrand's working method was highly individual. He appears to have taken photographs without looking through the viewfinder, at great speed, and using large quantities of film. In addition, he did not develop films straight away, but left them for a year or two in order to avoid recalling the specific circumstances in which a shot was taken. Just how obsessively Winogrand took photographs became clear when more than 2,500 exposed but undevel-

"Photography is a response that has to do with the momentary recognition of things. You look one moment and there's everything, next moment it's gone. Photography is very philosophical."

oped small-format films and thousands of developed but unedited films were found in his estate after his death.

European photographers have always been more literary than their American counterparts. In Europe, the influence of Cartier-Bresson and Frank was stronger than that of the aloof, impersonal eye of Walker Evans. Robert Doisneau, Elliott Erwitt (see *Comic Photography*), and Josef Koudelka are among the most important creators of European street photography.

Josef Koudelka (b. 1938), who became famous for his photographs of the Prague Spring in Czechoslovakia in 1968, eschews all forms of commercial photography and his work is therefore the very embodiment of street photography (fig. pp. 104–105). Although he too is a prolific photographer ("I have to shoot three rolls of film a day, even when I'm not taking photographs, in order to train my eye"), his pictures feel more selective, more composed, and more deliberate than those of, say, Winogrand. Koudelka stated: "I don't talk about my pictures. The pictures should speak to the viewer, not vice versa." And there is no need for him to add anything, as his photographs are often replete with entire dramas that unfold in front of our eyes. His photographs are often characterized by a slightly melancholy, poetic atmosphere that few other photographers can capture as skillfully.

For many years, Robert Frank's motto "Black and white are the colors of photography" applied to street photography in particular. The recognition of color photography in the artistic sphere during the 1970s soon led to its introduction to street photography, too. Joel Meyerowitz (b. 1938) was one of the trailblazers for this new form (fig. p. 102). For many photographers, color is a distraction; for Meyerowitz, by contrast, it is essential. His photographs record more in one moment than one usually perceives in the hustle and bustle of the big city: "Photography is a response that has to do with the

left—HENRI-CARTIER-BRESSON: THE VAR DEPARTMENT, HYÈRES | 1932

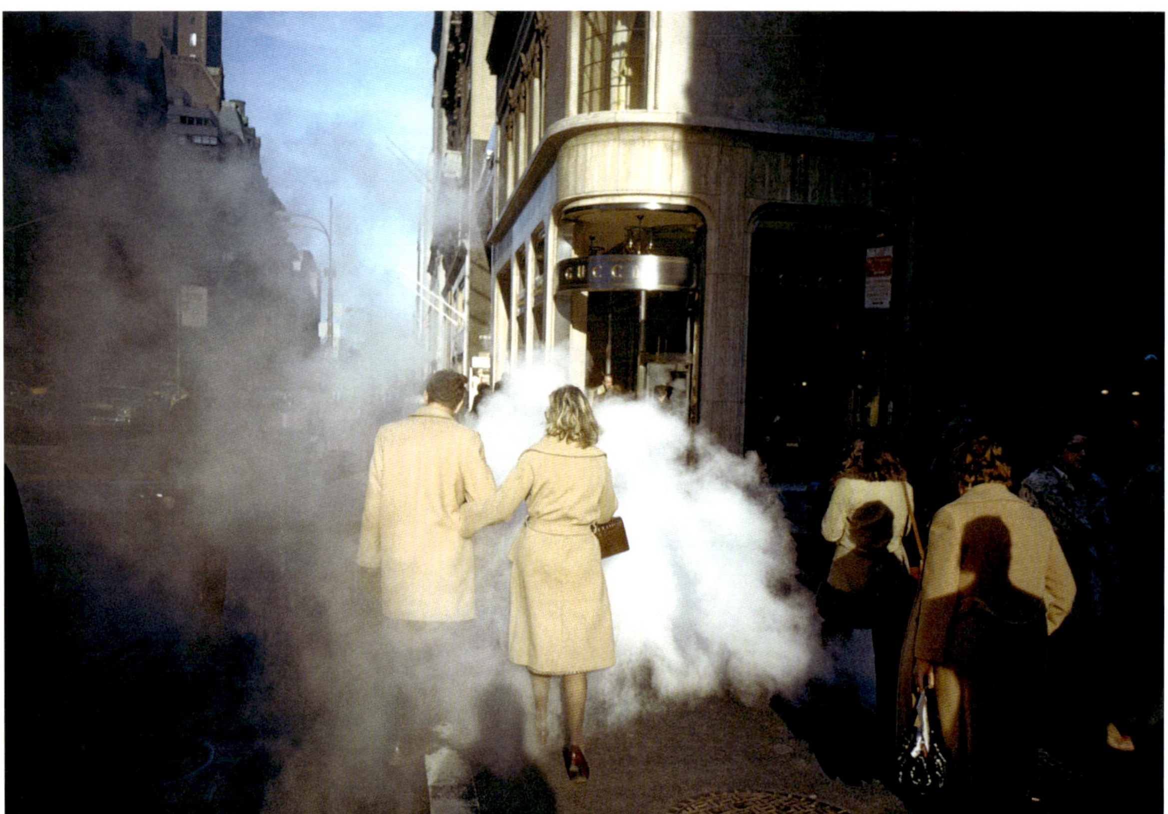

momentary recognition of things. You look one moment and there's everything, next moment it's gone. Photography is very philosophical."

Although the subjects of street photography are by their nature in constant flux, interest in it decreased towards the end of the 20th century, following the golden years of the 1960s and 1970s. And yet there are always some photographers who take an interest in it. The American Philip-Lorca diCorcia (b. 1951) is one of the most notable among them. His photographs of people on the street are so perfectly lit that at first glance they look like studio portraits. For his *Heads* series, he took photographs of strangers on New York's Times Square between 1999 and 2001. His approach is diametrically opposed to the standard practice of street photography, in which the photographer approaches people. DiCorcia, by contrast, attached flash units to scaffolding and positioned his camera a certain distance in front of it.

When people reached the place his equipment was set up for, he pressed the button. The background melts into darkness because of the short flash-synchronization time, and those who find themselves in the cone of light are singled out from the mass as they passed by. The result is a series of impressive portraits of unknown people whose thoughts and secrets are reflected in their faces. What they are and which stories accompany them is left to the imagination of the viewer.

above——Joel Meyerowitz: Camel Coats, 5th Avenue, New York | 1975

right——Garry Winogrand: Untitled | c. 1960

following pages——Josef Koudelka: Sceaux Park, France | 1987

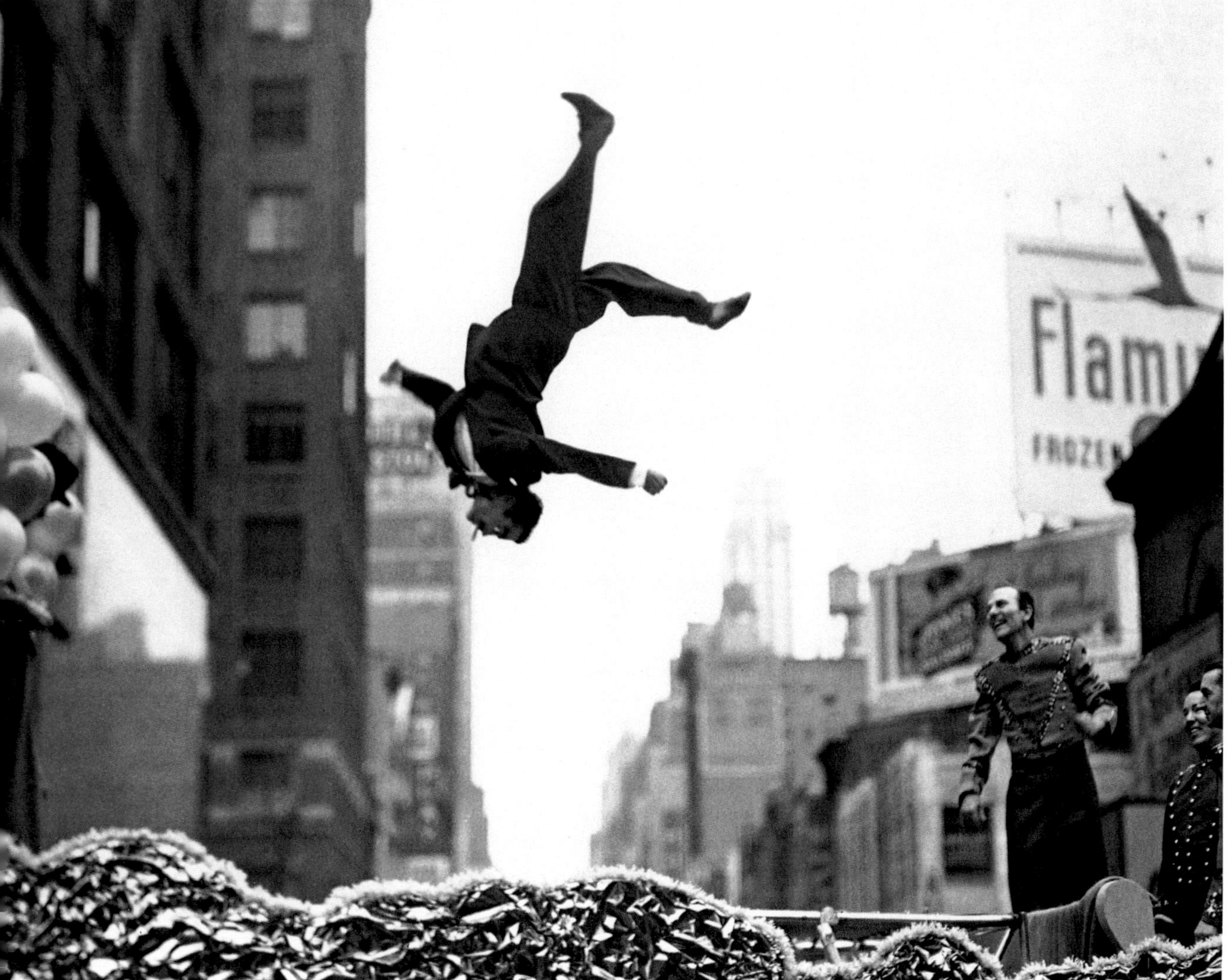
Flam
FROZEN

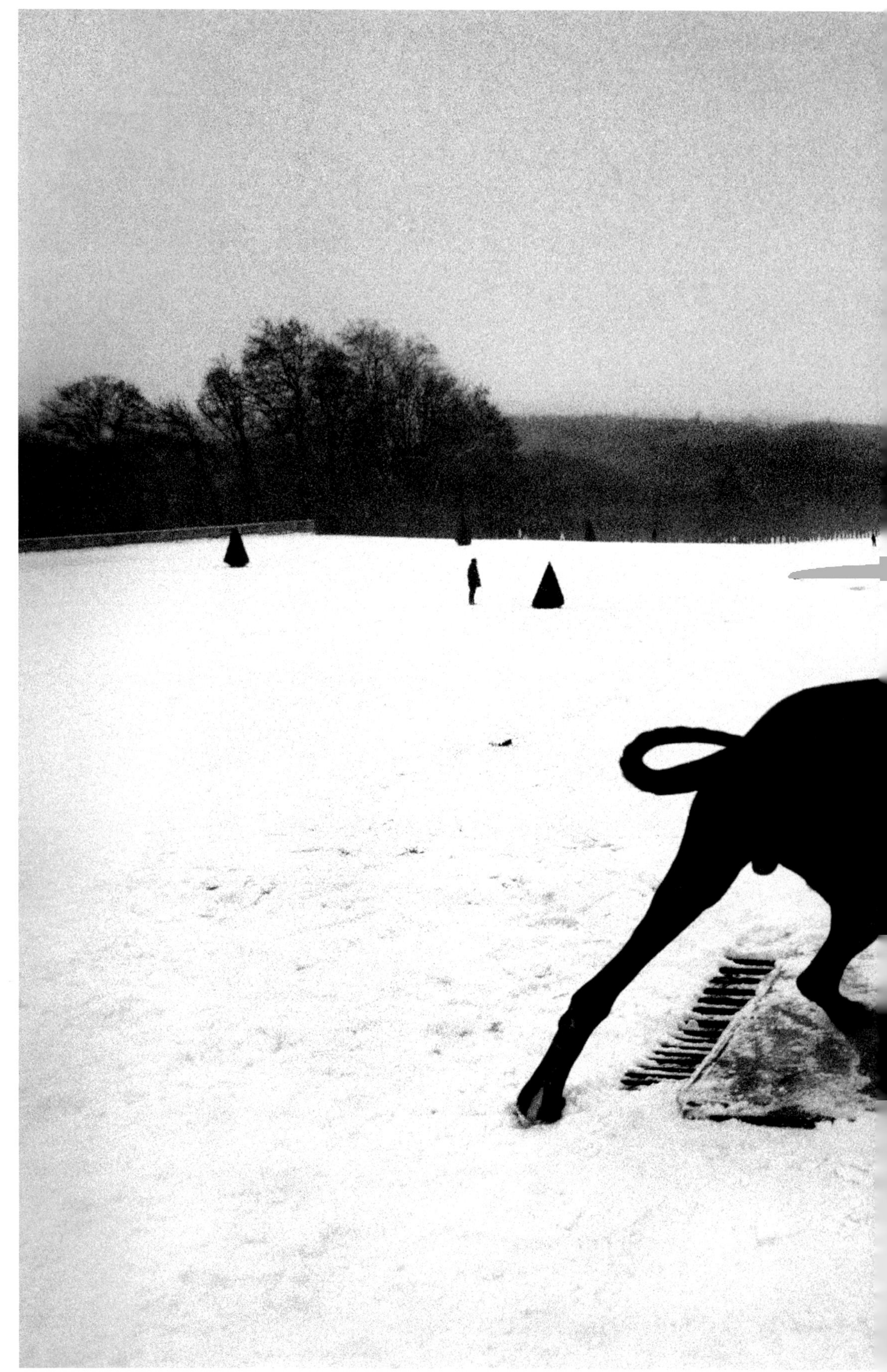

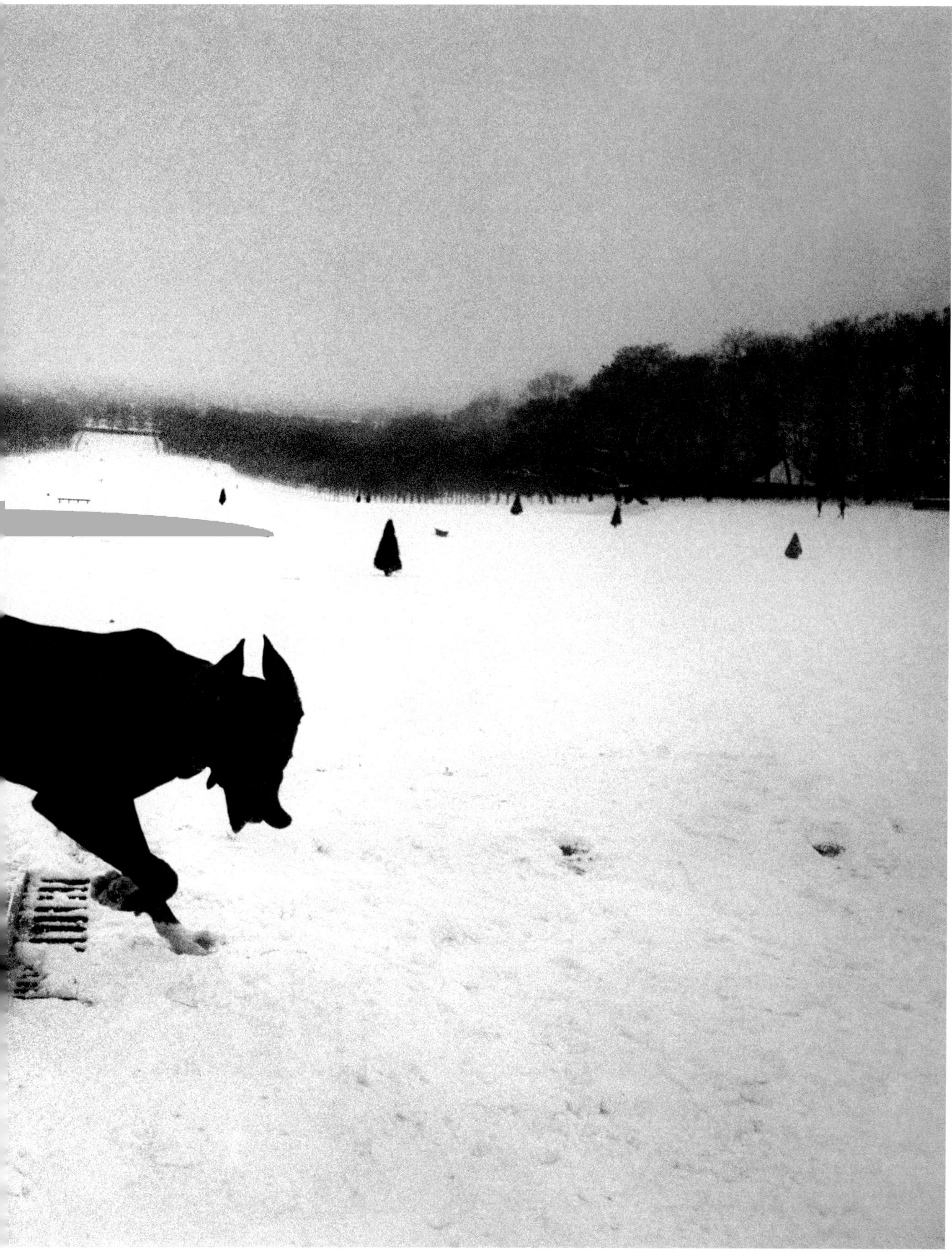

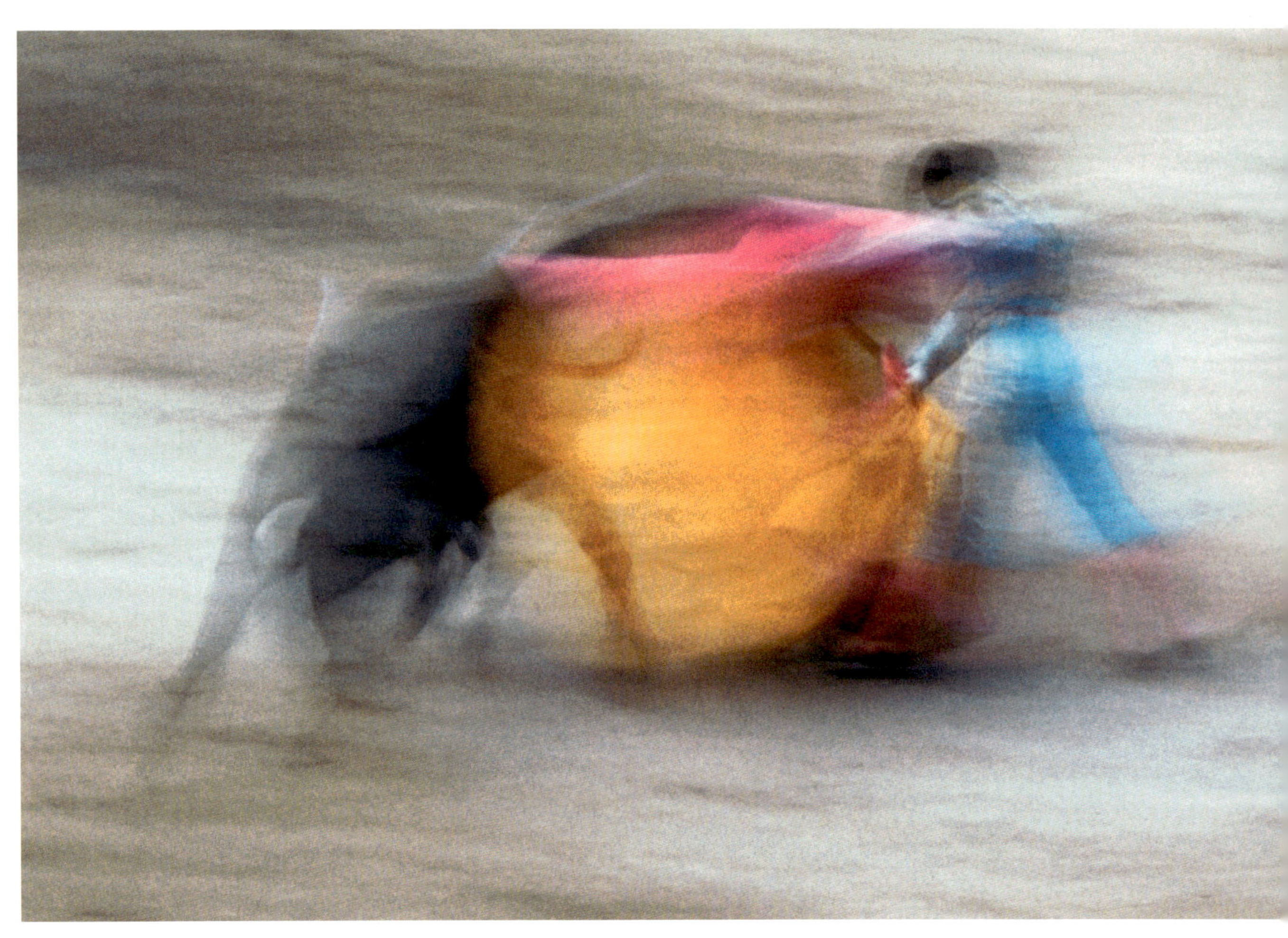

1837–1920 Louis Ducos Du Hauron   1845–1923 Wilhelm Conrad Röntgen   1857–1927 Eugène Atget

COLOR PHOTOGRAPHY

Even though enthusiasm for the daguerreotype and the calotype was great, many were aware of a weakness: these new pictures were "merely" black and white. For a long time, the only way to add color to photographs was to apply it by hand. Attempts to include color in the photographic process itself were long unsuccessful, and it was not until 1868 that Louis Ducos du Hauron (1837–1920) was granted a patent for a variety of techniques for color photography. Three photographs taken separately using red, green, and blue separation filters were lined up and placed on top of one another to create a color diapositive (a positive photographic image on a transparent material) (fig. p. 108). This procedure was, however, too laborious to gain a large following.

The first breakthrough in color photography was the so-called autochrome process, which was invented by the French brothers Auguste (1862–1954) and Louis (1864–1948) Lumière. It was the first technique that made it possible to create a color photograph using just one photograph (fig. p. 109). This was achieved by dyeing very fine particles of potato starch blue, green, or red and then mixing them together to create a thin coating that could be applied to a glass plate, which was then covered with a layer of gelatin bromide emulsion; the latter was placed farthest away from the lens, which meant that light had to pass through the color-sensitized starch before being recorded. In 1907 the brothers began to market the process they had invented, and were confident enough to claim that "from this day onwards, old, cold black-and-white photography is of limited interest."

The introduction of three-layer color films, produced by Kodak and Agfa from 1936 onwards, marked an important step in the popularization of color photography. Color was soon adopted in commercial photography, in other words advertising and fashion. The ability of the print media to reproduce images in color using three-color and four-color printing processes constituted another important development. Magazines in particular made use of this technique in the 1930s, which in turn led to an increased demand for color photographs. And yet black-and-white photography remained the standard, especially in art and photojournalism. The great expense, complexity, and unreliable color reproduction inherent in the process remained an obstacle to the popularization of color photography. Some photographers in the realm of art photography did concentrate on

left——Ernst Haas: La Suerta De Capa, Pamplona, Spain | 1956

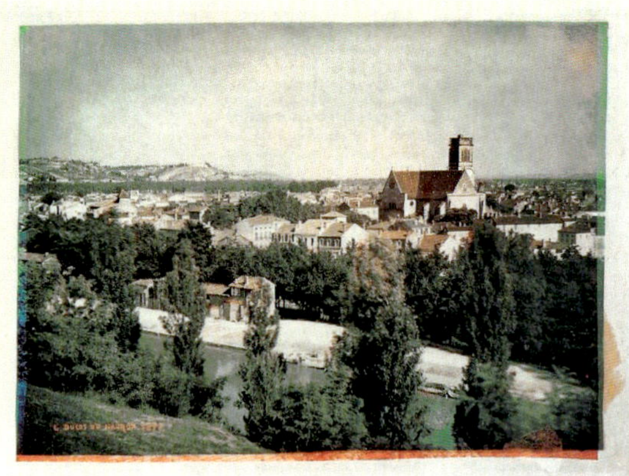

"'Color' does not mean 'black-and-white plus color,' just as 'black-and-white' is not simply a picture without color."

color from an early date, however, including the American Eliot Porter for landscape photography, Gisèle Freund for portraits, and Paul Outerbridge for still lifes and nudes (see *The Nude*).

The Danish photographer Keld Helmer-Petersen (b. 1920), who was strongly influenced by Renger-Patzsch's pictorial language (see *The Photobook*), and who worked exclusively with color photography, played an important role in changing attitudes to color photography. In 1948 he published a book entitled *122 Farvefotografier / 122 Color Photographs*; he shot all of the photographs using a Leica and Agfacolor film, which was still relatively new at the time, and they were all of subjects—everyday situations and objects—that worked best in color, which accounts for novel attraction of his images. Helmer-Petersen thought of color as form, and chose a large number of two-dimensional subjects in order to emphasize the importance of the color (fig. p. 110). His book ended up on the desk of the publisher of *LIFE* in New York, one of the most important publishers for photographers, and the magazine printed seven pages of his color images. With his apparently simple pictures, the Danish photographer was well ahead of his time. At about the same time, the Austrian photographer Ernst Haas (1921–1986) switched from black-and-white photography to color. For him, color photography symbolized the end of the war and of the

post-war years, which he once referred to as a "gray period." He wanted to rediscover the world and he wanted to do so in color (fig. p. 106). Haas began as a photojournalist, but saw himself increasingly as a poet of color photography. Like Helmer-Petersen, and in contrast to many other photographers, Haas made a clear distinction between black-and-white and color photography: "'Color' does not mean 'black-and-white plus color,' just as 'black-and-white' is not simply a picture without color." It was precisely this declaration that set these two early masters of color photography apart from many of their colleagues.

Haas emigrated from Vienna to New York and in 1953 published *LIFE*'s *Images of a Magic City*. This 24-page series of photographs was the first photo essay in color in the history of the magazine. His photographs were well received, even among photographers known primarily for their black-and-white work. Among these was Ansel Adams, who wrote in

above——**Louis Ducos du Hauron: Angoulême** | 1877 | George Eastman House | Rochester | New York

right——**Anonymous: Egyptian Dancer** | autochrome | c. 1915 | George Eastman House | Rochester | New York

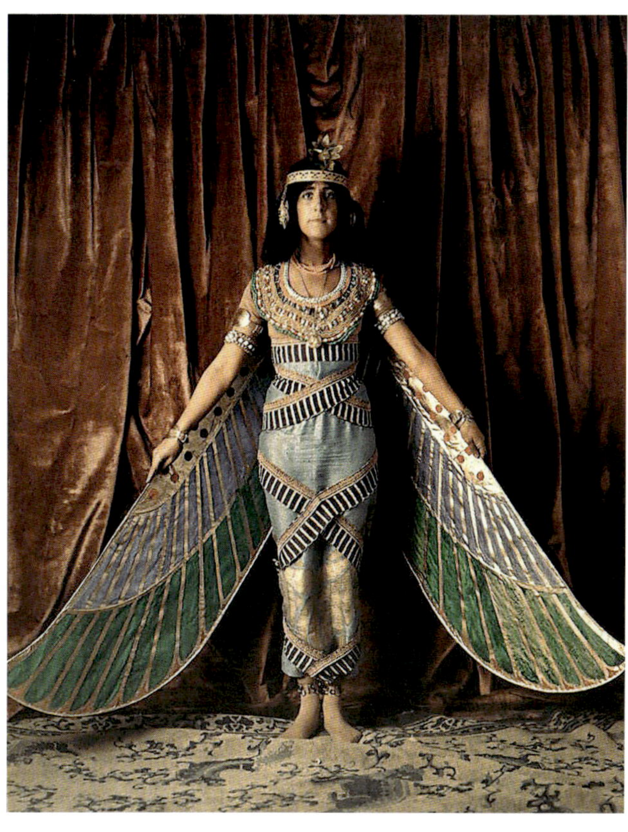

a letter to Haas: "Your work—although your sources were both simple natural situations and simple 'junk'—possess a direct quality of beauty which thoroughly transcends 'subject'." In 1962, the Museum of Modern Art (MoMA) in New York held an exhibition of his work entitled *Color Photographs*. This was the first exhibition of work by a photographer working exclusively in color. Although Haas would become one of the most-published and most-copied photographers of the 20th century, for many years he did not receive the recognition he deserved. As counterintuitive as this may sound, this was perhaps because of the poetry and beauty of his pictures. Members of the artistic avant-garde, who set the "impersonal" photographs of Walker Evans as a standard, considered color photographs too visually pleasing, not gritty enough. The fact that color printing remained a complicated and expensive process was also a problem. "The dilemma of color is still that it is not possible to make color prints as freely and as easily as black-and-white prints. When that becomes possible, the whole so-called art market and its incomprehensible hostility to color will change dramatically" (Ernst Haas).

This change finally began in 1976, and at the same place: MoMA in New York. This was the year that an exhibition of the work of William Eggleston (b. 1939) opened. This is nowadays considered to have been the start of color photography as art, though Eggleston was not the pioneer he is nowadays often thought to have been; in fact, Haas and Eggleston were not the first photographers to work in color. Some photographers in Europe, such as Luigi Ghirri (1943–1992) in Italy and Helmer-Petersen in Den-

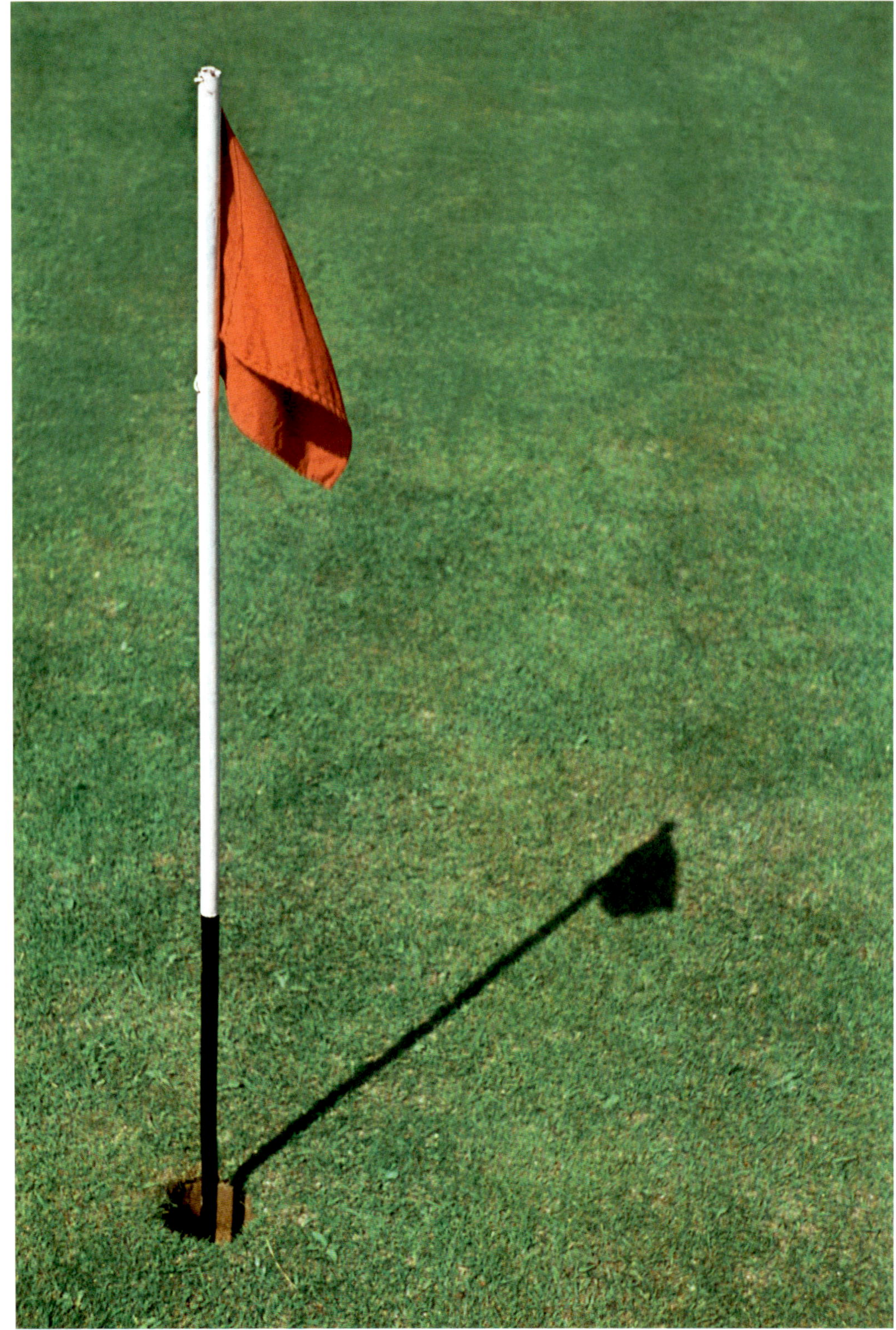

1974–today Damon Winter   **1976–today Pieter Hugo**   **1977–today Andrew Zuckerman**

"Helmer-Petersen thought of color as form, and chose a large number of two-dimensional subjects in order to emphasize the importance of the color."

mark, had been working in color for some time. The exhibition was highly controversial. Eggleston, who had worked exclusively in color from 1965 onwards, appeared to take photographs of random, everyday subjects and situations that had until then not been considered interesting or worthy, and certainly not suited to color photography. Now the mundane and the ugly also became a subject of photography. Eggleston, who had, like most photographers of his generation, been influenced by Walker Evans, appeared to point his camera at whatever he saw, without attention to composition: "I had this notion of what I called a democratic way of looking around, that nothing was more or less important." It was on this seeming arbitrariness and banality of the subjects that much of the criticism of the exhibition focused. It was accused of being "banal," "boring,"

and even of being "the worst exhibition of the year." Eggleston was not criticized for working in color, but for combining color and the mundane. Despite, or perhaps because of, the fierce debate on color photography caused by this exhibition, it opened up new horizons to young photographers such as Joel Meyerowitz (b. 1938) and Stephen Shore (see *Landscapes*). Slowly but surely, the use of color in photography came to be considered normal practice.

When considering the reception of the work of innovators such as Haas and Eggleston, it is important to bear in mind the era in which they worked. Their photographs were new and revolutionary at the time. If similarly ordinary subjects are photographed again and again, however, the view of the everyday becomes merely trite.

Color photography has become as normal as black-and-white photography was before the introduction of color. There has been a paradigm shift. Both types of photography are valid, and both must be used according to their own distinctive character. Paul Outerbridge, one of the pioneers of color photography, put it like this: "In black-and-white, you suggest; in color, you state. Much can be implied by suggestion, but statement demands certainty [...] absolute certainty."

left——Keld Helmer-Petersen: 122 Color Photographs (Golf)
1948 | lambda photography | 51 x 41 cm

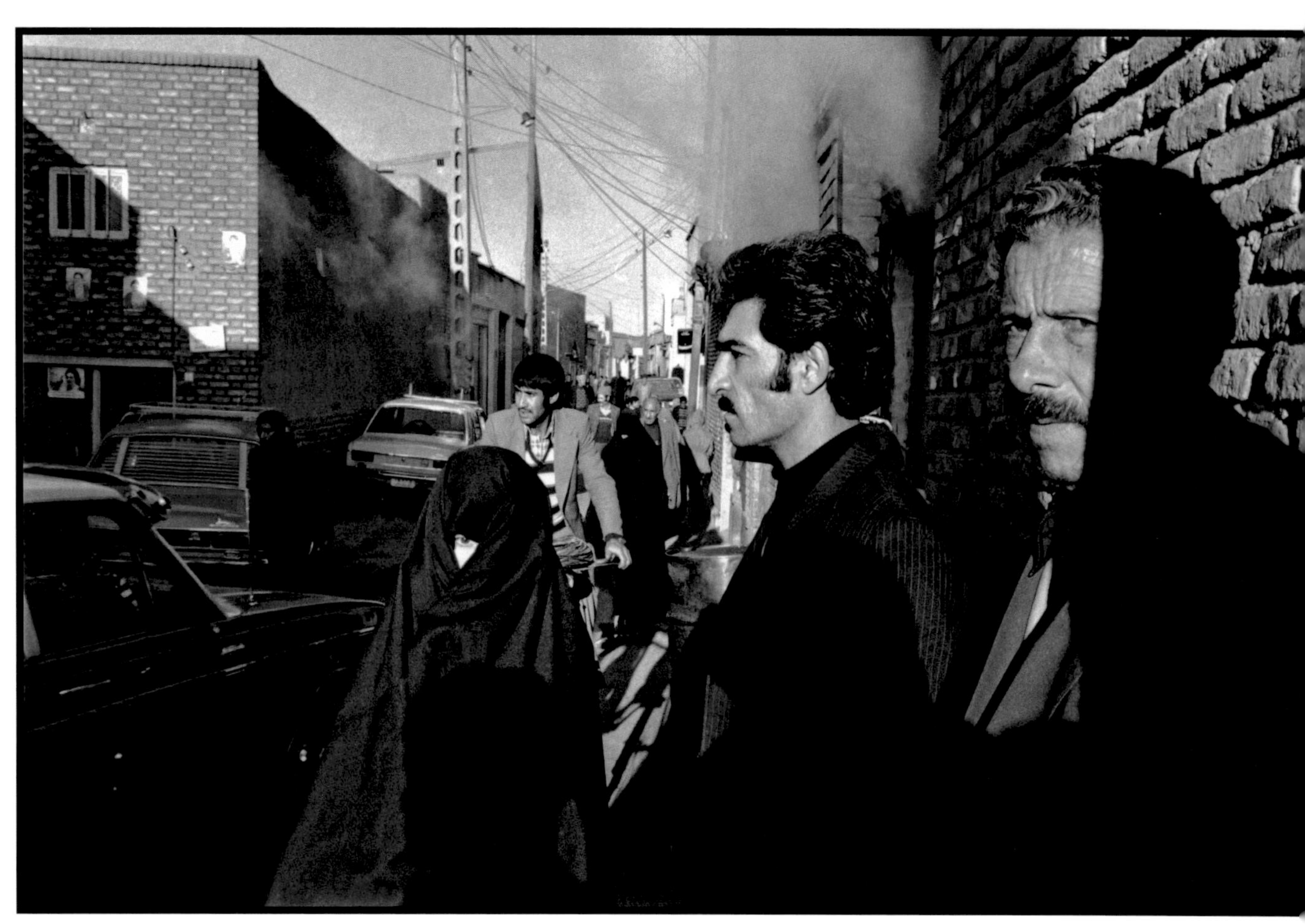

1864–1946 Alfred Stieglitz   **1868–1949 Baron Adolphe de Meyer**   **1879–1973 Edward Steichen**

PHOTOJOURNALISM (REPORTAGE)

One of the most important factors in the acceptance of photography by the press was the development of halftone, which emerged during the 1880s. Until then, photographs could be printed only if they were transferred to the medium of woodcut so that they could be printed at the same time as the text. Halftone permitted printing to be carried out for the first time not only in black and white, but also in all the tonal values in between, the so-called halftones. A photo was broken down into raster dots that were copied and etched onto light-sensitive metal plates. This produced a printing plate with raised dots that could be printed exactly as letters were. However, several years were to pass before the process had been developed to the point where it won wide approval, a delay caused by the skepticism of some newspaper publishers with regard to photography in general. In 1893, for example, the editor-in-chief of the *London Illustrated News* wrote: "I believe that in due course the public will become bored with the mere reproduction of photographs."

In spite of such reservations, halftone established its value, and with it that of photography, in the illustrated press—not least because photographs conveyed a higher degree of credibility and authenticity than traditional woodcuts. The golden age of the illustrated press had begun and with it the era of photojournalism and photo reportage. Its impact was felt first in Germany during the 1920s, where the *Berliner Illustrirte Zeitung* and the *Münchner Illustrierte Presse* took on pioneering roles and achieved circulations of over a million copies each. Also in Germany, Dr. Erich Salomon (1886–1944) produced photographic reportage from the world of politics and business, thereby becoming one of the founders of modern photojournalism. Salomon used small cameras with light-intensive lenses like the famous Ermanox, which enabled him to take undreamed-of pictures unobtrusively and without additional lighting. Another important technical development was the creation of the first small-format camera, the Leica, which, launched in 1924, soon became the quintessential reportage camera. Photo reportage occupied increasing amounts of space in periodicals and became the reader's window on the world. The weekly magazine *LIFE* was founded in New York in 1936; its innovative large-format illustrations and a circulation of millions made it one of the most important forms of publication for photographers and the yardstick of photo reportage in general. Among the most famous pho-

left——**Gilles Peress: Azerbaijan, Street** | 1979

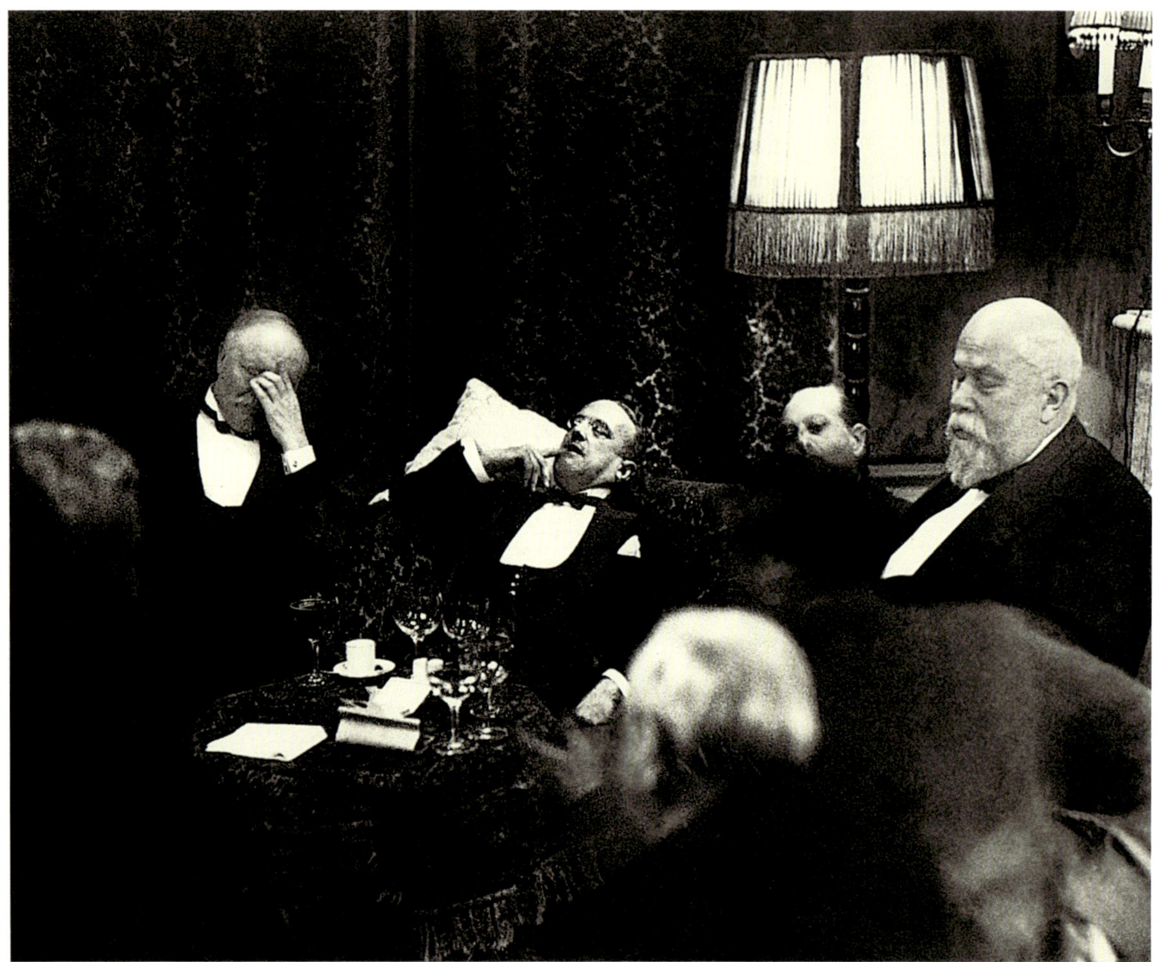

tographers to be employed by *LIFE* was W. Eugene Smith (1918–1978). He worked as a war reporter during World War II and initially produced the usual combat images. However, his experience of the suffering of the civilian population during his war assignments led him to change his style and to adopt a more emotive pictorial language. In 1948 he accompanied a country doctor near Denver for several months while researching a feature for *LIFE* (right, and fig. p 116). This was one of the first highlights of his journalistic career and a milestone in photo reportage. Smith saw in photography more than the mere illustration of a text. He subsequently planned his topics in an increasingly elaborate way and demanded more say in the selection of the photos and the layout. In 1955, when he was not granted his request, he switched to the Magnum Agency.

Magnum had just been established for the very same reasons that had prompted Smith to hand in his notice at *LIFE*. This innovative agency had been found in 1947 by Henri Cartier-Bresson, Robert Capa, George Rodger and others, all photographers

above——Dr. Erich Salomon: German and French Ministers during the Second Conference at The Hague | 1930
right——W. Eugene Smith: The Country Doctor | 1948

1912–1994 Robert Doisneau   1918–1978 W. Eugene Smith   1923–2004 Richard Avedon

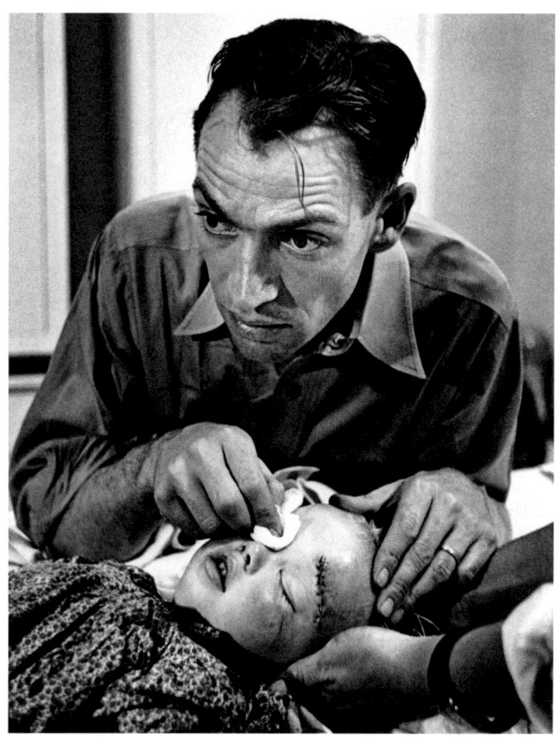

who had already made a name for themselves. Their aim was to maintain greater independence from publishers by protecting the copyright on their negatives, which was most unusual at the time. And at the same time they secured for themselves control over the publication and use of their pictures. This enabled them to sell them to several publishers at the same time, so that they earned more money and also achieved an increased media presence. With its many top-rank photographers, Magnum became the model for subsequent photo agencies and is still regarded as the Everest of photojournalism. Many of the "classics" of photography are by members of Magnum, including Elliott Erwitt, Josef Koudelka, James Nachtwey, Sebastião Salgado, Martin Parr, and many others.

In addition to their work for daily newspapers, the agency permits photographers to set up their own projects independently. Photographers can thus devote their attention to their work while the agency employees look after the sale of their pictures. An outstanding example of a cooperation of this kind, and a further milestone in photojournalism, is the reportage produced by the French photographer Gilles Peress (b. 1946) on Iran (figs. p. 117). Parts of it appeared in various newspapers and the entire reportage was published as a book with the title *Telex Iran: In the Name of Revolution*. Between December 1979 and January 1980, Peress traveled through Iran gathering his own impressions of the country during the Islamic Revolution under Ayatollah Khomeini following the flight of the Shah. It

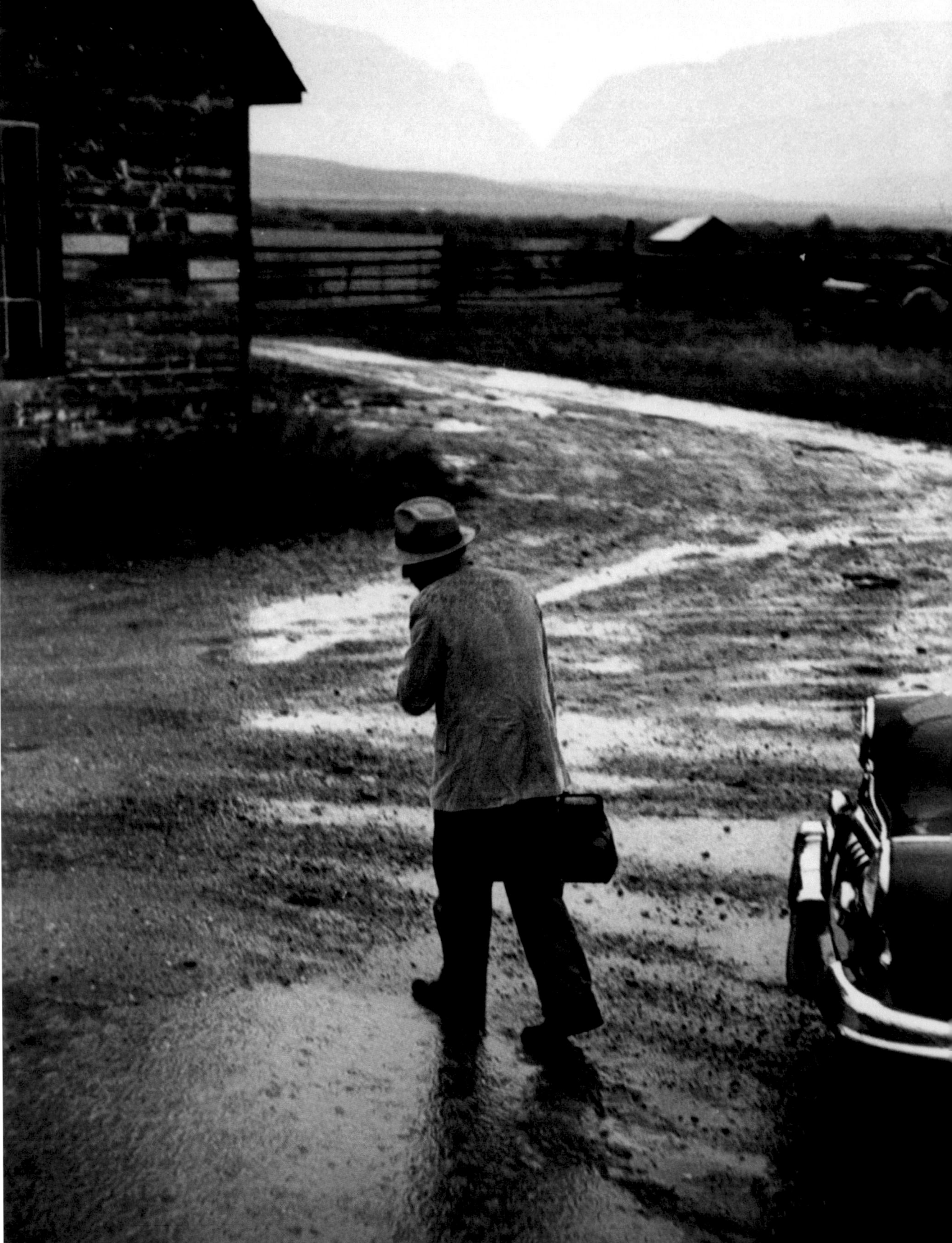

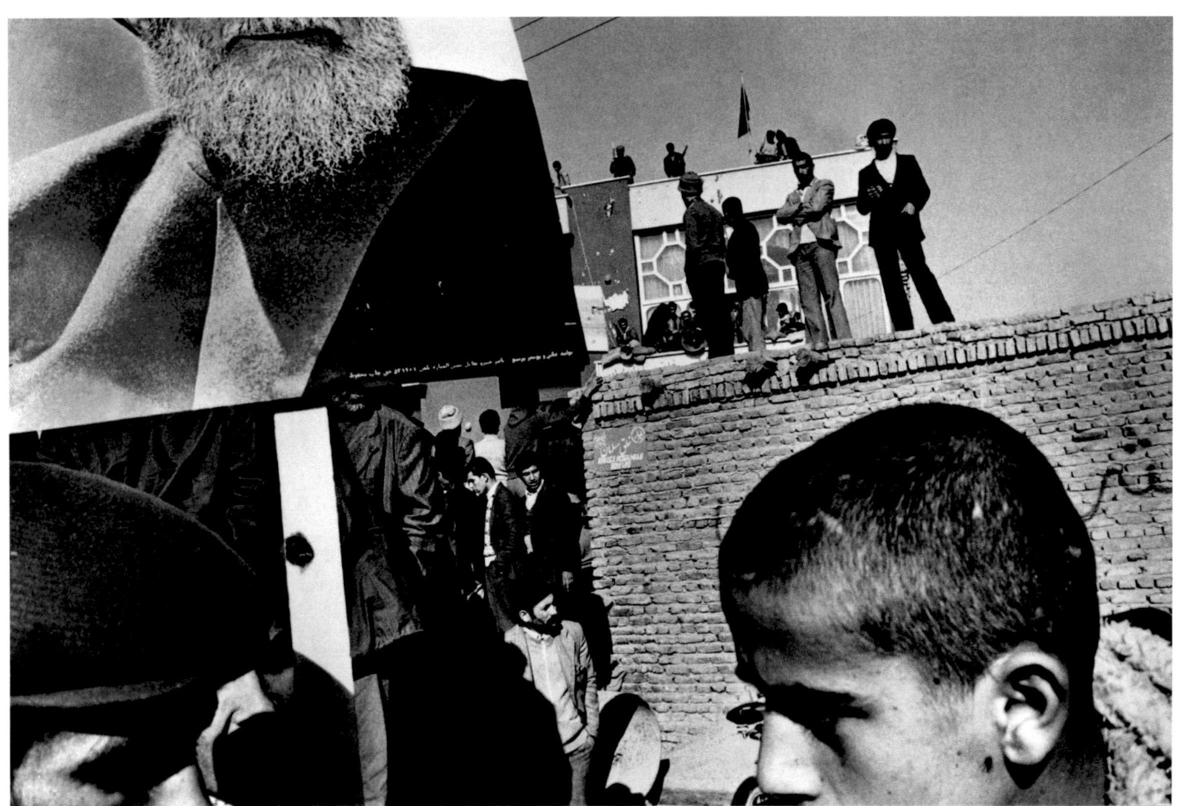

was the time when 52 employees of the American embassy were being held hostage. In the Western world, the image of Iran was colored by religious and political fanaticism. Peress wanted to understand the country and its people and to show his own personal view of things. He was not concerned about concrete events and he had no direct "message." He simply wanted to observe. But he did so in an innovative, artistically impressionistic way that no other photographer to date had ever attempted.

The photo captions in the latter part of the book provide little information about the content and the place where the photo concerned was taken. The only text accompanying the photos in the book consists of excerpts from telexes that Peress had exchanged with the office of his agency, Magnum, in Paris and New York (for example: "Attention: say to the lab to watch out particularly for a roll that might be in part ruined since the revolutionary guards opened my camera and tried to expose the film after I photographed heroin smokers. I hope they can save them. Thanks Gilles"). This combination lends the unusual reportage an intensity that was hitherto unknown. With *Telex Iran: In the Name of Revolution*, Peress showed a new approach to reportage that served to establish a distinctive style.

left——**W. Eugene Smith: The Country Doctor** | 1948

above——**Gilles Peress: Iran, Tabris** | 1980

1962–2010 Corinne Day **1968–today Rob Carter** **1976–today Pieter Hugo**

The era of *LIFE* ended in 1972 with what was the last issue for the time being. From 1978 it appeared again as a monthly in a considerably reduced print run; it finally closed in 2000. This event also marked the end of an era for photojournalism. By this point, television was omnipresent and had overtaken photography as the most important visual medium. The opportunities for publishing photos in the press diminished accordingly. However, this was by no means the end of photo reportage. Instead, it seems as if during this stage photographers had begun making more detailed reportage. This allowed them to take advantage of the new opportunities offered by the art world and they now increasingly presented their pictures in galleries, museums, and books that sold worldwide.

One of the outstanding exponents in this era of photojournalism is the Brazilian photographer Sebastião Salgado (b. 1944). He became famous for his images of the famine that devastated the Sahel region of Africa in 1984/85. Unlike those of many other photographers for the daily newspapers, Salgado's photos did not aim to present quickly grasped information, but to provide a profound documentation of the misery that was meant to shake the inhabitants of the industrialized world out of their complacency and to bring about an improvement in the situation. "For me it was never an individual photo that was important; it was always a sequence of photos that tell a story."

In the meantime, Salgado has started to specialize in large-scale photographic projects. They consist of individual reportages that he compiles to cover universal themes like migration or work. In 1986 he photographed gold prospectors in a mine in the Serra Pelada in Brazil, documenting "a dramatic spectacle of such gigantic dimensions, the like of which the world has not seen since the building of the pyramids" (right, and fig. p. 120). Every day, 50,000 people climbed down into the vast mine to dig for gold in the mud. By photographing this latter-day gold rush, Salgado created pictures of archaic quality, in which the men look like ants.

In order to finance his projects, Salgado publishes individual reportages in newspapers, organizes ex-

right——Sᴇʙᴀsᴛɪãᴏ Sᴀʟɢᴀᴅᴏ: Gᴏʟᴅ Pʀᴏsᴘᴇᴄᴛᴏʀs, Sᴇʀʀᴀ Pᴇʟᴀᴅᴀ, Bʀᴀᴢɪʟ | 1986

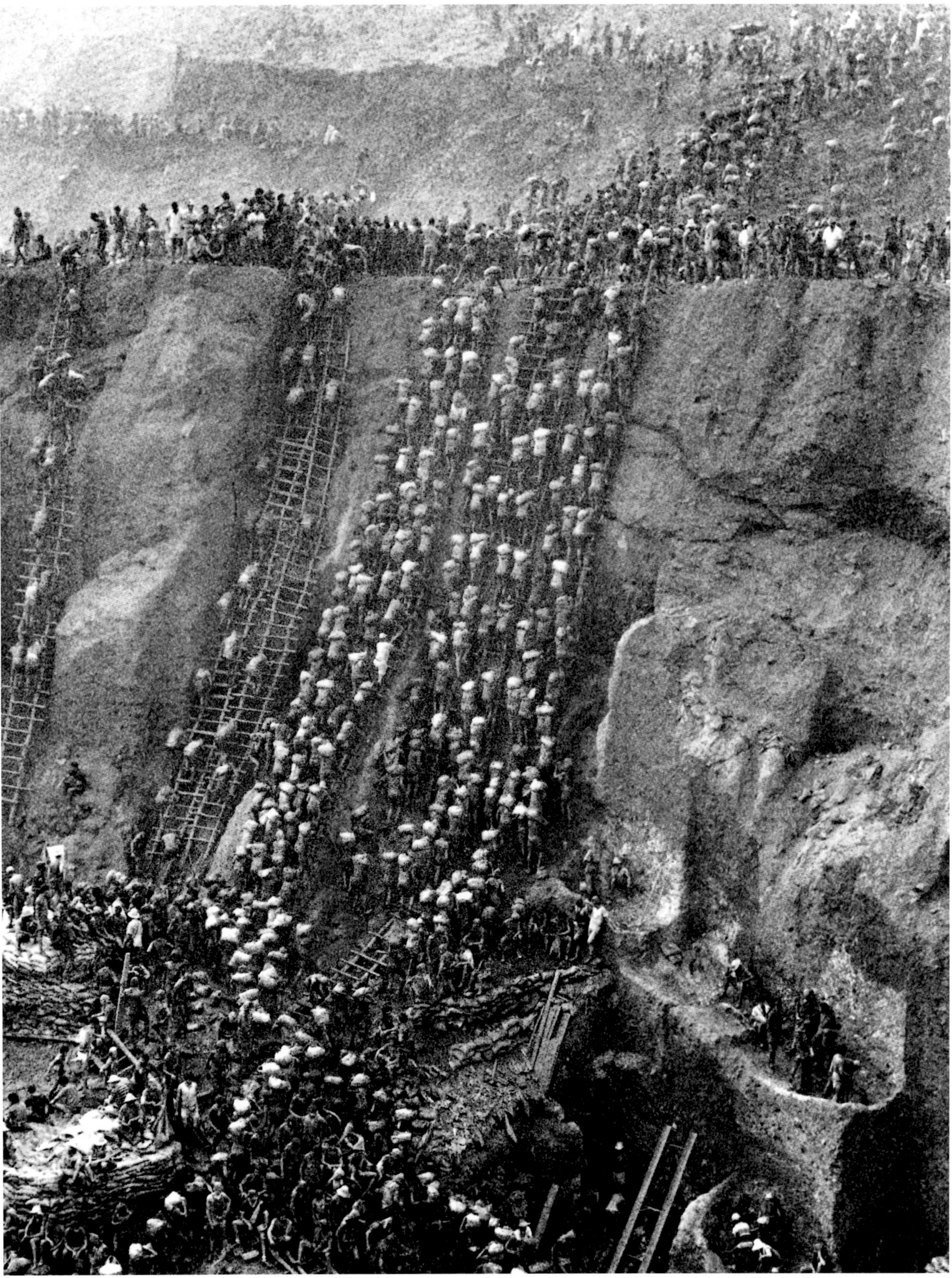

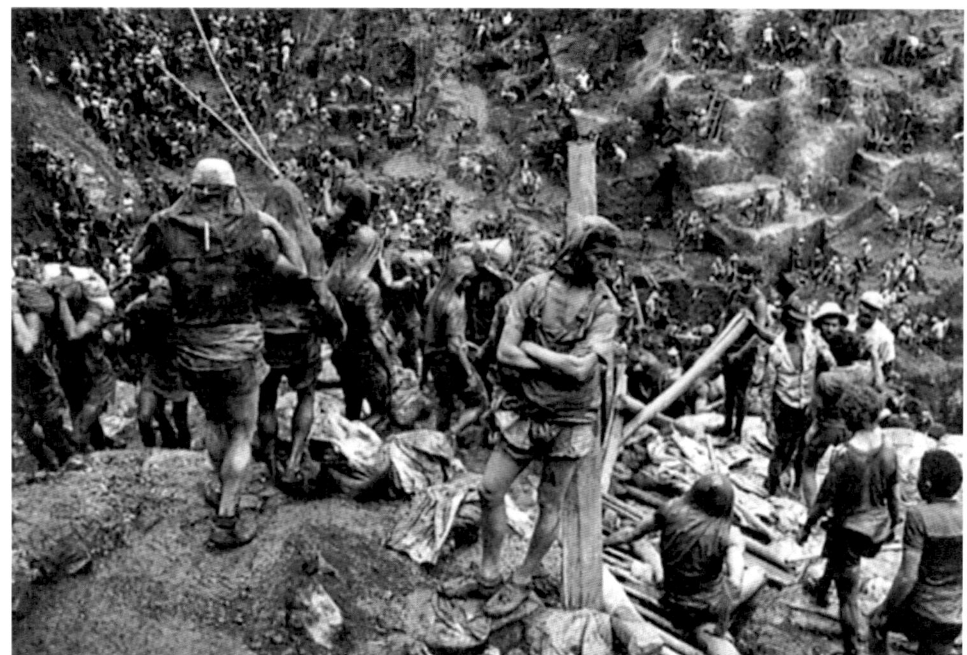

hibitions that travel the world, and publishes books in which the years of work invested in a project are summarized.

In their reportage, photographers repeatedly show extraordinary people and unusual living conditions, adopting new approaches in order to examine political and social problems.

The South African photographer Pieter Hugo (b. 1976) became aware of a group of traveling performers who attracted large crowds during their shows in the suburbs of Abuja, the capital of Nigeria. They were the Gadawan Kura, the so-called "hyena men" from the Hausa people (right). They are a mixture of acrobats and medicine men, who perform with hyenas, snakes, and baboons, and who sell tinctures, herbs, and amulets. Here an ancient world seems to encounter present-day reality, and the objective nature of the shots forms a stark contrast with the wild nature of the animals they present. The photos immediately aroused the ire of the animal welfare organizations in Europe and America, for the hyenas—which are powerful and very dangerous—are frequently forced to obey by being beaten with sticks. For Hugo, however, a more important question poses itself behind what is at first sight an apolitical reportage than that of animal welfare: "If we feel sorry for the animals, we should perhaps ask ourselves why these young men are forced to capture wild animals in order to survive in a country that is the world's sixth largest oil exporter." Despite the fascination exerted by these extraordinary images, Hugo's photos are an impressive and depressing record of the reality of life in the proliferating suburbs of the Third World. Hugo has created an unusual photo essay that demonstrates a departure from classic reportage and the emergence of a new artistic form of documentation.

above——**Sebastião Salgado: Gold Prospectors, Serra Pelada, Brazil** | 1986

right——**Pieter Hugo: Mallam Mantari Lamal with Mainasara, Nigeria** | 2005

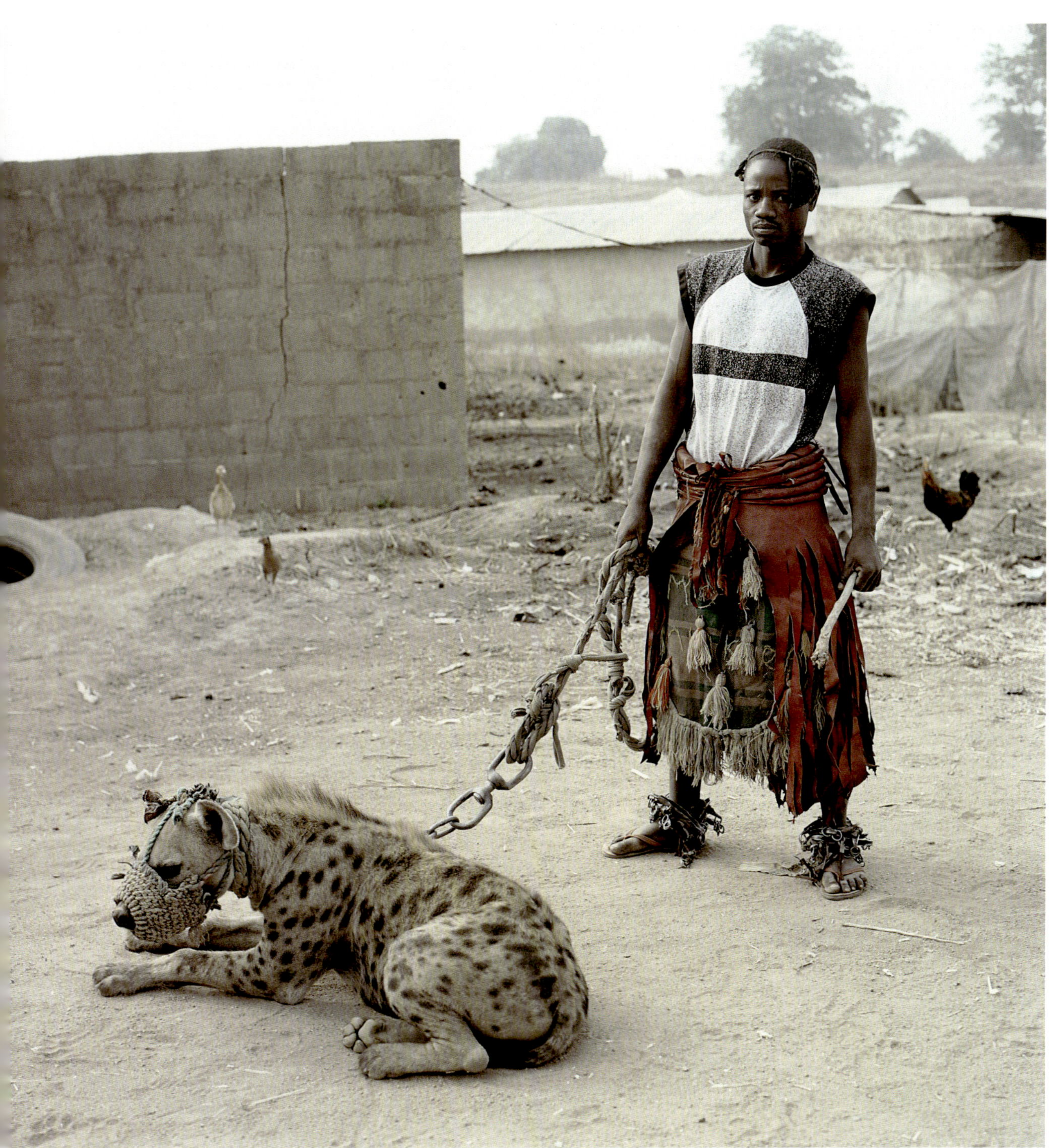

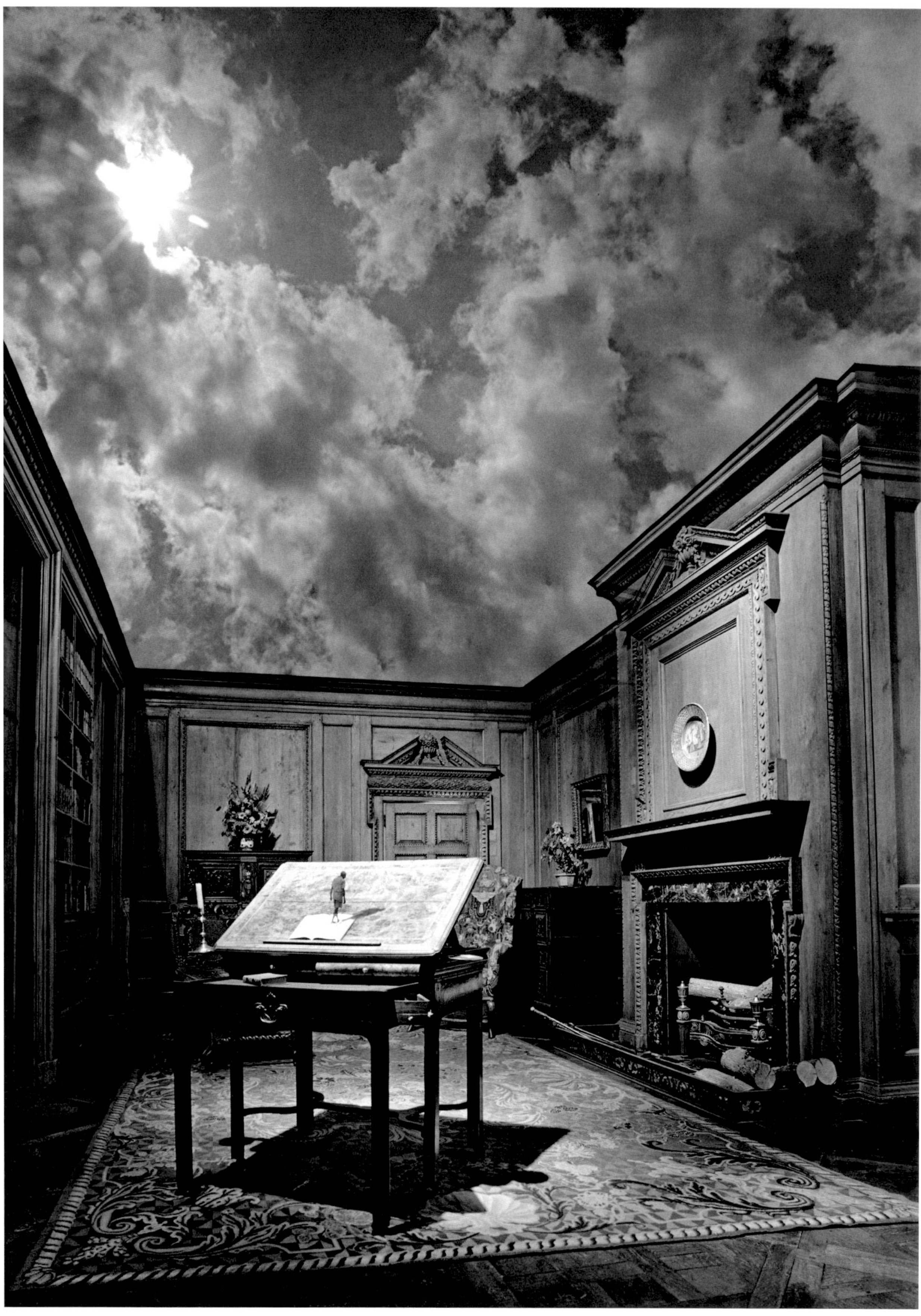

SURREALISM

Man Ray (1890–1976), one of the most important and influential photographers of the 20th century, came to photography almost by accident. He had studied painting and architecture in the United States, and initially planned simply to use photography to document his paintings.

Inspired by his acquaintance with the French artist Marcel Duchamp, who lived in New York from 1915 to 1921, and because he felt that he was not recognized as an artist in New York, Ray emigrated to Paris in 1921. Appreciation for his skill as a painter was not forthcoming in Paris either, however, and so he began to take photographs of the works of artists he met through Duchamp in order to make ends meet. Pablo Picasso, Henri Matisse, Jean Cocteau and others were among his clients. He became the portraitist of the arts scene and experimented with various techniques, notably "Rayography," to make his pictures even more interesting. These were photograms, a technique that William Fox Talbot had in fact already introduced to the public; Ray, however, rather immodestly treated it as his own invention and gave it his own name. He also experimented with "solarization," a method according to which light comes briefly into contact with photographic paper during the developing process, reversing the tonal values. Thanks to his innovative darkroom techniques, his imagination, and his versatility, Man Ray made a name for himself as one of the most creative photographers of his time.

In 1924 the poet André Breton published the *Manifeste du Surréalisme*, the key periodical of the Surrealist movement. The aim of Surrealism is to make the subconscious and the dreamlike visible. Objects from a variety of contexts are combined, apparently at random, to create "dream" scenes. Surrealist art makes reference to the insights of Sigmund Freud's psychoanalysis, and in particular to his interpretation of dreams. The Surrealists wanted to use their art to bridge the gap between the conscious and the subconscious, believing that true art could be created only when the rational mind is circumvented. From its inception, Surrealism, though it was initially a literary movement, fascinated both artists and photographers. For Salvador Dalí (1904–1989), probably the most famous Surrealist painter, it was in fact photography that was "the most stable medium for conveying poetry and the neatest procedure for capturing the subtlest of interactions that occur between reality and surreality." It took six hours to

left——**JERRY N. UELSMANN: UNTITLED** | 1976 | 49.3 x 36 cm | Metropolitan Museum of Art | New York

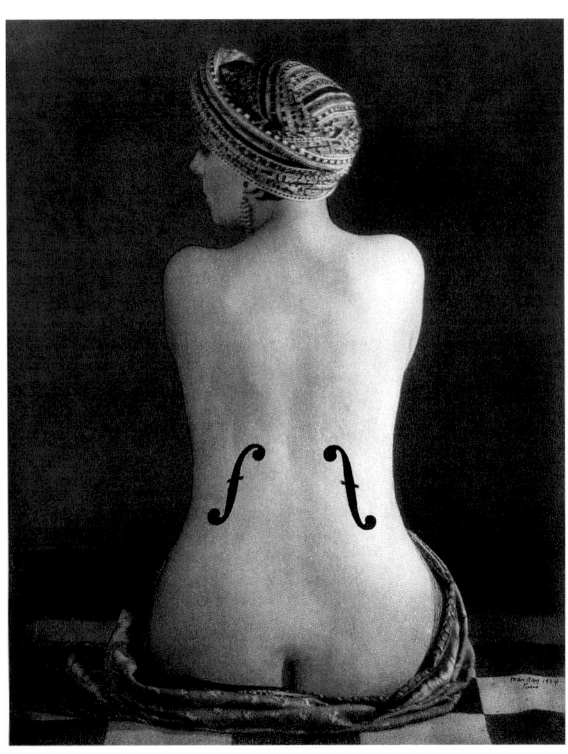

capture the portrait of Dalí by his friend Philippe Halsman (1906–1979) (right). Assistants had to throw buckets of water and three cats a total of 28 times for the sake of the perfect picture: "My assistants and I were wet, dirty, and close to collapsing from exhaustion; only the cats still looked fresh." Man Ray, who counted the Surrealists among his friends, never officially joined the group, but his work was certainly consistent with their beliefs. "For me, there is no difference between dream and reality. I never know whether what I do is a product of dreaming or of waking." The most famous photo by him from this period was created in 1924. It shows the back of his lover Kiki de Montparnasse (born Alice Prin), who was a well-known Parisian singer and friend of many artists. *Le Violon d'Ingres* (above) is a nude, photographed from behind to reveal her back, onto which Ray superimposed two f-holes (like those on a cello) in the darkroom. With this simple manipulation, Man Ray transformed the image of the model's back according to Surrealist theory, allowing viewers to form various associations. Man Ray makes playful reference to parallels

drawn between the musical instrument and the female body, and thus to the implication that cellists fantasize about holding a woman between their legs as they play their instruments. It also alludes to Jean-Auguste-Dominique Ingres's (1780–1867) famous painting *The Bather*, executed in 1808. Another association is concealed in the artwork's title: *Le Violon d'Ingres* could be translated as "hobby horse," or "hobby," so that Man Ray could have been referring to music, the cello, or his girlfriend Kiki as his "personal hobby horse."

Man Ray was one of the most versatile photographers of his time. He did not distinguish between art and commercial work, and took photographs in any field he found interesting, from art to fashion and advertising. Among his former assistants were Berenice Abbot, who essentially rediscovered the work of Eugène Atget with him; Lee Miller, a fashion model who would later become a successful photographer in her own right; and Bill Brandt, one of the best-known British photographers of the 20th century. Through his eclectic photographic oeuvre and his "inventions" in the darkroom, Man Ray liberated photography from its reputation as nothing more than a tool for the documentation of reality.

The ideas of Surrealism influence photography time and again. The connection of things that do not actually belong together and are instead brought together in "absurd" combinations gains an addi-

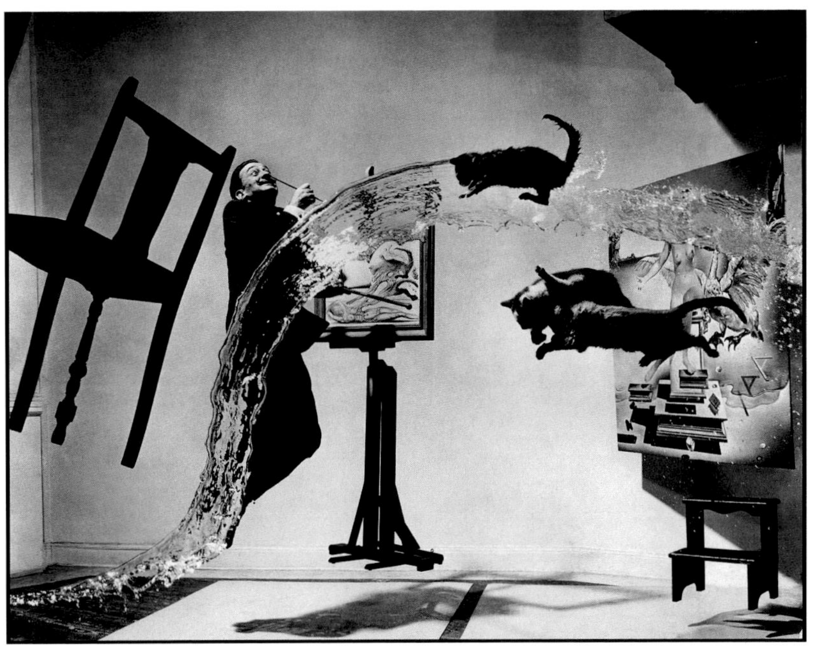

tional dimension from the realism of photography. The American Jerry Uelsmann (b. 1934) developed a special technique for the generation of Surrealist pictorial combinations. Uelsmann's pictures are the result of a sophisticated darkroom process according to which several negatives are superimposed on one another. The technique of photomontage was used as early as the 19th century, but Uelsmann refines it to achieve a new degree of sophistication (fig. p. 122). In his "visual research laboratory," he works with several enlargers that hold the various negatives he needs for a composition. The "realism of photography and the fluidity of our dreams" are combined in his work to form "a world of enigmas and mysteries." Uelsmann continues to be excited by "the alchemy of the photographic process." He does not use computers or Photoshop to process his pictures, and works with analog equipment to this day.

Ralph Gibson (b. 1939), whose roots are in street photography, and who worked on two films with Robert Frank in the 1960s, published a modern trilogy of Surrealist photography between 1970 and 1974: *Somnambulist*, *Déjà vu*, and *Days at Sea*. In contrast to the photographs of Man Ray and Jerry Uelsmann, his photographs are not the results of manipulation in the darkroom, but instead function as individual images for which he selects particular details that conjure up a surreal atmosphere. Going one step further, Gibson creates combinations of two photographs that are in fact quite unrelated. The juxtaposition of two photographs that were taken at different times in different places creates associations that the individual images could not (fig. pp. 126 and 127). Gibson compares the effects of these juxtaposition to overtones in music that can result from the combination of different notes in chords. "What is interesting is that my photographs are in fact, in the end, documentary photographs, even if they have an intentionally surreal effect. This has to be the case because photography forces us to accept reality; we cannot escape it."

left——**MAN RAY: LE VIOLON D'INGRES** | 1924
above——**PHILIPPE HALSMAN: DALÍ ATOMICUS** | 1948

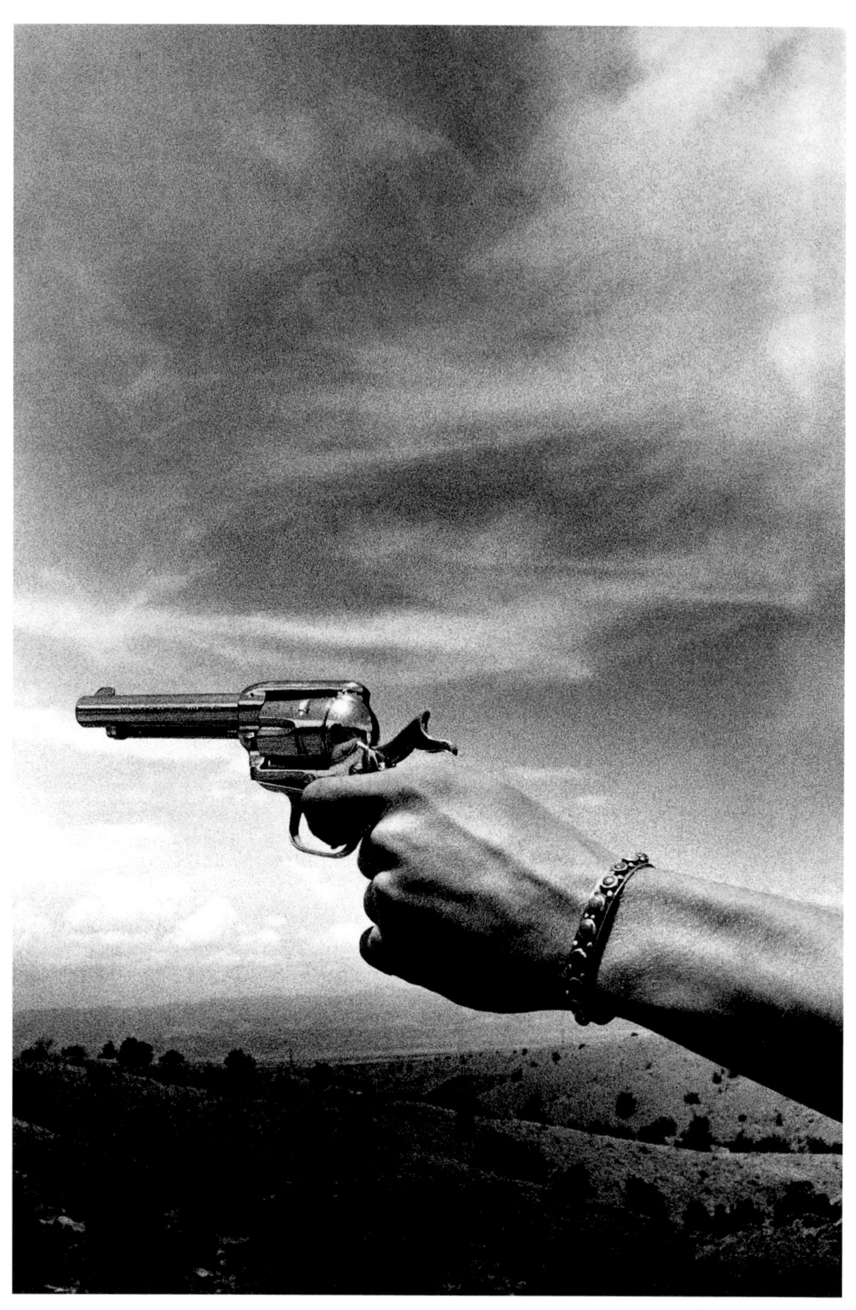

above and right——**RALPH GIBSON: UNTITLED (HAND WITH PISTOL)** | from
Déjà vu (New Mexico/New York) 1972

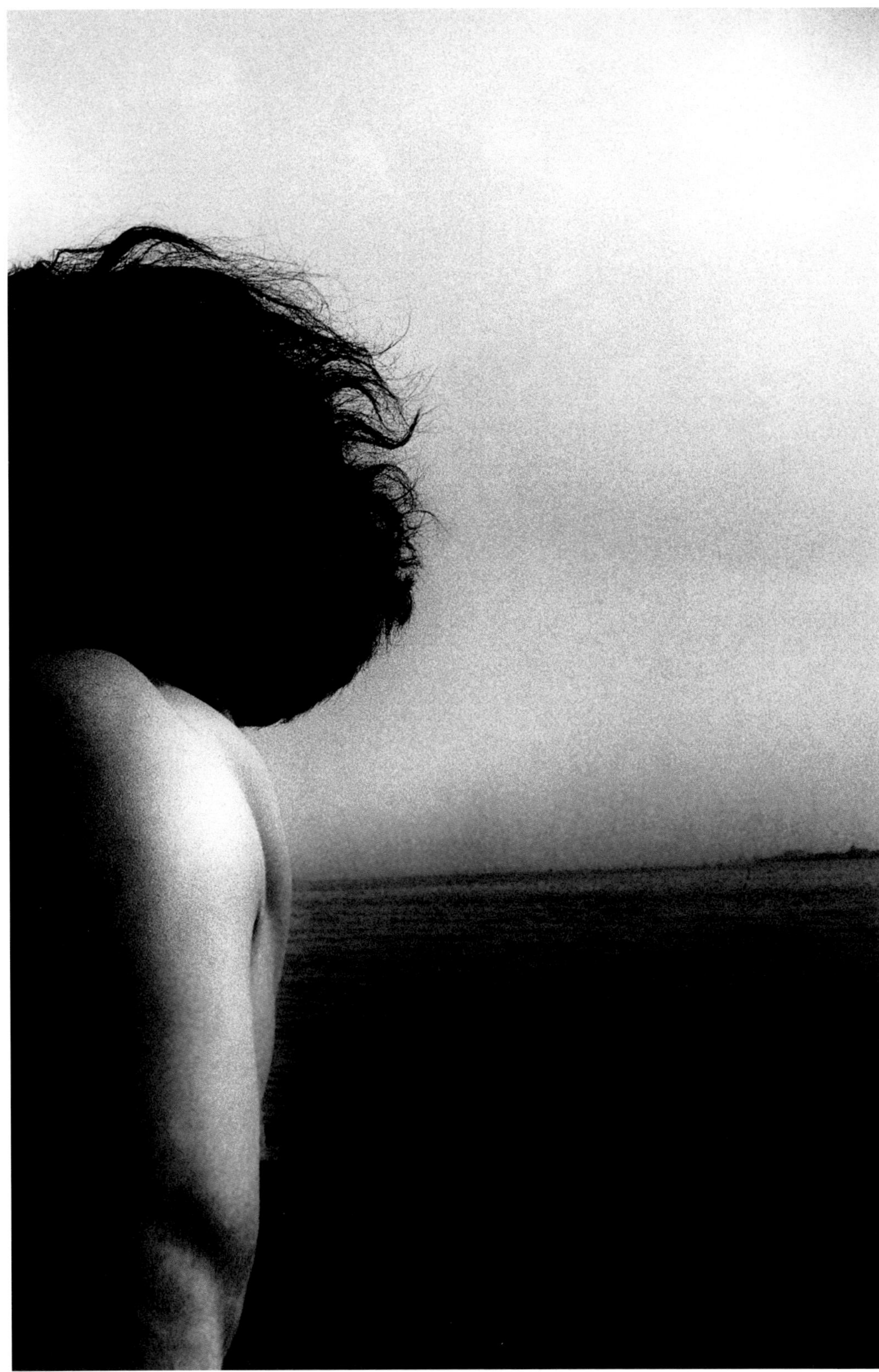

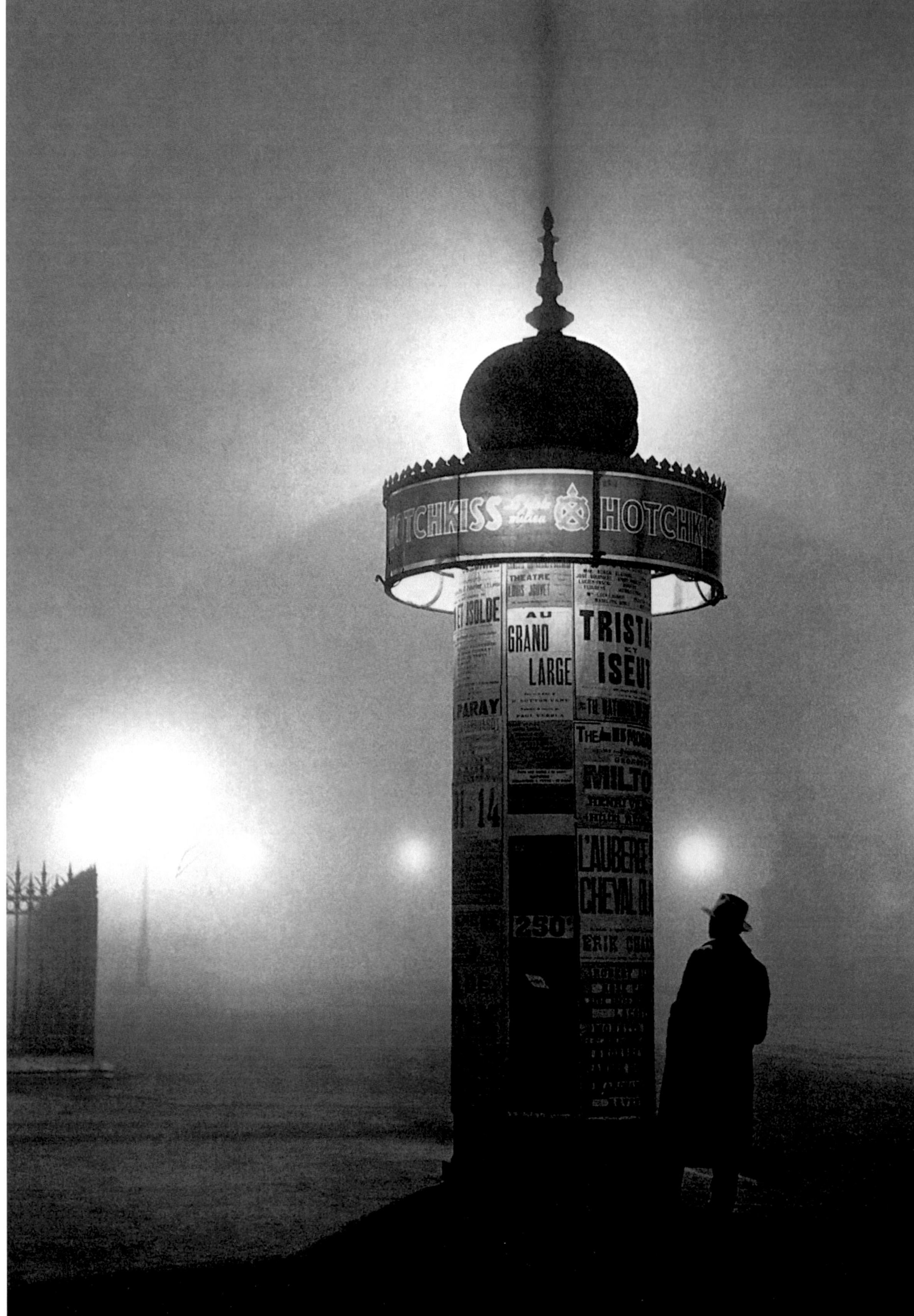
HOTCHKISS
HOTCHKI
THEATRE
LOUIS JOUVET
AU
GRAND
LARGE
TRISTA
ET
ISEUT
PARAY
MILTO
L'AUBERG
CHEVAL
ERIK CHA

NIGHT PHOTOGRAPHY

The word "photograph" means "to write with light," and so to take photographs at night would seem to be paradoxical. Not until the development of film emulsions that were very sensitive to light was it possible to take photographs during the nighttime, too. The alternative was to use artificial light. In the late 19th century, magnesium flash lamps were used to light up the darkness, until these were replaced in the 1930s by flashbulbs. The electronic flash unit in use today owes its invention to the research of Harold E. Edgerton (see *Chronophotography*). Although there are now many methods for taking pictures of the night, it continues to exert a particular fascination on us. To take photographs at night, no matter which technique is used, always feels special.

Published in 1933, the photobook *Paris de Nuit* by the Paris-based Hungarian photographer Brassaï (Gyula Halász, 1899–1984) was a milestone of nighttime photography. "It all started because I was a sleepwalker, and I was enchanted and excited by the pictures of the city at night. I asked myself how on earth I could capture and record these great impressions—which medium would allow me to do so." Brassaï worked as a journalist and painter and was introduced to photography by his compatriot André Kertész. He immediately recognized that this was the medium he had been looking for.

Brassaï worked without a flash, using only the light already present at a scene. He positioned his camera in such a way that sources of direct light, such as street lamps, were as far as possible obscured by trees and walls in order to avoid excessive contrasts of light and dark. Furthermore, he often took photographs in foggy conditions, which also evened out the contrasts (left). Using this technique, Brassaï created what is at times an almost sinister atmosphere in which people make shadowy appearances before fading back into the darkness. He took pictures of everything that occurred on the streets of Paris at night, and proved to be an unobtrusive observer. He was interested specifically in the nighttime activities that remain inaccessible to the "virtuous citizens" who go to bed in good time. Brassaï was entranced by the world of brothels and seedy bars. Here too he continued to act as the quiet observer, and was satisfied merely to suggest. The story of the man who is about to step into the brothel called "Suzy" is only hinted at (fig. p. 130, left).

Brassaï leaves it to the viewers to imagine what lies behind the scenes he captures.

Weegee (Arthur Fellig, 1899–1968) was in every respect the opposite of Brassaï: both intrusive and indiscreet.

left——Brassaï: Avenue de l'Observatoire, Paris | 1933

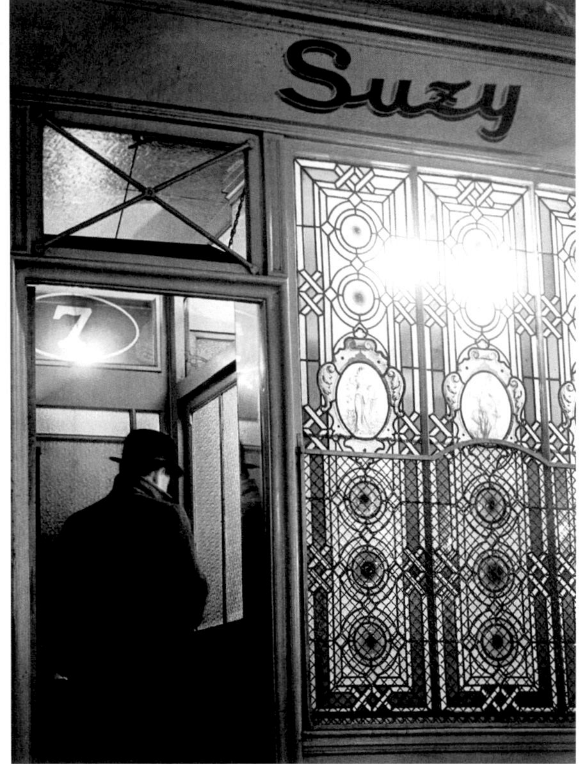

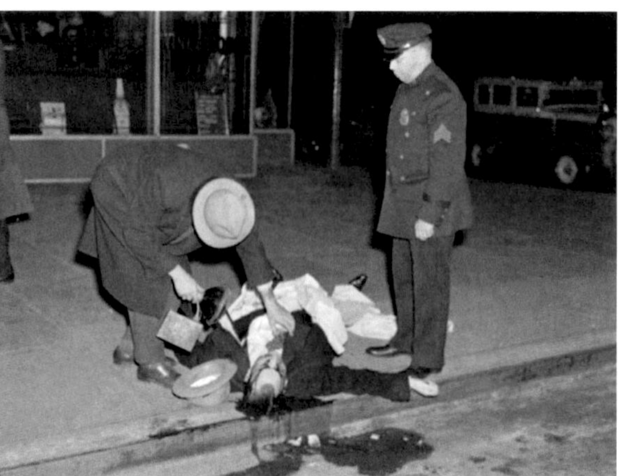

He was a photojournalist who specialized in crimes and scandals for the popular press in New York during the 1930s and 1940s. Whereas Brassaï took a more poetic approach to the night, Weegee focused on cold, hard facts and did nothing to try to embellish them in his photographs.

New York crime was his subject, and he captured it in a relentlessly honest, direct, and brutal light (above, right). According to the man himself, he covered more than 5,000 murders during his ten years as a yellow-press journalist. He was not a photographer who produced work appreciated by art aficionados with subtle tastes, but one whose work was published in the popular press. The aim of his photographs was to shock and titillate in order to encourage passersby to buy the newspapers in which they were printed. His subject matter made him a specialist in nighttime photography, which in turn had an impact on his style in both creative and technical terms. The defining characteristic of his pictures is the use of flash. This literally highlights those objects that are close to the camera and causes the background to melt into the darkness. Gray tones are reduced, leaving a harsh contrast between black and white that was well suited to newspaper printing. Weegee did not hesitate to drag his "victims" into the limelight. His photographs are striking and brash—we are confronted by the brutal reality of a scene, and have no choice but to come to terms with it. Some of his pictures, however, are not what they seem at first glance. In *Their First Murder* (fig. pp. 132–133), a group of excited children are transformed by the title of the photo into a scandal-hungry crowd jostling to see their first dead body. What would otherwise be a carefree scene thus becomes a macabre moment in which the children learn about the harsh realities of the world in which they live.

Weegee was interested in the depiction of the depths of the human soul. In his photographs, he displayed a comprehensive and unrelenting picture of the dark side of society. His book *Naked City*, published in 1945, and an exhibition at the Museum of Modern Art that same year, finally led to a critical recognition of his work as a photographer that had previously been withheld from him during his career as a photographer for the popular press.

Michael Kenna (b. 1953), an Englishman and one of the most widely discussed landscape photographers

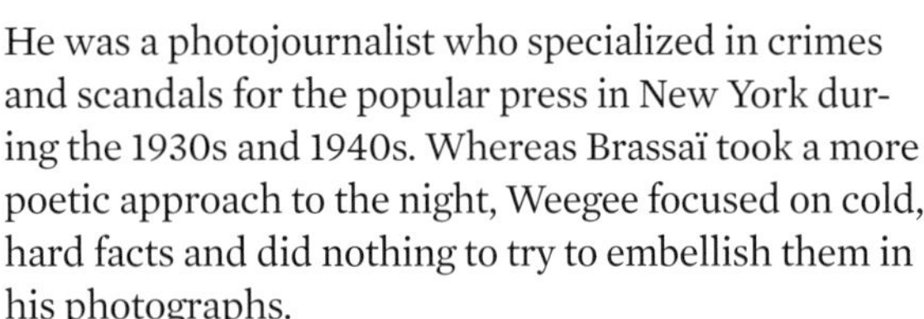

above left——**Brassaï: Chez Suzy, Paris** | 1932
above right——**Weegee: Murder, New York** | *c.* 1938
right——**Michael Kenna: Twenty Sticks, Kohoku, Honshu, Japan** | 2003
following pages——**Weegee: Their First Murder, New York** | 1941

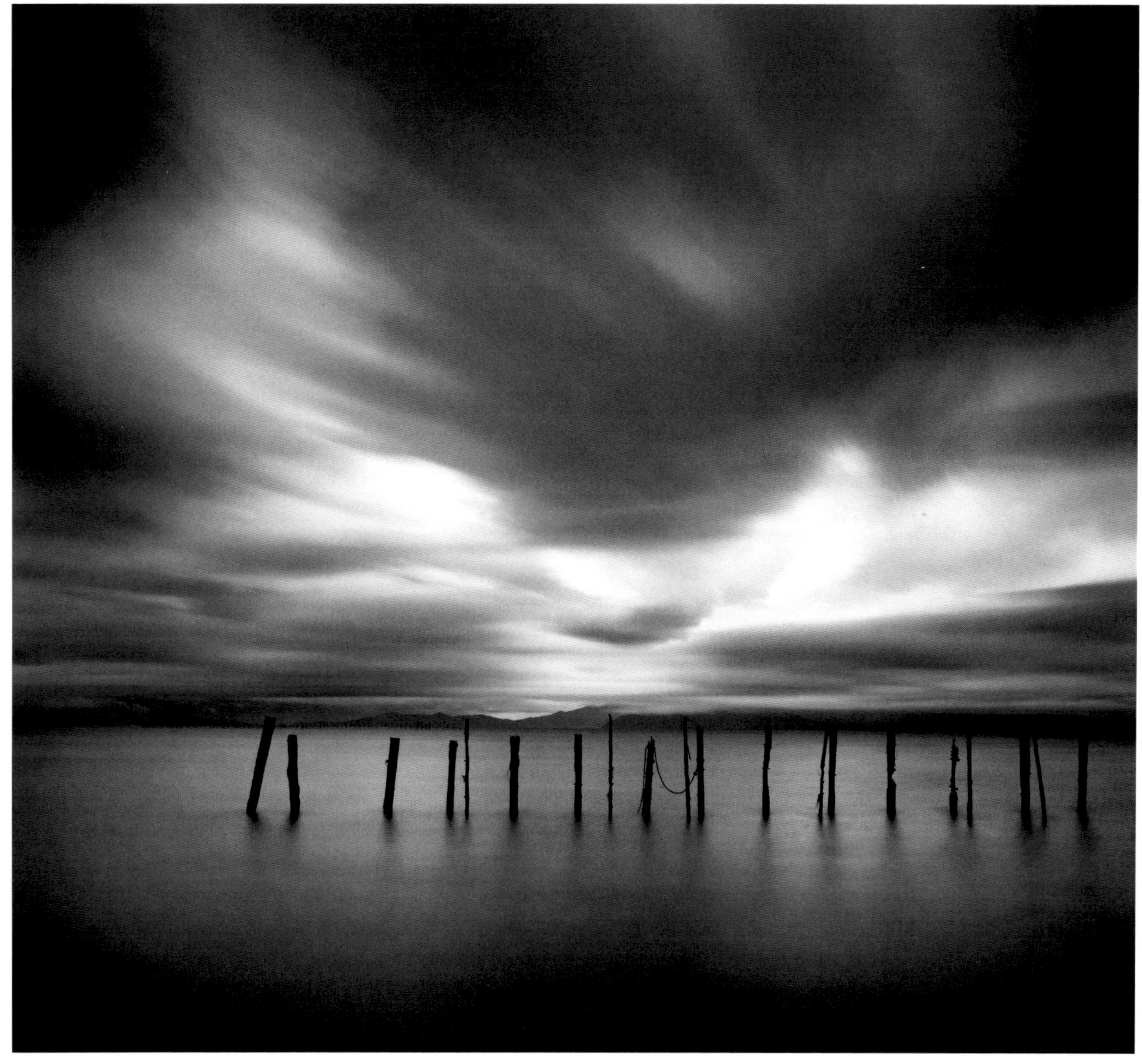

of our time, has a particular penchant for nighttime photography. Depending on the subject, his exposure times vary from ten minutes to eight hours. In the midst of our hectic lives, he enjoys sitting quite calmly next to his camera, waiting to see what the negative will reveal. It is the unpredictability of the outcome of such long exposure times that makes photographs taken at night so special for Kenna. Water is transformed into an even gauze-like texture, and clouds take on an undefined appearance that is shaped through wind and time into unpredictable forms (above). Whereas there is only one main source of light during the daytime—the sun—at night there can be several different sources coming from various, often unpredictable, directions. He comments: "Perhaps most intriguing of all is that it is possible to photograph what is impossible for the human eye to see—cumulative time." Photographs usually capture a single moment in a fraction of a second. In Kenna's nighttime pictures, by contrast, a multitude of moments are superimposed on one another in one photograph. Perhaps it is precisely because of these cumulative moments in time that Michael Kenna's photographs have a meditative air.

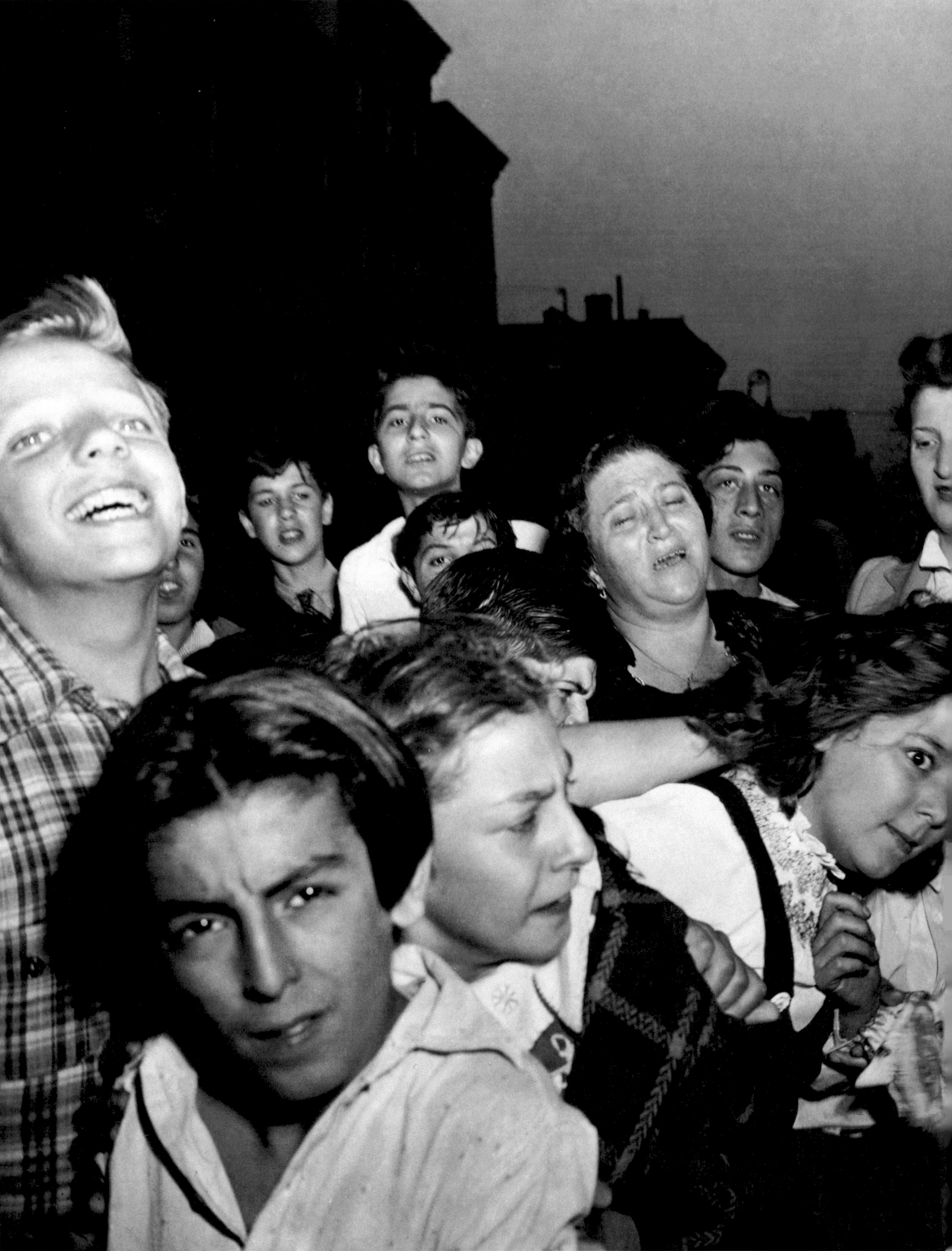

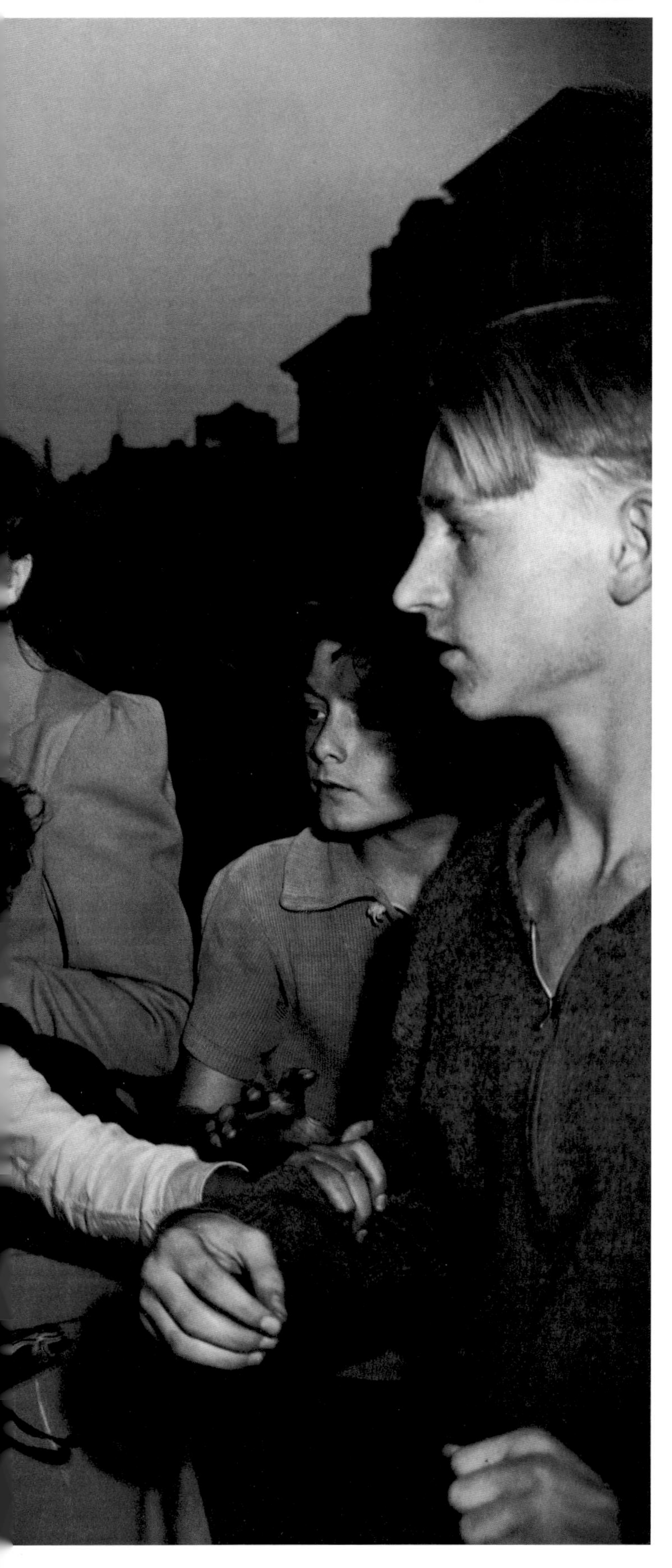

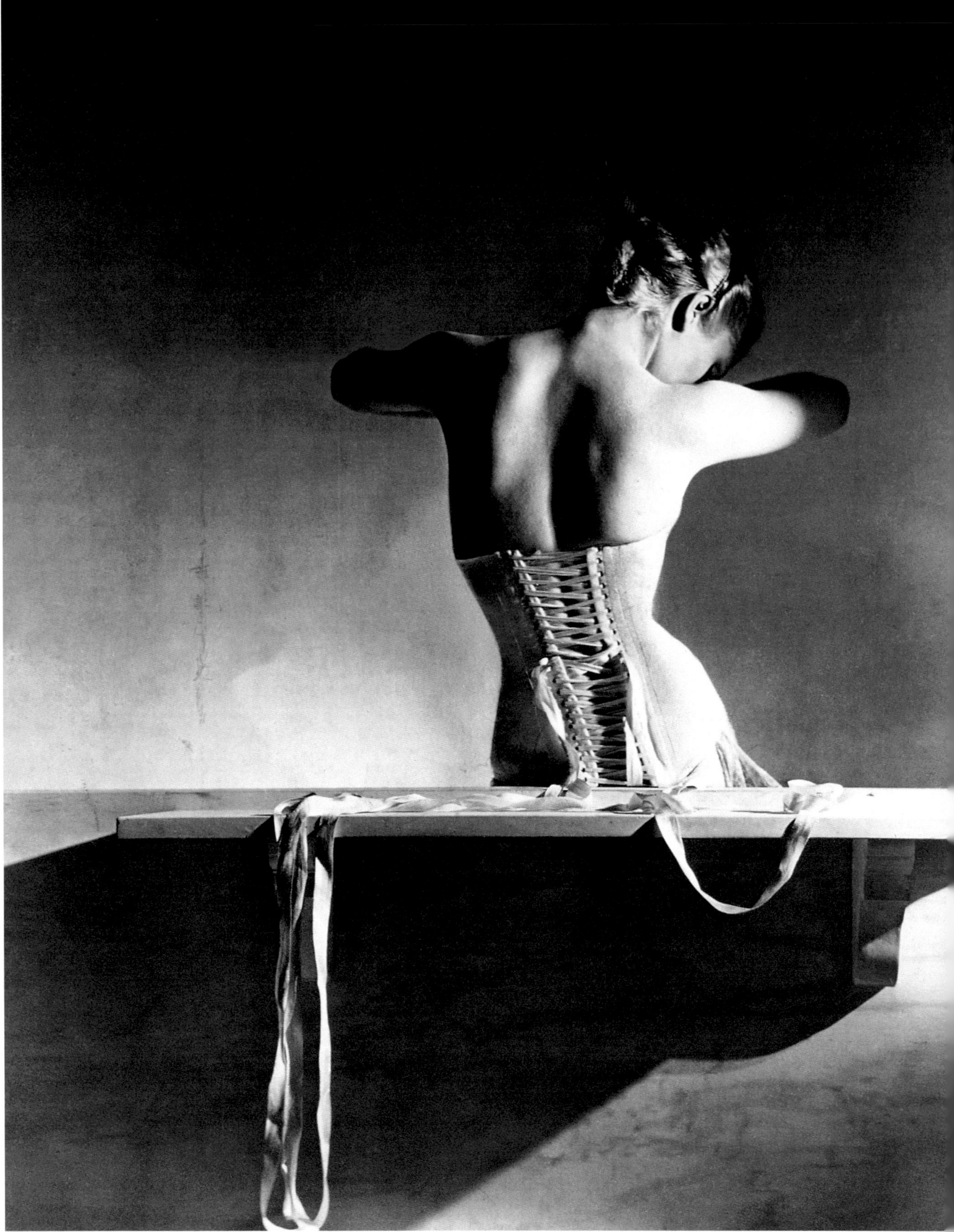

FASHION PHOTOGRAPHY

Fashion expresses the spirit of the times and fashion photography is the photographic translation of what fashion designers, art directors, marketing specialists, and photographers have created. It is the attitude to life that fashion is intended to convey that is to be captured and communicated by photography. The task of fashion photographers is to reconcile their artistic aspirations with commercial needs. The grand masters of early fashion photography were Baron Adolphe de Meyer (1868–1949), who still created fashion photographs in the Pictorialist style, and Edward Steichen (1879–1973), who succeeded de Meyer as chief photographer of *Vogue* in 1922. They were also the first photographers to unite art and commerce in photography. Georg Freiherr von Hoyningen-Huene (1900–1968) and his pupil Horst P. Horst (1906–1999), both of whom moved from Europe to the United States, were leading figures in the fashion photography during the 1920s and 1930s, their style being strongly influenced by Greek antiquity and Art Deco. One of the most famous fashion photographs of the time was the so-called *Main-*

bocher Corset (left), which Horst photographed in Paris in 1939. The elegant simplicity of the photo is derived not only from the subject but also from a complicated lighting arrangement possible only in a studio: "Light is more complex than we imagine. It looks as if there is only one source of light, but I added reflectors and other spotlights. I don't know how I did it. I couldn't repeat it." At times the models in early fashion photography look almost like statues; the principles of composition and pose were derived from the art of classical antiquity and the paintings of artists like Jean-Auguste-Dominique Ingres (1780–1867), and relied heavily on elaborate studio techniques. The large-format cameras were heavy and cumbersome; flash had not yet become standard as studio lighting for fashion photography; and the exposure times were still lengthy. Thus the technical necessity of a static pose was transformed into an aspect of style.

At the same time, the sports photographer Martin Munkácsi (1896–1963), a native of Hungary, was also working as a fashion photographer in the United States. He left Europe in 1934 and worked for *Harper's Bazaar* and later also for *LIFE*. Munkácsi created his own dynamic and innovative style by using his experiences of sports photography when taking fashion shots. He dispensed with large-format cameras on tripods and instead took his photos with small,

left——**HORST P. HORST: MAINBOCHER CORSET** | 1939

"While the pictures by Hoyningen-Huene and Horst suggested a timeless world of apparently unattainable ideals, Munkacsi's photos evoked the modern woman whose carefree lifestyle was a goal that could be reached by all women."

portable cameras like the Leica, with which he could react quickly to changes in light, composition, and pose. He had the models running or jumping along a beach or in the street, thereby introducing movement and dynamism into fashion photography (right). And Munkácsi's pictures brought about a further change in fashion photography. The image of women shown in his photos differed markedly from the familiar statuesque fashion icons posed in luxurious studio settings. While the pictures by Hoyningen-Huene and Horst suggested a timeless world of apparently unattainable ideals, Munkácsi's photos evoked the modern woman whose carefree lifestyle was a goal that could be reached by all women. They were active women who seemed to have been photographed by chance and who therefore looked more natural and "ordinary."

The development of fashion photography is closely linked to *Vogue* and *Harper's Bazaar*, for many years the most important magazines in fashion. They in turn were dependent on their art directors, who determined their looks and style, selecting photographers who corresponded with their artistic concept. One of the most influential art directors was Alexey Brodovitch (1898–1971), who not only engaged Richard Avedon, William Klein, and many other photographers, but also worked as the art director at *Harper's Bazaar* for 20 years, from 1938 to 1958.

He had a decisive influence on the development of photography, especially on the so-called "New York School."

The period just after World War II was characterized on the one hand by the dreary aftermath of the war, and on the other by a desire for change that Richard Avedon in particular translated into dynamic photographs filled with *joie-de-vivre*. He took up the ideas of Munkácsi and photographed his models on the streets of Paris. While Munkácsi "showed that the models had legs," Avedon imbued his models with personality and emotions. He became one of the most influential fashion photographers, along with his colleague and friend Irving Penn (1917–2009). The latter continued to prefer studio photography in a stricter, more classical style (fig. p. 138), thereby presenting a contrast to the work of Avedon. These two photographers and their differing styles determined the development of fashion photography until well into the 1970s.

The 1980s saw the marriage of glamour, design, and fashion. They also marked the birth of the so-called

right——**Martin Munkácsi: The Puddle Jumper** | 1934

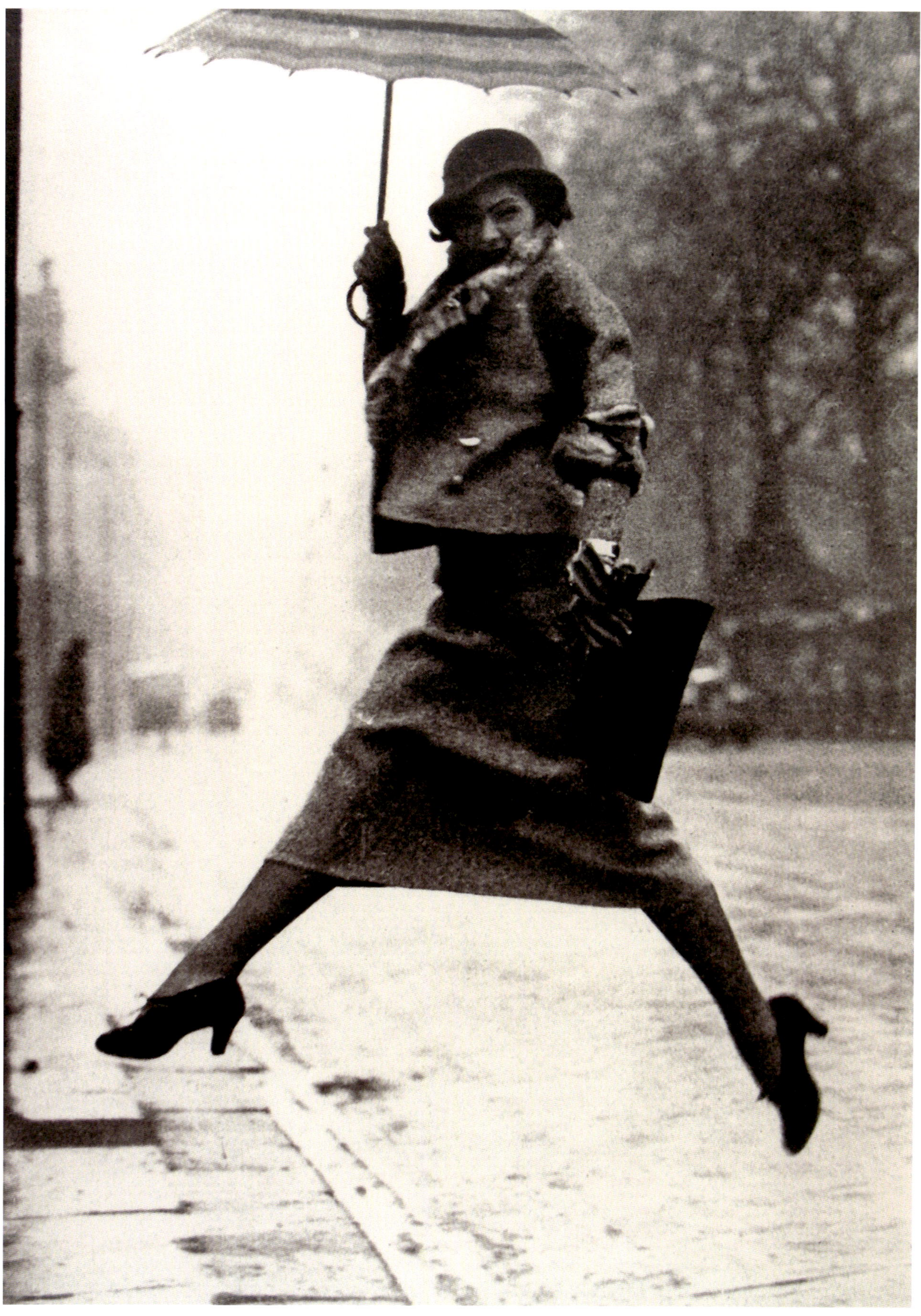

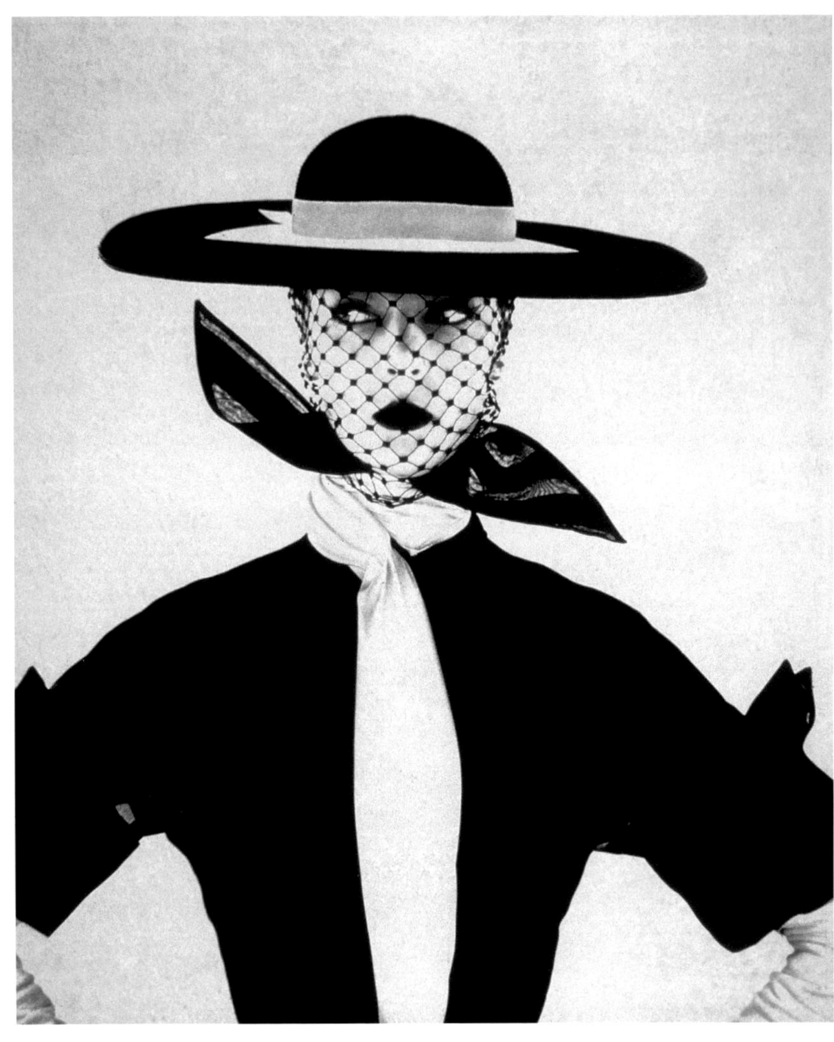

supermodels like Naomi Campbell, Claudia Schiffer, and Linda Evangelista, the new stars alongside film divas. They were at the center of interest in the photographed narratives of artists like Peter Lindbergh (b. 1944) and the classic compositions of photographers like Herb Ritts (1952–2002). With his stylized black-and-white photos, Ritts left a deep impression on the sleek aesthetic of the 1980s, which was characterized by unusual but plain backgrounds, elegant compositions, and by a marked sense of corporeality. But during the 1990s, the aestheticization of all aspects of life provoked a counter-movement led by young photographers, their anti-glamour pictures quickly becoming all the rage. In this context, Herb Ritts's photographs look like the swan song of the highly aestheticized glamour world of the 1980s. As in the fashion photography of the past decades,

above ——**Irving Penn: Black and White** | cover of *Vogue* | New York 1950

right——**Jürgen Teller: Fashion Photo for Marc Jacobs** | 2009

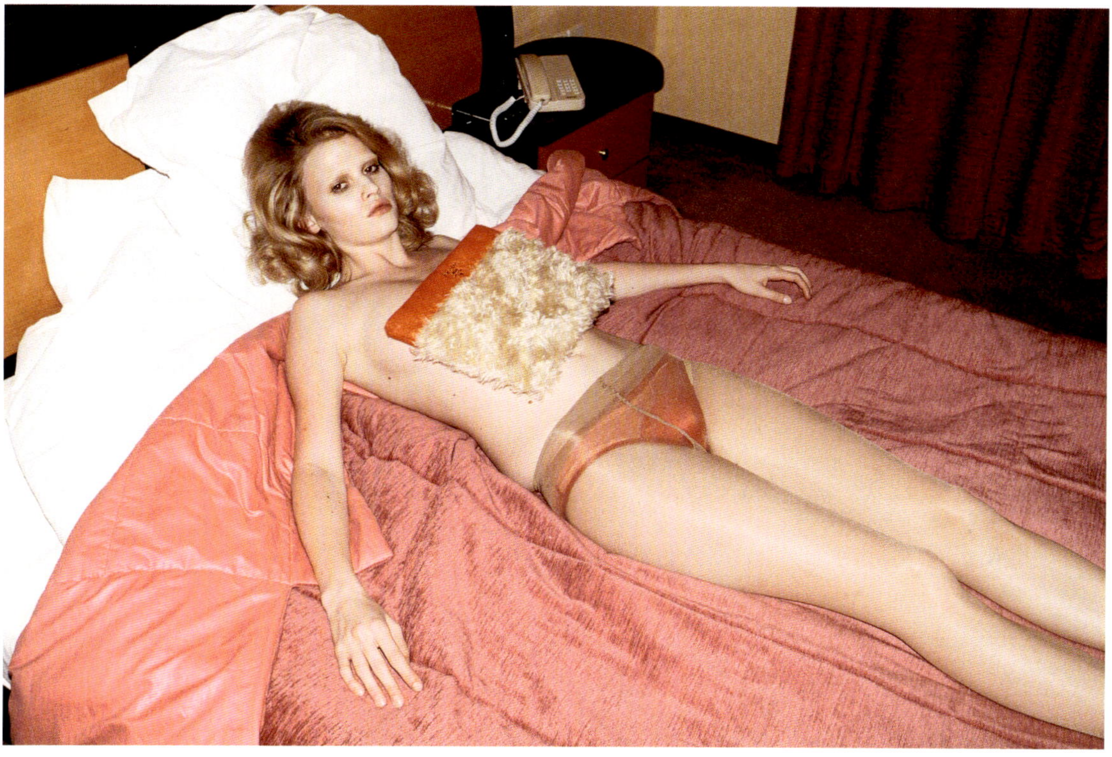

this aesthetic "riposte" also had its inspiration in art photography. Nan Goldin's book *The Ballad of Sexual Dependency*, published in 1986, showed a completely different picture of society. Her subject was the New York subculture of drag queens, addicts, and the club scene, of alcohol, drugs, and Aids. The "horribly authentic" photos, taken with flash, were unprettified and raw, but also intimate and emotional; all in all, they were the opposite of the photos of, for example, Robert Mapplethorpe or Herb Ritts. With her "trashy" pictorial aesthetic, Nan Goldin (b. 1953) had found a new form of expression, which the younger generation of photographers adopted with enthusiasm and modified to suit their purposes. Photographers like Corinne Day (1962–2010), who "discovered" Kate Moss, Jürgen Teller (b. 1964) (above), and Wolfgang Tillmans (b. 1968) continue to influence the scene in some respects to this day. *Vogue* and *Harper's Bazaar* were suddenly faced with competition from younger magazines like *i-D*, *The Face*, and *Dazed & Confused*, the last founded by the fashion

photographer Rankin (John Rankin Waddell). The provocative, "ugly," unsanitized pictures were an attack on the perfect, carefully styled aesthetic of their predecessors. Personal, intimate, documentary, they opposed the idealization of the body that is usually found in the fashion sector.

But despite this new "trash aesthetic," the classic, "attractive" fashion photography has continued to this day, though its computer-optimized figures and faces are increasingly subjected to criticism.

The German journalist Ulf Poschardt observed: "The greatest success of fashion photography is its power of definition with regard to what characterizes our time." This may be true, in that fashion photography has always taken up current trends—indeed, that is its *raison d'être*, so to speak. It is also correct that fashion photography, whose aim is ultimately to sell a product, fashion, has always operated in the realm of extremes, both glamour and trash. The lives of its consumers no doubt mostly lie somewhere in between.

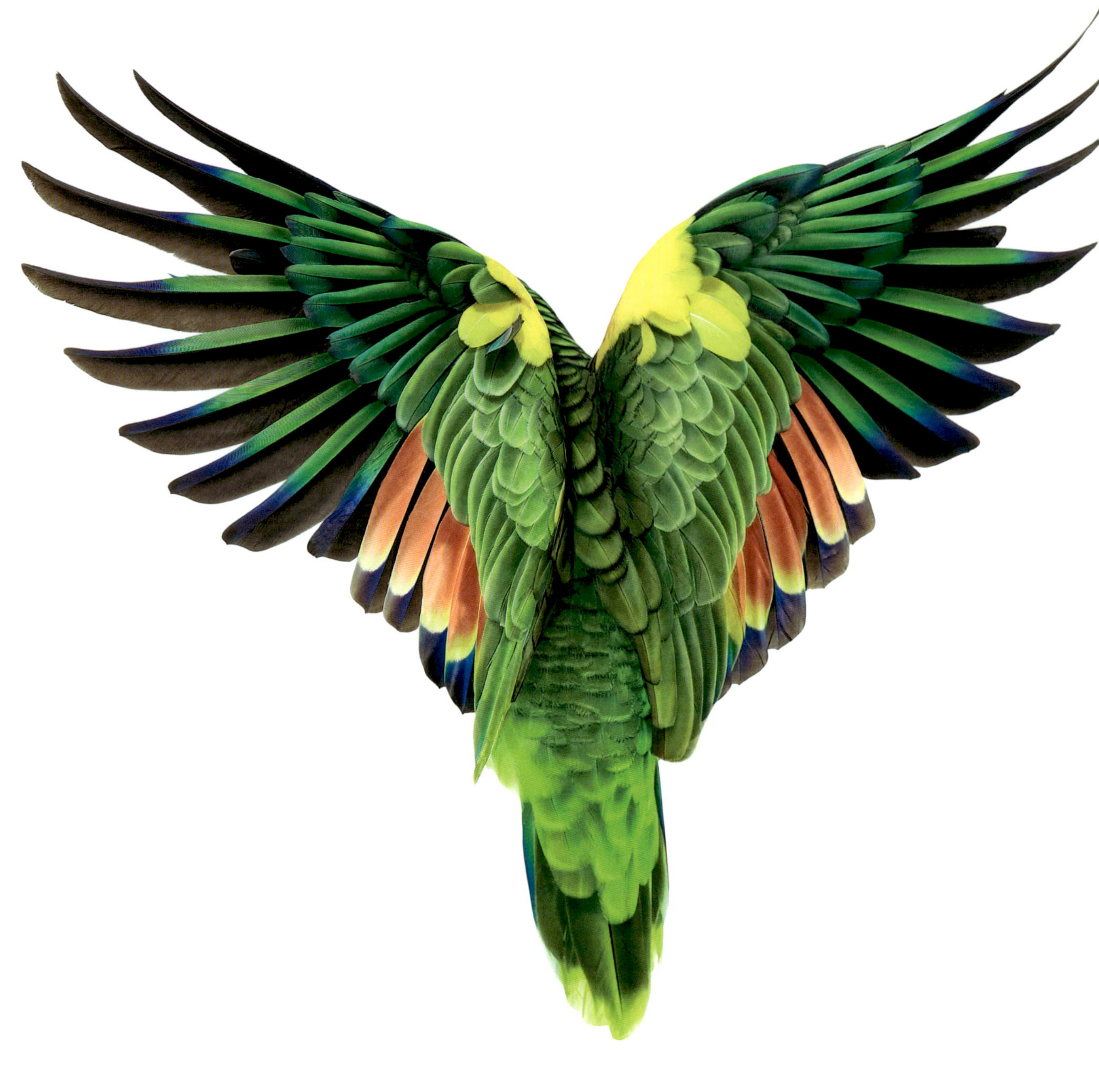

ANIMAL PHOTOGRAPHY

During the 19th century and at the beginning of the 20th century, the purpose of animal photography was mostly to record the results of a big game hunt. The photos showed the tiger, lion, or elephant "courageously" killed by the intrepid hunters. The awareness that nature was a valuable asset worth protection, and that wild animals do not exist simply so that someone can shoot them, did not exist at that time. This awareness developed only slowly and was first introduced to a broader public during the 1950s and 1960s by animal filmmakers such as Bernhard Grzimek, Marlin Perkins, Jacques Cousteau, and Joan and Alan Root. The books produced to accompany the films enjoyed a wide circulation. Magazines like *National Geographic* or *Geo,* which was founded somewhat later, published photographic animal reportage that introduced people in industrialized countries to nature and the wilderness. Animal photographers became "reporters of creation," and as such they strove to show their audience unique features of nature and to make them aware of the relentless destruction of the environment and the animal world.

Animal photographers often spend months pursuing their subjects and then often wait for days or weeks in order to take the perfect picture. The American photographer Jim Brandenburg (b. 1945) is a master in his field; he takes on long-term projects covering specific subjects. It was during a project of this kind that he traveled through the far north of Canada in 1986 in search of Arctic wolves. He accompanied and photographed the pack initially from a safe distance using telephoto lenses, until they had got used to him. This permitted him to reduce the distance gradually to such an extent that he was able to photograph the Arctic wolves at close quarters. The result is an extraordinary animal reportage culminating in a photo of a wolf leaping from ice floe to ice floe in search of food (fig. p. 142). In 2010 the photo was chosen by the International League of Conservation Photographers (iLCP), an association of the best nature photographers, as one of the best 40 nature shots in the history of photography.

The art of animal photographers consists initially of studying the habits of animals and then patiently waiting for the decisive moment at which an animal reveals its unique character. As in "normal" reportage, it is important to touch the viewer emotionally but without humanizing the animals. Most wildlife photographers regard environmental protection

left——**Andrew Zuckerman: Blue Fronted Amazon** | 2008

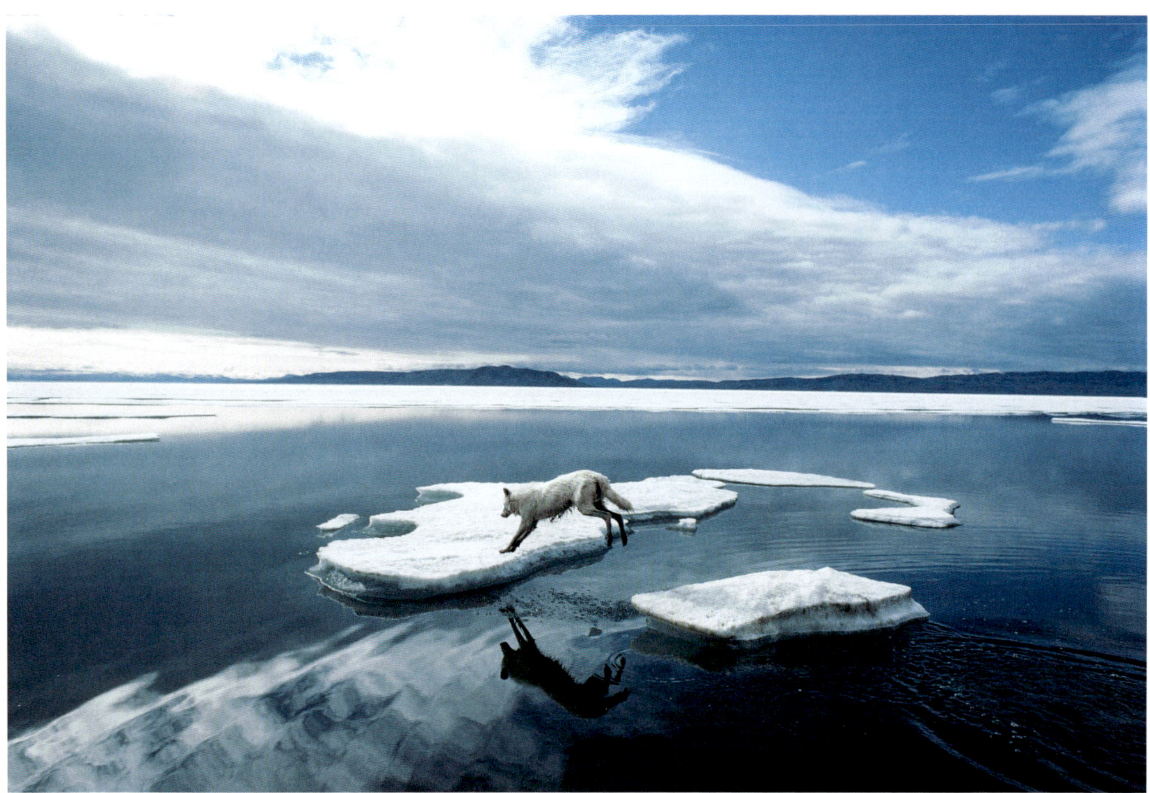

as one of their main aims. The era of the big-game hunters is fortunately more or less over, though illegal poachers have since taken their place. It is necessary to produce ever new, more impressive, and more moving pictures in order to make people aware of how important it is to protect nature and the animal kingdom.

Nick Brandt and Andrew Zuckerman pursue the same goal, albeit with quite different photographic means. Nick Brandt photographs animals in the wild, using an analogue camera and black-and-white film. Andrew Zuckerman, by contrast, films in the studio, digitally, and in color. Both have found a new, individual way of expressing their interest in with the animal world, thereby creating an awareness of the importance and infinite variety of nature—and also of the dangers that now threaten the natural world.

Nick Brandt (b. 1966) worked initially as a director of music videos, and in 1995 he directed the video for Michael Jackson's hit *Earth Song*. Part of the shooting took place in Tanzania, and from the very first moment Brandt was fascinated by the landscape and animals of the region, and he pondered how he could translate this fascination into pictures. When he started photographing animals in 2000, his aim from the start was to take pictures unlike any taken by other photographers. He decided on photographs taken with an analogue camera and in black and white. That alone is most unusual in the 21st century, the age of digital photography. Even more unusual was his decision not to use telephoto lenses. Brandt did not want to produce normal animal reportage that documented the lives of animals, the way they hunt and are hunted. His aim was to produce portraits of animal personalities (right): "I try to capture animals as they are—their personality, their soul—and to photograph them as I would photograph people. And you don't do that at a distance using a telephoto lens."

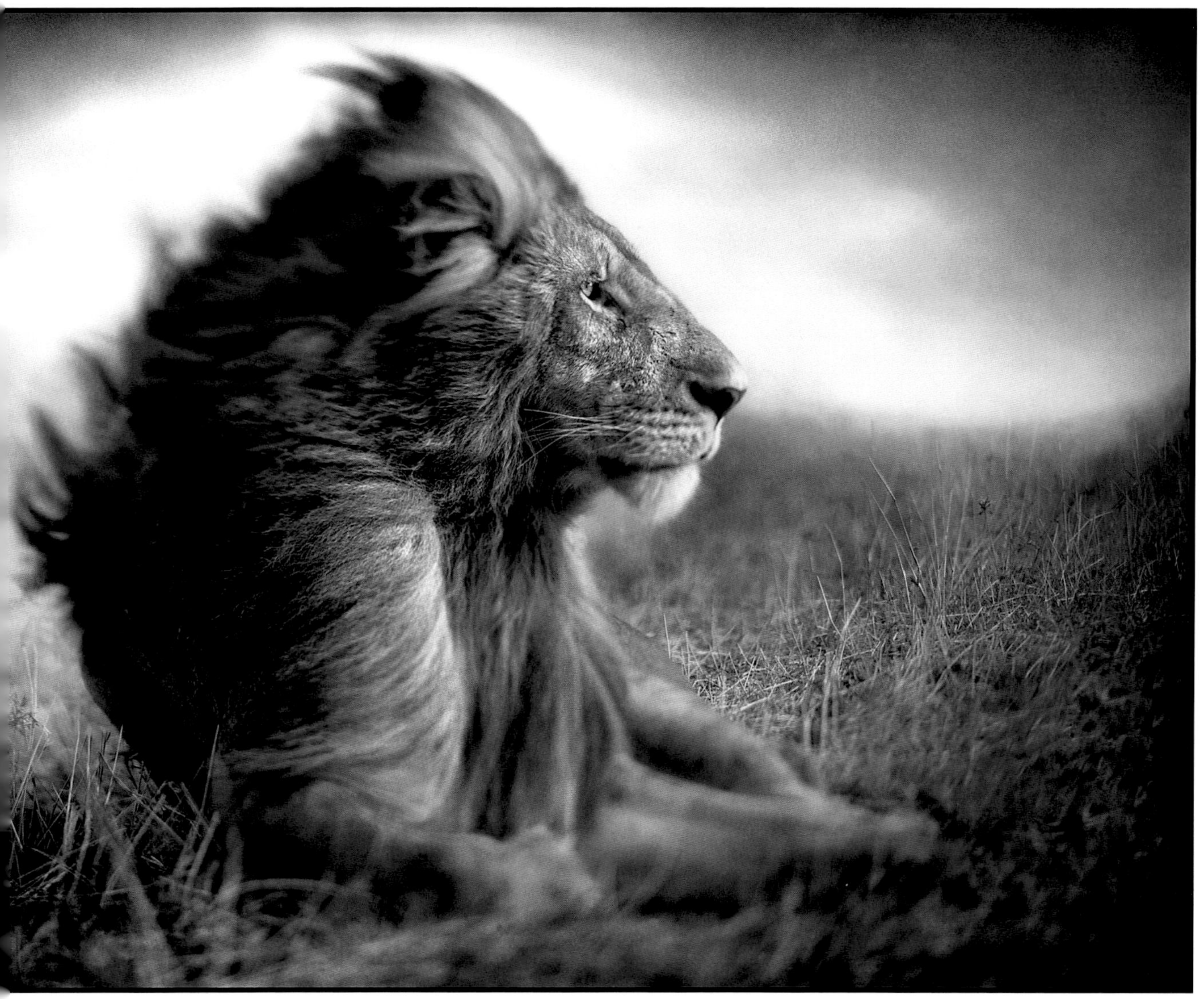

left——Jim Brandenburg: Arctic Wolf (WW133 White Wolf Leaping) | 1986
above——Nick Brandt: Lion Before Storm II, Sitting Profile, Maasai Marai | 2006

"My photos are idyllic and romantic; I portray an enchanted Africa. They are my elegy for a world that is tragically disappearing."

Brandt's unusual decision to photograph animals in black and white was taken to ensure visual impact—the absence of color results in a simplification of the graphic effect, focusing attention on essentials. But there was also another reason: black-and-white photographs create an impression of timelessness. For Brandt, they are already images of animals from a past era, of a vanishing world increasingly threatened by man: "My photos are idyllic and romantic; I portray an enchanted Africa. They are my elegy for a world that is tragically disappearing."

Andrew Zuckerman (b. 1977) has chosen a different path. He brings the animal kingdom and especially the world of birds into his (sometimes mobile) studio, where he photographs his subjects in the same way he photographs fashion accessories for magazines: puristically and against a white background (fig. p. 140). His photos have no narrative context and they are not "portraits" of animal personalities like those Nick Brandt photographs in the wild. Zuckerman's photos are minimalist in style and at the same time present a fireworks display of lively and bright colors whose intensity is increased by the brilliant white of the background. With his high-resolution digital technology and a studio setting, which is unusual for animal photos, Zuckerman is able to achieve a hyper-realistic reproduc-

tion of every feather. The variety and the brilliant colors of birdlife have never been shown in this way before. Zuckerman "transforms birds into mythical paradisiacal objects" (Massimo Vignelli).

In a way similar to that of Brandt with his use of black and white, Zuckerman also harks back to the art of the past. The reference points for his photos of birds are the watercolors of the celebrated American artist John James Audubon (1785–1851), who catalogued the birdlife of America in magnificent paintings during the first half of the 19th century. Unlike Zuckerman, however, Audubon drew the birds after he had shot them with a small-bore shotgun.

Animal photography can also take other routes, however, as the American artist William Wegman (b. 1943) shows with his Weimaraner dogs (right). The Polaroid company supplied him, like numerous other artists, with a 24 x 20 inch (60.9 x 50.8 cm) instant picture camera. His photos of his dogs Man Ray and Fay Ray—sometimes comical and sometimes Surrealistic—made him famous.

right——**William Wegman: Walker** | 1990

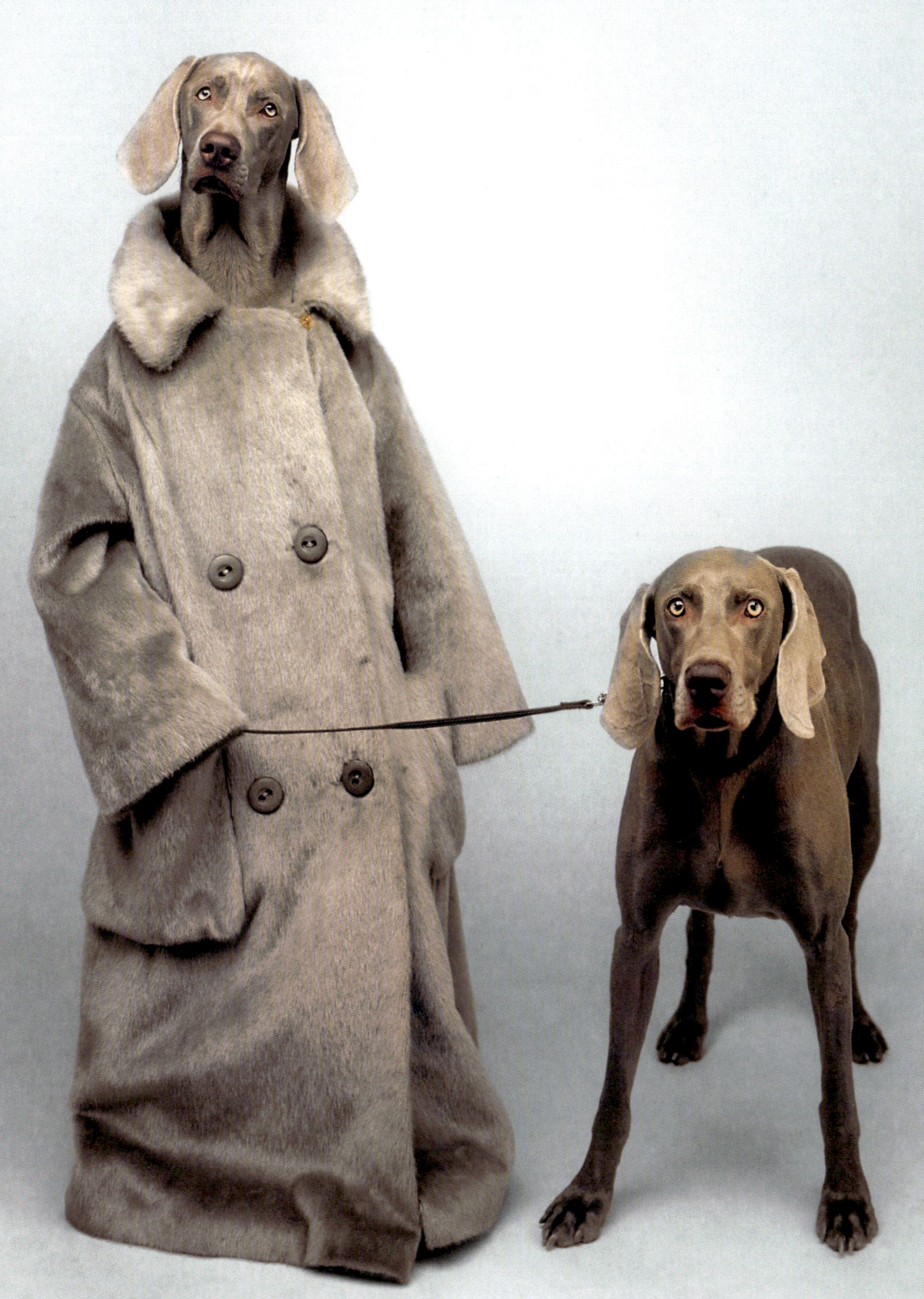

THE AMERICANS

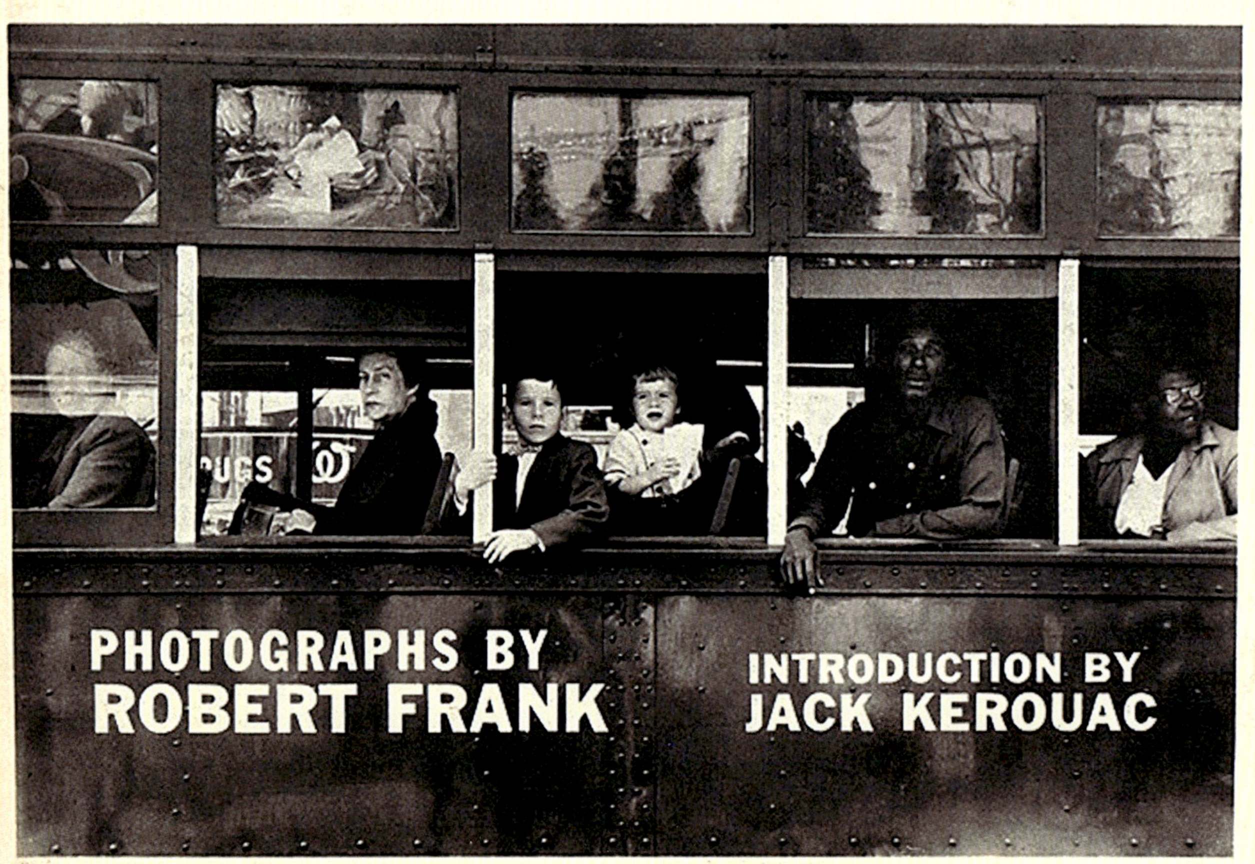

THE PHOTOBOOK

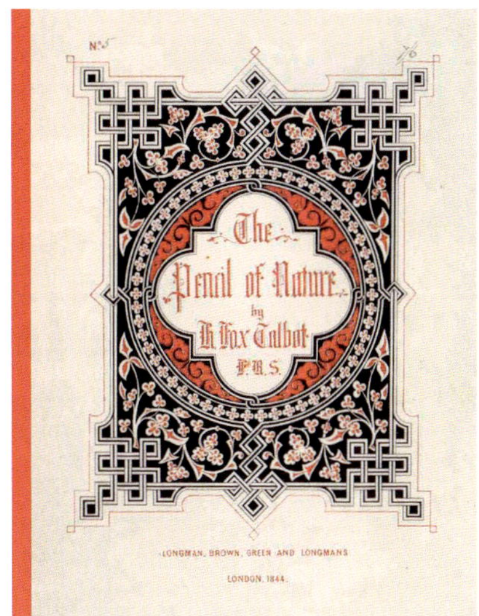

The wild euphoria that the daguerreotype created in 1839 made William Fox Talbot doubt that his own method had any chance of commercial success. But when he had recovered from his initial shock he turned his attention to perfecting his process and making it more widely known. He had the idea of publishing a book of his calotypes as a sort of selection of samples meant to demonstrate the advantages of his method; the very fact that reproduction was possible using his negative-positive process was one of the greatest advantages of all. *The Pencil of Nature*, published between 1844 and 1846, was the first photobook in history (right).

Talbot felt it was important to make it clear that no graphic artist had been involved in his pictures: "The pictures in this publication were achieved purely through the effects of light, without the help of an artist's pencil." Twenty-four calotypes that he had produced between 1841 and 1844 were used to illustrate the 80-page book. Talbot selected the photos in such a way that the reader was presented with the full range of the new medium's possibilities, and he wrote a commentary for each picture that was designed to explain it in more detail. He included calotypes of articles made of glass to show the effects of light and transparency; photograms of leaves; and, in order to encourage the use of the calotype as a reference source for artists, pictures of antique sculptures. He also showed a number of photographs of his home, Lacock Abbey, such as *The Ladder* (fig. p. 148), the only picture in the book on which people are to be seen. Talbot probably wanted to demonstrate that his method could also be easily used to produce portraits. The text accompanying this photo sounds strange today, but the explanation was clearly necessary at the time: "The production of a group photograph does not take any longer than that of an individual portrait, because the camera records all the figures at the same time, regardless of how many are involved."

Talbot produced about 200 copies of *The Pencil of Nature*, which was published between June 1844 and April 1846. But in spite of the numerous explanations and the pioneering photographs, the publication disappointed some: it took nearly two years to appear in full, and was extremely expensive. The journal *The Atheneum* concluded: "All this proves that the efforts required for the realization of a photograph are too great for it to be of any general use in the field of illustration."

left——**ROBERT FRANK: THE AMERICANS** | cover 1959
right——**WILLIAM FOX TALBOT: THE PENCIL OF NATURE** | 1844–46 | cover

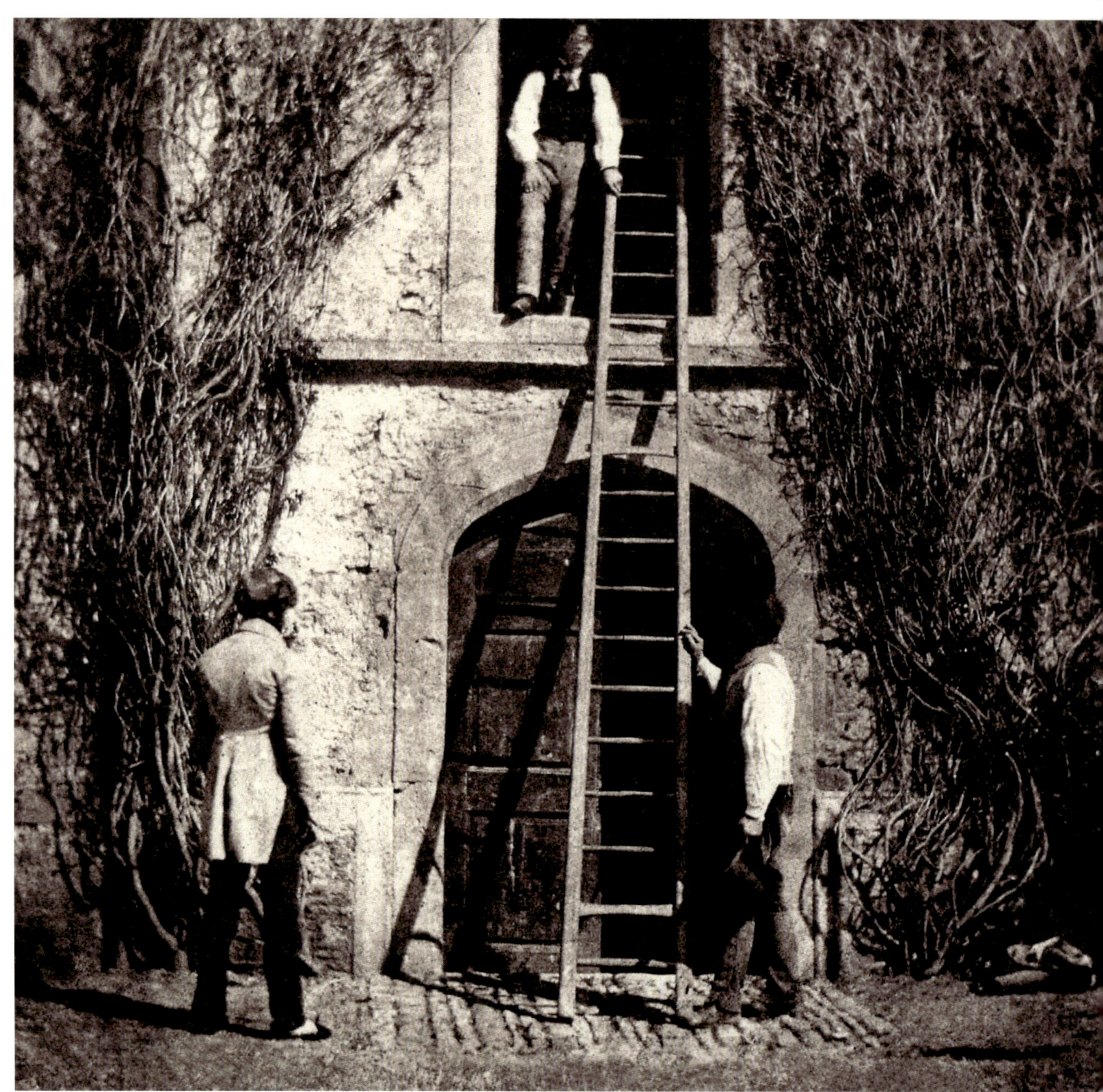

above——**WILLIAM FOX TALBOT: THE LADDER** | 1843 | Royal Photographic Society | London

right——**WILLIAM FOX TALBOT: COPYING THE CALOTYPES** | c. 1844

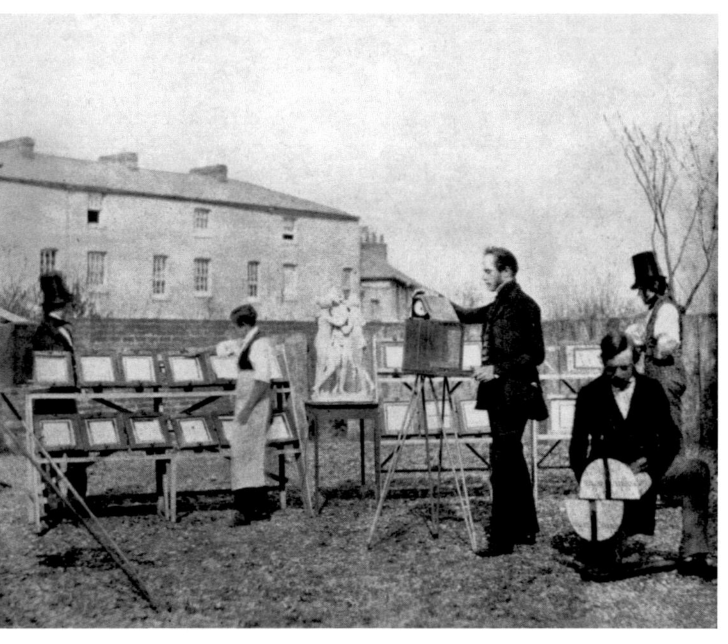

Nevertheless, photobooks became an important market for publishers and photographers, and before long two fundamentally different types could be distinguished. On the one hand there were books in which photographs were use to illustrate texts; and on the other there were the photobooks produced by photographers. The latter have always provided photographers with the opportunity to present a particular view of a subject or to develop and present their own concept regarding content and style, completely free from any restrictions on subject matter. Of the vast number of photobooks produced, three pioneering works will be presented here, works that set standards and had a lasting influence on photography.

Die Welt ist schön (The World is Beautiful) by the German photographer Albert Renger-Patzsch (1897–1966) was published in 1928 (fig. p. 150, left). Renger-Patzsch was an object photographer in Germany who adapted the ideas of straight photography to his own particular style. Kurt Tucholsky commented: "This purely visual pleasure in concrete objects, in material, in living things is [...] otherwise found only in American photographers." Like Edward Weston,

Renger-Patzsch photographed objects as they really were. However, unlike Weston he did not aim to evoke unrelated associations. Renger-Patzsch was interested only in the objects themselves and their unadorned photographic representation. In the 100 photos in his book he showed—apart from everyday objects (fig. p. 150, right)—landscapes, details from nature, and animals (fig. p. 151). The photographer himself wanted to call his book, logically enough, *Die Dinge* (Things); for sales purposes, however, the publishers decided on the more effective title *Die Welt ist schön*.

Renger-Patzsch's book and its approach became a milestone in photography. "Let us leave art to the artists and attempt, using the means of photography, to produce photographs that can survive by virtue of their photographic qualities" (Renger-Patzsch). With his rigorous way of concentrating on the shape of objects and their relationships to each other, he became a model not only for advertising photographers but above all for those who practiced photography as an art, especially Bernd and Hilla Becher and those who were influenced by them (see *Conceptual Photography*).

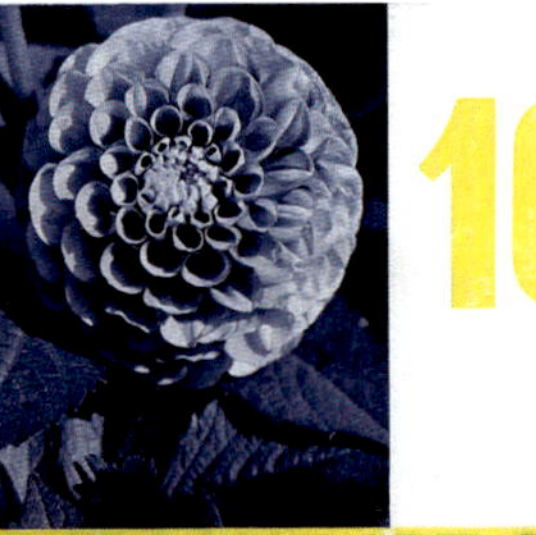
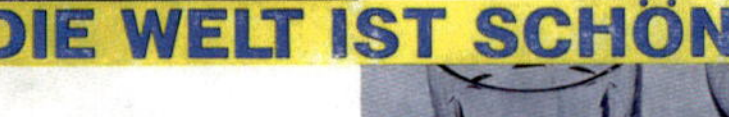

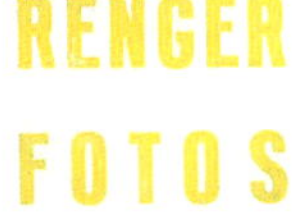

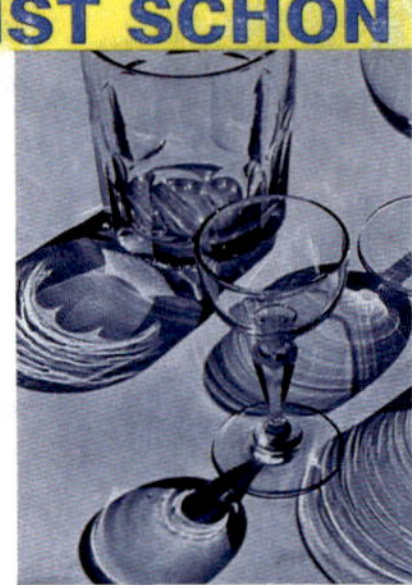
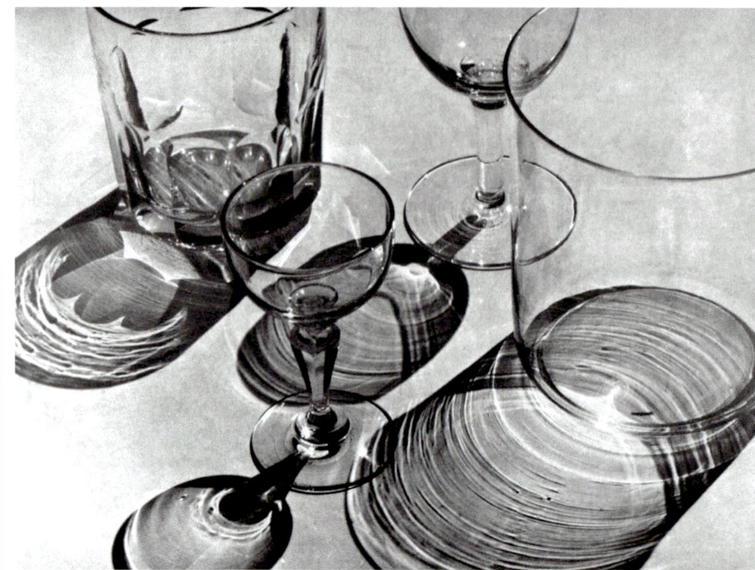

Four years after the publication of *Die Welt ist schön*, the extraordinary career of Henri Cartier-Bresson (1908–2004) began with his purchase of a Leica. "It became the extension of my eye and never left me. All day long I walked with my senses alert, scouring the streets for pictures in order to catch life in the act. What I wanted to do was to capture the essential elements in a picture." Few photographers became one with their cameras in the way that Cartier-Bresson did with his Leica. In his first exhibition in New York in 1932, his photos provoked surprise and wonder. Most visitors thought they were the results of pure chance. In an age in which photography still involved large-format cameras on tripods, most people could not imagine that photos like these were composed consciously and after a great deal of thought. A photo like *Place de L'Europe* (fig. p. 153) of 1932 was completely new and demonstrated at the same time Cartier-Bresson's motto that a photograph is created by the "simultaneous instant recognition of the inner significance of an event on the one hand, and, on the other, the strict and uncompromising

creation of a world of shapes that can be perceived visually and can express that event." Snapshots were already commonplace, but what was completely new was that a photographer should, for example, spot the man leaping and the ballet poster in the background and the bent steel pipe—and then release the shutter at the very same moment. Cartier-Bresson presented this and 125 further photographs he had taken since 1932 in his photobook *Images à la Sauvette*, which was published in 1952 (fig. p. 152, left and right). It was not only a summary of his work as a photo reporter to date, but also a programmatic statement of his way of taking photos. The English title, *The Decisive Moment*, describes even more accurately the nature of photography à la Cartier-Bresson. His approach was to take his photos as unobtrusively as possible, without flash, and to record a story with as few shots as possible, ideally—but very rarely—with a single photograph. He photographed street scenes all around the world, and also famous personalities such as Jean-Paul Sartre and Henri Matisse, who drew the cover picture for *Images à la Sauvette*

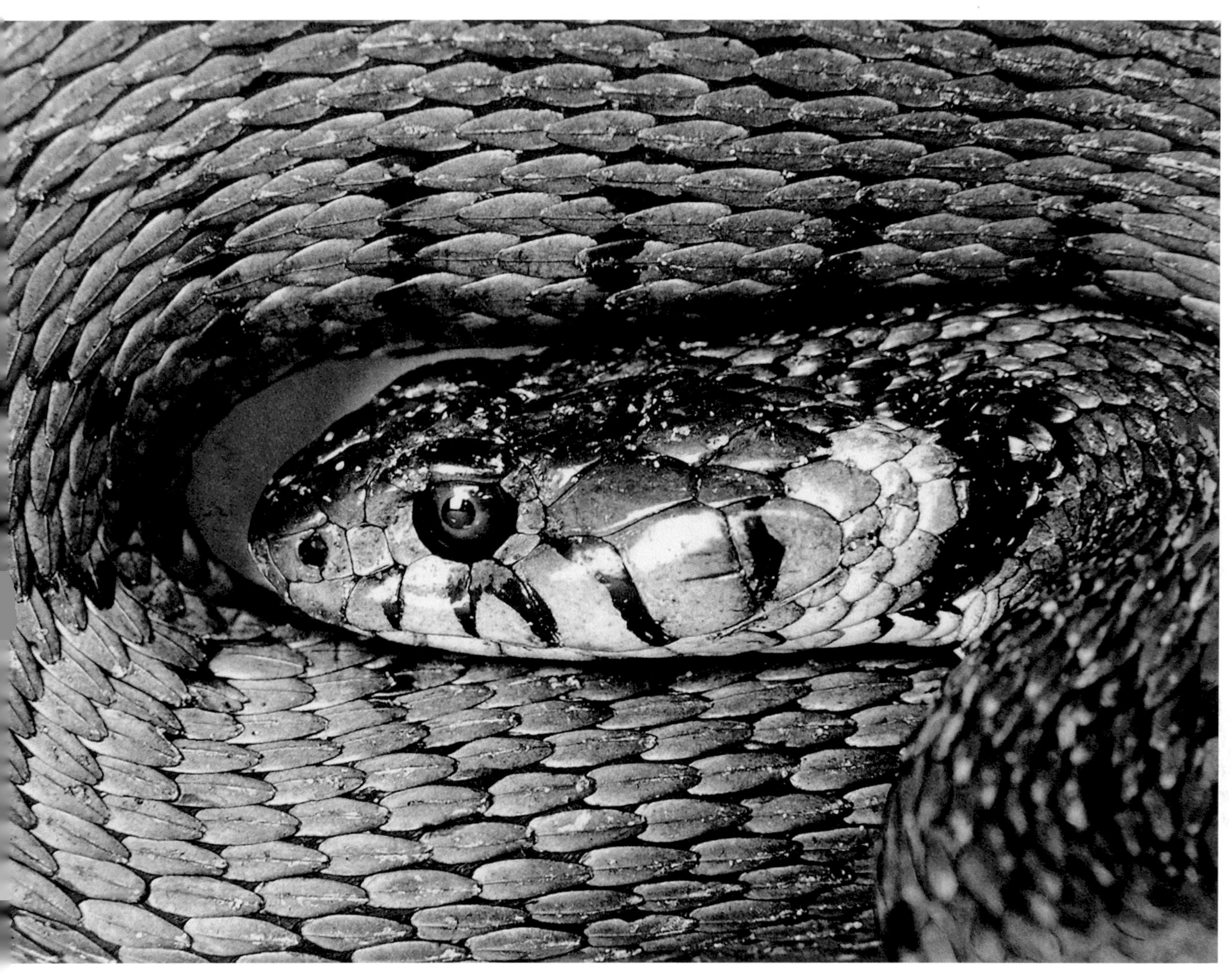

far left——**ALBERT RENGER-PATZSCH: DIE WELT IST SCHÖN** | 1928 | cover
left——**ALBERT RENGER-PATZSCH: GLASSES** | 1927 | Metropolitan
Museum of Art | New York
above——**ALBERT RENGER-PATZSCH: SNAKE** | 1927 | Metropolitan Museum
of Art | New York

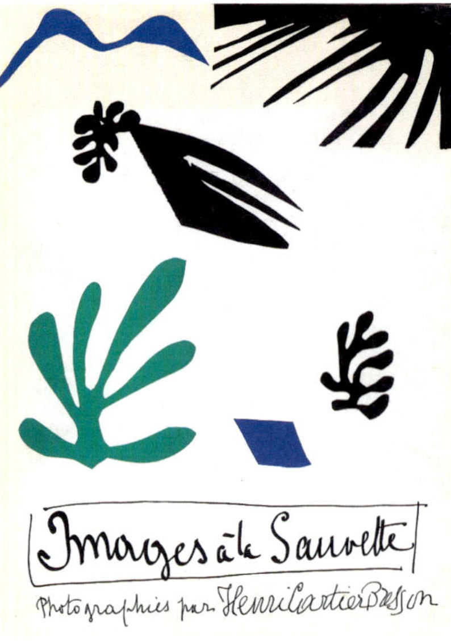

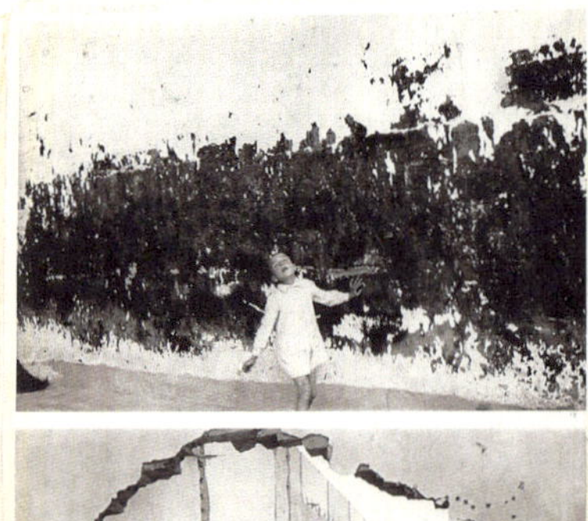

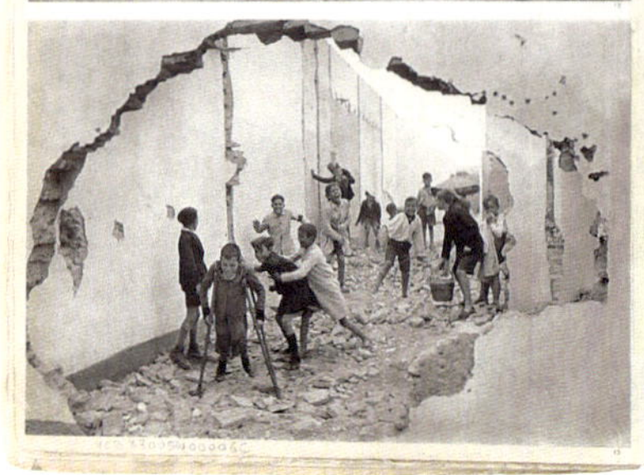

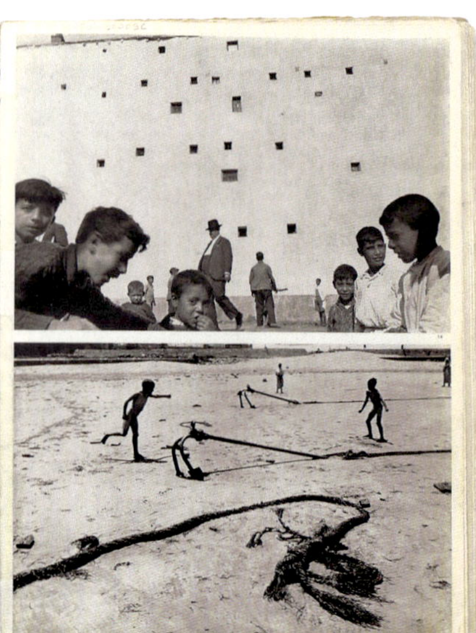

(above, left). His type of photography, which he determined more precisely still with the founding of the Magnum agency in 1947, became the yardstick for many and left its mark on photography for many decades.

Unlike Cartier-Bresson, Robert Frank (b. 1924) did not seek the "decisive moment," but photographed moments that were apparently fluid and "unresolved." Arranged as a book, however, they acquired a cumulative intensity that Cartier-Bresson could not achieve with single pictures.

"Robert Frank, Swiss, unobtrusive, nice, with that little camera that he raises and snaps with one hand he sucked a sad poem right out of America and onto film, taking rank among the tragic poets of the world." This sentence can be found in Jack Kerouac's foreword to *The Americans*, which was published in the United States in 1959 (fig. p. 146). Robert Frank arrived in America in 1947 and worked initially as a fashion photographer, before being awarded a Guggenheim Scholarship in 1955. He used it to travel throughout the United States in order to create a "visual study of a society." The result was a shock for Americans and a revelation for the photographer himself. For Americans, the 1950s were a time of

change and economic prosperity. But this was also an era of racial segregation and other social problems. Although Frank did not set out to produce political photos, the book as a whole shows an aspect of the country that Americans did not want to believe was true. Of the 27,000 photos taken during the trip, Frank laboriously compiled 83 to create a series unlike anything previously seen. He did not photograph "decisive moments," but seemingly random shots of jukeboxes, filling stations, people engaged in monotonous work, people who appeared to be lonely in the crowd (figs. pp. 154, 155). The photos are not beautiful in the classical sense. They are rough and coarse-grained, sometimes out of focus, sad, and in their own way poetic. Frank consciously photographed in black and white: "Black and white are the

above left —— HENRI CARTIER-BRESSON: IMAGES À LA SAUVETTE | 1952
cover
above right—— HENRI CARTIER-BRESSON: IMAGES À LA SAUVETTE
pp. 14–15
right——HENRI CARTIER-BRESSON: PLACE DE L'EUROPE, PARIS | 1932

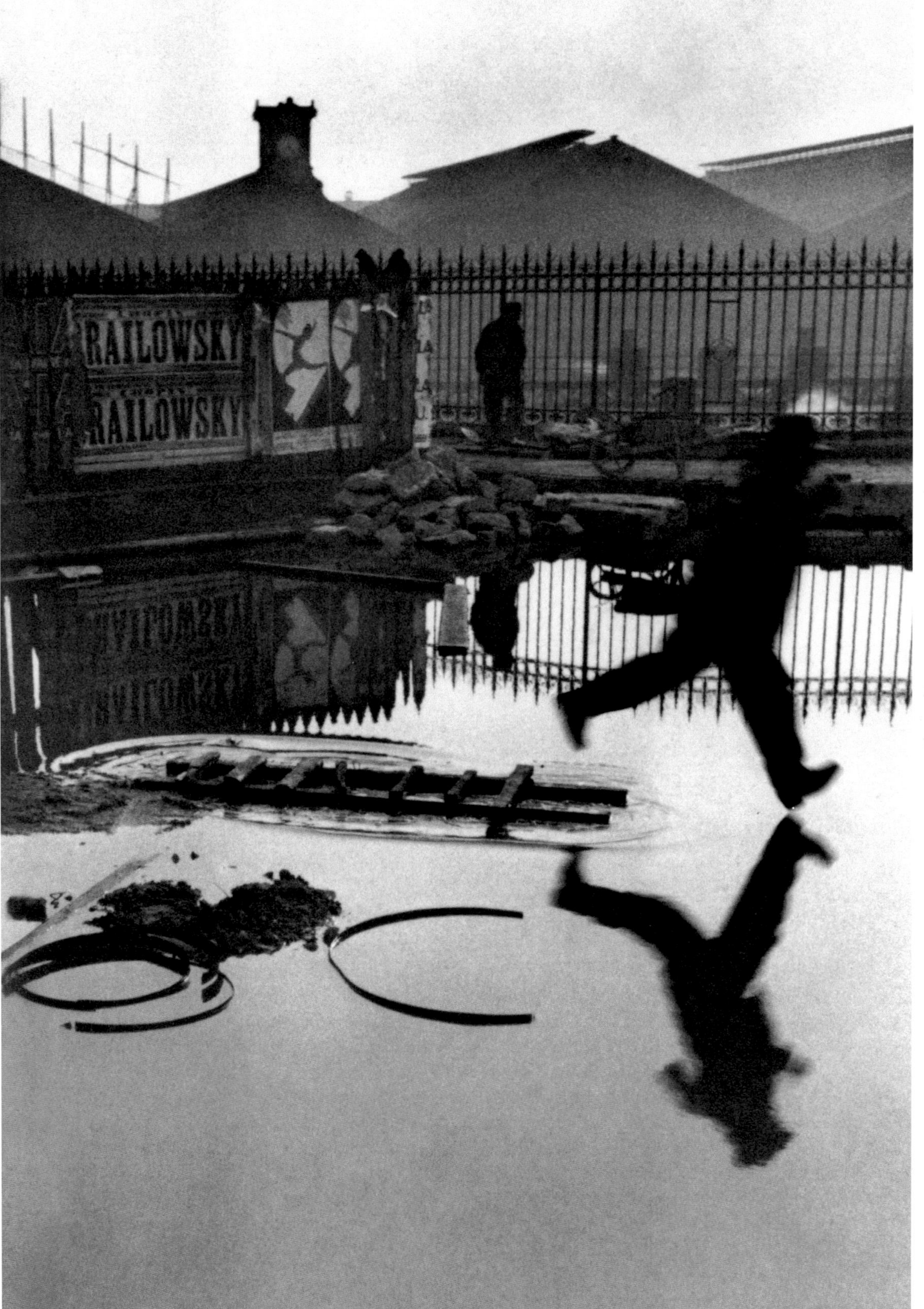
RAILOWSKY
RAILOWSKY

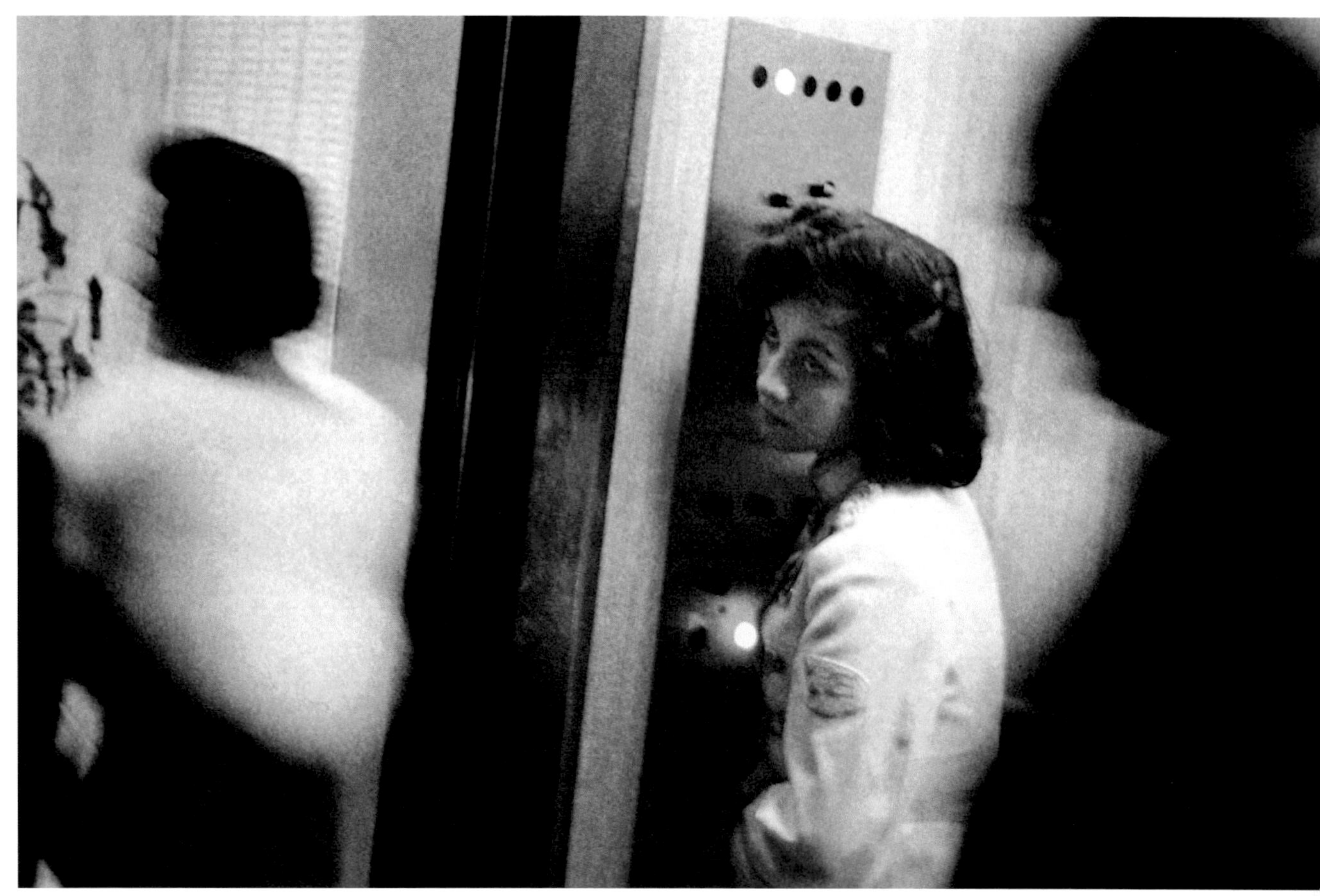

colors of photography. For me they symbolize the opposites hope and despair to which mankind is always subject." This contrast determines the overall mood of the book, in which despair is the dominant mood. The book was an alarm call for the younger generation of photographers who had grown up with the elegant and aesthetically subtle pictures of Cartier-Bresson and Ansel Adams.

The book was initially published in France because American publishers refused to present such a negative view of their country. "We all knew that these things existed, but the way they had been photographed made them harder to accept" (John Szarkowski). But it was not only his subject matter; it was also the way he photographed. Frank showed photographers a new approach. This is true of individual photos but especially to the photobook, in which the totality of the photos adds up to more than the sum of its parts.

Through their photobooks, Frank and Cartier-Bresson became the cornerstones of modern photography. It was between these two cornerstones that photographers developed during the 1960s and 1970s. Today, when television has become the dominant medium and very few magazines provide a suitable platform for an extensive series of photographs, photobooks offer photographers virtually the only opportunity of publishing comprehensive reportage, of examining subjects precisely and in depth. Although the Internet also provides a platform for photographers, it cannot be compared with the intensity, power, and concentration of a book.

1974–today Damon Winter   **1977–today Andrew Zuckerman**

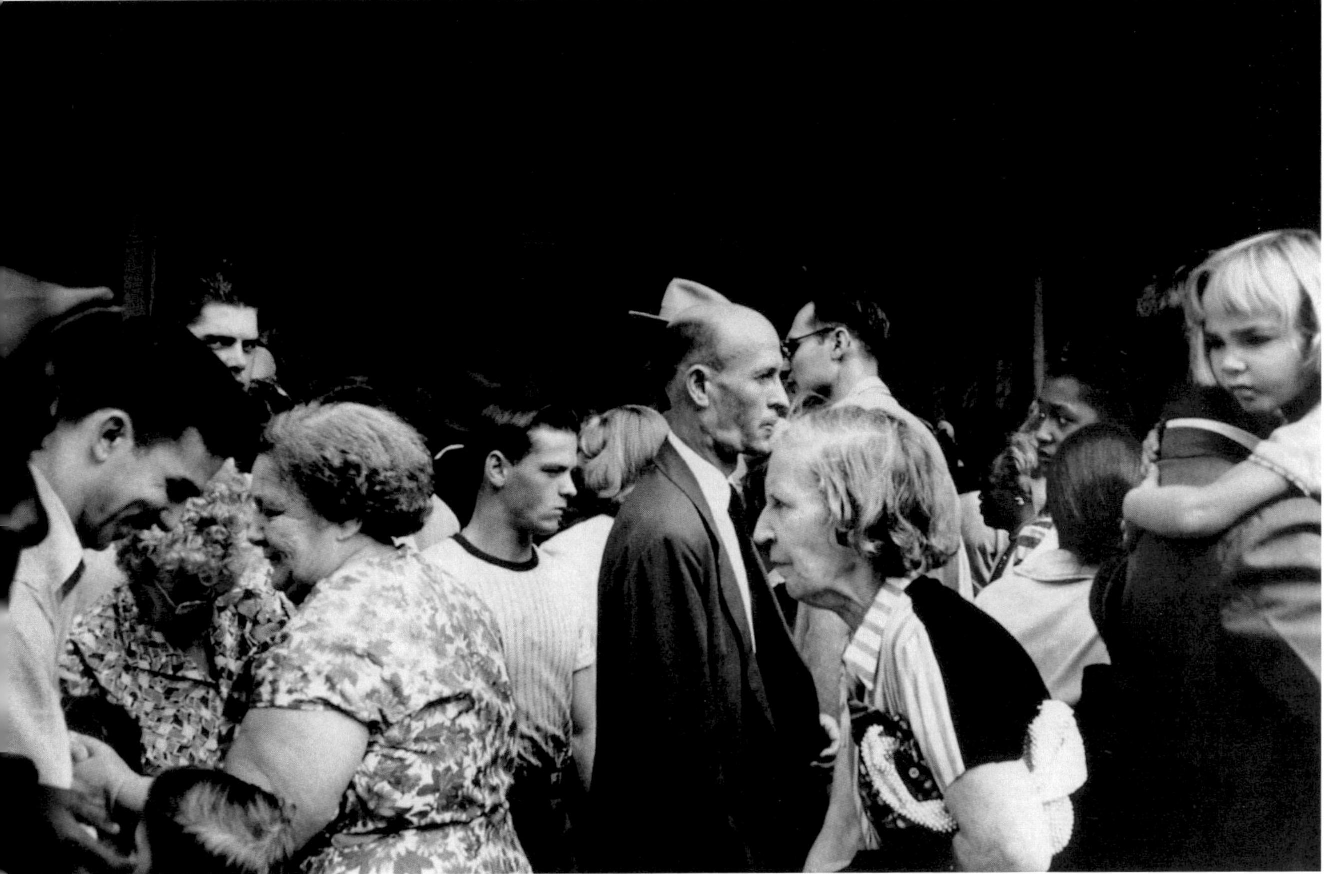

left——ROBERT FRANK: ELEVATOR – MIAMI BEACH | 1955
from *The Americans*
above——ROBERT FRANK: CANAL STREET – NEW ORLEANS | 1955
from *The Americans*

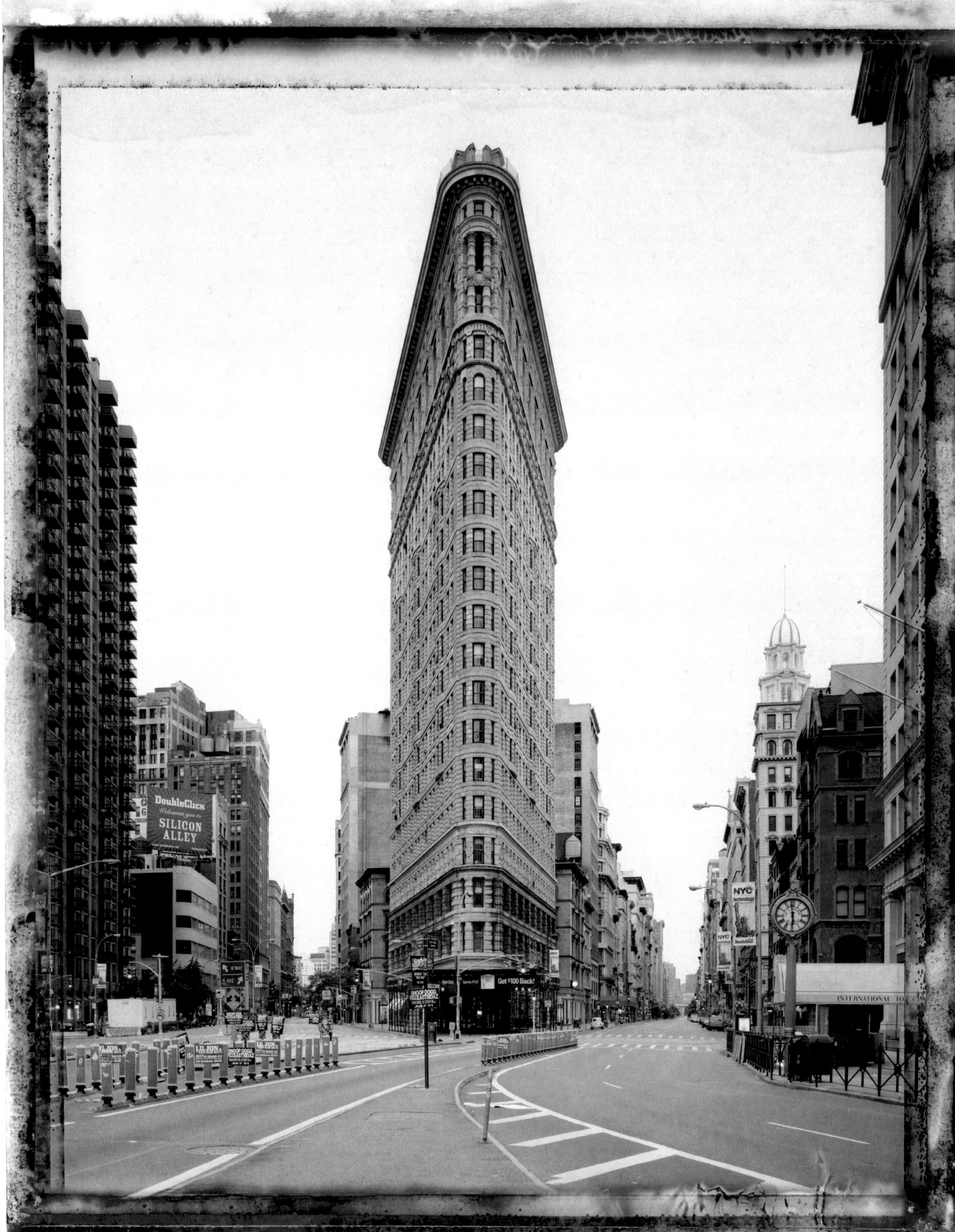
DoubleClick
Welcomes you to
SILICON
ALLEY
Get $100 Back!
SNOOP DOGG
NYC
technology
INTERNATIONAL

INSTANT PHOTOGRAPHY

"To shake or not to shake?" That was the question that always provoked keen debate among photographers using instant film. Immediately after the little picture was ejected by the legendary SX-70 or other instant camera, it was shaken, rubbed, or left in peace until it developed in full glory before the photographer's eyes. In fact, it made no difference as regards the development of the photo whether it was shaken or not. Be that as it may, 2008 marked the end of the era of Polaroid photography when the last production site closed down—for the time being. It had begun in 1947, when the American inventor Edwin Land (1909–1991) dreamed up a process that combined negative and positive as well as developer and fixer. The instant photo, or Polaroid, as it is usually called today, was born. After exposure in a specially created camera, the negative and positive were drawn through two rolls that spread both developer and fixer evenly between the layers of film. The development process began and after a few minutes the negative and positive could be separated—and the photo was ready.

The instant photo was a revolution. Never before had it been possible to develop and see a photo so quickly. Edwin Land had liberated the photographer from the technicalities of the production process. He wanted to make available a method that required no special knowledge of photographic techniques: "The aesthetic goal of instant photography is to provide all those who have an artistic interest in the world with a new means of expression."

In 1949, Land engaged the famous landscape photographer Ansel Adams (1902–1984) as technical and artistic advisor; his job was to suggest improvements from a photographer's point of view (fig. p. 159). As a result of this partnership, Land developed a clever marketing strategy: he provided well-known photographers and artists with cameras and films, and they, in return, provided him with a range of pictures. He thus involved creative people in the development process and profited both from their experience and their fame. In addition to artworks that were unique items, the instant photo offered photographers the possibility of checking composition and exposure before taking photos using a more traditional camera. Ample use was made of this advantage, especially in architecture, landscape, and above all number studio photography. Apart from the "artistic interest in the world," this use was important for professional photography,

left—**Christopher Thomas, Flatiron Building** | 2001

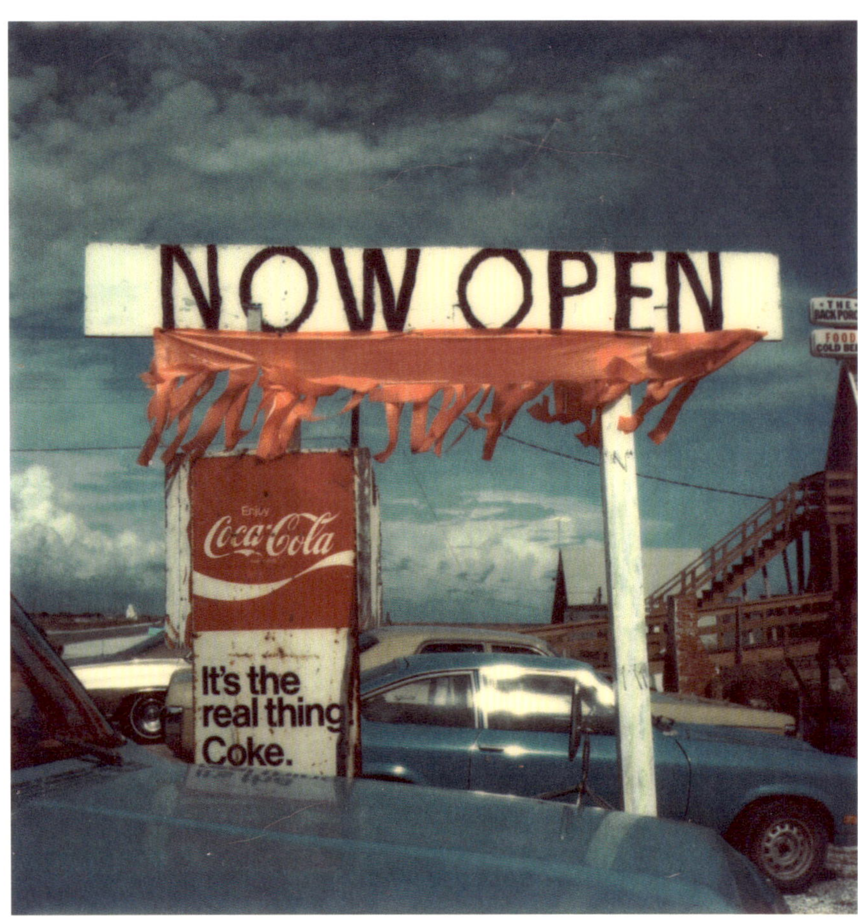

especially once colored Polaroids appeared on the market in 1963.

The Polaroid BigShot was launched in 1971. It cost less than 20 dollars and in its way made art history because it became the preferred portrait camera of Andy Warhol (1928–1987), who used instant photos as references for his portraits of both the famous (fig. p. 160) and the unknown, which he produced as silkscreen prints (fig. p. 161). With the Polaroid differences disappeared, because Warhol photographed everyone the same way—in fact, with this camera it was not possible to do anything else. They all appeared in the same colors and they all had the same white frame. With his Polaroid portraits, Warhol blurred the borders between fame and obscurity,

between photography and art, and between art and commerce.

In 1972, an "integrated" film appeared through which Polaroid finally became a cult brand. This was the famous SX-70 film, with its associated folding

left——**Walker Evans: Roadside Advertisement for the Back Porch Restaurant, Destin, Florida** | 1974 | Metropolitan Museum of Art | New York

right——**Ansel Adams: Yosemite** | 1955 | PolaPan 200 Land Film Type 42 | Ansel Adams Publishing Rights Trust

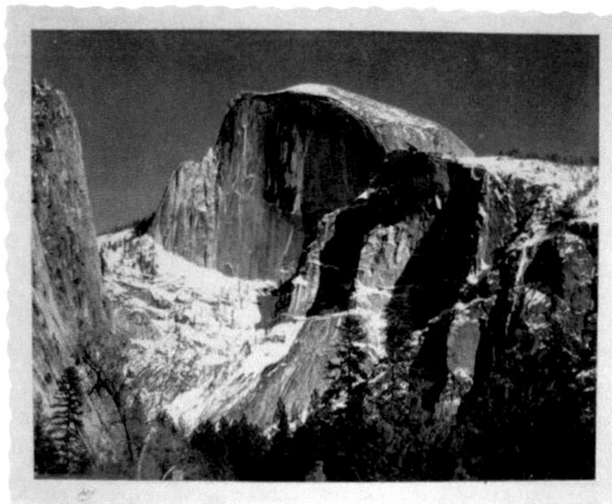

"Nobody should touch Polaroid until he's over sixty."

camera. Now the picture no longer had to be separated; there was no waste and no wet chemistry, and the picture even came complete with a frame. As Land had done at the beginning, so now he also made the "integrated film" and the SX-70 cameras available to artists and photographers. One of the first was the 70-year-old photographer Walker Evans, by this time a legend, who was very enthusiastic about the new technique. Polaroid made available an unlimited number of films and from then until 1974 Evans created his last body of work consisting of over 2,500 Polaroids. The camera seemed to be ideally suited to Evans's precise but poetic view of the world. With this technique he returned to the subjects he had studied at the beginning of his career: signs, ad, and posters, which he interpreted as independent artworks. He saw in these symbols the essence of the modern world (fig. left). Because of the concentration solely on the moment of releasing the shutter, and because of the uncorrectability of the result, instant photography faced him with a new challenge that he felt he was able to meet only with the experi-

ence of age: "Nobody should touch Polaroid until he's over sixty." It is impossible to say nowadays whether he was entirely serious.

Before the production of Polaroids stopped in 2008, the German photographer Christopher Thomas (b. 1961) was able to secure sufficient material to create a photobook focusing on Venice. A dying technique for a portrait of a sinking city—there has never been a more appropriate combination of subject and photo material (fig. pp. 162–163).

Today, in the age of digital photography, traditional large-format photography as practiced by Thomas is surrounded by an aura of the unusual, sometimes with a hint of the archaic. A photographer with a black cloth over his head recalls the very origins of photography. When this is paired with pictures of a city that has changed very little in its outer structures across the years, the viewer has the impression of being transported back to another century. Thomas used a Type 55 film that made it possible to produce not only the usual positive but also a normal negative that can then be reproduced.

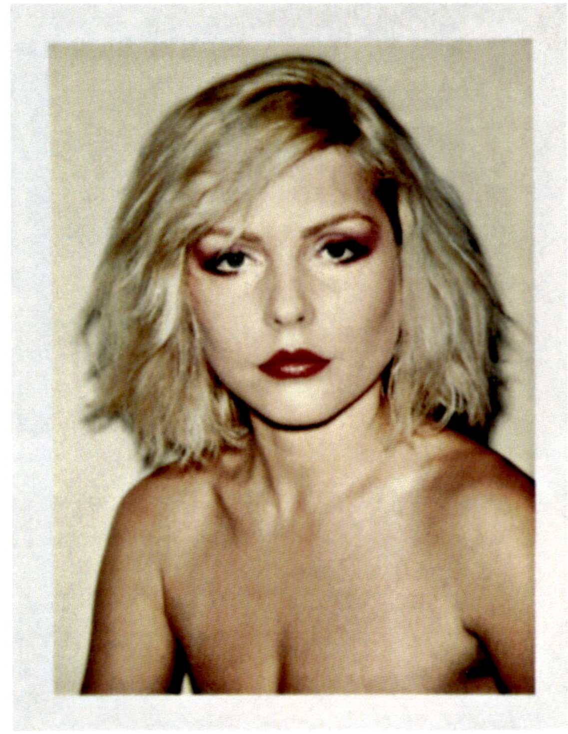

Thomas, who had already photographed Munich and New York (fig. p. 156) using Polaroid, attempted to capture the unique atmosphere of Venice, which is usually overcrowded with tourists, by taking his photos in the early morning hours or at night, when the scenes were free of the masses of people who usually impede the view of the architecture and ruin the romantic atmosphere. "It is an attempt to recapture the tranquillity of Venice during the 19th century and to extract the city from its mass tourism" (Christopher Thomas).

Instant photography is not finished yet. The sophistication and slickness of today's digital photography have provoked a photographic counter-movement. Many photographers are attempting to revive old techniques—or develop computer programmes—in order to simulate instant photography and give their photographs a nostalgic air. Following the end of Polaroid production, several like-minded enthusiasts tried to revive instant photography under the name of "The Impossible Project," using an old production machine to manufacture instant films again.

left——**ANDY WARHOL: DEBBIE HARRY** | 1980 | Polacolor Type 108 Polaroid | 10.8 x 8.9 cm

right——**ANDY WARHOL: DEBBIE HARRY** | silkscreen print

following pages——**CHRISTOPHER THOMAS: CAMPO DELLA PESCHIERA I**

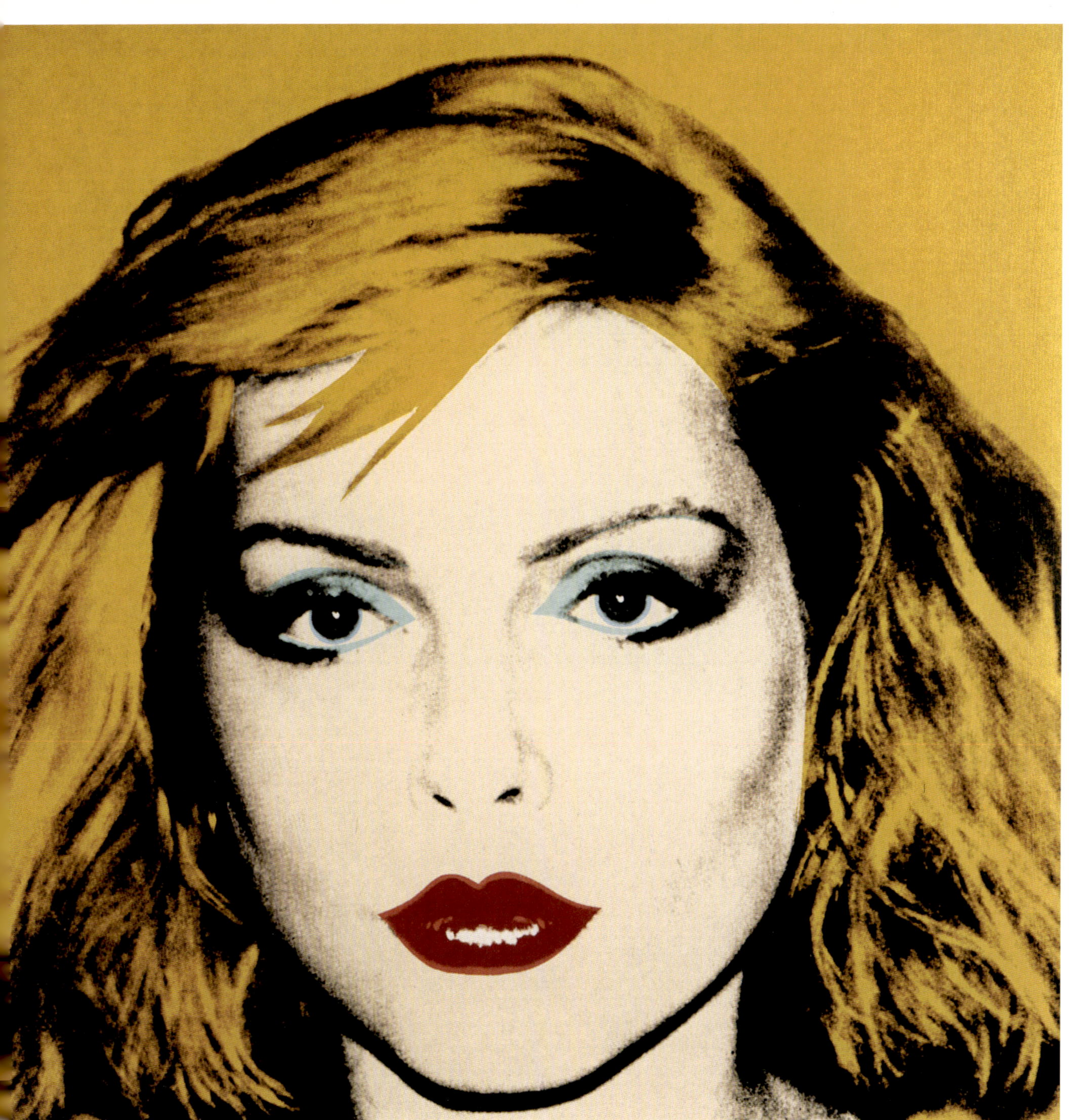

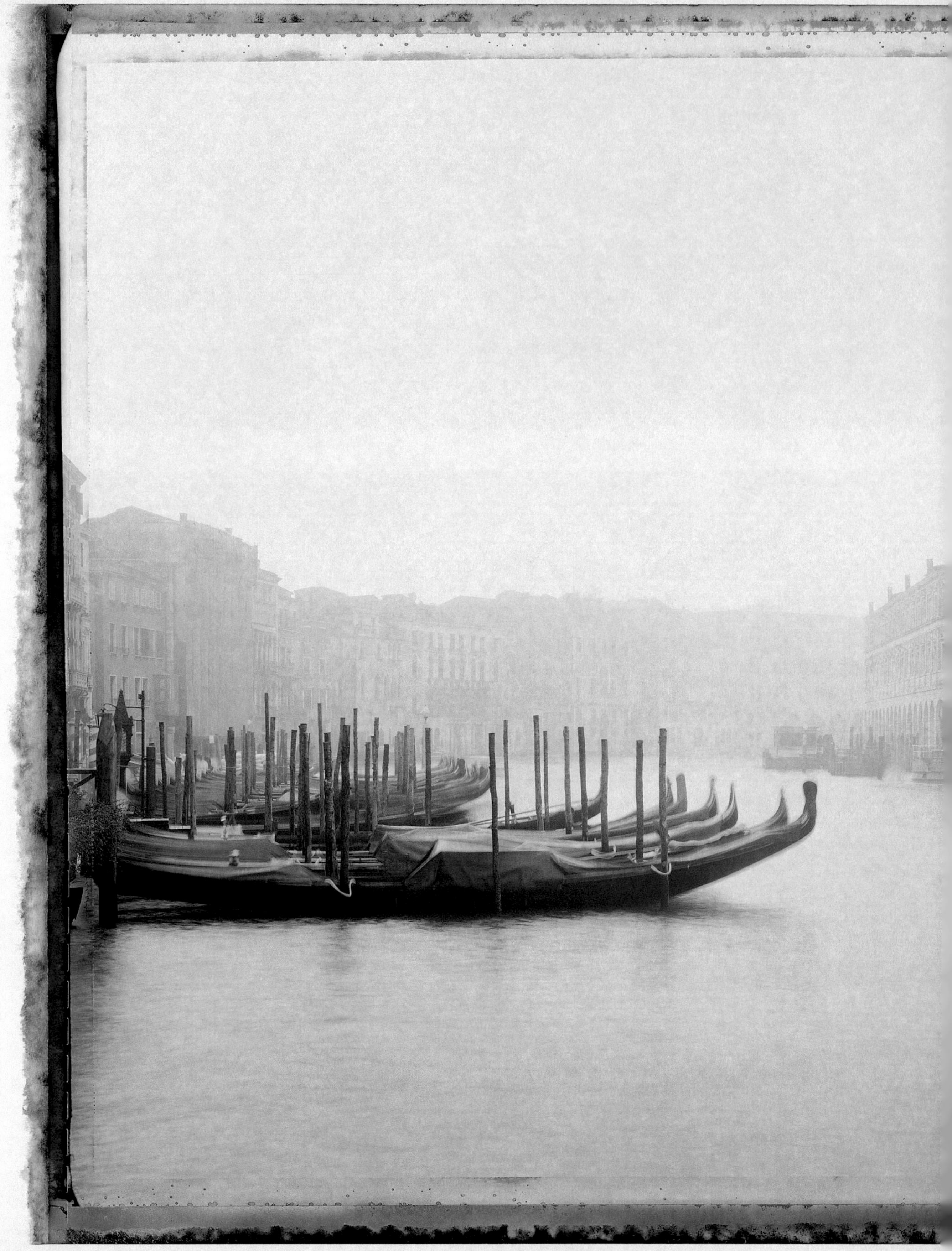

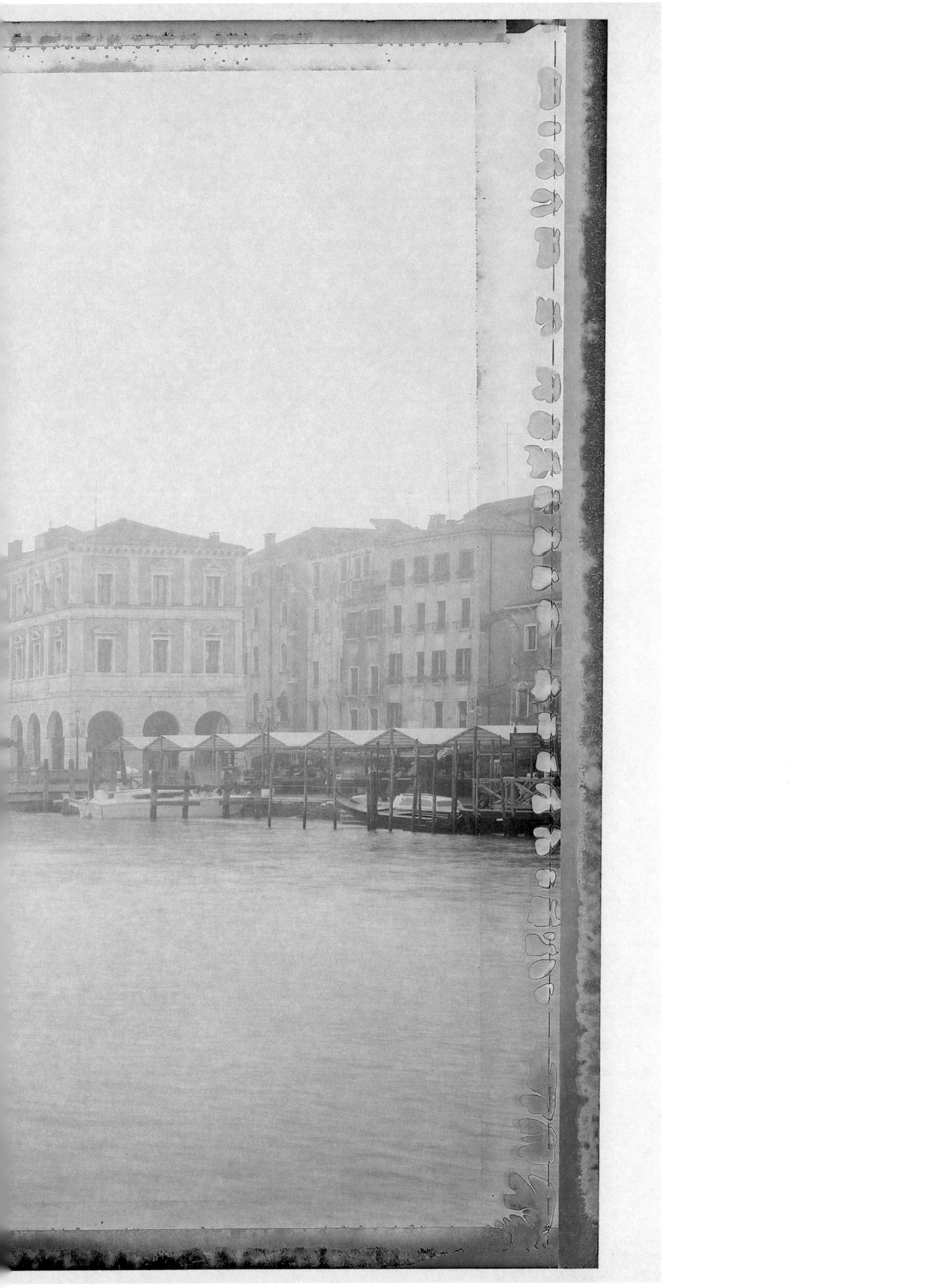

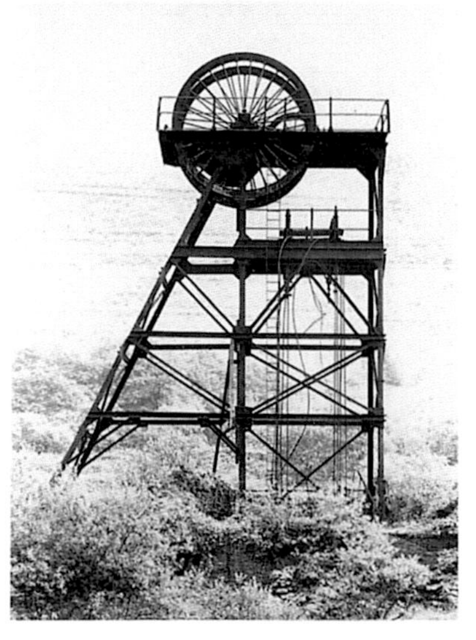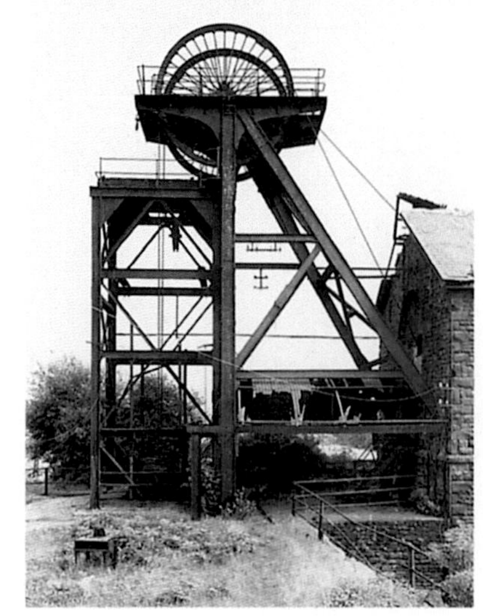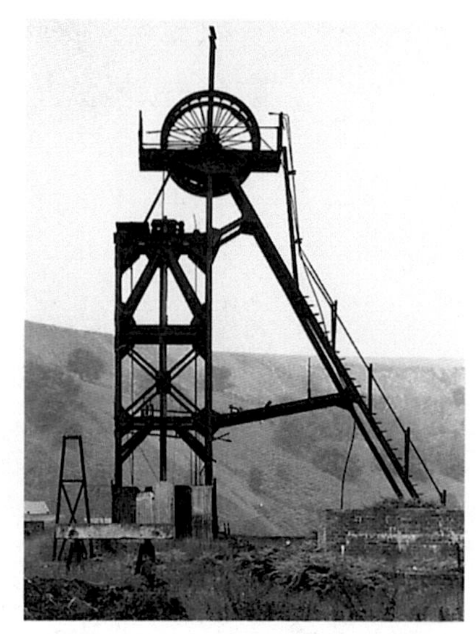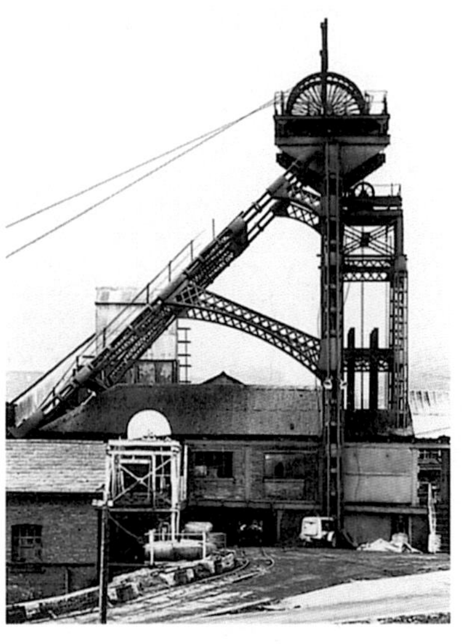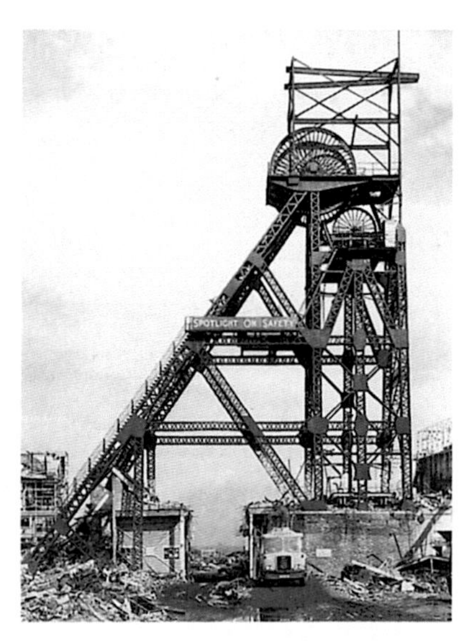
SPOTLIGHT ON SAFETY
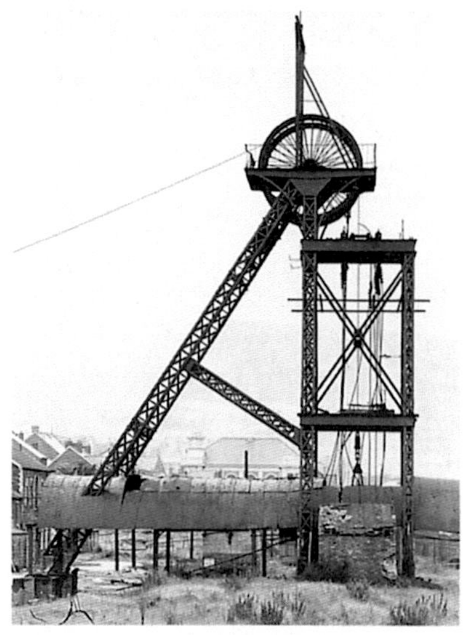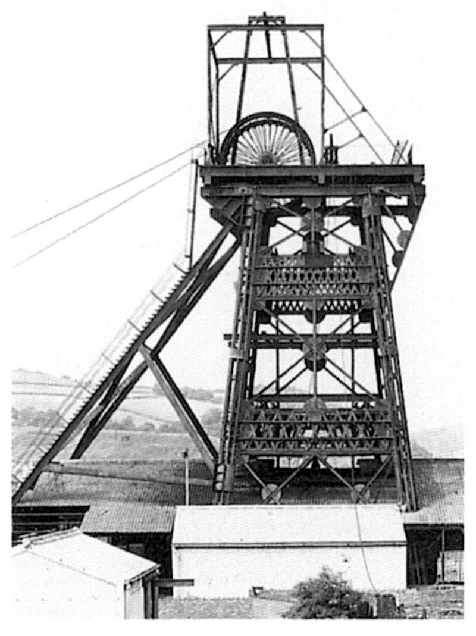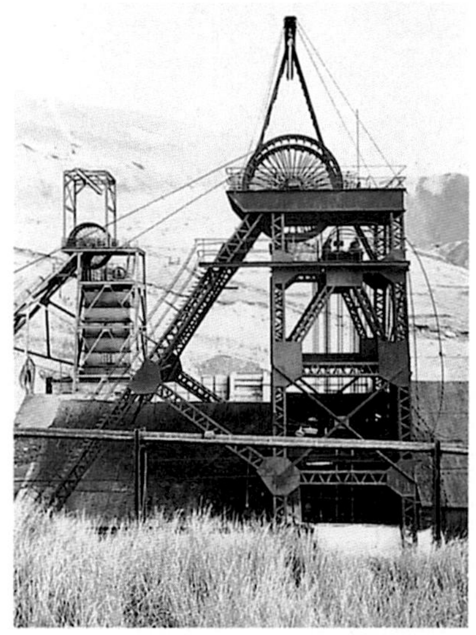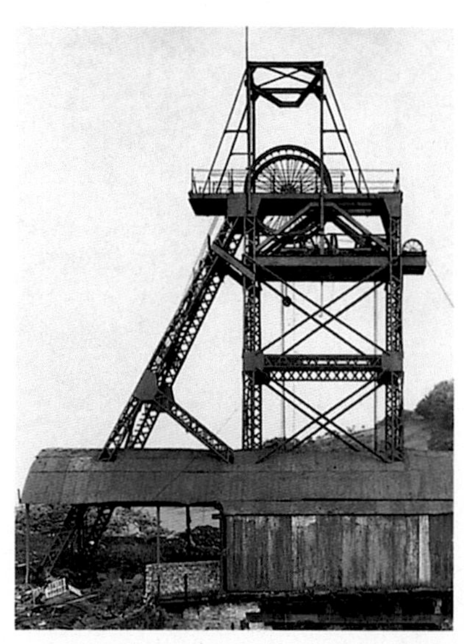

CONCEPTUAL PHOTOGRAPHY

"I am often asked how I had the idea of creating this work. Seeing, observing, and thinking, and the question is answered. [...] We find writings and books with illustrations from all periods in the past, but photography has given us new opportunities and tasks different from those of painting." The German photographer August Sander (1876–1964) wrote these lines in November 1927 about an exhibition of his wide-ranging photographic work *Menschen des 20. Jahrhunderts* (People of the Twentieth Century). In 1929 his book *Das Antlitz der Zeit* (The Face of the Times) appeared, the first part of his planned project. Sander's aim was no less than to produce an "inventory of the German people" at the beginning of the new century. The project, designed in its entirety to extend through 45 portfolios of 12 photographs each, was to assemble "all occupations, all classes and estates" in a typology, and to present a stock-taking of the social reality of the population. Sander portrayed people from all social classes, occupations, and population groups. He was less interested in the individual than in his or her membership of a group. Kurt Tucholsky described the task as follows in 1930: "Sander did not take photographs of individuals, but of types. People who represented their class, their status, their caste to such an extent that the individual could be taken as representing the whole." From the industrial tycoon to the junior manager and the match-seller, from the hack lawyer to the notary, from boxers (fig. p. 166) and cyclists to National Socialists and persecuted Jews, Sander photographed all possible representatives of the German social classes, which he intended to bring together as his life's work. He employed a precise photographic language, or as he expressed it, "precise photography." He mostly photographed people in their own environment, with the available light, and as a full-length portrait. He aimed to make his protagonists look as natural as possible: "Nothing seemed to me to be more appropriate than to present a contemporary picture of our age through photography that is absolutely true to nature." Sander's diverse, in many respects problematic, image of the Germans did not suit the National Socialists and their distorted racial ideas, and in 1936 they destroyed all the printing plates and the remaining copies of *Antlitz der Zeit*. Sander refused to be deterred and continued to take photos. However, he failed to complete the monumental and encyclopedic work in its entirety.

left——**Bernd and Hilla Becher: Shaft Towers, Germany** | 1971–1991
Museum of Modern Art | New York

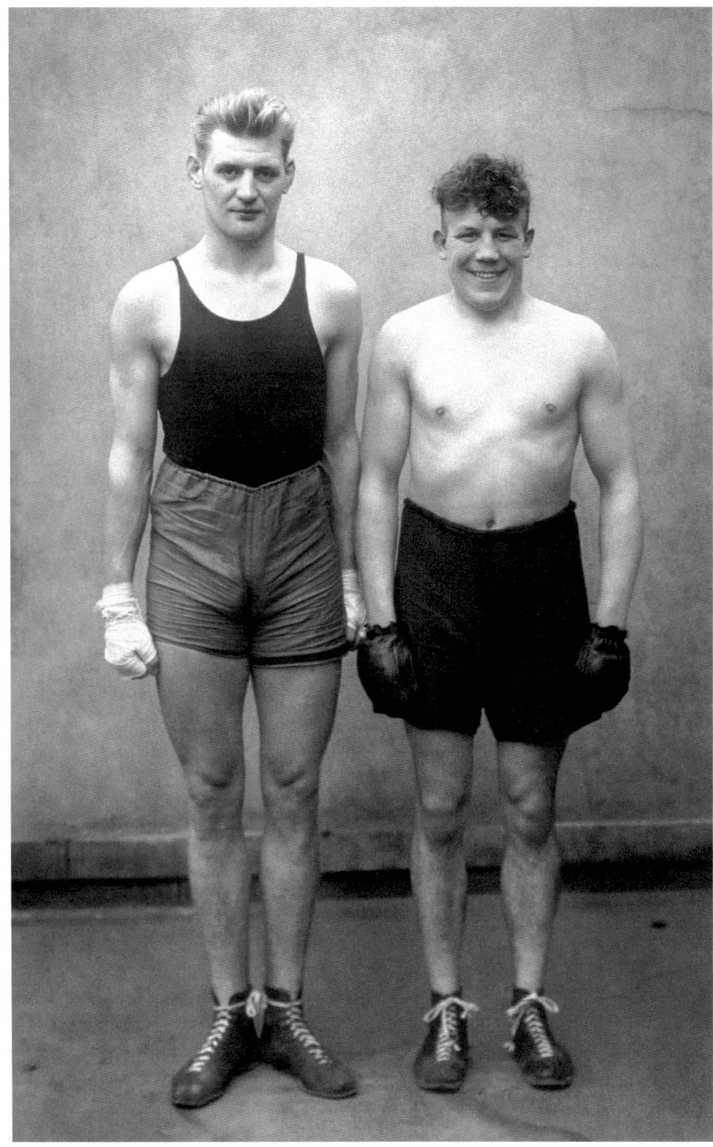

With his photographs, and especially with the idea behind it of a photographic archive in the form of a survey, Sander anticipated conceptual photography, an art movement that became an important aspect of art photography during the 1970s, notably through the work of Bernd (1931–2007), and Hilla (b. 1934) Becher. It is still important today.

The essence of conceptual photography is the series: in a series, the individual picture (which generally resembles the others formally) loses its significance and becomes part of a whole, subsumed under the linking idea, the concept. Just as Sander's intention was to document "all occupations, all classes and estates," so the Bechers' aim was to record industrial architecture (figs. p. 164). They documented the vanishing world of the coal mines in the Ruhr district and later other traditional locations of heavy industry in the United Kingdom and the United States.

"The essence of conceptual photography is the series: in a series, the individual picture loses its significance and becomes part of a whole, subsumed under the linking idea, the concept."

The Bechers developed a documentary style in which they strove for the greatest possible objectivity, so that it is not easy to discern a specific "style": "The lack of style became the characteristic of their style" (Peter Sager). They always took their photographs in the same way: with a large-format camera; diffuse light, which provides an even illumination of objects; no distorting perspectives; a low horizon; no people; and, above all, in black and white, in order to avoid drawing attention away from the form. "There are plenty of objects where the color is not only not important, but actually detracts from the form" (Hilla Becher). Form is the essential element in their pictures. Their standardized mode of representation, made as objective as possible, allows the buildings and structures to be closely compared. The Bechers recognized certain typologies, which are constantly repeated. They arranged the photographs in groups of nine to thirty pictures to form tableaux whose arrangement gains its fascination from the rhythm of the architecture. Through these juxtapositions, both the typical characteristics and the variations of a building type can be discerned.

The danger for conceptual photography is the boredom this type of documentary photography may induce because of the similarity of the images, both in subject and treatment. Interest lies not in a question of a single, fascinating image, as in reportage, but in the overall idea that lies behind the series as a whole. That was certainly a problem affecting the reception of the Bechers' works at the beginning of their project. Only over time has the attitude to their work changed; the idea of the conceptual has become established and the reception of their work has changed from "boring" to "modern" and even "pioneering." In 1990 Bernd and Hilla Becher were awarded the Grand Prize at the Biennale in Venice—not for photography, but for sculpture, the focus being on the "anonymous sculptures" of industrial architecture that they have recorded in their own distinctive way.

Bernd and Hilla Becher taught at the Academy of Art in Düsseldorf from 1976 to 1996, passing on their objective approach to their students and followers, thus creating the so-called "Düsseldorf School." Members included Andreas Gursky (see *Photography and Painting*), Thomas Struth, Thomas Ruff, and other photographers who are considered to be among the most important "artist photographers" of today. They

left——**August Sander: Boxers** | 1929 | Die Photographische Sammlung/ SK Stiftung Kultur | Cologne

"The result is at worst a bored public, who have to endure an 'Inventory of the Manhole Covers of Ottawa' or the 'Storefronts of Schenectady' being eulogized as conceptual art."

have taken up the Bechers' ideas and continued to develop them. Sander's principle of "seeing, observing, and thinking" remains as relevant as ever for modern photographers.

The "Becher influence" can be clearly discerned in the early series of Thomas Ruff (b. 1958); nowadays, however, he has developed conceptual photography in his own way. Like most conceptual photographers, Ruff uses the same technique continuously throughout a series. Today, however, he does not take photos himself, he works with images from observatories, high-resolution data from NASA, or images downloads from the Internet. Such photos form the basis of the series *jpegs*, in which he prompts a discussion of photographic assumption in the digital age (right). Jpeg is a common form of compression of digital photos, used in order to save storage space and send images more quickly within the Internet; the name derives from the **J**oint **P**hotographic **E**xperts **G**roup, which developed this now-commonplace method in 1992. During compression, blocks of up to 8 x 8 pixels are formed. This may lead to the formation of disruptions to the pictures, so-called "artifacts." One day Ruff noticed this. They can scarcely be seen on small computer screens; however, if the compressed digital photos are enlarged to museum size, as Ruff did, they can be recognized so easily that in close-up one sees only these artifacts and not the actual picture, which seems to disintegrate into its pixel structure. This creates a painterly quality which, when blown up to museum format, looks at times like (digital) Pointillism. Ruff has transformed images taken from the computer screen into the museum-sized artwork. As in many of his series, in *jpegs* Ruff calls photography into question on a meta-level: its significance and its claim to authenticity in spite of, or because of, the digital processing opportunities available today.

The concepts, or rather the photographic series based on the concept concerned, consist of a theoretically unlimited number of pictures. Unfortunately, today it seems as if many photographers simply photograph similar objects in the same manner under the banner of conceptual photography, thereby producing a vast number of photos. The result is at worst a bored public, who have to endure an "Inventory of the Manhole Covers of Ottawa" or the "Storefronts of Schenectady" being eulogized as conceptual art. If the ordering basis in line with Sander's "seeing, observing, and thinking" is absent, photographers are in danger of losing themselves in photographic formalism.

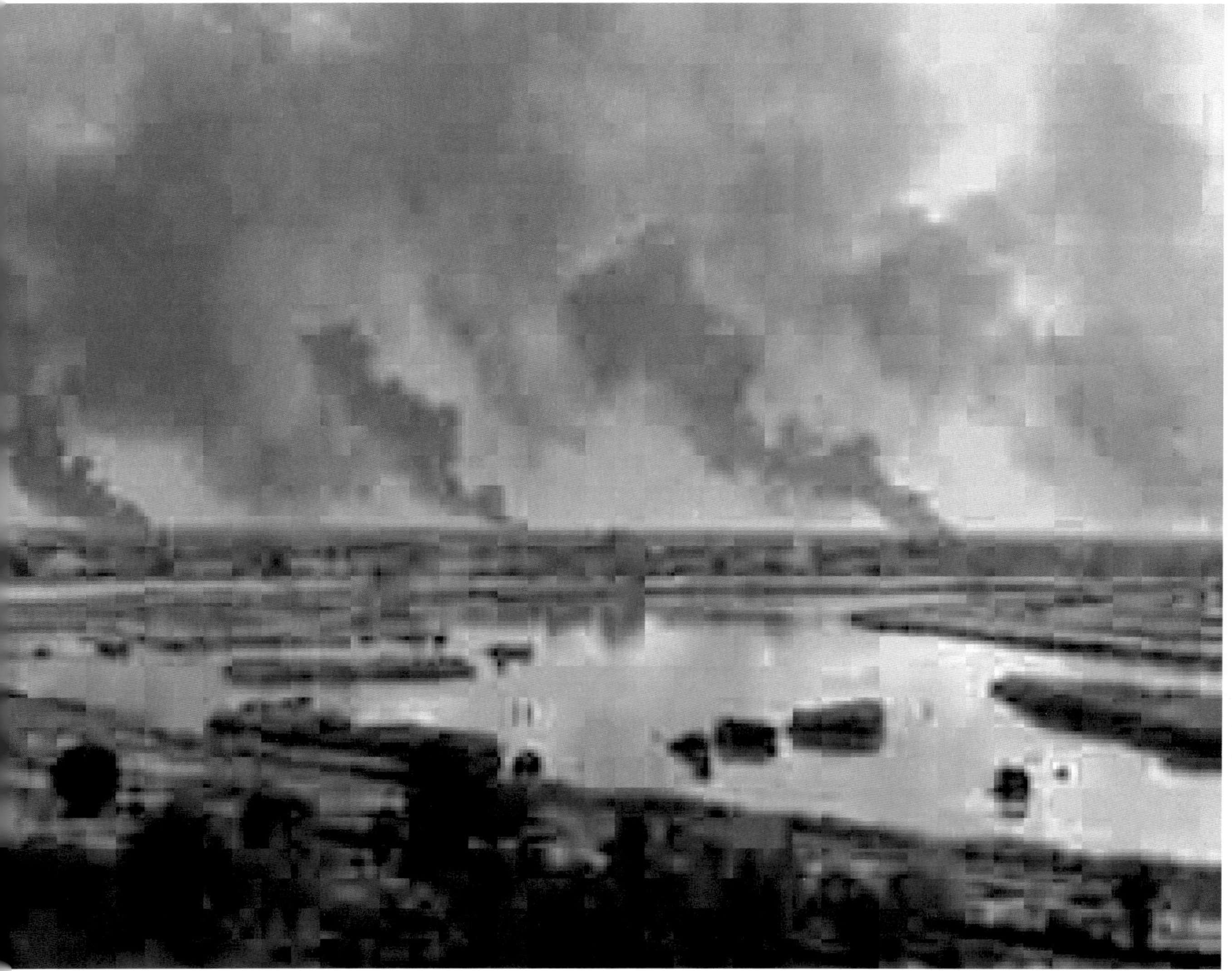

above——THOMAS RUFF: JPEG BO02 | 2004 | 188 x 243 cm

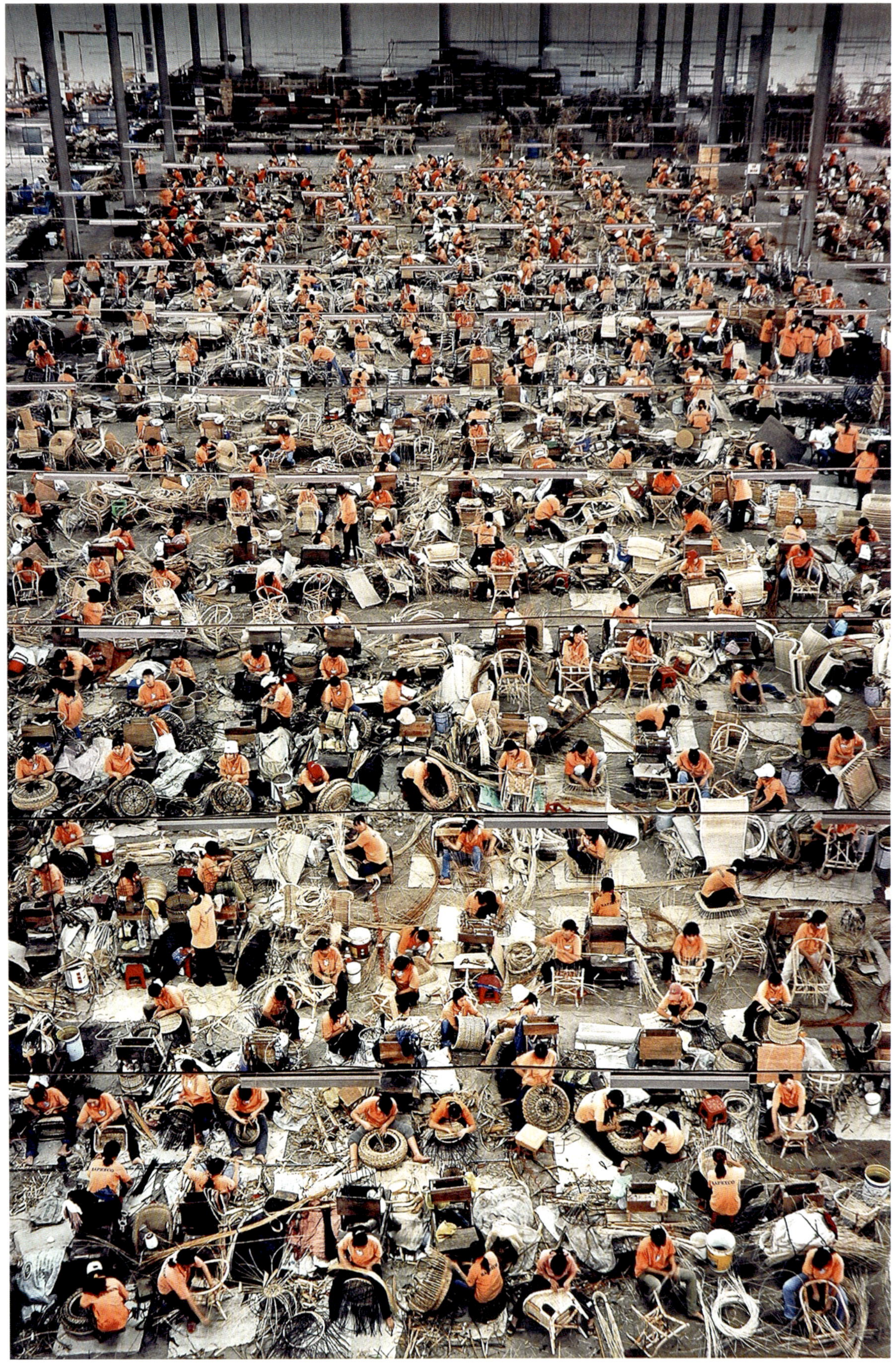

PHOTOGRAPHY AND PAINTING

"Photography should be the humble servant of science and art, just as the printing press and shorthand have neither created nor replaced literature." This comment comes from the French poet Charles Baudelaire (1821–1867), one of the greatest art critics during the 19th century. In fact, countless artists have used photography as an aid to painting and drawing. For them the camera became a new form of sketchbook, an aid to the study of form, pose, and composition, as we have seen in the case of David Octavius Hill (see *Portraits*). Eugène Delacroix (1798–1863) also used photography as a "humble servant"; he engaged a photographer, Eugène Durieux (1800–1874), to take photos of male and female models, according to his instructions, which he then used as studies for his paintings. Jean-François Millet (1814–1875) recommended the study of photographs in order to improve drawing skills, and we know that Edgar Degas (1834–1917) photographed dancers (fig. p. 173) and horse races so that he could base his drawings and paintings on them; the apparently casual composition of some of his paintings clearly reveals a photographer's eye.

To the extent that art aimed to reproduce the world as accurately as possible, photography represents the culmination of the development of painting. Photography was able to carry out this task faster and more efficiently, as the artist Paul Delaroche (1797–1856) was one of the first to recognize in 1839: "From today, painting is dead!" Fortunately, his famous prediction has not come true. As a result of the rapid development of photography, painting was forced to seek new tasks and therefore experienced a freedom that previously could not have been dreamed of. Photography liberated artists from the need to reproduce nature accurately and thus allowed them to develop new styles and interests. Color acquired a greater importance in painting, and the fantasies of some artists were impossible to translate into a photograph. This freedom led to the emergence of Impressionism, Symbolism, and ultimately also of Cubism and abstract painting. The question is how, when, and indeed whether painting would have undergone these changes if photography had not been invented.

But that was not the end of photography as an inspiration for painting, and to this day artists use photographs as the basis for their paintings. The most famous examples of the close partnership between photography and painting are the works of Andy Warhol (see *Instant Photography*) and those of

left——ANDREAS GURSKY: NHA TRANG | 2004 | C-print | 295.5 x 207 x 6.2 cm

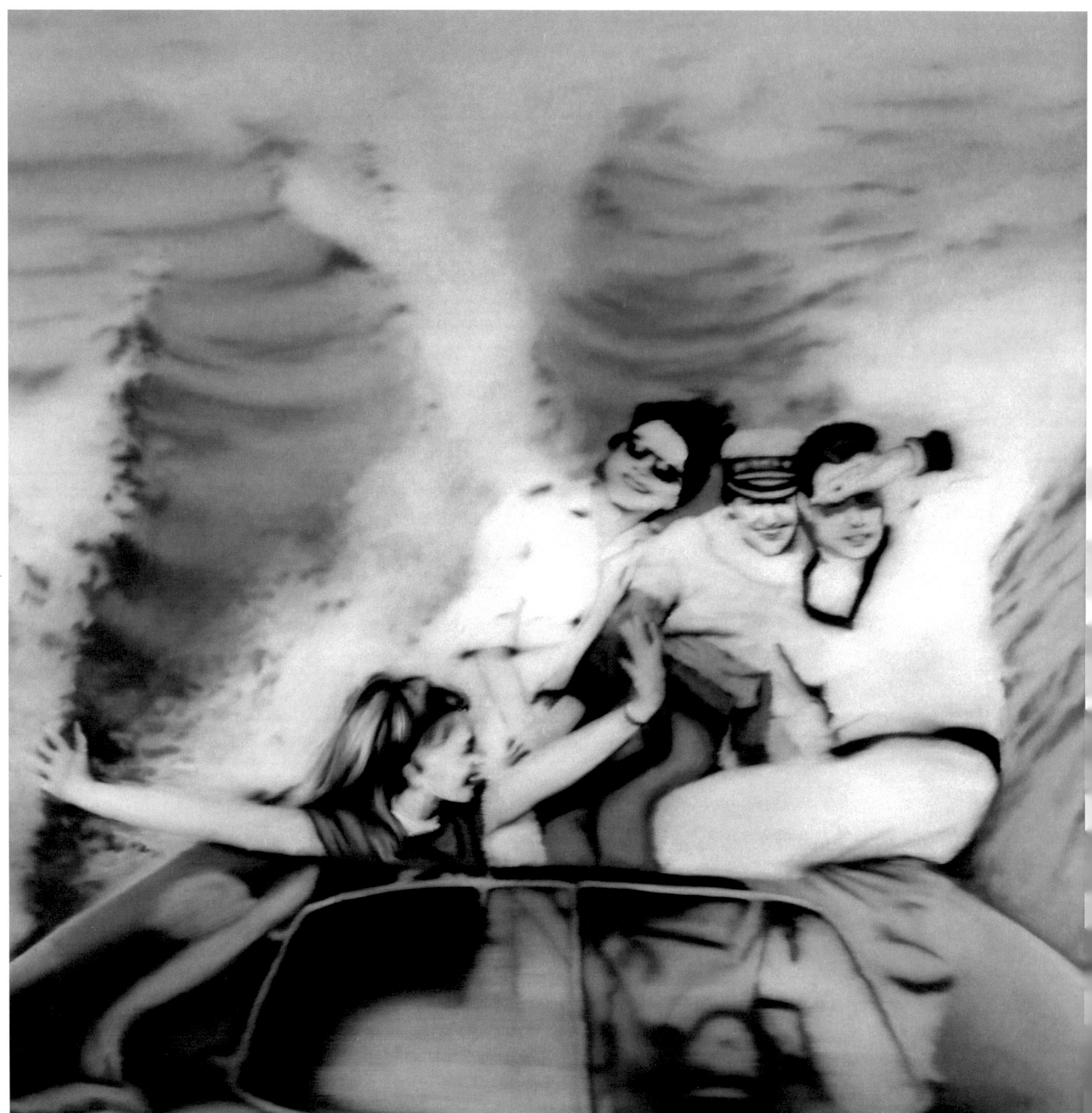

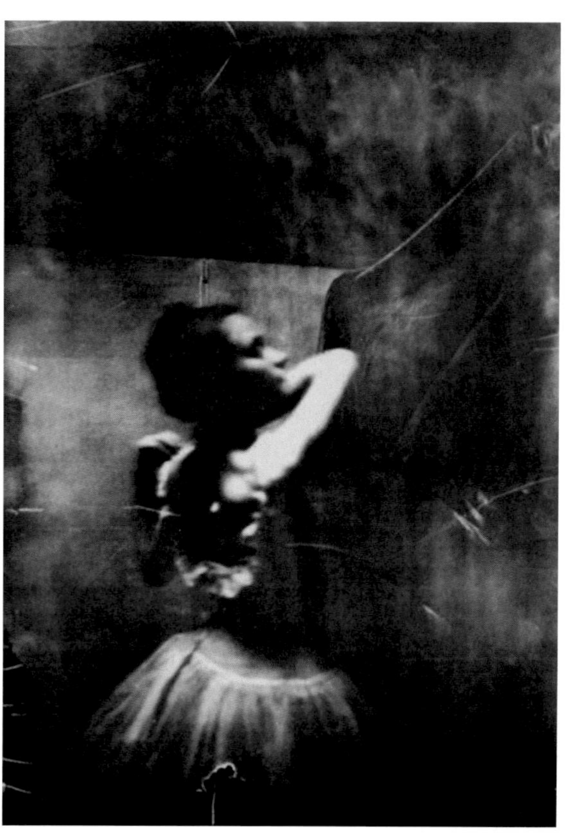

the German artist Gerhard Richter (b. 1932). A large part of the latter's work is based on photographs: old family photos, either taken by himself or others, or press photos, which he translates into large-scale paintings (left). However, Richter does not simply enlarge and copy them as a large-format painting. While copying a photo, Richter transforms it. The very fact that a newspaper photo is enlarged to over two meters in itself changes it. Furthermore, while painting, Richter introduces a blurring of the focus of his picture. Photography is transformed into art.

Through this transformation, he imbues a picture with a completely different aura and in its new context as an artwork it acquires an entirely different meaning.

Other artists approach photography in a very different way. David Hockney (b. 1937), a British artist living in the United States, does not use photos as a reference, but takes a large number of individual pictures that he then assembles like a collage to create a "photo painting" (fig. p. 175). In doing so he works with photographs but uses them in the same way as an artist who paints a series of brushstrokes until the entire picture has been created. Hockney does not like the way photography is limited to a single perspective and a single moment. Through the many photos of a motif that he assembles to form a picture, he expands, as it were, not only time but also space. Thus he also changes the role of the viewer, who must now examine the entire picture

left——**GERHARD RICHTER: MOTOR BOAT** | 1965 | 170 x 170 cm | Kunstmuseum Basel

right——**EDGAR DEGAS: DANCER** | photograph | 1895 | Bibliothèque Nationale de France | Paris

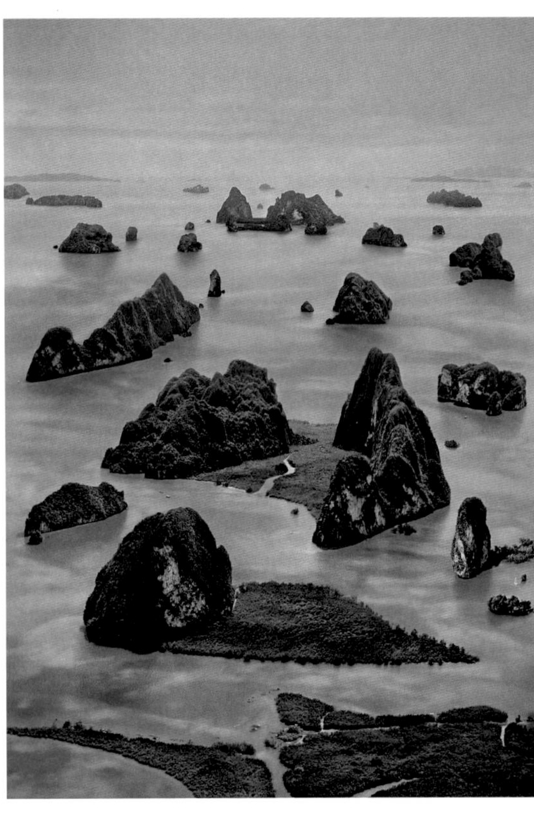

"I really think that now, with the digital possibilities we have today, there is no longer any difference between photography and painting."

actively, from one pictorial component to the next. It is no coincidence that Hockney's photo collages bear a vague resemblance to the multiple perspectives of Analytical Cubism.

If we compare Hockney's pictures with the large-format photographic works of the German photographer Andreas Gursky (b. 1955), we might at first conclude that Hockney is the analogue precursor of digital picture-making. Gursky, who comes from the so-called "Düsseldorf School" (see *Conceptual Photography*), has developed a new kind of photography, which proceeds in a similar manner to painting in its basic approach, with the difference that here not the paintbrush but the computer is the main tool. The introduction of digital technology enabled photography to emancipate itself from "simply recording" and to create its own realities. Nevertheless, photography still needs an object as the source of a photographic likeness. Just as artists withdraw to their studios in order to create paintings with the sketches they have made on location, so Gursky uses photographs taken in situ, in front of a subject, as merely the first (important) step on the way to the final work: "I really think that now, with the digital possibilities we have today, there is no longer any difference between photography and painting."

The process by which Gursky's pictures are created is in a sense parallel to the major theme that he examines in his photos—modern mass society and all its attendant aspects: mass production and mass products, battery farming and large-scale ag-

left——**ANDREAS GURSKY: JAMES BOND ISLAND II** | 2007 | C-Print 307 x 223.3 x 6.2 cm

right——**DAVID HOCKNEY: PAINT TROLLEY, L.A. 1985** | 1997 | photographic collage | 104 x 155 cm

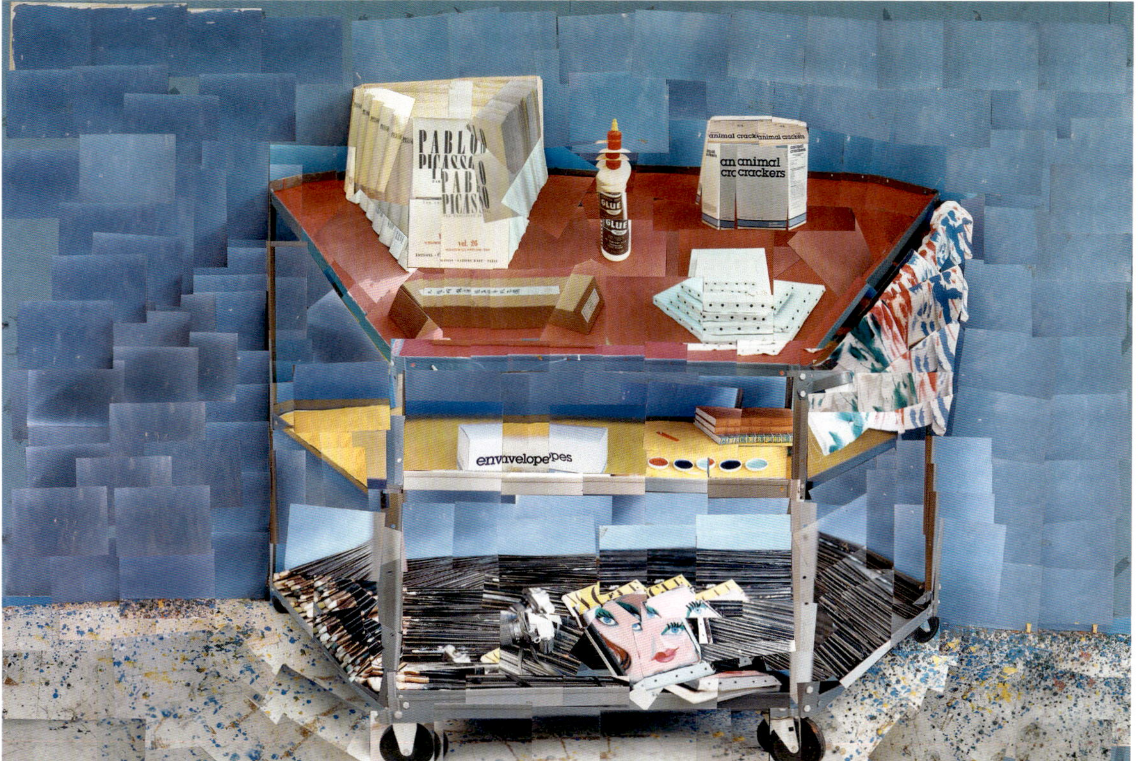

riculture, sports and political mass events, and mass leisure pursuits. Gursky also composes entire landscapes like *James Bond Island II* (left) in his own characteristic style, though the effect is sometimes less convincing because these pictures seem to be too close to a possible real model.

Gursky's photographs are close to painting in that the photographer creates his pictures piece by piece. His pictures are not created in the instant the camera shutter opens and closes. He takes several shots of a scene and then combines them on a computer to form a new whole. In this way he creates pictures in which a large number of moments seem to be united. And it is here that Gursky shows his true mastery. His method allows him to create pictures of a size and precision that was previously not possible. The remarkable thing about his pictures is the combination of distance and detail: "My pictures are always composed from two sides. They can be read in extreme close-up down to the very last detail. And at a distance they become mega-signs." His pictures do indeed need the "museum scale," because this ambiguity between near and far is ultimately recognizable only in the large scale of his exhibition works.

The starting point of a work is an actual situation, but the picture itself is an artistic translation of it; or, in Gursky's own words: "The picture is not true, but it is truthful." In his pictures Gursky plays with the trust we habitually place in photography, which has always been regarded as incontrovertible proof of a real situation or state of affairs. What the eye of the camera sees must have actually happened in that way or must have existed at that moment. This also applies to Gursky's works, but with an important proviso: "Any claim to truth in my pictures can only be satisfied to the extent that a particular event actually happened in the here and now."

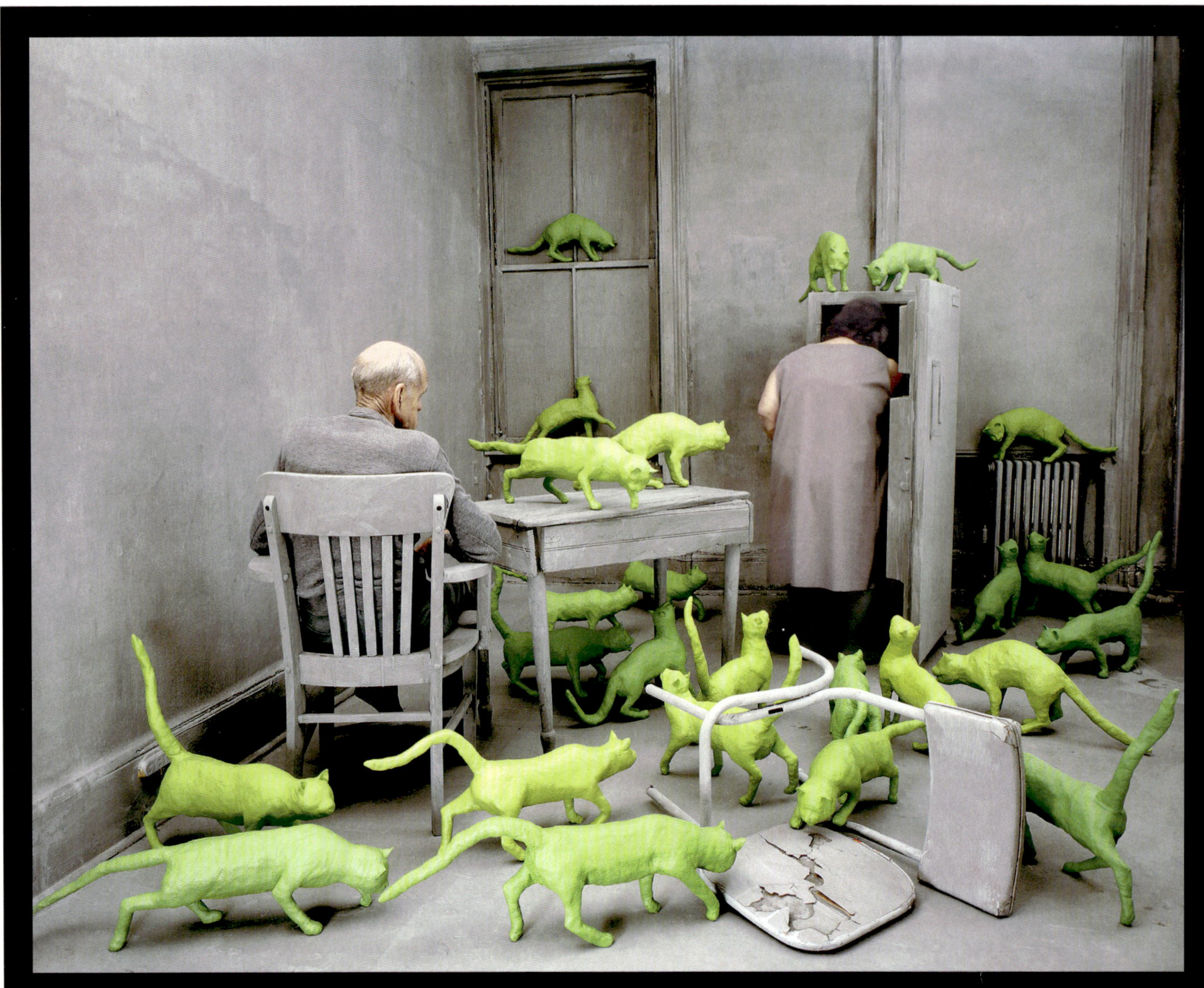

RADIOACTIVE CATS © 1980 Sandy Skoglund

STAGED PHOTOGRAPHY

Until the 1970s, the art of photography mostly lay in the reproduction of reality with the greatest possibly objectivity, whatever the defining style or concept—whether the modernism of Paul Strand, the "decisive moment" of Cartier-Bresson, or the "sad poem" of Robert Frank. Apart from the photographers who chose the still life as their art form, staging was the preserve of commercial photography, in other words in fashion and advertising.

Since the 1970s, photography has developed into a medium of modern art. Artists, most of them not "trained" photographers, use photography as an alternative to painting in order to realize their ideas. In staged photography, artists create their own stories and thus become modern "history painters" who have exchanged the paintbrush for a camera. The American photographer Sandy Skoglund (b. 1946) photographs worlds of her own making. In her elaborate Surrealist pictures, the viewer is confronted with scenes that recall nightmares or strange visions of the future. In *Radioactive Cats* (left) from 1980, we see an elderly couple in a gray, cheerless kitchen. The woman is clearly busy get-

ting food out of a refrigerator for 25 bright-green cats. It looks like a scene from a science-fiction film. The question is: What is the picture meant to show? Is it the vision of a world after a nuclear catastrophe, as the title and the radioactive green cats seem to indicate? Or is it a quirky examination of old age, in which lack of interest and lethargy go so far that even 25 irradiated cats are not disconcerting? The question remains unanswered. Skoglund created a number of similar scenarios that may even contain comic elements. "Since the Eighties, I have been fascinated with interiors and invading interiors with problems and interruptions, usually by animals."

For Sandy Skoglund, photography is only part of her art. The other, equally important, part lies in her carefully crafted scenarios. She laboriously produces by hand the settings and the various animals, such as goldfish, dogs, squirrels, and especially cats, which appear in her pictures repeatedly. Cindy Sherman (b. 1954) always stages herself— albeit not as Cindy Sherman, but as her own model, her only one—in her pictures, which pose questions about reality and identity. Sherman became famous with her series *Untitled Film Stills* (fig. p. 178), which she created between 1977 and 1981. It consists of black-and-white photos that look like stills from films. In them, Sherman appears in ster-

left——**Sandy Skoglund: Radioactive Cats** | 1980 | 64.7 x 82.5 cm

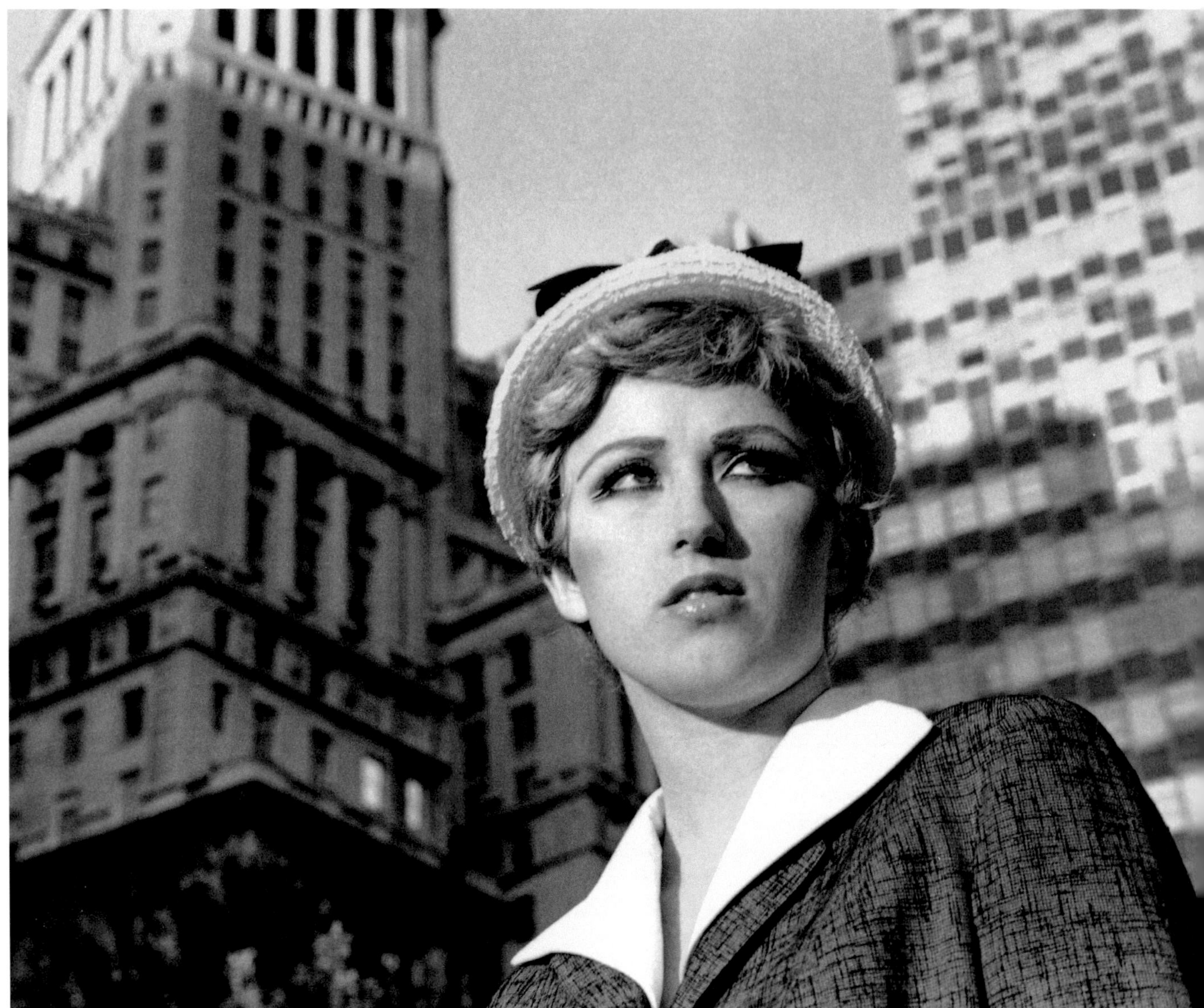

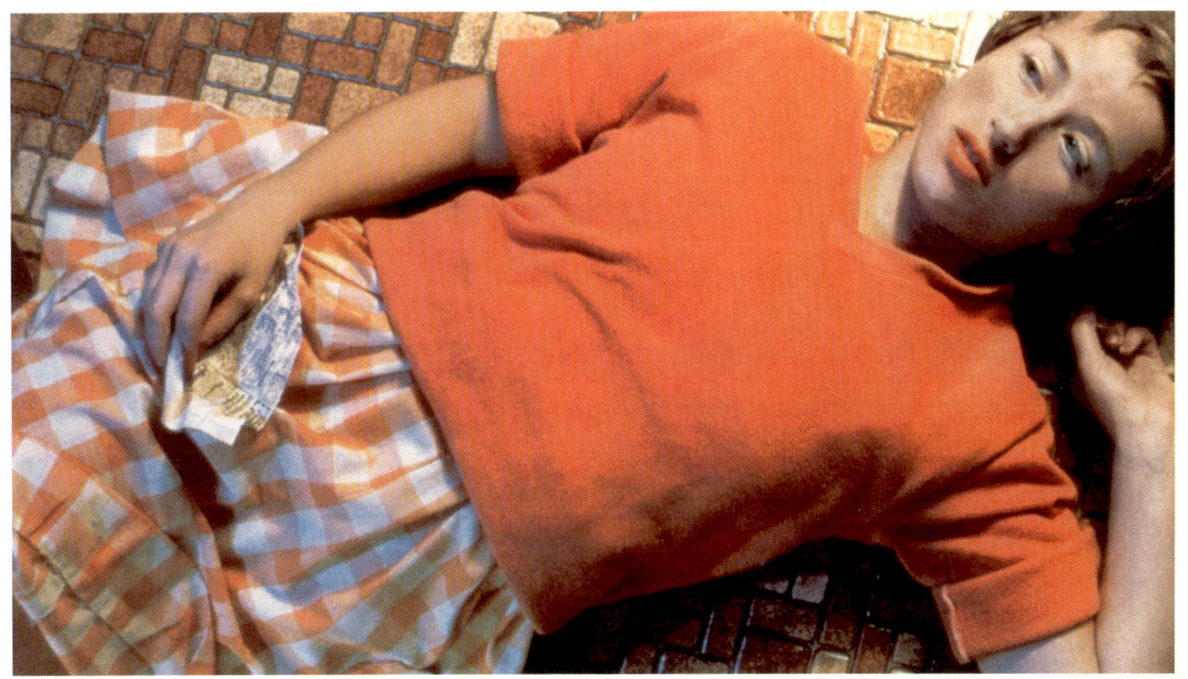

eotyped female roles intended to evoke the cliché of the female image of Hollywood and the film noir of the 1950s and 1960s. One has the feeling of having seen the film from which the scenes appear to come. The film, however, does not exist, nor does the scene represented. It exists only as a photo. Sherman uses lighting, camera settings, costumes, and poses that correspond with the film in question. In order to present the staging consistently in its external form, the format of the relatively small photos (19 x 24 cm, just under 7½ x 9 ½ in) recalls press material. She does not give her works titles but simply numbers them, in order to leave all possibilities of association open: "The still must tease with the promise of a story the viewer itches to be told."

That also applies to her numerous other series in which she stages herself. In the series *Clowns*, she contrasts overt displays of happiness with inner sadness; in *Society Portraits*, she appears as a sophisticated lady who is desperately clinging to her lost youth, like those frequently seen in magazines; and in the series *Centerfolds*, she plays with the expectations that the expression prompts—in men's magazines like *Playboy*, it refers to the foldout photo in the center of the magazine. One of these photos, with the typical Sherman title *Untitled #96* (above), was auctioned in 2011 for 3.89 million dollars and is thus one of the most expensive photos in history.

Unlike Cindy Sherman, who works in series, Jeff Wall (b. 1946) focuses on individual images. They are like reportage photos, but without the real-life background, for Wall's pictures are also staged photographs, not only as regards content, but also—one might say—as regards their presentation. His meter-high pictures are exhibited as slides in a light box, rather like advertising posters in a public space. That underlines, so to speak, the artificial and artistic character of his works.

left——CINDY SHERMAN: UNTITLED FILM STILL #21 | 1978 | 19 x 24 cm Museum of Modern Art | New York

above——CINDY SHERMAN: UNTITLED #96 | 1981 | 61 x 122 cm | Museum of Modern Art | New York

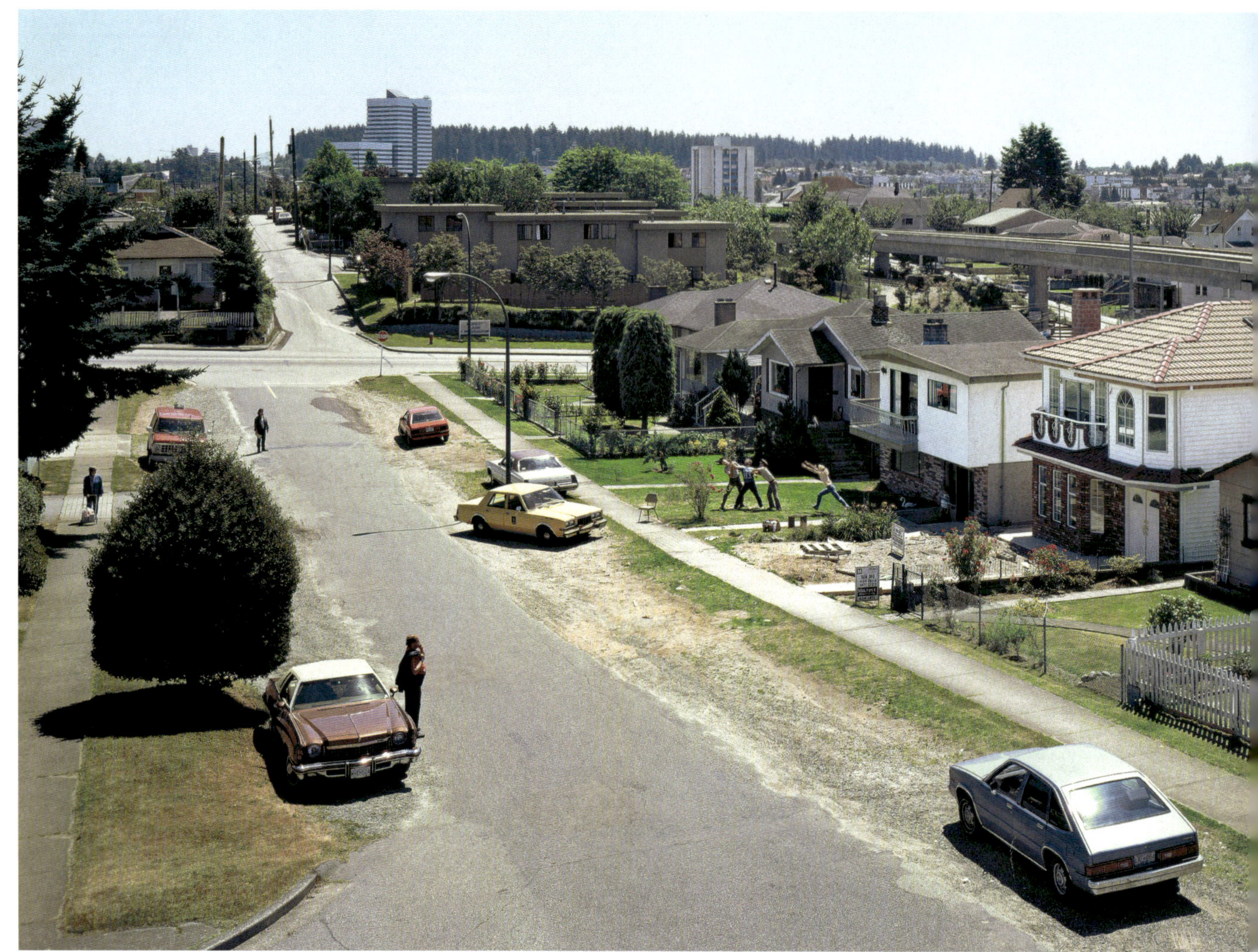

With the staged photograph, photography was up-graded to an artistic medium that in museums was beginning to take its place on equal terms beside traditional forms of art. The size of the work plays an important role in this respect. Unlike "classic" photos that were initially intended for publication in magazines and books, the photographs of Jeff Wall were designed from the outset for presentation in museums. This applies not only to the form of presentation, but also to the details in the pictures. Through them the viewer is drawn into the picture and can for this very reason recognize and study the staged scene they present. A good example is the picture *Eviction Struggle* (above) of 1988. It shows a typical suburban scene, as if taken from a tall build-ing. Everything looks real and the viewer has the impression of looking at a snapshot of a neighbor from an apartment located a few floors higher. As the title reveals, it shows a dramatic but probably by no means unusual scene. Two policemen have just arrived in a front garden and are attempting to arrest a man. His wife rushes over to help him. At first sight it all looks like a snapshot or a piece of reportage. If we look more closely, however, its

1970 – today Jonathan Meese

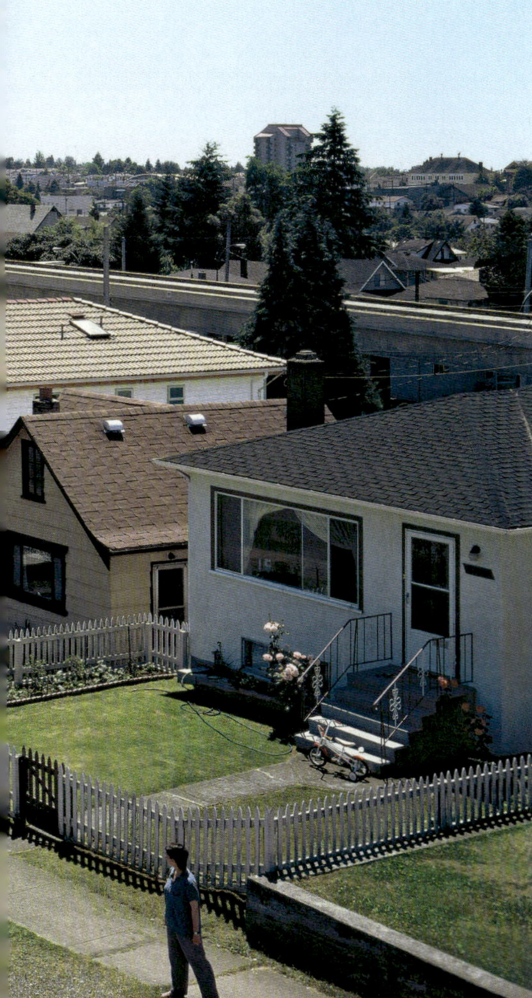

"Wall shows in his picture the story of a suburb that looks tranquil at first sight, and in the same instant he destroys this illusion by means of his staged scene."

"artificiality" is evident: the gestures and poses of the protagonists are too exaggerated and the precision of the vast print does not correspond to the resolution of the reportage cameras of the time. Wall shows in his picture the story of a suburb that looks tranquil at first sight, and in the same instant he destroys this illusion by means of his staged scene.

With staged scenes like this, which pretend to be authentic situations, Wall plays with photography's credibility and its claim to authenticity. Until recently, anything that had been photographed was considered to have really happened. Wall questions this "that's how it was" just as Cindy Sherman does in her *Untitled Film Stills*.

During the 19th century, photography was often only an aid to painting, but now it has become art in its own right by appropriating the staged elements of painting.

above——**Jeff Wall: Eviction Struggle** | 1988 | 249 x 434 cm | Pinakothek der Moderne | Munich

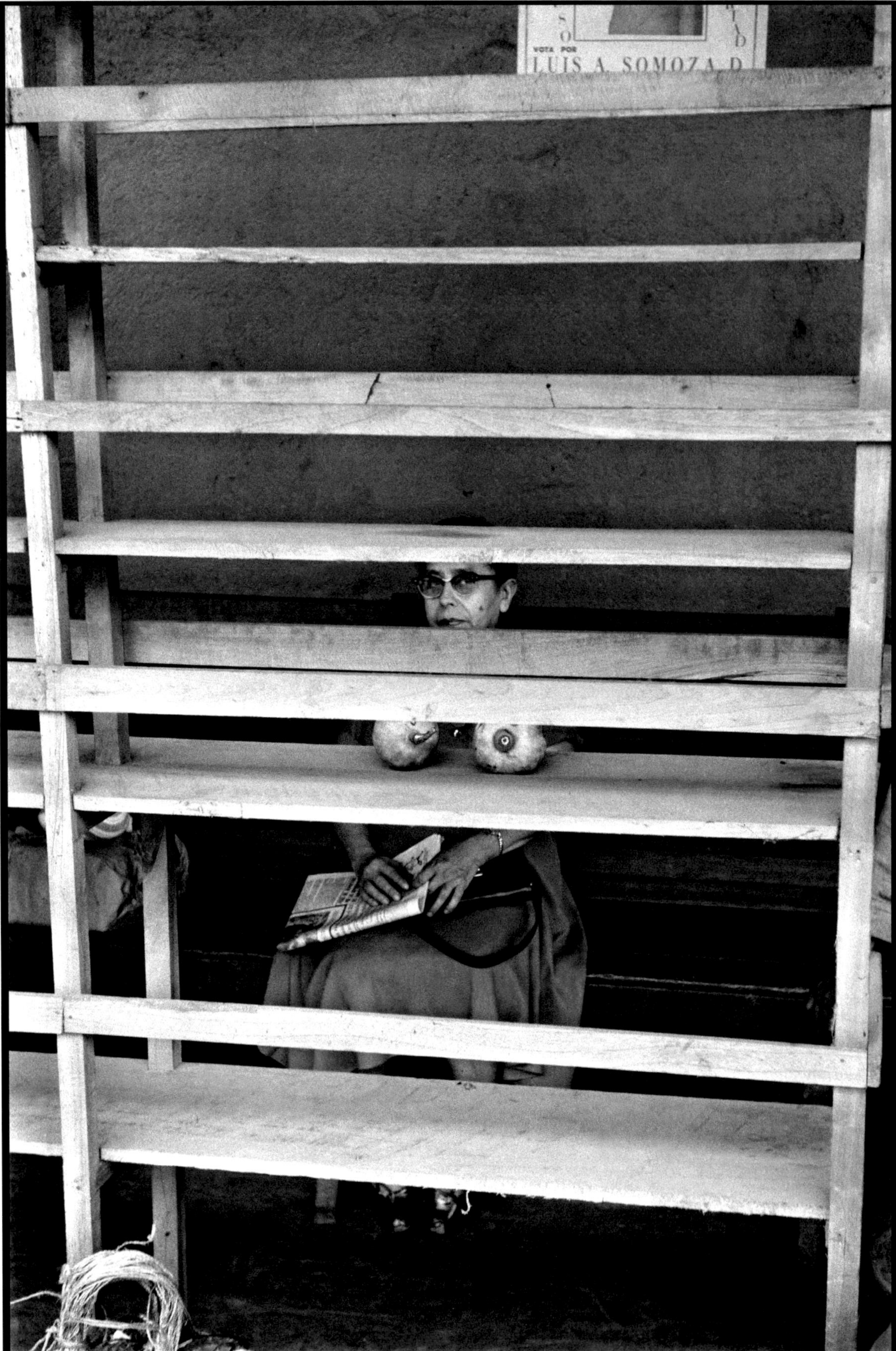
S
O
VOTA POR
LUIS A. SOMOZA D.
D

HUMOR IN PHOTOGRAPHY

There is surprisingly little humor in art. Perhaps this is because many people still believe that art is a serious affair, and that entertainment can never be art. The conductor Leonard Bernstein once said that "there is no such thing as pop music and serious music, only good and bad music." The same is true of art and photography. It is easy to forget that entertainment and humor are in fact high art forms! For great artists, tragedy and humor are two sides of the same coin as both are connected to our deepest emotions. In art, humor is often left to caricaturists. This may be because it requires too much effort to paint a large oil painting "simply" in order to provoke a laugh or a smile. Photography is different. Many situations reveal their humorous sides precisely in the fraction of the second that it takes to capture them in a photo. It goes without saying that coincidence plays an important role in this. The skill lies in the ability to see these moments, and perhaps even to anticipate them, in order to capture them at just the right moment. There can be no question that there are considerably fewer high-quality humorous pictures than

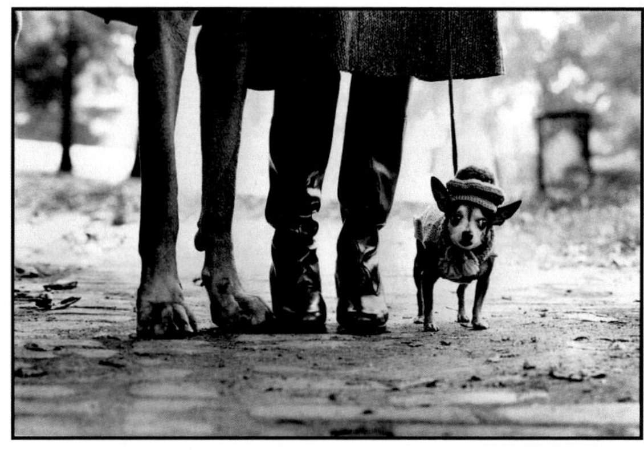

serious ones because they are generally either very good or very bad: there is little scope for mediocrity. The photographer either has or has not captured precisely the right moment, the moment in which a scene reveals its comedy. And whereas it is possible to imbue certain mediocre works with significance through intellectual interpretation, it is not so much intellect as emotion that determines our responses to humorous photographs.

"To me, photography is an art of observation. It's about finding something interesting in an ordinary place [...] I've found it has little to do with the things you see and everything to do with the way you see them," observed Elliott Erwitt (b. 1928), one of

left——**Elliott Erwitt: Managua, Nicaragua** | 1957
right——**Elliott Erwitt: Felix, Gladys and Rover, New York** | 1974

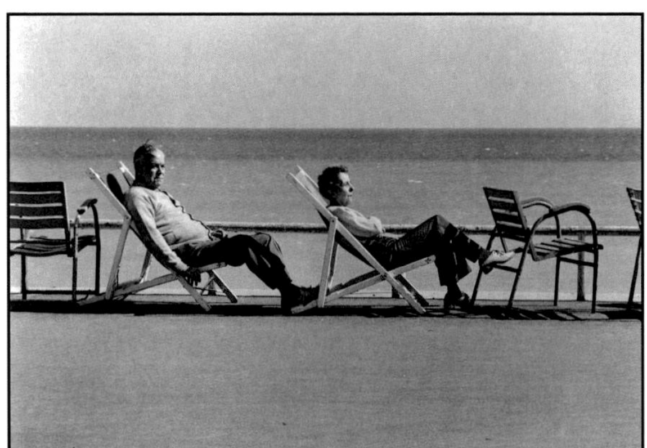 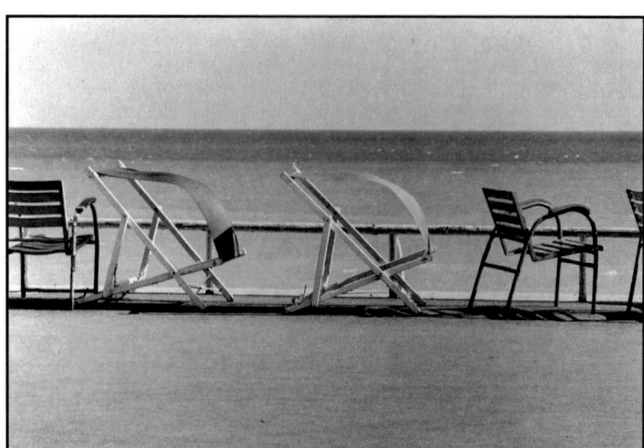

the few humorists among photographers. His skill at teasing out the funny moments of life is virtually unsurpassed (fig. p. 182), and he has become famous in particular for his pictures of dogs, a subject he has returned to many times (fig. p. 183). "Dogs are just really funny if one catches them in certain situations [...] There is also a human side to dogs, and I think that part of the power of my pictures of them lies in the fact that they are so human." This also seems to be true of William Wegman, who has also become well known for his photographs of dogs (see *Instant Photography*). Erwitt specializes in short sequences of pictures with unexpected punch-lines (above, left and right). He uses these sequences again and again to tell new and surprising stories that could not be narrated in the same way in any medium other than photography. As in a comedy, which depends entirely on getting the timing right, amusing photographs are contingent upon capturing the precise moment. A contact print by the photographer Richard Kalvar (b. 1944) shows how a photographer approaches a scene in the expectation of taking a funny photograph. Kalvar, another of the small number of true humorists in photography, tries to get as close as he possibly can to the people he wants to photograph: "I use people as unconscious actors in little dramas they don't know they're in." To this end, he pretends to be interested in something else as he approaches his "victims." In this case, he was in Rome when he spotted a man with heavy glasses listening intently to another man (opposite, left). Kalvar noticed the fountain behind the two men at the same time, and already had an idea of the composition of the picture in his mind. The contact print allows us to follow the development of the composition (opposite, right). "I continued to experiment with the two men and the spout in the background, and took a picture whenever I felt I was not being observed. Just as I stood in a place from which it looked in the viewfinder as though the jet of water were hitting the young man on the back of the neck, the *miracolo* happened: he unexpectedly lifted his head and revealed an astonished expression. I had therefore got my picture, but that was not the reason for which I let it rest after that; I had simply run out of film."

"The miracles of everyday life are exciting; no film director can arrange the unexpected that one stumbles upon in the street." As a photographer, one certainly can, however, lend a helping hand. The Parisian photographer Robert Doisneau (1912–1994) was a master storyteller. It is in part thanks to his photographs, which fill postcard stands to this day, that we have a romantic picture of Paris that can be

above——**ELLIOTT ERWITT: CANNES I & II** | 1975

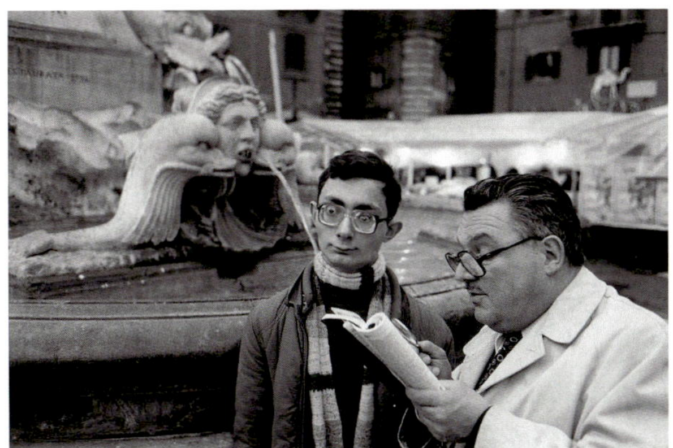

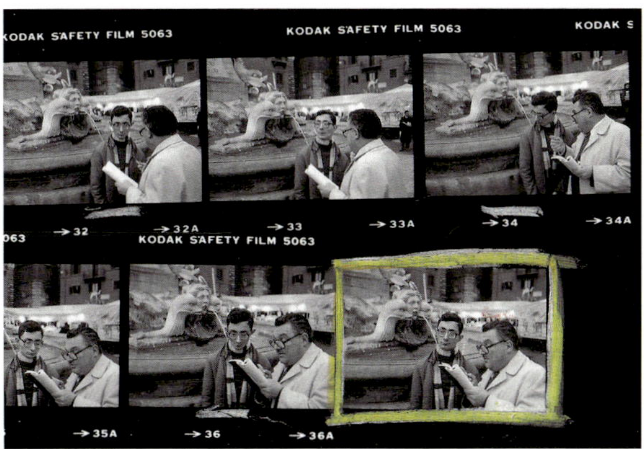

matched only by films like *Amélie* and drawings by Sempé. Doisneau combed the streets of his hometown in search of poetic and amusing moments, which he captured with his Rolleiflex. But Doisneau was also brilliant at staging scenes inconspicuously. The most famous example of this is his *Kiss by the Hôtel de Ville* (1950), which was not revealed to have been staged until much later. This knowledge has done nothing to diminish the quality and the success of the picture, however. For a series of photographs, Doisneau placed a painting of a nude woman in the display window of an antiques store, and used his camera to capture the reactions of passersby (fig. p. 186). This images tell us much about the people in front of the display window, but are equally eloquent on the subject of the photographer himself and his attitude to life.

The Englishman Martin Parr (b. 1952) is one of the few photographers of our time to cultivate the humorous in his pictures (see *Self-Portraits*). His photographs work differently from those of Erwitt, Kalvar, and Doisneau. Parr's pictures are funny, bizarre, and occasionally biting comments on the ways in which we present ourselves in everyday life, in our free time and as tourists (figs. pp. 187, 56, 60 and 61). We frequently find ourselves laughing out of *schadenfreude* when looking at his photographs. Just as often, we choke on our laughter, however, because we recognize ourselves in them. "If people simultaneously laugh and cry when looking at my pictures, then that is exactly the same reaction they provoke in me, too. Things are neither fundamentally good nor fundamentally bad. I am always interested in portraying both extremes" (Martin Parr).

Most photographers are reluctant to comment on their photos, and leave it to others to discuss them: "A picture should be looked at, not talked about," as Elliott Erwitt put it. There is a valid reason for that: if a photo is good, it speaks directly to us, stimulating our own thoughts and feelings. These are generally the pictures that become milestones of photography because they etch themselves into our minds.

above left——**RICHARD KALVAR: PIAZZA DELLE ROTONDA** | 1980
above right——**RICHARD KALVAR: PIAZZA DELLA ROTONDA** | 1980
contact print

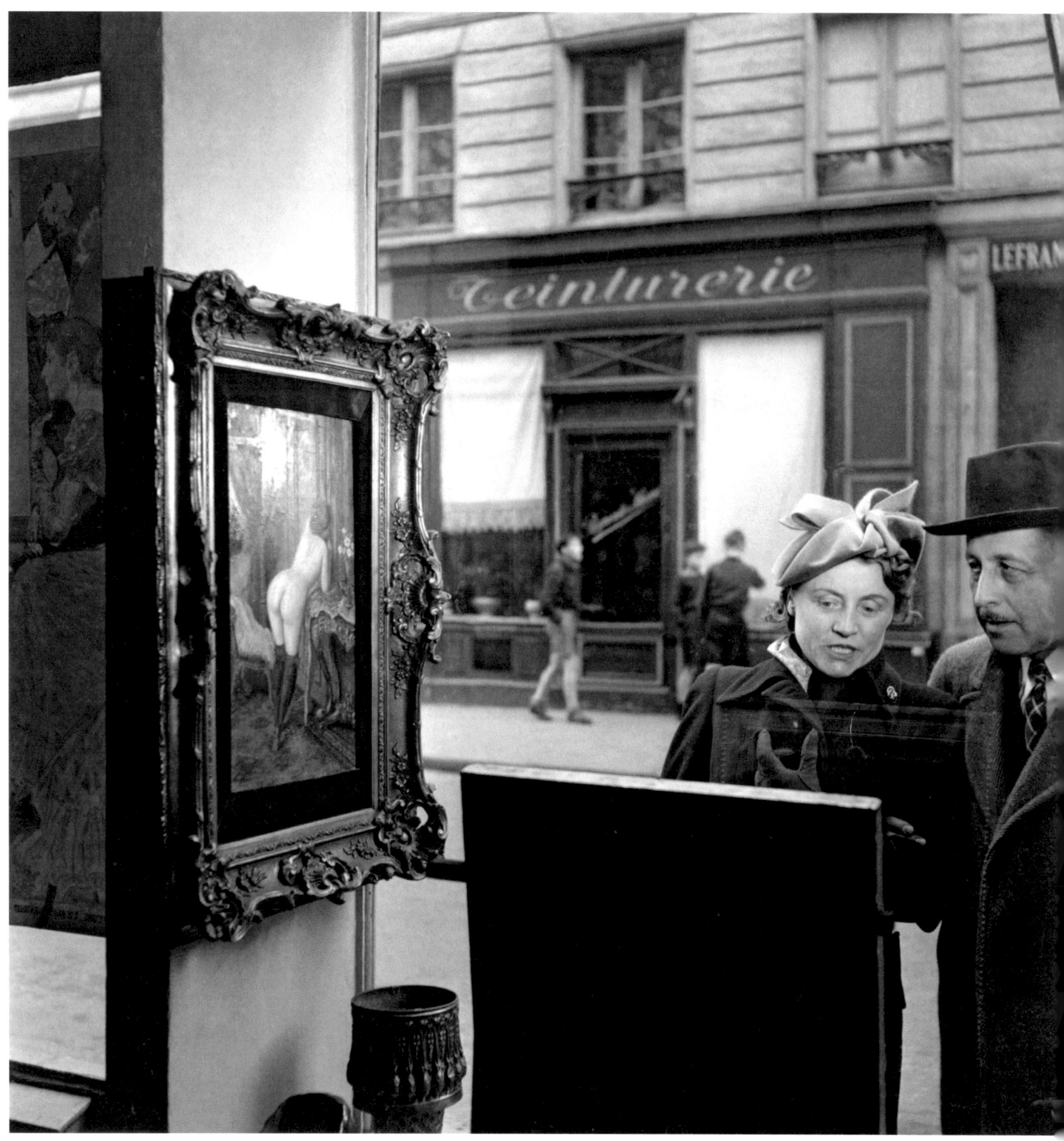

above——**Robert Doisneau: Romi Gallery, 12 rue de Seine, Paris** | 1947

right——**Martin Parr: Turkey, Kalkan** | 1994

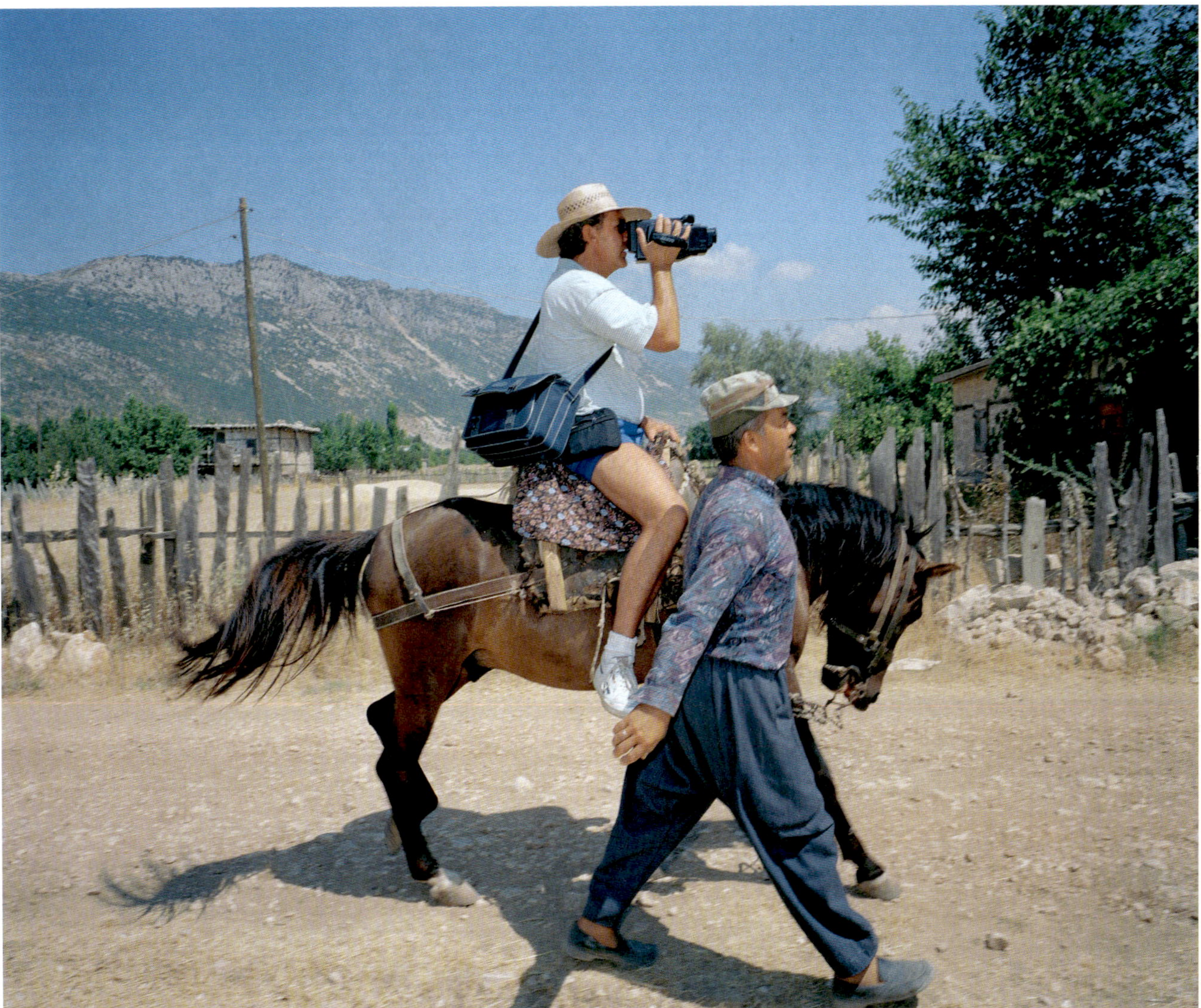

PHOTOGRAPHERS AND ARTISTS

ADAMS, Ansel: born February 20, 1902, in San Francisco; died April 22, 1984, in Carmel-by-the-Sea, California

ADAMSON, Robert: born April 26, 1821, in Burnside, Scotland; died January 14, 1848, in St. Andrews

ARNOLD, Eve: born April 21, 1912, in Philadelphia; died Januar 4, 2012, in London

ATGET, Eugène: born February 12, 1857, in Libourne, France; died August 4, 1927, in Paris

AVEDON, Richard: born May 15, 1923, in New York City; died October 1, 2004, in San Antonio, Texas

BALLEN, Roger: born 1950 in New York City

BARNBAUM, Bruce: born 1943 in Chicago

BAYARD, Hippolyte: born January 20, 1801, in Breteuil-sur-Noye, France; died May 14, 1887, in Nemours

BECHER, Bernd: born August 20, 1931, in Siegen, Germany; died June 22, 2007, in Rostock

BECHER, Hilla: born September 2, 1934, in Potsdam, Germany

BISSON, Louis-Auguste: born April 21, 1814, in Paris; died May 12, 1876, in Paris

BISSON, Auguste-Rosalie: born May 1, 1826, in Paris; died April 22, 1900 in Paris

BRASSAÏ (Gyula Halász): born September 9, 1899, in Bra̦sov (Brassó), now Romania; died July 7, 1984, in Nice, France

BRANDENBURG, Jim: born 1945 in Luverne, Minnesota

BRANDT, Nick: born 1966 in London

CAPA, Robert (Endre Ernő Friedmann): born October 22, 1913, in Budapest; died May 25, 1954, in Thai Binh, Vietnam

CAMERON, Julia Margaret: born June 11, 1815, in Calcutta; died January 26, 1879, in Kalutara

CARTER, Rob: born 1968

CARTIER-BRESSON, Henri: born August 22, 1908, in Chanteloup-en-Brie, France; died August 3, 2004, in Montjustin

DAGUERRE, Louis Jacques Mandé: born November 18, 1787, in Cormeilles-en-Parisis, France; died July 10, 1851, in Bry-sur-Marne

DAY, Corinne: born February 19, 1962, in Ickenham, England; died August 27, 2010, in London

DEMACHY, Robert: born July 7, 1859, in Saint-Germain-en-Laye, France; died December 29, 1936, in Hennequeville

DELACROIX, Eugène: born April 26, 1798, in Charenton-Saint-Maurice, France; died August 13, 1863, in Paris

DEGAS, Edgar (Hilaire Germain Edgar de Gas): born July 19, 1834, in Paris; died September 27, 1917, in Paris

DICORCIA, Philip-Lorca: born 1951 in Hartford, Connecticut

DOISNEAU, Robert: born April 14, 1912, in Gentilly, France; died April 1, 1994, in Paris

DU HAURON, Louis Ducos: born December 8, 1837, in Langon, France; died December 31, 1920, in Agen

DURIEUX, Eugène: born 1800 in Nîmes; died 1874 in Paris

EDGERTON, Harold E.: born April 6, 1903, in Fremont, Nebraska; died January 4, 1990, in Cambridge, Massachusetts

EGGLESTON, William: born July 27, 1939, in Memphis

ERWITT, Elliott: born July 26, 1928, in Paris

EVANS, Walker: born November 3, 1903, in St. Louis, Missouri; died April 10, 1975, New Haven, Connecticut

FENTON, Roger: born March 28, 1819, in Crimble Hall near Heywood, England; died August 8, 1869, in Potters Bar

FRANK, Robert: born November 9, 1924, in Zurich

GHIRRI, Luigi: born January 5, 1943, in Scandiano, Italy; died 1992

GIBSON, Ralph: born January 16, 1939, in Los Angeles

GOLDIN, Nan: born September 12, 1953, in Washington, DC

GREEN, John Beasley: born 1832 in Le Havre; died 1856 in Cairo

HAAS, Ernst: born March 2, 1921, in Vienna; died September 12, 1986, in New York

HALSMAN, Philippe: born May 2, 1906, in Riga; died June 25, 1979, in New York

HELMER-PETERSEN, Keld: born August 23, 1920, in Copenhagen

HILL, David Octavius: born May 20, 1802, in Perth, Scotland; died Ma 17, 1870 in Edinburgh

HOCKNEY, David: born July 9, 1937, in Bradford, England

HORST, Horst P. (Horst Paul Bohrmann): born August 14, 1906, in Weissenfels, Germany; died November 19, 1999, in Palm Beach Gardens, Florida

HOYNINGEN-HUENE, Georg Freiherr von: born September 4, 1900, in St. Petersburg; died September 12, 1968, in Los Angeles

HUGO, Pieter: born 1976 in Johannesburg

JACKSON, William Henry: born April 4, 1843, in Keeseville, New York; died June 30, 1942, in New York

KALVAR, Richard: born 1944 in New York

KÄSEBIER, Gertrude (Gertrude Stanton Kasebier): born May 18, 1852, in Des Moines, Iowa; died October 13, 1934, in New York

KENNA, Michael: born 1953 in Widnes

KERTÉSZ, André (Andor Kertész): born July 2, 1894, in Budapest; died September 27 or 28, 1985, in New York

KOUDELKA, Josef: born January 10, 1938, in Boskovice, Czechoslovakia

KÜHN, Heinrich: born February 25, 1866, in Dresden; died September 14, 1944, in Birgitz, Austria

LARTIGUE, Jacques Henri: born June 13, 1894, in Courbevoie, France; died September 12, 1986, in Nice

LINDBERGH, Peter (Peter Brodbeck): born November 23, 1944, in Reichsgau Wartheland (now Leszno, Poland)

MAN RAY (Emmanuel Rudnitzky): born August 27, 1890, in Philadelphia; died November 18, 1976, in Paris

MAREY, Étienne-Jules: born March 5, 1830, in Beaune, France; died May 15, 1904, in Paris

MCCULLIN, Don: born October 9, 1935, in London

MEYER, Baron Adolphe de: born September 3, 1868, in Paris; died January 6, 1949, in Los Angeles

MEYEROWITZ, Joel: born March 6, 1938, in New York

MUNKÁCSI, Martin (Márton Marmelstein): born May 18, 1896, in Kolozsvár, Transylvania; died July 13, 1963, in New York

MUYBRIDGE, Eadweard (Edward James Muggeridge): born April 9, 1830, in Kingston upon Thames, England; died May 8, 1904, in Kingston upon Thames

NADAR (Gaspard-Félix Tournachon): born April 6, 1820, in Paris; died March 21, 1910, in Paris

NEWMAN, Arnold: born March 3, 1918, in New York; died June 6, 2006, in New York

NEWTON, Helmut (Helmut Neustädter): born October 31, 1920, in Berlin; died January 23, 2004, in Los Angeles

NIÉPCE, Nicéphore: born March 7, 1765, in Chalon-sur-Saône, France; died July 5, 1833, in Saint-Loup-de-Varennes

OPPENHEIM, Meret: born October 6, 1913, in Charlottenburg, Germany; died November 15, 1985, in Basel

OUTERBRIDGE, Paul: born August 15, 1896, in New York; died October 17, 1958, in Laguna Beach, California

PARR, Martin: born May 23, 1952, in Epsom, England

PENN, Irving: born June 16, 1917, in Plainfield, New Jersey; died October 7, 2009, in New York

PERESS, Gilles: born December 29, 1946, in Neuilly, France

RANKIN (John Rankin Waddell): born 1966 in St. Albans, England

RENGER-PATZSCH, Albert: born June 22, 1897, in Würzburg, Germany; died September 27, 1966, in Wamel, Germany

RHEIMS, Bettina: born December 18, 1952, in Neuilly-sur-Seine, France

RICHTER, Gerhard: born February 9, 1932, in Dresden

RITTS, Herb: born August 13, 1952, in Los Angeles; died December 26, 2002, in Los Angeles

RUFF, Thomas: born February 10, 1958, in Zell am Harmersbach

RÖNTGEN, Wilhelm Conrad: born March 27, 1845 in Lennep, present-day Remscheid, Germany; died February 10, 1923, in Munich

SALGADO, Sebastião: born February 8, 1944, in Aimorés, Brazil

SALOMON, Dr. Erich: born April 28, 1886, in Berlin; died July 7, 1944, in Auschwitz

SANDER, August: born November 17, 1876, in Herdorf, Germany; died April 20, 1964, in Cologne

SHERMAN, Cindy: born January 19, 1954, in Glen Ridge, New Jersey

SHORE, Stephen: born October 8, 1947, in New York

SKOGLUND, Sandy: born September 11, 1946, in Quincy, Massachusetts

SMITH, W. Eugene: born December 30, 1918, in Wichita, Kansas; died October 15, 1978, in Tucson

STEICHEN, Edward (Edouard Jean Steichen): born March 27, 1879, in Bivange, Luxembourg; died March 25, 1973, in West Redding, Connecticut

STIEGLITZ, Alfred: born January 1, 1864, in Hoboken, New Jersey; died July 13, 1946, in New York

STRAND, Paul: born October 16, 1890, in New York; died March 31, 1976, in Orgeval

TALBOT, William Fox: born February 11, 1800, in Melbury, England; died September 17, 1877, in Lacock Abbey, England

TELLER, Jürgen: born 1964 in Erlangen, Germany

THOMAS, Christopher: born 1961 in Munich

TILLMANS, Wolfgang: born 1968 in Remscheid, Germany

TOSCANI, Oliviero: born February 28, 1942, in Milan

UELSMAN, Jerry N.: born June 11, 1934, in Detroit

UT, Nick (Huynh Cong Út): born March 29, 1951, in Long An, Vietnam

VEASEY, Nick: born 1962 in London

WALL, Jeff: born September 29, 1946, in Vancouver

WARHOL, Andy (Andrew Warhola): born August 6, 1928, in Pittsburgh; died February 22, 1987, in New York

WEDGEWOOD, Thomas: born May 14, 1771, in Etruria, England; died July 10, 1805, in Eastbury

WEEGEE (Arthur Fellig): born June 12, 1899, in Zloczow (Zolochiv) near Lemberg, Ukraine; died December 26, 1968, in New York

WEGMAN, William: born December 2, 1943, in Holyoke, Massachusetts

WESTON, Edward: born March 24, 1886, in Highland Park, Illinois; died January 1, 1958, in Carmel-by-the-Sea, California

WINOGRAND, Garry: born January 14, 1928, in New York; died March 19, 1984, in Tijuana, Mexico

WINTER, Damon: born December 24, 1974, in Elmira, New York

ZUCKERMAN, Andrew: born 1977 in Washington, DC

LITERATURE

General

Badger, Gerry: *The Genius of Photography*, London 1996
Bate, David: *Photography: The Key Concepts*, Oxford 2009
Chermayeff, Cathrine: *Fashion Photography Now*, New York 2000
Edwards, Steve: *Photography: A Very Short Introduction*, Oxford 2006
Freund, Gisèle: *Photography and Society*, London 1980 (a translation of the thesis she published in 1936)
Frizot, Michel (ed.): *A New History of Photography*, Cologne 1994
Gee, Helen: *Photography of the Fifties: An American Perspective*, Tucson 1980
Green, Jonathan (ed.): *Camera Work: A Critical Anthology*, New York 1983
Greenough, Sarah, Joel Snyder, and others: *On the Art of Fixing a Shadow* (exh. cat., National Gallery of Art, Washington), Boston 1989
Jeffrey, Ian: *Photography: A Concise History*, London 1981
Livingston, Jane: *The New York School: Photographs 1936–1963*, New York 1992
Lubben, Kristen (ed.): *MAGNUM – Contact Sheets / Kontaktbögen*, London and Munich 2011
Maddow, Ben: *Faces: A Narrative History of the Portrait in Photography*, New York 1977
Manchester, William (ed.): *In Our Time: The World as Seen by MAGNUM Photographers*, London 1989
Marien, Mary Warner: *Photography: A Cultural History*, London 2010
Meyerowitz, Joel, and Colin Westerbeck: *Bystander: A History of Street Photography*, London 1994
Newhall, Beaumont (ed.): *Photography: Essays and Images*, New York 1980
Parr, Martin, and Gerry Badger: *The Photobook: A History*, Vols. 1 & 2, London 2004/2006

Poschardt, Ulf, Marion de Beaupre, and Stephane Baumet (eds.): *Archeology of Elegance – 1980-2000 – 20 Years of Fashion Photography*, London 2002
Rosenblum, Naomi: *A World History of Photography*, New York 1984
Sobieszek, Robert (ed.): *Masterpieces of Photography*, George Eastman Collection, New York 1985
Sontag, Susan: *On Photography*, New York 1977
Tausk, Petr: *Photography in the 20th Century*, London 1980
Wells, Liz: *Photography: A Critical Introduction*, London and New York 1997

Monographs

Atget, Eugène, and Berenice Abbott: *The World of Atget*, New York 1964
Avedon, Richard, and Mary Shanahan (eds.): *Evidence 1944–1994*, New York 1994
Barnbaum, Bruce: *Visual Symphony*, Toronto 1986
Brandt, Nick: *On this Earth*, San Francisco 2005
Brassaï: *Paris de Nuit*, New York 1987
Brassaï: *Letters to My Parents*, Chicago 1997
Cartier-Bresson, Henri: *Images à la Sauvette*, Paris 1952
Erwitt, Eliot: *Personal Exposures*, New York 1988
Evans, Walker: *Evans at Work*, New York 1982
Frank, Robert: *The Americans*, New York 1959
Frank, Robert: *New York to Nova Scotia* (exh. cat., Museum of Fine Arts, Houston), Boston 1986
Gautrand, Jean Claude: *Robert Doisneau*, Cologne 2003
Gibson, Ralph: *Tropism*, New York 1987
Goldin, Nan: *The Ballad of the Sexual Dependency*, New York 1986
Hawkins, G., G. Howe, and J. Markham: *Paul Outerbridge Jr. Photographs*, New York 1980
Kertész, André: *Ma France*, Paris 1990
Kertész, André, and John Szarkowski: *André Kertész Photographer* (exh. cat., Museum of Modern Art, New York), New York 1964
Mapplethorpe, Robert: *Ten by Ten*, Munich 1988
Nachtwey, James: *Inferno*, London 1999
Newton, Helmut, and Felix Zdenek (ed.): *The Best of Helmut Newton*, Munich 1993
Parr, Martin, and Val Williams: *Martin Parr*, London 2002
Penn, Irving: *Passage*, Munich and London 1991
Peress, Gilles: *Telex Iran: In the Name of Revolution*, Zurich 1997
Purcell, Kerry William: *Weegee*, London 2004
Ray, Man, and Manfred Heiting (eds.): *Man Ray*, Cologne 2004
Rheims, Bettina, and Serge Bramly: *Chambre close*, Munich 1992
Salgado, Sebastião: *Workers*, New York 1993
Sander, August, with Susanne Lange and Gabriele Conrath-Scholl (eds.): *People of the 20th Century*, New York 2002
Stange, Marin (ed.): *Paul Strand: Essays of his Life and his Work*, New York 1990
Stieglitz, Alfred, and Eva Weber: *Alfred Stieglitz*, London 1994
Strand, Paul, and Sarah Greenough (eds.): *An American Vision* (exh. cat., National Gallery of Art, Washington), Washington 1990
Talbot, William Fox: *The Pencil of Nature*, New York 1989
Tillmans, Wolfgang: *truth study center*, Cologne 2005
Toscani, Oliviero, and Olivier Saillard: *Workwear: Work Fashion Seduction*, New York 2009
Tucker, Anne Wilkes, Richard Howard and Avis Berman: *Brassaï: The Eye of Paris*, Houston 1997
Weegee: *Naked City*, New York 1946
Wegman, William: *Polaroids*, New York 2002
Weston, Edward, and Nancy Newhall (eds.): *The Flame of Recognition*, New York 1993
Witkin, Joel-Peter, and Germano Celant: *Witkin*, Zurich 1995
Zuckerman, Andrew: *Bird*, San Francisco 2009

INDEX

Numbers in *italics* refer to images.

IMPRINT

© Prestel Verlag, Munich · London · New York, 2012

© for the works reproduced is held by the artists and photographers, their heirs or assigns, with the exception of: © Eve Arnold/Magnum Photos/Agentur Focus; Richard Avedon: © 1985 The Richard Avedon Foundation/Photograph by Richard Avedon; © 1963 Arnold Newman/Getty Images; © Stephen Shore/Courtesy 303 Gallery, New York; © Joel-Peter Witkin/Image: courtesy Catherine Edelman Gallery; Robert Mapplethorpe: © Robert Mapplethorpe Foundation; © Wolfgang Tillmans/Courtesy Galerie Buchholz, Köln/Berlin; © Nick Ut/AP Photo; © Damon Winter/Laif; Robert Capa: © International Center of Photography/Magnum/Agentur Focus; © Don McCullin/Agentur Focus; Oliviero Toscani, Meret Oppenheim, Giacomo Balla, Thomas Ruff: VG Bild-Kunst, Bonn 2012; © Martin Parr/Magnum Photos/Agentur Focus; Edward Steichen: Permission of the Estate of Edward Steichen; Paul Outerbridge, Jr.: © 2012 G. Ray Hawkins Gallery, Beverly Hills, CA; Irving Penn: © The Irving Penn Foundation/Condé Nast Publications Inc.; Jacques Henri Lartigue: Donation Jacques Henri Lartigue © Ministère de la Culture et de la Communication – France/AAJHL, Paris 2012; Heinrich Kühn: © Estate of the Artist/Courtesy Gallery Kicken Berlin; Alfred Stieglitz: © Georgia O'Keeffe Museum/VG Bild-Kunst, Bonn 2012; Paul Strand: © Aperture Foundation, Inc./Paul Strand Archive; Edward Weston: © 1981 Center for Creative Photography; Walker Evans: © Walker Evans Archive, The Metropolitan Museum of Art; André Kertész: © Estate of André Kertész/Higher Pictures; © Henri Cartier-Bresson/Magnum Photos/Agentur Focus; Garry Winogrand: © The Estate of Garry Winogrand/Courtesy of Fraenkel Gallery, San Francisco; © Josef Koudelka/Magnum Photos/Agentur Focus; © Ernst Haas/Getty Images; © Keld Helmer-Petersen/Courtesy Rocket Gallery; © Gilles Peress/Magnum Photos/Agentur Focus; © W. Eugene Smith/Magnum Photos/Agentur Focus; © Sebastiao Salgado/Agentur Focus; © Pieter Hugo/Courtesy of Stevenson Cape Town/Johannesburg and Yossi Milo, New York; Man Ray: Man Ray Trust, Paris/VG Bild-Kunst, Bonn 2012; © Philippe Halsman/Magnum Photos/Agentur Focus; Weegee: © International Center of Photography/Getty Images; Horst P. Horst: © Horst Estate; Martin Munkacsi: © Estate of Martin Munkacsi/Courtesy Howard Greenberg Gallery, New York; Copyright by Andrew Zuckerman from BIRD; © Jim Brandenburg/National Geographic Stock; © William Wegman/Courtesy Senior & Shopmaker Gallery; Robert Frank/Courtesy Pace/MacGill Gallery, New York; Albert Renger-Patzsch: © Albert Renger-Patzsch Archiv/Ann und Jürgen Wilde/VG Bild-Kunst, Bonn 2012; Ansel Adams: © 2012 The Ansel Adams Gallery; Andy Warhol: © ARS, New York 2012; © Bernd und Hilla Becher/Sonnabend Gallery, New York; August Sander: © Die Photographische Sammlung/SK Stiftung Kultur – August Sander Archiv, Köln; VG Bild-Kunst, Bonn 2012; Andreas Gursky: © Courtesy Sprüth Magers, Berlin, London/VG Bild-Kunst, Bonn 2012; © David Hockney/Photo: Steve Oliver; © Elliott Erwitt/Magnum Photos/Agentur Focus; © Richard Kalvar/Magnum Photos/Agentur Focus; Robert Doisneau: © Gamma-Rapho/Getty Images

Front cover: Andreas Gursky, *James Bond Island II*, see p. 174
Back cover, from left to right: Eadweard Muybridge, *Galloping Horse*, see p. 76; Stephen Shore, *Presidio, Texas, February 21, 1975*, see p. 36; Andrew Zuckerman, *Blue Fronted Amazon*, see p. 140
Frontispiece: Eugène Atget, *Cour de Rouen, passage du commerce*, 1908, George Eastman House/Kontributor/Getty images

Prestel Verlag, Munich
A member of Verlagsgruppe Random House GmbH

Prestel Verlag, Munich
Neumarkter Straße 28
81673 Munich
Tel. +49 (0)89 4136-0
Fax +49 (0)89 4136-2335
www.prestel.de

Prestel Publishing Ltd.
4 Bloomsbury Place
London WC1A 2QA
Tel. +44 (0)20 7323-5004
Fax +44 (0)20 7636-8004
www.prestel.com

Prestel Publishing
900 Broadway, Suite 603
New York, NY 10003
Tel. +1 (212) 995-2720
Fax +1 (212) 995-2733
www.prestel.com

Library of Congress Control Number is available; British Library Cataloguing-in-Publication Data: a catalogue record for this book is available from the British Library; Deutsche Nationalbibliothek holds a record of this publication in the Deutsche Nationalbibliografie; detailed bibliographical data can be found under: http://dnb.d-nb.de

Prestel books are available worldwide. Please contact your nearest bookseller or one of the above addresses for information concerning your local distributor.

Translated by: Jane Michael, Munich
Editorial direction: Claudia Stäuble and Julie Kiefer
Copyedited by: Chris Murray
Picture editor | Timelines: Andrea Jaroni
Index: Katharina Knüppel
Cover design: Joana Niemeyer, April
Design concept: LIQUID Agentur für Gestaltung, Augsburg
Layout: Wolfram Söll, Munich
Production: Nele Krüger
Art direction: Cilly Klotz
Origination: ReproLine Mediateam, Munich
Printing and binding: Druckerei Uhl GmbH & Co. KG, Radolfzell

Printed in Germany

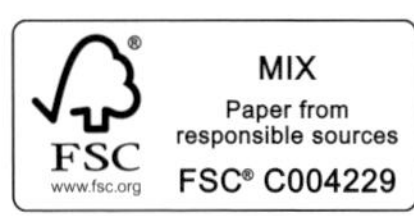

Verlagsgruppe Random House FSC©-DEU-0100
The FSC©-certified paper Hello Fat Matt has been produced by mill Condat, Le Lardin Saint-Lazare, France.

ISBN 978-3-7913-4669-4
(German edition: ISBN 978-3-7913-4672-4)